Manly Traditions

MANLY TRADITIONS

The Folk Roots of American Masculinities

EDITED BY
SIMON J. BRONNER

With an afterword by Alan Dundes

INDIANA UNIVERSITY PRESS
Bloomington & Indianapolis

This book is a publication of

Indiana University Press
601 North Morton Street
Bloomington, IN 47404-3797 USA

http://iupress.indiana.edu

Telephone orders 800-842-6796
Fax orders 812-855-7931
Orders by e-mail iuporder@indiana.edu

The paper used in this publication meets the minimum requirements of American National Standard for Information Sciences—Permanence of Paper for Printed Library Materials, ANSI Z39.48-1984.

Manufactured in the United States of America

Library of Congress Cataloging-in-Publication Data

Manly traditions : the folk roots of American masculinities / edited by Simon J. Bronner ; with an afterword by Alan Dundes.
p. cm.
Includes bibliographical references and index.
ISBN 0-253-34613-4 (cloth : alk. paper)—ISBN 0-253-21781-4 (pbk. : alk. paper)
1. Men—United States—Folklore. 2. Masculinity—United States—Folklore. 3. Men in popular culture—United States. 4. Masculinity in popular culture—United States. I. Bronner, Simon J.
GR105.M36 2005
398'.35—dc22
2005008305

1 2 3 4 5   10 09 08 07 06 05

*Dedicated to Ronald L. Baker,
in appreciation of forty years of folklore scholarship, service,
and teaching at Indiana State University*

CONTENTS

ACKNOWLEDGMENTS

I am eternally grateful to Ron Baker for inspiring this book and enriching us all with his wisdom and charm. Catherine Baker, Ron's wonderful partner and scholar in her own right, urged us on. Indiana State University kindly provided a subvention for this volume to honor Ron, and the university's Joseph Schick Memorial Lecture Endowment gave opportunities for many of us to share our ideas face to face in Terre Haute. Back in Harrisburg, I am grateful to staff member Sue Etter and graduate assistants Gwendollyn Wind and Michael McCombs at the Center for Pennsylvania Culture Studies for their help. Michael Barton, Charles Kupfer, Jessica Dorman, John Gennari, John Haddad, and Karin Thomas—valued colleagues in Penn State Harrisburg's American Studies Program—prodded my thinking about interdisciplinary approaches to American diversity. I am indebted to all the contributors here, but I want to give special credit to Jay Mechling and Bill McNeil for helping me focus the concept in its early stages, and to Alan Dundes for his close reading as the manuscript took shape. Margaret "Peggy" Yocom provided valuable comments on a panel with Jay Mechling and me at the American Studies Association meeting in 2002 when early forms of our essays were first presented. Polly Stewart and Yolanda Hood also helped clarify feminist perspectives on folklore in dialogues with me that informed the present volume. Charles "Terry" Zug at the University of North Carolina, Michael Christensen at the Utah Cultural Celebration Center, Eric Eliason at Brigham Young University, and Catherine Johnson-Roehr, curator of art, artifacts, and photographs at Indiana University's Kinsey Institute for Research in Sex, Gender, and Reproduction, brought significant visual and material resources to my attention. At Indiana University Press, Michael Lundell gave a sure guiding hand as editor for the project.

I have gained much from vigorous discussion of gender issues at American Studies Association, American Culture Association, American Folklore Society, Organization of American Historians, American Sociological Association, American Anthropological Association, American Men's Studies Association, and National Women's Studies Association meetings, among others in which I and other contributors here participate. Less formal, but nonetheless enlightening, the steam-room sessions with fellas at the Y deserve recognition; you might be surprised by the revealing conversations that occur sitting naked with sweat pouring down. I am also grateful for the interest of my neighbors in what I was doing, and for introducing me to Pennsylvania's hunting-camp culture, which set me to thinking about manly traditions in new ways. I benefited, too, from discussion about the subject with Theresa and Ed Lanza in Harrisburg; they generously sent me many variations of "guy and gal folklore" found in the introduction, and Ed assisted me in the translation and editing of Spanish texts. Finally, I am driven always by the encouragement and womanly advice of my partner, Sally Jo Bronner, and the lessons that the boy and girl she mothers provide daily about the significance of gender and human development in American culture.

Simon J. Bronner

INTRODUCTION

My neighbor is a doctor who would never be accused of being the Marlboro Man. Slight of build, known in the area for quiet sensitivity, and a father of three girls, he can often be seen in his yard playing dolls with his daughters. One day he rolled into the driveway and stopped suddenly to see that his front door and shutters had been painted pink. Spying me taking out the trash, he turned and snickered, "Times like this, I need a good manly tradition like hunting."

He was not really going hunting, but he sought some symbol to express his manliness in relation to what he perceived as an overly feminine public statement. My rolling out the garbage, somehow a man's duty in my neighborhood, hardly sufficed. He mocked himself for losing his manhood when he gave up his heavy sport utility vehicle for a light minivan. He liked to joke about being emasculated in a female-dominated home and had a repertoire of what he called "manly humor," touching on themes of sports, bars, and Viagra. He could discern American masculinity in this humor as being about aggressiveness, sexual prowess, muscular strength, social dominance, and competition. As he reflected further on his life experience, however, he realized different social contexts that shaped his nuanced views of being a man—his family dynamic in a female-centered home, his Italian-American upbringing with his brothers, his midlife age beyond the age of forty culturally associated with the end of youth, occupational training with its professional class orientation, and, not insignificantly, the social pressure of feminist values at the turn of the new millennium. In often privatized traditions of his raising and those of his choosing, he understood sources of his manhood.

This book gets at the roots of being a man in America. More to the point, it interprets the ways that manliness is expressed, symbolized, and perceived for people like my neighbor and others. Those roots, the contributors argue, are in the traditions men inherit and often adapt for their own purposes in contemporary life. By focusing on traditions, the book seeks to interpret the mechanisms by which masculine values are maintained, adapted, invented, and discarded, especially in situations where manliness has been challenged. These traditions are critical in explaining socially particularized states of masculinity because they are by their nature vessels for creating meaning, producing metaphors, reinforcing beliefs, and transmitting values through time.

Whereas many studies focus on popular culture as "reflections" of taste and values because imaginative evidence is broadcast in media, the contributors here intentionally go beyond the commercial products to locate in everyday life those traditional, often longstanding practices in which manliness is socially constructed, widely shared symbolic texts are apparent, and men are engaged cultural participants. To get at the behaviors and symbols of everyday life, contributors observe practices in ethnographic fieldwork and collect texts for comparative content analysis. Outside of the cultural scenes they observe and the texts they analyze, they take into consideration the dynamic between men's and women's cultures, and perceptions and uses of manly activity—by both men and women—in public or mainstream culture.

For all the reminders that men are different from women in ways other than anatomy, the distinctive cultural traditions that contribute to a conveyable sense of masculinity still need definition, especially in an era when manliness, if given consideration, is often criticized and suppressed. If masculinity has a certain objective ring to it as the bearing of being a man, then use of "manliness" and "manly" connotes social activities distinctively, conspicuously, and intensively male. Masculinity implies that being a man involves social and cultural differences, inherited to be sure, in relation to femininity—a state of being. Manliness involves characteristics that extend, and typically symbolize, the cultural values and traditions of being a man. Before moralists pass judgment on such values and traditions, we encourage an understanding of their contexts and purposes, which cannot and should not be narrowly reduced to oppression. The "traditions" men know are those they communicate to one another in their social interaction and are shaped by what women do, and such traditions often are inherited from a previous generation. They embody and express manliness, and provide common fonts of symbols, images, and practices from which to derive and shape meaning. Even if not "performed," such traditions provide metaphors to think with, and sometimes to live by. As traditions, they are typically subject to variation and adaptation in different ethnic, regional, familial, age, and occupational contexts where symbols, rituals, and narratives of masculinity are enacted in a system of communication. It is those texts and contexts that contributors to this volume uncover and interpret. Once thought to be restricted to the heterosexual male, manliness here includes homosexuals in its definition and indeed attempts to show diversity of masculinities within sexual orientations and gray areas in between. The approach here shows that gender display is not a simple binary relationship but a range of identities variously expressed and negotiated.

The context of national experience adds to the query of what drives men to do what they do, judging from cross-cultural analyses of masculine traits in the United States and other countries. Questions of national conditions arise, for example, from controversial attempts to quantify masculinity such as the one formulated by Geert Hofstede in *Culture's Consequences* (2001). Masculinity there is ascribed to a traditional masculine work role model of male achievement, control, and power. A "High Masculinity" ranking on a scale of 100 indicates the country experiences a high degree of gender differentiation. Men are supposed to be "assertive, tough, and focused on material success; women are supposed to be more modest, tender, and concerned with the quality of life" (Hofstede 2001, 297; see also Hofstede 1998). A wide gap exists between Japan (close to 100), the nation he measured as having the highest ranking in the world, and the United States (62), just above the world average of 50. At the low end, close to zero—where the quantifiers claim hardly any gender differentiation and discrimination exist—sit the Scandinavian countries of Norway, Sweden, and Denmark. While criticisms of methodology hound such attempts to measure "character," the positioning of the United States near the middle of the scale often draws relative views of the country's gender relations as half full or half empty. It also raises qualitative questions about the role of perception, since as Hideyo Konagaya points out in this volume, Japanese Americans in *taiko* performance emphasize manly performance in response to the American perception that they are feminized, and one of the manly images found in American folk humor is of the Scandinavian Viking as an alpha male.

Among the first qualitative observations of a national character, Alexis de Tocqueville's *Democracy in America* (1835, 1840) pointed out that American patriarchal authority is distinctive for its weakness in comparison to European traditions. More than 150 years later, American textbooks, while acknowledging similar national patterns, were declaring the end of the national model of a father's patriarchal role as "the good provider" and "male breadwinner." A widely used sociological textbook, the sixth edition of *Family in Transition* (1989) by Arlene and Jerome Skolnick, claimed that the intensity and effect of the women's movement were distinctively American to the point that "men perceive their roles as being under threat in a world that is different from any in the past" (Skolnick and Skolnick 1989, 177). The modern American norm was the *Feminized Male,* as Patricia Sexton pronounced in a provocative book title of 1969, and she associated this status in her subtitle with the *Decline of Manliness* in the contemporary United States. She was hardly alone in her observation, as popular titles such as *The Feminization of American Culture* (Douglas 1978) and *The Last American Man* (Gilbert 2002) avowed.

Accordingly, with the beginning of a new millennium, the revisionist question broached by philosopher Waller R. Newell in his book *What Is a Man?* (2000) was echoed in many public forums. He based his query on the observation that "As America heads into the twenty-first century, there is an increasingly widespread feeling that we have forgotten the meaning of manliness" (xvii). Loudly sounding alarms on the public radar, many so-called manly traditions became suspect because of the connotations of aggressiveness and violence treated as undesirable in building a civil society. Such traditions did not disappear but went underground and remained sources, sometimes roots, for men to draw on and for popular culture to caricature. Because of the lack of documentation of folk activities in all-male groups and settings, such traditions were often assumed to be brutish, and the range of masculine identities available to men remained unconsidered. Responding to public stigma of men's ways, and skeptical of the likelihood or desirability of a genderless society in the new millennium, Newell reworded many of the manly traits as virtues in his pointed question, "How might we recover an understanding of what it means to be a man in the positive sense—brave, self-restrained, dignified, zealous on behalf of a good cause, imbued with sentiments of delicacy and respect for one's loved ones?" (xviii).

Contributors to this volume necessarily broach the question of what national conditions as well as local contexts allow or curtail the expression of manliness. But they do not share a single ideology or narrow judgment on the value of manly traditions, except to say that it is high time to discern rather than dismiss these activities. The role of these traditions in both American imagination and practice needs charting. Nationalistic images of dominating the American frontier and a reassurance of material abundance or nature's bounty in the perception of hunting, for instance, are hard to shake. The folktype of the cowboy is recognized internationally as an American representation of a manly man and contributes to the normative, or some may say "mainstream," construction of American masculinity characterized by independent, competitive, and aggressive behaviors and outward signs of rugged muscularity, physical dominance, and social ganging.

Other combinations, often paradoxical, of manly traits that emphasize male difference often enter into the mix: display of facial hair and yet shaving one's head, an affinity for primitive outdoor life coupled with an attraction to technical control and gadgetry, fondness for boisterous exuberance and of stoic suppressions of emotion. For many critics, the ultimate physical difference of the male penis translates culturally into a manly preoccupation with size, sexual prowess, hardness, toughness, and endurance. Further, Freudian psychoanalytical perspectives often claim a concomitant preoccupation with fear of feminization or anal penetration and homosexual attack, while sociological studies still cite Lionel Tiger's hypothesis of *Men in Groups* (1969) that male bonding in all-male groups is not just a symptom of formalized hostility to females, but significantly a "positive valence" or attraction among men.

For all the discussions of national traits and their value, one discovers in discussions with men connections of masculinity they make with their subcultural backgrounds and identities. Many Orthodox Jews comment on ethnic definition of the bearded and studious man as an ideal. Interviews with men of Japanese and Korean ancestry reveal the importance placed on manly silence. Surveys within Mexican American communities refer to *machismo* as a culturally important term for exaggerated aggressiveness in male-to-male and male-to-female relationships or repudiation of feminine characteristics. In many parts of the United States associated with "sportsman" culture, men like my Pennsylvania neighbor worry that their masculinity will be questioned if they do not hunt or fish. Some occupations traditionally are associated with manliness, such as plumbing, trucking, and construction trades. Cooking and washing, often considered effeminate in many ethnic family dynamics, have been part of the heritage of Chinese male labor. Various cultural expectations also exist for men's familiarity with speech and narrative traditions, such as erotic joke telling and salty swearing.

Symbolic associations for men continue to be perpetuated within American culture, such as the colors blue and black, machinery such as trucks and guns, and animals such as wolves and bears. One can point to folklore for longstanding values embedded in sayings such as "talking man to man" to represent forthright honest dialogue or "being man enough" to signify courageous action. American culture recognizes men's gendered behavior as somehow instinctual in the popular saying "A man's gotta do what a man's gotta do" and its roots in developing boyhood in "Boys will be boys." One may also hear in various contexts the declaration "Be a man!" suggesting gendered behavior as constructed rather than inherited, for it is often used in reference to the perceived need to perform manliness by being strong and aggressive or avoiding crying. In fact, in a sweeping survey of American folklore texts, folklorist Alan Dundes offered a hypothesis in 1976 worthy of continued testing that American culture exhibits a "male bias," even "male chauvinism." The significance of these texts, he asserted and we agree, is that biases, prejudices, beliefs, and values are not just reflected passively in America's folk roots but are actively transmitted through time and space, often unconsciously or unselfconsciously, through folkloric means. Moreover, underscoring the significance of such investigations, he reminds us of Richard Dorson's pronouncement in *American Folklore and the Historian* (1971) that "popular prejudices and stereotypes nourished by oral tradition have affected the course of history." As cultural critics, the writers here find that in interpreting expressions of beliefs and values, particularly when cultural conditions change and traditions become contested, challenged, or threatened, they can investigate the very texture of American consciousness in the pressures that build, conflicts that occur, and the choices that ensue around manliness.

Awareness of gendered traditions invites questioning of the customs and narratives men learn, adapt, and perpetuate—and those they discard and invent—as part of their realization, indeed embodiment, of themselves. In contrast to the number of tomes showing male representations in films, literature, and television, often in a negative light, this volume interprets what men *do* as a result of their cultural inheritance—and construction. By reaching into the often hidden roots of longstanding and invented manly values, the volume's primary objective is to contribute to contemporary discourse on the redefinition of gendered practices. Its broad purpose is to add to the inquiry into the role of tradition in social change. In its suggestion of closer examinations of different versions of masculinity, it may also help address the increasingly felt societal need to counsel boys in their development and men—young and old and of various ethnicities and backgrounds—in their attainment of social comfort under changing conditions.

Our claim is that this book is the first to focus on the problem of the construction of manliness in American folklife. This may come as a surprise, considering the feminist assertion expressed in complementary collections of essays such as *Women's Folklore, Women's Culture* (1985), edited by Rosan A. Jordan and Susan J. Kalčik, that men are known through folklore, women are not. They emphasized that research of men's public settings and forms of tradition has dominated discourse, while women's folklore has been largely ignored or underrated. Many studies have been undertaken since that time in women's domains by both men and women and have helped build a solid foundation for discussions of gender in culture. They have established that a women's culture emerges from traditions shared and maintained by women, and prompted new insights into men's culture by forcing queries of the ways in which the two cultures affect each other—"whether the relationship be one of contrast or one of complementarity," as Jordan and Kalčik state (x). Yet we cannot accept the notion that men's culture is well documented or understood. Many of the cultural scenes and texts discussed in this book are revealed for the first time, and others are refreshingly unpacked in the light of manliness as a concept. The contributors as a group point out a need to expand the inquiry into men's subcultures and identities from the young raver to the old carver, especially as we are increasingly more sensitive to the cultural implications of gendered behavior. As new research into women's worlds has taught us, we want to avoid the temptation to overlook, marginalize, underrate, dismiss, caricature, and silence men's traditions.

One self-reflective trend in the push to study enactments of gender is consideration of the influence of the researcher's identity on one's conclusions, and particularly the access to domestic settings offered by women ethnographers. A special feminist concern has been for examination of power relations. Many folkloristic studies by women of female traditions seek to prove that women are empowered by those traditions, rather than being victims or failures in an essentially male world. As Jordan and Kalčik assert in their volume, "Despite male domination of one sort or another many of the women studied here are very much in control of themselves and their worlds, and a sense of real power is communicated by their folklore" (xii). In another anthology, *Feminist Theory and the Study of Folklore* (Hollis, Pershing, and Young 1993), the editors claim further that the role of women is one of relative powerlessness, and the feminist agenda is to change the academic "tradition that has silenced and marginalized us" (13). These keywords come up again in reference to cultural traditions when the editors state, "From generation to generation, women's traditions have had their own part to play in countering the patriarchal tradition that has marginalized and silenced women" (13). Consequently, feminist researchers hypothesize the social support of female bonding and the social construction of femininity as responses to oppressively patriarchal cultural conditions.

The essays in this volume also deal with power relations but do not necessarily assume the exertion of oppression by, and silencing power of, men. That is not to say they deny it, but they question it in action. Indeed, many essays explore the restrictions placed upon men in their development and social relations with one another and examine the conditions to which men's traditions respond. In several cases, they find that men perceive themselves as stigmatized and marginalized by processes of feminization or the social structures of cultural scenes with which they identify. In this regard, the essays consistently address the creation of potent symbols in performance and text that are meant to resolve conflicts in gender identity or clarify manliness in an increasingly elastic definition of gender difference. To be sure, they often refer to feminist theory in the conception of a developed masculinity separate from the culture of men, but they often have different takes on the ideological basis of study. And it should be emphasized that in an effort to focus multiple lenses on the male subject, contributors are men and women from different ethnic backgrounds.

There is no denying that men's spheres have previously been featured in the literature, but the inquiry represented here addresses the situations in which manliness is an issue as part of new directions for gender and cultural studies. In this new men's studies, or what some might call post-feminist studies, the issues of human development and identity are paramount and raise new questions about assumptions of normative roles ascribed to gender in the field. In addition to considerations of patriarchal influence, the role of powerful women—mothers and teachers—regarding the developing boy receives attention. Not stopping at coming-of-age, writers here also take into account the extent and extension of the life span through the invented tradition of the male-centered midlife crisis to old age in changeful times. These writers consistently had to probe the maturation process that produced men from boys, and the cultural passages that guided it and the social forces that affect it. Instead of simply assuming that men are preoccupied with the anatomical distinction of their penises, dominance over women, or their size and muscular development, the writers here explain the texts and performances of male display and why at bottom they become necessary to display. Whether it is a Japanese American using drumming to heighten perceptions of his manliness in ways that would never be performed in Japan, or Ozark men expressing simultaneous images of a sexually masterful or sexually naïve mountain man, the explanations of these expressions push beyond formulations of performance and function to find social psychological factors in human development and the socialization process. They are also forced to address the cultural process by which these folk roots, often with bounded subcultural characteristics, relate to or form representations within an encompassing mass culture.

One may reasonably ask whether this new direction constitutes a "masculinist" answer to feminist interpretation. The writers do not identify themselves by that label and resist creating a parallel universe of exclusion and ideological bias. They bring various methodologies and interpretative tools to bear on manly traditions and call upon the significant explorations of women's worlds in cultural scholarship. But rather than getting past the male subject as having been covered, they ask anew whether it has been adequately *discovered*. They share, however, in the endeavor of men's and women's studies to find appropriate cultural explanation drawing on the understanding of situations in which gendered behavior is evident, indeed necessary, and they are not averse to questioning common assumptions of male privilege and dominance, especially ethnographically in subcultural contexts. This movement is not backlash, then, but instead is progress toward fuller consideration of the way that gender is enacted, indeed embodied, in lived experience. In fact, some writers apply what they would call a feminist perspective on men's spheres to illuminate socially particular references to the feminine and the gendered "other" in the discourse of masculinity. And it is fair to say that all the writers give special attention to the process of social construction in the formation of ideas of male display and accounting of American consciousness.

The genres featured in this volume are those in which symbols of male socialization are especially apparent. They include humor evident in joke telling, recitation, and woodcarving; male initiation in rites of passage and occupational rituals; and performances of intimacy in dance and music performances. As expressions that are especially prevalent culturally to broach disturbing or taboo subjects, they often include symbolism of attitudes and feelings that do not come out in conversation, especially when some of the values involved are considered publicly stigmatized. They are indeed found as symbols meant for social commentary at the folk roots because that is the most appropriate location to resolve conflicts and address problems, clarify or question identities, and express desires and fantasies. The writers do not retread male-centered "public settings and forms of tradition" by the emphasis in this volume on these genres. Rather, they bring out ways in which many texts and performances have been previously suppressed in scholarship because of their obscene content or not given adequate analytical attention for their contribution to gender construction.

When folkloric genres are expressed in locations where sexual and gendered boundaries are vague, they often take on especially fascinating forms that raise questions about the "gray areas" between spheres. Consider, for instance, the ethnographies of the rave and gay "circuit" scenes in this volume in which normative assumptions of manliness are intentionally appropriated and altered. The genres are probably presented with a greater sensitivity to audience than in many other treatments. Tom Mould examines the changing function of staged "step shows" of African American men for audiences of blacks and whites, men and women. In my essay on woodcarvers, I point out differences between products shown publicly and those displayed privately among men. W. K. McNeil discusses jokes of the mountain man folktype known widely and those told by mountain men among themselves.

The structure of the volume is in two parts, with the first part emphasizing displays and performances to highlight *enactments* of manliness, typically public in nature, and the second part featuring male expressions and texts to draw attention to more private *rhetoric* of folkloric communication. Both deal significantly with the process of cultural production and metaphor building related to gender. For the purposes of overview, in "Menfolk" I survey prominent concepts of, and approaches to, men's cultural production and the role of tradition in the enactments and rhetoric of manliness.

Part 1 opens with Gary Alan Fine's sociological inquiry into social changes in occupational settings engendered by the entrance of women. He asks pointedly, whose traditions change—those of the women who adapt to the male workplace, or those of the men who accommodate the women? Fine uses several case studies to offer theoretical insights into the social behavior of men in groups and the classic idea of male bonding. Following this exploration of contact between spheres, Tom Mould explores the condition of complementarity in his study of African American "stepping"—staged performances of dance and march routines popular on many college campuses. Although both men and women in African American Greek life share the tradition of step shows, Mould observes, they differ in the style and content of their performances to effect distinctively gendered racial personas. Norma Cantú focuses her study on Chicano rites of passage from adolescence to manhood in light of the emphasis within Mexican American border culture on the maturation of the girl and expectations of the *macho* Chicano boy. Having previously applied feminist perspectives to Chicana traditions, she refocuses her lens here on the difficult transition of Chicano boys into men in Texas border towns.

Continuing inquiry into definitions of masculinity within different American ethnic groups from a woman's perspective, Hideyo Konagaya considers the conspicuously noisy display of strength by Japanese American men in *taiko*, immense sets of drums requiring hyperkinetic, strenuous bodily activity. A native of Japan, Konagaya compares *taiko*'s social functions of performing manliness in Japan and the United States. She finds explanation in normative mass cultural perceptions of the Japanese American male as effeminate because of stereotypes of a slight build and quiet demeanor.

The last two essays in the section discuss the key display of dancing as a sign of intimacy in the construction of masculinity. Often associated with femininity, dancing has been a central tradition in the definition of rave and gay subcultures. Emergent traditions within these communities, the authors find, appropriate or extend normative ideas of masculinity in the mass culture for their own purposes. Therefore, the groups are not the antithesis of manliness, as some folklore might suggest, but instead are a variation of it. Anthony Avery in his study of the rave scene in Albuquerque, New Mexico, calls this variation an "alternative masculinity" and examines symbols of cross-dressing and feminine bodily performance by men within a distinct cultural setting. Mickey Weems offers an opportunity for comparison with his study of another contemporary DJ-led event, and he focuses especially on the symbols of shirtless muscularity and mood-altering drugs appropriated for the construction of an assertive folk display of gay masculinity.

In Part 2, writers draw attention to material and oral texts for the analysis of symbol communication within and outside men's expressive culture. Especially in this section, contributors refer to standard references documenting types of the folktale. Citations of numbers as "Aarne-Thompson" types refer to Antti Aarne's *Verzeichnis der Märchentypen,* translated and enlarged as *The Types of the Folktale* by Stith Thompson (Aarne 1987 [1961]). You also may run across references to Grimm numbers, shorthand for the classic nineteenth-century folktale compendium of Jacob and Wilhelm Grimm in *Kinder und Hausmärchen* (see *The Complete Fairy Tales of the Brothers Grimm,* translated into English by Jack Zipes [2003], and for a German text, see Uther 1996), and Child ballad numbers, for Francis James Child's *The English and Scottish Popular Ballads* (2003, 2002–2004, and digital edition 2002). The references serve as tools of comparison, and they are also reminders of the circulation of a cultural repertoire of narrative themes and types.

Many of the texts in this book, because of their sexual content, go beyond the scope of the above references. Avoiding the analysis of these kinds of expressions, typical of earlier scholarship, has resulted in the loss of opportunities for confronting the folklore and folklife of men as men. When Stith Thompson prepared his monumental *Motif-Index of Folk-Literature* (revised and enlarged, 1955–1958, and digital edition, 1993), he gingerly sidestepped material he listed as "X700–X799 Humor concerning sex" by stating "Thousands of obscene motifs in which there is no point except the obscenity itself might logically come at this point, but they are entirely beyond the scope of the present work. They form a literature to themselves, with its own periodicals and collections." While the challenge of filling in this textual information has been subsequently taken up notably by Frank Hoffmann in *Analytical Survey of Anglo-American Traditional Erotica* (1973), Gershon Legman in *Rationale of the Dirty Joke* (1968, 1975), and Vance Randolph in *Pissing in the Snow* (1976), the contextual and thematic understanding of this material as gendered expressions remains an analytical priority for cultural studies in our time. Besides typologies of bawdy jokes associated with men's performances, major inventories and analyses are now available for limericks, poetry and recitations, photocopied folklore, and songs (see Legman 1964, 1974, 1977; Dundes and Pagter 1978, 1987, 1991, 1996, 2000; Randolph 1992a, 1992b). Rarely documented, and even more rarely interpreted, such material is crucial to the analysis of the folk roots of American masculinities. All this is to say that the contributors in this volume deal with uncensored material, specifically because it comes out of oral tradition and the customs of some male groups. You should be prepared to encounter some sensitive material that may appear obscenely aggressive and bigoted, and therefore offensive, in the earnest pursuit of comprehending what people really do and why they do it.

In the second part of the book, for example, Jay Mechling's opening essay broaches the inevitable, although often suppressed, question of why men tell so many narratives about the penis as their defining bodily part. In his revisionist analysis, he considers feminist and psychoanalytical perspectives and offers provocative new insights into the gendered role of joke telling in American culture.

Greg Kelley's texts are more common in literature as marvel tales of wish fulfillment, often associated with European *Märchen* and not usually viewed as expressions of masculinity. He shows the relations of these texts to male contexts and questions the male-centeredness or phallocentrism of their content in American settings.

W. F. H. "Bill" Nicolaisen also examines common texts—these from contemporary legendry—and poses questions about the role of manly characters within them. Looking for a corpus of legends for the purpose of analysis, comparable to the folktale and ballad references above, he offers some hypotheses based on his summary of the accumulated legend texts in the books of Jan Harold Brunvand in the 1980s and 1990s (see Brunvand 1981 for the first in the series; a "type-index of urban legends" is provided in Brunvand 1993; Brunvand 1999 and 2001 alphabetically list and summarize legends with cross-references to texts previously published in the series).

W. K. "Bill" McNeil focuses on one common American folk character—the hillbilly or southern mountaineer—frequently appearing in jokes with erotic content and presents his fieldwork on the jokes that southern mountain men intend to be shared privately among themselves. He finds that these narratives show awareness by tellers of the stereotyped public image of the southern mountaineer as the primal man within mass culture, while specially dealing with conflicts raised by simultaneous images of sexual mastery and naïveté among mountain men.

The last two essays deal with expressions and texts produced by men for other men in privatized situations. My essay follows from my previous publications about woodcarving among old men in which crafted items were shown to both men and women. In the course of fieldwork, I found that special carvings with erotic content were reserved for private "showings" among other men. Using psychoanalytical and social interactionist perspectives, I propose in the essay that elderly carvers crafted symbolism of the surprisingly large erect member in "barrel men" and "coffin men" to confront the impotence and infirmity of their aging set against the public association of manliness with youthful sexual prowess.

In the last essay, Ronald L. Baker and I discuss the most popular, if hardly published, recitations performed by men for other men, especially by adolescent males. We trace the available literary and historical evidence on the interrelated traditional recitations of Lady Lil, Eskimo Nell, and Pisspot Pete as a manly genre and present an analysis using developmental psychology of the young male who deals symbolically in folklore with a dominant woman authority figure.

The understanding of manly traditions owes much to Alan Dundes's trailblazing essays beginning in the 1960s, and he gets an opportunity to comment on the directions suggested by the volume in his afterword (see his oft-cited essays on masculinity and psychoanalytical approaches in 1978, 1980, 1987, 1989, 1997). He offers sources for a cross-cultural and symbolist interpretation of masculinity in folklore, considers such interpretation in manly traditions such as cockfights and verbal duels, reviews his contributions to theories of male display and aggression, and shows their relevance to widely publicized incidents of public concern in the war with Iraq in 2004.

While Ronald Baker's contribution is at the end of the book, it marked the beginning of this project. He presented his research on men's erotic recitations in 1983 when he chaired a special panel at the American Folklore Society entitled "Men and Manliness." It was a bold title and set of presentations for the time. Its purpose, he declared, was to illustrate how males view themselves and declare their masculinity. Speaking in part to emerging feminist perspectives on male genres, he explained the need for the attention to "manliness" as an esoteric concept, that is, an expressive construction of participants within a culture. He wrote, "Most studies of men and manliness in folklore emphasize exoteric concepts. They examine the representations of women in folklore presumably collected from male informants and claim masculine folklore is 'sexist' or 'male chauvinistic.' The orientation of this panel is somewhat different. Panel members will emphasize esoteric concepts." Bill McNeil and I both participated in that session, and in retrospect, it was well ahead of its time for cultural studies, and even ahead of the men's studies movement.

Baker continued to collect material in the intervening years, and the essay included here is a substantial revision of his early presentation (Baker 1987). He also produced source material for the study of the folk roots of American masculinities in his books of legends, jokes, and slave narratives (1982, 1986, 2000). He had a pivotal role as editor of the journals *Midwestern Folklore* and *Folklore Historian,* publishing the work of others contributing to the scholarship of gendered folklore. He has also been instrumental as the driving force behind folklore programming at Indiana State University for forty years, including organizing important Hoosier Folklore Society conferences featuring issues of gender in folklore studies. In so many other ways, he was influential within American folklore studies, and we want to recognize his inspiration by dedicating this volume to him.

It took time for the post-feminist perspectives presented here to take shape, and they benefited from developing theories of gender, tradition, and sexuality advanced as the new millennium forced reflection on identities past and future. Indeed, all the essays are original and timely for today. They can be especially useful within new developments of American studies, men's studies, women's studies, and cultural studies. It was especially important to me in taking on the project to represent a variety of regional, ethnic, and sexual groups culturally expressing masculinity in changing times. In addition to featuring senior folklorists Alan Dundes, Ronald Baker, Bill Nicolaisen, Gary Alan Fine, Jay Mechling, Bill McNeil, and Norma Cantú, the volume includes contributions from a promising young generation of folklorists working in a variety of institutional settings: Anthony Avery of the University of New Mexico, Greg Kelley of Indiana State University, Hideyo Konagaya of Siebold University in Japan, Mickey Weems of Ohio State University, and Tom Mould of Elon University. They barely came of age when Ronald Baker suggested manliness as an analytic concept for folklore studies, and they are actively expanding its possibilities and applications for a new generation of students and public audiences.

REFERENCES

Aarne, Antti. 1987 [1961]. *The Types of the Folktale: A Classification and Bibliography.* Translated and enlarged by Stith Thompson. 2nd ed. Helsinki: Suomalainen Tiedeakatemia Academia Scientiarum Fennica.

Baker, Ronald L., ed. 1982. *Hoosier Folk Legends*. Bloomington: Indiana University Press.

———. 1986. *Jokelore: Humorous Folktales from Indiana*. Bloomington: Indiana University Press.

———. 1987. "Lady Lil and Pisspot Pete." *Journal of American Folklore* 100: 191–99.

———. 2000. *Homeless, Friendless, and Penniless: The WPA Interviews with Former Slaves Living in Indiana*. Bloomington: Indiana University Press.

Brunvand, Jan Harold. 1981. *The Vanishing Hitchhiker: American Urban Legends and Their Meanings*. New York: W. W. Norton.

———. 1993. *The Baby Train and Other Lusty Urban Legends*. New York: W. W. Norton.

———. 1999. *Too Good to Be True: The Colossal Book of Urban Legends*. New York: W. W. Norton.

———. 2001. *Encyclopedia of Urban Legends*. Santa Barbara, Calif.: ABC-CLIO.

Child, Francis James, ed. 2002. *The English and Scottish Popular Ballads*. Digital ed. 2 CD set. New York: Heritage Muse.

———. 2003 [1882–1898]. *The English and Scottish Popular Ballads*. 5 vols. New York: Dover.

———. 2002–2004. *The English and Scottish Popular Ballads*. 3 vols. Corrected edition prepared by Mark Heiman and Laura Saxton Heiman. Northfield, Minn.: Loomis House Press.

Dorson, Richard M. 1971. *American Folklore and the Historian*. Chicago: University of Chicago Press.

Douglas, Ann. 1977. *The Feminization of American Culture*. New York: Avon.

Dundes, Alan. 1978. *Essays in Folkloristics*. Meerut, India: Folklore Institute.

———. 1980. *Interpreting Folklore*. Bloomington: Indiana University Press.

———. 1987. *Parsing through Customs: Essays by a Freudian Folklorist*. Madison: University of Wisconsin Press.

———. 1989. *Folklore Matters*. Knoxville: University of Tennessee Press.

———. 1997. *From Game to War and Other Psychoanalytic Essays on Folklore*. Lexington: University Press of Kentucky.

Dundes, Alan, and Carl R. Pagter. 1978 [1975]. *Work Hard and You Shall Be Rewarded: Urban Folklore from the Paperwork Empire*. Bloomington: Indiana University Press.

———. 1987. *When You're Up to Your Ass in Alligators: More Urban Folklore from the Paperwork Empire*. Detroit: Wayne State University Press.

———. 1991. *Never Try to Teach a Pig to Sing: Still More Urban Folklore from the Paperwork Empire*. Detroit: Wayne State University Press.

———. 1996. *Sometimes the Dragon Wins: Yet More Urban Folklore from the Paperwork Empire*. Syracuse, N.Y.: Syracuse University Press.

———. 2000. *Why Don't Sheep Shrink When It Rains? A Further Collection of Photocopier Folklore*. Syracuse: Syracuse University Press.

Gilbert, Elizabeth. 2002. *The Last American Man*. New York: Viking.

Hoffmann, Frank. 1973. *Analytical Survey of Anglo-American Traditional Erotica*. Bowling Green, Ohio: Bowling Green University Popular Press.

Hofstede, Geert H. 1998. *Masculinity and Femininity: The Taboo Dimension of National Cultures*. Thousand Oaks, Calif.: Sage.

———. 2001. *Culture's Consequences: Comparing Values, Behaviors, Institutions, and Organizations across Nations*. 2nd ed. Thousand Oaks, Calif.: Sage.

Hollis, Susan Tower, Linda Pershing, and M. Jane Young, eds. 1993. *Feminist Theory and the Study of Folklore*. Urbana: University of Illinois Press.

Jordan, Rosan A., and Susan J. Kalčik, eds. 1985. *Women's Folklore, Women's Culture*. Philadelphia: University of Pennsylvania Press.

Legman, G. 1964. *The Horn Book: Studies in Erotic Folklore and Bibliography.* New Hyde Park, N.Y.: University Books.

———. 1968. *Rationale of the Dirty Joke: An Analysis of Sexual Humor—First Series.* New York: Grove Press.

———, ed. 1974 [1969]. *The Limerick: 1700 Examples, with Notes, Variants and Index.* New York: Bell.

———. 1975. *Rationale of the Dirty Joke: An Analysis of Sexual Humor—Second Series.* New York: Breaking Point.

———, ed. 1977. *The New Limerick: 2750 Unpublished Examples, American and British.* New York: Crown.

Newell, Waller R., ed. 2000. *What Is a Man? 3000 Years of Wisdom on the Art of Manly Virtue.* New York: Regan Books.

Randolph, Vance. 1976. *Pissing in the Snow and Other Ozark Folktales.* Urbana: University of Illinois Press.

———. 1992a. *Roll Me in Your Arms: "Unprintable" Ozark Folksongs and Folklore.* Vol. 1: *Folksongs and Music.* Ed. G. Legman. Fayetteville: University of Arkansas Press.

———. 1992b. *Blow the Candle Out: "Unprintable" Ozark Folksongs and Folklore.* Vol. 2: *Folk Rhymes and Other Lore.* Ed. G. Legman. Fayetteville: University of Arkansas Press.

Sexton, Patricia C. 1969. *The Feminized Male: Classrooms, White Collars, and the Decline of Manliness.* New York: Random House.

Skolnick, Arlene S., and Jerome H. Skolnick. 1989. *Family in Transition: Rethinking Marriage, Sexuality, Child Rearing, and Family Organization.* 6th ed. Glenview, Ill.: Scott, Foresman.

———. 2003. *Family in Transition,* 12th ed. Boston: Allyn and Bacon.

Thompson, Stith. 1955–1958. *Motif-Index of Folk-Literature: A Classification of Narrative Elements in Folktales, Ballads, Myths, Fables, Mediaeval Romances, Exempla, Fabliaux, Jest-Books, and Local Legends.* Rev. ed. 6 vols. Bloomington: Indiana University Press. Digital ed. CD. Bloomington: Indiana University Press, 1993.

———. 1993 [1955–1958]. *Motif-Index of Folk-Literature: A Classification of Narrative Elements in Folktales, Ballads, Myths, Fables, Mediaeval Romances, Exempla, Fabliaux, Jest-Books, and Local Legends.*

Tiger, Lionel. 1969. *Men in Groups.* New York: Random House.

Tocqueville, Alexis de. 2004 [1835, 1840]. *Democracy in America.* New York: Library of America.

Uther, Hans-Jörg, ed. 1996. *Kinder- und Hausmärchen: Nach der Grossen Ausgabe von 1857, Textkritisch Revideiert, Kommentiert und Durch Register Geschlossen.* 4 vols. Munich: Diederichs.

Zipes, Jack, trans. 2003. *The Complete Fairy Tales of the Brothers Grimm.* 3rd ed. New York: Bantam.

Manly Traditions

Menfolk

SIMON J. BRONNER

When ex-football player and all-around tough guy "Iron" Mike Ditka announces in a magazine advertisement, "Never let an evening with a lady become an excuse to look like one," he is clearly talking to other men. Self-assuredly brandishing a hefty cigar held between thick fingers, he has taken off his tie and is talking to the viewer "man to man." In apparent answer to promoters of beauty products that appeal to the feminized "metrosexual," he reminds the consumer to "never use girly hair stuff." Why? In his gritty vernacular he explains, " 'Cuz guys are different" (*Sports Illustrated,* July 29, 2002).

Biologically, they definitely are. And conspicuous in those differences, as any parent-to-be will tell you in confirming the baby's sex, is the presence of a penis. Other notable physical differences that become pronounced in our lore are body shape (especially in the breasts and pelvic structure), chromosomal composition, hair patterns, vocal quality, and hormonal balance. In addition to men's issues that enter humor such as male pattern baldness and erectile dysfunction, there are other absences that figure in cultural as well as physical differences. As women will avow, men cannot get pregnant, menstruate, or lactate. From this biological inquiry, inevitably the question arises whether men's and women's brains are different. In lore, offhand references to men being thick-headed and women having maternal "instincts" abound, but neuroscientific work on brain function carries serious implications for the heated discussion of whether men and women inherently think and behave differently (Baron-Cohen 2003; Blum 1998; LeVay 1994; Moir and Jessel 1992; Treadwell 1992).

Folklore abounds to explain how guys are different and, indeed, the difference between "guys" and contemporary feminized "men." Photocopied and e-mailed lists of definitions circulate from office to office—usually among women—with humorous contrasts such as these:

Men: claim to be feminist but still insist on opening doors, driving, and paying for dinner.
Guys: claim to be feminists so they can let *you* open doors, drive, and pay for dinner.

Men: are experts on women's erogenous zones.
Guys: are experts on their own erogenous zone.

Men: put you on the phone when their mothers call.
Guys: pretend you're not there when their moms call.

Men: are afraid of becoming their fathers.
Guys: are afraid of becoming men. (Collected 2004)

Implicit in this distinction is the linkage of the development of masculinity from the mother and father to a new generation, and the effectiveness of such masculinity in maintaining modern relationships with potential partners. "Guys," it appears, stands for traditional stereotypes, conflated with working-class images, deemed inappropriate in a modern age of "sensitivity." This folklore of "guys" has precedents in humor of "real men" differentiated from modern or "gentle" men, who have supposedly abandoned their manly traditions. In an informally circulating test to see if you are a real man, for example, one finds

You think today's sensitive, caring man is:
a) A myth
b) An oxymoron
c) A moron. (Collected 1984)

In following the line of thinking that presumptions about sexual roles and relations between the sexes are challenged, new rules need to be established. A variety of bestsellers have, in fact, proposed to set in print such rules for a culture in flux, reminding one of the upsurge of gendered etiquette books and advisers in the late nineteenth century for a new American urban culture (see Bronner 1986b, 42–55; Kasson 1990; Fein and Schneider 1995; De Angelis 1997). Iron Mike's "rules," which, unlike most of the new manner books, come from an apparently masculinist perspective, have folk sources in humor of the "guy code of conduct" and "rules that guys wish women knew." The former speaks to men, while the latter addresses women. In the folkloric "code," one encounters images of the boisterous joke telling, homophobic, insensitive, violent, beer-swizzling, sports-crazy, oversexed male. Here are some samples:

1. You may exaggerate any anecdote told in a bar by 50% without re-crimination; beyond that, anyone within earshot is allowed to call bullshit.
2. Under no circumstances may two men share an umbrella.
3. Any man who brings a camera to a bachelor party may be legally beaten and killed by his fellow partygoers. (Collected 2003; cf. Dundes and Pagter 1991, 350)

In folk humor circulated primarily among women in e-mails and photocopies is a portrayal of men as easily understood, signified by simplicity, immaturity, lack of concern for appearance, and boorish behavior—in desperate need of reform, at least as perceived by women. Indicative is a list making the rounds of the Internet under the title of "Why Men Are Just Happy People":

What do you expect from such simple creatures?
The world is your urinal.
The occasional well-rendered belch is practically expected.
One mood, ALL the time.
One wallet and one pair of shoes, one color all seasons.
You can play with toys all your life. (Collected 2004)

Responding to the view that women really do not know or understand men, even though they swear otherwise, the folk rules emphasize special interests distinguishing American men:

1. Do not ask us what we are thinking about unless you are prepared to discuss such topics as navel lint, the shotgun formation and monster trucks.
2. Sunday = sports. It's like the full moon or the changing of the tides. Let it be.
3. Come to us with a problem only if you want help solving it. That is what we do. Sympathy is what your girlfriends are for. (Collected 2003)

An implication of this humor is that mass society has changed according to women's perspectives; therefore a complaint can be heard that men are supposed to change while women do not. This view can be summarized as fear of "domestication." Such humor in its exaggeration establishes that men still have interests and traditions that distinguish them as a group, and even if they comply with the new order of gender roles, they still have a need to express themselves as men. There may also be the view that they, in fact, may be treated unfairly because of the weight of folklore from childhood establishing boys as inherently evil and disobedient, in need of being controlled and changed, whereas girls are naturally good and cooperative. Many rhymes such as the one below are prevalent in America and express such deep-seated assumptions:

Boys are rotten
made out of cotton.
Girls are handy
made out of candy.

What are little boys made of?
What are little boys made of?
Snips and snails and puppy-dogs' tails,
That's what little boys are made of.

What are little girls made of?
What are little girls made of?
Sugar and spice and everything nice,
That's what little girls are made of. (Dundes 1980, 163–64)

Indeed, the common saying that "Boys will be boys" is used typically in folk speech to explain male aggressive or mischievous behavior as instinctual.

Often unexamined because it seems so ordinary, such folklore is essential for historical, social, psychological, and cultural inquiry precisely because it represents core values of a society and provides metaphors by which people live, often inculcated in traditions from generation to generation, group to group. The collection of this material as the folklore of gender serves, as Alan Dundes has emphasized, to make "the unconscious or unselfconscious conscious" (Dundes 1980, 175). Seeking to apply the lessons of this uncovering project, Dundes offers that people can hold folklore "up to the light of reason and through the unrivaled picture it provides" they can see "what wrongs need righting" (175). Political judgments aside for the moment, folklore is arguably unrivaled as evidence of gendered behavior because of the symbolic communication it encapsulates, the potential for structural, situational, and comparative analysis it suggests, and yes, the values, metaphors, and beliefs it embodies, sometimes outside the awareness of its bearers. And maybe because such symbols, metaphors, structures, values, and beliefs are outside of awareness is precisely why they find their way onto the canvas of folklore.

MASCULINE TRAITS, TEXTS, AND SETTINGS

Intriguing questions arise out of folkloristic inquiry into how masculine traits are nurtured, or "normalized," by traditions. Contributors to this volume follow the inquiry to traits that are socially "constructed," that is, created and maintained ritually through customary events and messages, and resultant values and beliefs consented to, or imposed upon, society or a group (see Berger, Wallis, and Watson 1995; Cornwall and Lindisfarne 1994; Brod 1988). Such perceived male traits include toughness, aggressiveness, independence, competitiveness, egotism, and dominance, although some may spin these loaded terms positively to assertiveness, goal orientation, courage, and self-assuredness. While attempts to universalize and nationalize the male "character" abound, challenges and exceptions to such generalizations may be made when considering men's traits in the contexts of particular groups or even particular settings. Further, by thinking of gender as a continuum rather than as a binary, it is also possible to envision complications to the neat divisions of masculine and feminine traits when considering sexual-social identities of hyper-masculine, metrosexual, transgender, bisexual, transvestite, and gay. For that matter, masculinity among women and femininity among men (in pejorative folk speech what might be called being "butch" and "sissy," respectively) are topics that not only raise the psychological issue of men and women dealing with the integration of their feminine and masculine "sides" but also the cultural manner in which displays of dress, hair style, cosmetics, jewelry, and body shape construct alternative identities or criticize normative expectations (see Pleck 1992, 32–33). Too little or too much male display may be considered a problem to others, legislated socially in the former with the cajole to "Be a man!" or the question "Are you man enough?" while in the latter with the derogatory comment about a "macho" or "testosterone" man. But how do we define what is in the middle, and for whom?

The popular notion of individuals having a dynamic of masculine and feminine sides harks to ideas of a fundamental "androgyny" introduced by influential psychologist Carl Jung. Resisting rigid definitions of masculine and feminine roles, which he recast as men's *anima* and women's *animus* working in a "contrasexual psyche," Jung inspired the modern view of pathological problems arising from polarization and denial of opposite-sex characteristics (Jung 1989; Pleck 1992, 32–33; Brookes 1996). The notion can be seen in post-feminist inquiries into female aggression and female masculinity as well as in psychobiographies of "strong" male tradition bearers (i.e., a controlling or leading influence on cultural practices) and male organizational leaders (see Kirsta 1994; Simmons 2002; Mechling 1987; Niles 1999, 173–93; Jones 1989). Female masculinity is challenging as a concept, as Judith Halberstam has observed, because it is "masculinity without men": "female masculinities are framed as the rejected scraps of dominant masculinity in order that male masculinity may appear to be the real thing" (Halberstam 1998, 1).

Folkloristically, such analysis of a contrasexual psyche has a bearing in male initiation rites and ritualized male roles in birth practices such as the couvade (Munroe and Munroe 1971; Munroe and Munroe 1973; Munroe, Munroe, and Whiting 1973; Dundes 1987, 145–66). In many male initiation rites into fraternities, sports teams, or dangerous occupations, an acknowledgment may be given for the gentle or feminine side appropriate to an earlier novice stage. The feminine is often ritually suppressed or rejected by celebrating brotherhood as the man's only need. Sometimes this rejection involves symbolic equivalence of homosexuality with femininity as in submitting as a fraternity pledge to paddling on the rear end (see Nuwer 2004). In the couvade, the expectant father experiences somatic symptoms such as indigestion, headache, and constipation typically associated with the women's pregnant state. Since there is not a substantial biomedical explanation for the couvade, many analysts have looked to the onset of conditions in the male as a self-imposed initiation into paternity. The contrasexual comes into play because as ritual, the transition signifies an ambivalence toward fatherhood by simultaneously expressing anxiety for the emasculating effect of caring for a child and sympathy for the feminine birth role (see Hall and Dawson 1989). Others may take a more masculinist stance, asserting that the couvade is, in fact, a result of psychological conflicts caused by fear of retaliation by the man's father symbolized in the image of the child as an extension of the man as a child (Reik [1931]; see also Dundes 1987, 145–66).

Frequently writers in many gender studies assume that masculine identities are total, yet ethnographic literature suggests the use of occasional settings to enact a range of masculinities, from the locker room to the living room for the same individual. In my trips to all-male hunting camps in Pennsylvania, for example, I have found that many men look forward to "getting away" to what they consider a manly tradition and *expect* to be able to act differently there. Part of the tradition is to emphasize manliness by braving the elements and refraining from shaving or bathing; indeed, many men go to camp to take in the scene but do not pursue game. Even though hunting is no longer necessary for food gathering, those who do hunt may talk about the pioneer heritage of the male provider in the woods they perpetuate. Some will say that they come not for the game but for the male camaraderie—and "the traditions and rituals" setting the scene apart from domestic life. A longtime member of one camp I attended liked to tell me about hunters he knew who acted like a lion at camp and a lamb at home. You could not guess their occupations or class from attendance at camp, as they were dressed alike in burly flannel shirts and heavy boots. The dress code identifies them as manly hunters. One can detect the construction of ritual events with different expectations of masculine display. At one camp where members are mostly married men in their forties, the tradition on Friday night before the opening of deer season is to cook a hearty dinner of man-sized steaks, with a side of baked potatoes, and wash them all down with beer. Conversation moves from one adventure story to the next, often repeated from year to year; after recounting last year's hunt and inviting hunters who have recently bagged game to regale the group, the storytelling typically becomes raunchy. On Saturday night, however, the wives attend a dinner ceremonially cooked by the men where the conversation and the meal are much more sedate. The women are served and flattered. It is as if with this gesture, permission is granted to return to the primal man of the wild, at least temporarily.

And what about those rituals that allow men to perform femininity? One thinks of cross-dressing and role reversals such as sailors' dressing in drag at crossing-the-equator rituals on board ships at sea, Halloween parties that invite masquerading, or mock beauty pageants staged by fraternities. Anthony Avery, in his essay in this volume, finds that unlike such

Hunters pose with their "bagged" buck and masculine symbols of cigar, guns, and booze, Washington, 1949. *Photograph courtesy Simon J. Bronner.*

performances that ridicule the idea that men could assume a women's identity, constructed rave events encourage men to symbolically embrace the positive aspects of femininity through dress for their masculine identity. These events raise questions about the prevailing gender model of "separate spheres" and the idea of total identity. Examining the notion of normative masculine traits over time, do we see stability or change? Many settings in which manly traditions are expressed, such as hunting, sporting, building, and soldiering, change over time, and there has been the historical argument that American society has progressively become feminized as either genteel values prevail or manly behaviors are suppressed in the name of social progress and advancing civilization (Douglas 1977; see also Pendergast 2000; Kimmel 1996; Rotundo 1993). Another historical take on this development is the spread of public education through the nineteenth and twentieth centuries and the suppression of brutish manly "in-

Hunters gather at camp on Friday night before opening of antlered deer season with storytelling and steak dinner, Pennsylvania, 2003. *Photograph by Simon J. Bronner.*

stincts," because of an inculcated middle-class morality based on feminine, Christian values in the reformist call for a civil society (Mangan and Walvin 1987; see also Ames 1992; Bederman 1995; Sommers 2000). A frequent feminist perspective is to view the entrenchment of patriarchy or male privilege in society despite public moves toward equality. In answer to the historicist argument for a progressive feminization in American culture, a counter-argument is made for "male hegemony," that is, the cultural illusion of reform consented to by an invisible, controlling male superstructure because it actually serves men's interests or persists in marginalizing women (see Herb Goldberg 1976; Friedan 1983; Lears 1984; Chafe 1991; Farrell 1993; Hollis, Pershing, and Young 1993; Faludi 1999; Bourdieu 2001). Debate then shifts to the nature and source of competition between the sexes (is it a dysfunctional war or a functional system?) and the political (some may say post-modern) question of who dominates and who is a victim (and as many book titles have claimed, whether male privilege is a "myth").

HISTORICALLY SPEAKING: FEMINIZATION, RITUALIZATION, AND MANLINESS IN AN AMERICAN ETHOS

If the overarching folklore of gender I cited previously indicates that men are forced to change toward a feminine model of sensitivity in the company of women, then arguably all-male groups and their folklife are discouraged in the new American ethos. All-female groups physically separated in a "room of her own" tend to be validated more because they allow for a safe, undominated space to build women's confidence in a patriarchal society. This is a striking historical development after a period when social separation of boys and men to attend to their special needs was considered desirable. Examples of institutions coming out of the early twentieth century seeking to build "strength of character," folk masculine values adapted for modern civilization, include Boy Scouts, Boys Clubs, college fraternities, fraternal organizations, bachelor or gentleman clubs, organized sports including Little League, athletic organizations and gyms including the YMCA, and boys' schools (see Chudacoff 1999; Mechling 1987, 2001; Kasson 2001; Fine 1987b). The culprit then for boys' troubles was reported to be the crowding of urban spaces, disruption of traditional family structures, and emasculating effects of industrialization. Programs to bring boys out to the country, provide a nurturing social environment, or engage in supervised confidence-building activities such as contact sports were considered the proper correctives. Reformers sought to adapt boys' values of toughness, loyalty, competitiveness, and aggressiveness for a new industrial society. Indeed, in many states, "reform schools" for delinquent boys were "industrial schools" intended to give boys training in the responsibility of work.

One can find ample references to concern for the consequences of "feminizing of culture" in America not only for the plight of the maturing boy but for society as a whole. Earl Barnes, writing in the popular magazine *Atlantic Monthly* in 1912 in his essay "The Feminizing of Culture," claimed that the process had became evident since 1870, when women became dominant in institutions of school, church, and press as part of a distinctive American democratization, removal of legal restrictions on women's freedom, and weakening of "sex prejudice." He was an advocate for the enfranchisement of women but worried, though, that "As to the feminizing influence of women teachers on manners and morals and general attitude toward life, there can be no real doubt. Boys and girls cannot spend eight or twelve impressionable years of childhood and youth under the constant daily influence of women without having the lady-like attitude toward life strongly emphasized" (Barnes 1912, 775). He thought the male teacher provided a balance to the authority of the mother, but with the rise of the female teacher, the boy's maturation would be dominated by women. This historical context becomes especially important in adolescent folk recitations emerging in the period with the "schoolmarm" figure combining roles of maternal and institutional authority over the increasingly rebellious boy, discussed by Ronald Baker and me in this volume.

Outside the classroom and home, changes in the structures of play as metaphors for American society came under scrutiny during the period of industrialization and urbanization. Referring to the power of play in shaping character, Barnes declared that "playgrounds are laboratories of conduct, and they should not only give physical exercise, but should also furnish standards and ideals" (Barnes 1912, 774). Implying that competitive play traditions strengthened character, he asked "can dancing, marching, and gymnastics" characteristic of women's grace and restraint "take the place of more aggressive, direct, and violent contests in the training of boys?" (774). He predicted that emasculation of modern boys as women strip away their manly traditions in school, church, and community in favor of genteel "liberal culture" would assuredly be a result. Although he worried about the ability of boys to be decisive, creative, and assertive under these new conditions, he also welcomed the refinement and intellectualism ushered by women in their authority of boys.

Many social leaders assumed feminization to be an inevitable result of modernization and welcomed the result as a sign of cultural progress toward an enlightened civilization (Conger-Kaneko 1906; see also Campbell 2004, 1–65). Using evolutionary models of progress, moralists argued that industrial civilization with its cosmopolitan, feminine values was a natural step up the ladder over lower rungs of brutish values of savagery and barbarism marked by the "rudeness" of primitive male manners. Intellect and reason triumphed in civilization over rugged manly physicality, evolutionists declared, and implied that civilization, like femininity, was cultivated in a process of refinement. Aggressive and antisocial, masculinity resided symbolically in the wild, in nature, while femininity was located in the home and domestic settings. Aggressive masculinity was innate—and problematic. Also viewing maturation in developmental terms, moralists frequently assumed that because of their "primeval" or "savage instincts," as well as their physicality, boys naturally had a harder time than girls in "progressing" beyond childhood. Particularly since the pubescent period was considered dangerous for boys because of their sexual excitement and aggressive phallic competition, much of the reformist attention focused on introducing activities to displace or suppress boys' "natural" tendencies. Thus began a rhetoric of criticizing manly traditions as "barbaric" or "adolescent" that still echoes into the twenty-first century.

In the nod to evolutionary or developmental thinking, masculinity appeared to be something to get above and beyond, rather than acquire and adapt. In response, some commentators tried to convince reformists that manly traditions were a resource to tap rather than to displace in character formation. Prominent writer Henry Childs Merwin, for example, asked in *Atlantic Monthly* at the end of the nineteenth century what was sacrificed for this progress? His answer was "closeness to nature" associated with primeval instincts and muscular vigor of the pre-industrial age. In this natural association of maleness with the untamed outdoors, he found positive values of "pity or benevolence, pugnacity, and pride" that needed to be recovered from manly traditions (Merwin 1897, 841).

Perhaps the most notable voice in the chorus calling for reinvigorating boys' hardy character through adoption in industrial civilization of the "strenuous life," associated with an earlier era, was President Theodore Roosevelt, who promoted the appreciation by Americans of the "rougher, manlier virtues" in traditions such as rough-hewn cowboy and frontier songs, wildlife hunts, and boxing matches (Roosevelt 1926; Garraty 1967; Porterfield 1996, 150–52; Bronner 2002, 3–7). The embattled tone of his appeal indicated, nonetheless, that these traditions increasingly become metaphors counter to the rising tide of civilization. The "economic man of the present day," he admitted, is bound to be gentler and more tender than "martial" men of the past (Roosevelt 1926, 257).

In light of post-feminist perspectives, however, revisionist interpretation is possible. Jay Mechling, for example, argues that many male youth leaders at the end of the nineteenth century attacked "feminization" (i.e., traits of weakness, dependence, lack of self-reliance, lack of trustworthiness, and lack of honor) but actually had a feminist goal of building an androgynous ideal. The founder of the Boy Scouts, Mechling asserts, devised games and customs drawn from American Indians, whom he considered manly (i.e., independent, self-reliant, trustworthy, and honorable). Calling the founder's program "conflict enculturation," Mechling found in them "experiences structured by feminist principles, teaching the young people of both sexes that a workable and satisfying alternative existed to the masculinist institutional structures that young people encountered elsewhere in their everyday lives in America" (Mechling 1987, 57). The "feminization" encountered later in the twentieth century has continuities with this period but is distinctive because of its multicultural implications and its representation of peacefulness and civility.

We can understand the late twentieth-century discouragement of men's folklife, sometimes provocatively called "the war against boys," for a multicultural society when considering the background and rhetoric of contemporary character education (Sommers 2000). In the wake of various human rights and liberation movements during the 1960s and 1970s, educators and reformers concerned with building a civil, egalitarian society berated segregation that could be perceived to perpetuate dominant social structures. Presuming that boys and men in groups would segregate themselves and gravitate toward dominance, prejudice, violence, and abuse, educators and reformers railed against many traditions and rituals involving

Contrast in visual culture of the nineteenth century of the pre-industrial rugged man close to nature and the industrial, feminized gentleman. Top, "The Beginning," from *Eighty Years' Progress of the United States* by "Eminent Literary Men" (Hartford, Conn.: Stebbins, 1868), xvii. Bottom, "Salutation," from *Our Manners at Home and Abroad* (Harrisburg: Pennsylvania Publishing, 1883), 92.

all-male groups as much as exclusively white organizations. The "real man" of this era was categorized in the guises of folktypes such as construction workers or situation-comedy character "Archie Bunker": working class, conservative, and biased (Sexton 1969); by the 1980s, a best-selling guidebook entitled *Real Men Don't Eat Quiche* satirized the anachronistic manly man (Feirstein 1982). Using ecological metaphors, educators and reformers devised "sensitivity training" and "diversity training" to produce a social "climate" diminishing bias, hostility, and conflict characteristic of patriarchy. In an environment emphasizing "diversity" to increase cultural sensitivity, women became a diversifying and moderating presence in society rather than men, and reformers sought ethnic traditions to introduce in the schools to de-emphasize white middle-class male hegemony (see Stern 1991; Mechling 1993). Some traditions, such as games and play at school recess, were, in fact, reconstituted to emphasize a new American ethos based on feminine social models such as cooperation (replacing competition or ego-centrism), congeniality (replacing conflict and toughness), equality (replacing leadership or dominance), and inclusiveness (replacing exclusiveness) (see Pleck 1992; Sherrod 1992, 237–38; Mergen 1995; Bishop and Curtis 2001). The ideal of the "new man" or "new lad," as cultural historian John Beynon calls the reconstructed industrial man, emerged as sensitive nurturer and narcissist (Beynon 2002, 198–221). "Traditional" men reported feeling stigmatized, raising the question that if society was so patriarchal, and men privileged, then why did they feel so disempowered and beleaguered (Brooks 1998)?

Along with the mainstreaming of feminine sensitivity in schools was a new intensification of masculine intimidation in other institutions. In response to the concern for curbing rampant youth violence, penal institutions pushed to treat delinquent boys and gang members with "shock" measures. These "ultra-masculine" or "hyper-masculine" environments, as they were called, implemented in youth boot camps and juvenile reform facilities try to show the boys the brutal treatment they can expect by staying along their manly criminal path (McCombs 2004; Lutze and Murphy 1999; Miller 1958). The folk roots of this controversial approach to rehabilitation, according to two criminologists, is the prevalent "instinctual" attitude of "Boys will be boys," or at least boys on the street (Lutze and Murphy 1999). In this thinking, boys cannot change their basic instincts but may be able to control them. Since boys respond to social dominance structures and displays of strength, the idea is to have the institution provide brutal leaders in the form of "drill instructors" and impose military-styled rules. In an ethnography of a boys' boot camp in Florida, Michael McCombs found that hyper-masculine status was assigned by demonizing the feminine as soft and weak. Upon entrance to the institution, drill instructors ridicule the boys as "pussy," "sissy," "little girl," "cry baby," "mama's boy," "baby girl," "bitch," "punk," "faggot," and "little Annie crotch-rots." The boys gain status by displays of muscular strength and mark their "promotion" by different hats adorning their heads. As feminized and infantilized newcomers, they must wear feminine red and move to novice green before attaining the more masculine blue and gold. In a ritual called the "coverboard ceremony" held in the drill instructor's "house," actually his office, the boy presents his case for promotion. If accepted, the boy is ritually required to stomp, bite, and kick the old hat (McCombs 2004). While perhaps appearing pathological in its demonization of the child and the feminine in the boys, it is also possible to see in the boot camp's use of metaphors an extension of mainstream society's assertion of gender difference in the contrast of masculine hardness and feminine/infantile softness (Murphy 2001).

Many other examples can be cited for the importance of ritual initiations marking separation from, indeed the rise above, a presumably lower infant and feminine stage of a male's maturation or experience. In some all-male groups, another strategy for gaining manhood is to symbolically replace the father. In hunting, for instance, where the emphasis is on transmission from father to son, the boy tests his mettle by killing the fatherly buck, often described as the monarch or lord of the woods. After the first kill, the father commonly smears blood from the buck on the boy's face or invites him to drink it, suggesting a loss of virginity (Huffman 1997, 60, 96–99; Sterba 1947, 425). In many army units the loss of virginity for the soldier is explicitly made when the initiate wears a red hat inscribed with the picture or word "cherry." His seniors inform him after his first jump that he just "popped his cherry." Or they force him to carry a cherry pie on the jump, resulting in a gooey red mess smeared on his face. Whether constituting appropriation of feminine traits or symbolic patricide, infanticide, or matricide, initiation is functionally central in many all-male groups not only for supposedly hyper-masculine military or correctional institutions, but also for businesses, fraternities, teams, clubs, and other mainstream organizations.

More than providing male bonding, the tests of endurance and infliction of duress in many initiations require boys to shed their maternal-controlled pasts by symbolically ridiculing the initiates as unsocialized, feminized infants and then impelling them to adopt senior paternal models. And as Alan and Lauren Dundes point out, for fraternity initiations, "the more initiates are feminized, the more macho or masculine the senior members appear to be by comparison" (Dundes and Dundes 2002a, 119). The value system implied in sorority pledging is arguably different, since sororities place great demands on pledges to show qualities of caregiving and cooperation, in addition to expressing creative abilities. Fraternities, often in manly military style, tend to reward values of toughness, physicality, and competition (Bronner 1995, 137). Although fraternities claim to use initiations for positive consequences of building trust and brother-

A soldier from 1st Battalion, 19th Special Forces, Camp Williams, Utah, prepares for his first airborne operation with his unit after completing paratrooper school. He is wearing the traditional red "cherry helmet" of first-time jumpers, October 4, 2003. *Photograph by Eric Eliason.*

hood, the appearance of physical and mental abuse in their initiations has created a public outcry against abusive practices under the label of hazing (Nuwer 2004).

In the landmark Supreme Court case of *United States v. Virginia* (1994), the Virginia Military Institute (VMI) in fact argued against the admission of women on the grounds that it would destroy the rituals and traditions designed specifically for an all-male institution. The central initiation is the "adversative system" of Rat lines. As described by Colonel Norman M. Bissell, VMI's commandant of cadets, a Rat "is a term we affectionately tied to the classmen that come to VMI, referred to as probably the lowest animal on earth and part of our humbling experience where we try to bring everybody into a basic commonality, everybody is very spartan, very—they are all treated exactly alike and the rat term kind of defines that very appropriately. They are referred to as a rat through about seven months, until such time as they break out of the rat line in the March time frame and then they become fourth classmen" (Strum 2002, 43). To break out, the first-year students withstand verbal barrages by gangs of upperclassmen in a formal ceremony. Upperclassmen can order Rats to drop down for penalty push-ups or stand naked for inspection in communal bathrooms. According to Colonel Bissell, the practice of depersonalization and resocialization at VMI "has far more dramatic, more pressure, more stress than boot camp or basic camp," but the result for the successful cadet is "you are brimming with confidence to undertake anything else in life" (45). VMI lost its case, although the Court did not dismiss the argument about the value of the Rat tradition but found that it was debatable, stating, "The notion that admission of women would downgrade VMI's stature, destroy the adversative system and, with it, even the school, is a judgment hardly proved" (289). The institution countered that traditions were all part of building strength of character in isolation; the rituals intentionally created a separate world, and since they were developed for a man's world, they would have to change for a co-educational environment. At the Citadel, female cadet Nancy Mace recalled, the system of intense hazing of first-year "knobs" was maintained; women became initiated as men, "bonded in a *brotherhood* of survival with roots that ran deep" (Mace 2001, 207; emphasis added).

In initiations for crossing the equator on military ships, the adversative system thrives. Sailors crossing the "line" for the first time, infantilized in folk speech as "pollywogs," "tadpoles," or "slimy wogs," are awakened by experienced "trusty shellbacks" and forced to appear before a Royal Court with King Neptune and Davy Jones, where they are accused of various mock crimes (Richardson 1977; Arnold 1986). Emphasizing their status as messy anal infants, they display their degradation by "kissing" the Royal Baby or Royal Belly. That means taking a homoerotic position and having their heads immersed in representations of semen such as raw oysters, eggs, and grease. Other related degradations applied may be having their heads shaved, often with comically oversized razors (suggesting symbolic castration), wearing clothes backward (suggesting that their faces are their "backsides" and their penises are converted to receptive buttocks), or being confined in stocks and beaten with phallic clubs. The pollywogs gain notice even before the ritual that they will be "pulled apart" before being reconstructed as shellbacks in the Loyal Order of the Deep. The shellbacks suggest manly images of hardness, endurance, and seniority; in circulated photocopies hung on walls, the shellbacks are shown dismembering the pollywogs, and the "Deep" is visually associated with sexual prowess of phallic penetration.

At daybreak of the initiation, the pollywogs are typically hauled and kicked through long tubes filled with garbage before emerging in a "coffin" filled with liquid. There, they are dunked and emerge to be herded

"King Neptune" holding a trident, his cross-dressed "Queen Aphrodite," and Royal Scribes dressed as pirates. Brandishing a pirate flag, the shellbacks take over the ship and submit pollywogs to punishments and initiations. One scribe is holding a shillelagh made from a fire hose used for punishments. *Photograph courtesy Perry Christensen, USS Oxford, 1966.*

together naked and hosed down in full view of a ridiculing crowd of shell-backs. But in the process, they get down on all fours as if they will evolve like creeping reptiles from the ocean or crawling infants to erect, manly humans. They ritually die in the coffin and are reborn into the new manly world. That evening, the sailors often gather for a Neptune's Ball, mytholo-gizing the men's world of the sea. Neptune appears as a bearded elderly man carrying an intimidating trident, an implement that carries phallic symbolism (see Dundes and Dundes 2002b). In some accounts, members of Neptune's court include men dressed in drag flattering the god of the sea and also serving to humiliate the feminine. As with the Rat line at VMI, "crossing the line" is a depersonalization and resocialization into a tightly bonded, separate world, necessitated, so officers insist, by the demands of the stressful teamwork of military duties. There is also the implication that mainstream society does not adequately socialize boys for the new task at hand. In references to the need to "break down," "dissect," and "pull apart" the novice are suggestions of a feminized mass culture in which sons as well as daughters model after their mothers. Therefore, the thinking goes, boys need ritualized transitions, or initiations, to re-create themselves with new manly parentage.

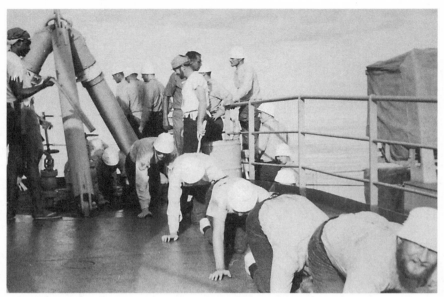

Pollywogs forced to crawl on all fours into garbage chute. *Photograph courtesy Perry Christensen, USS Oxford, 1966.*

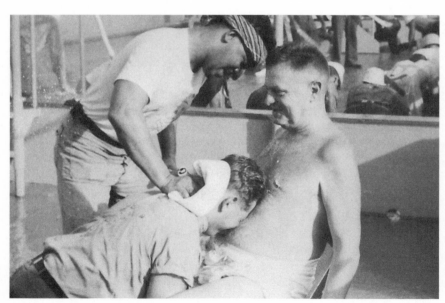

Pollywog forced to kiss the Royal Baby's belly, covered with raw eggs and oysters. *Photograph courtesy Perry Christensen, USS Oxford, 1966.*

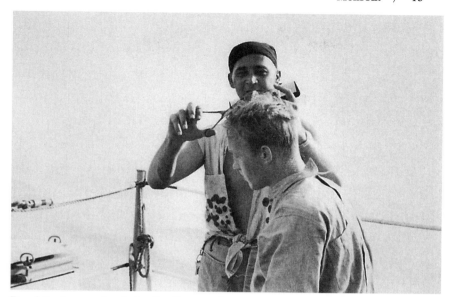

Royal Barber cutting hair of pollywog, who is forced to wear clothes backward.
Photograph courtesy Perry Christensen, USS Oxford, 1966.

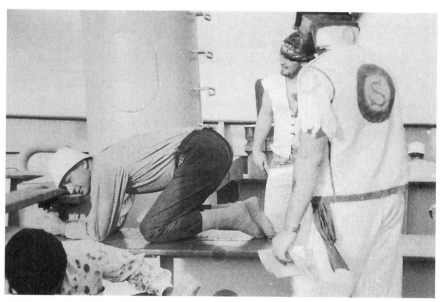

Pollywog prostrates before King Neptune's court, while being beaten with shillelaghs from shellbacks (note the shellback insignia on the back of the shirt).
Photograph courtesy Perry Christensen, USS Oxford, 1966.

Pollywogs dunked in the "coffin" after crawling through the garbage chute.
Photograph courtesy Perry Christensen, USS Oxford, 1966.

THE ETHNOGRAPHY AND FOLKLORE
OF MEN IN GROUPS

Considering the claims for the historical and social feminization of American culture, how does Iron Mike's assertion of manliness fit in? Do viewers see it as humorous or even folksy because his rhetoric, and his image, seem strangely anachronistic or incongruous? Or did the advertising agency think that it appealed to "guys" as the primary group who read *Sports Illustrated* and covet the famed women's swimsuit issue and photographs of men in sporting combat? There is evidence of recovering a sense of "guy culture" in other advertisements in the magazine, such as one for Valvoline oil tapping into the connection of men with machinery, blaring the message about manly tradition, "Guys don't pass down recipes. They pass down cars" (see Horowitz 2001). A photograph of a young boy admiringly watching his father working under the hood accompanies the text. And there is a proverb that bespeaks a male metaphor of hardness and aggressiveness: "Life Is Sport, Play Hard."

Is there a sense of Iron Mike's staged scene that rings true ethnographically within genteel society? After all, one can perceive customary associations of his blue-collar vernacular, a pronounced heterosexual stance, and smash-mouth football toughness heightening an air of manliness. Is the image presented, in fact, more manly because he is defying polite, or feminine, society's rules, coming up with his own (the one above is "Ditka's Rule #32")? The advertisement's popular culture "representation" invites ethnographic inquiry into everyday practice and the structure of men's social worlds. Such inquiry identifies and interprets bounded cultural scenes to uncover the distinctive symbols and systems evident from the scenes' customary social behavior and cultural expressions.

Some examples of that ethnographic inquiry bear mention for exploring the social construction of gender and the varied cultural maintenance of men in groups. James Spradley and Brenda Mann in their 1975 ethnography of a male-dominated bar exposed a bounded cultural scene that they thought represented the frustration of woman's work in a man's world. They found repressive expressions in cultural features such as "joking relationships" between men and women ("permitted disrespect" to women, the authors claimed), the division of labor (women were prohibited from being bossy bartenders), the kinds of space customarily granted to men and women (women were segregated in areas away from the bar), and even speech acts such as ordering drinks (men exhibited camaraderie by ordering beer in "rounds," while women ordered cocktails individually) (Spradley and Mann 1975). Twenty years later, students reading the text in my classes reported abundant examples of women bartending and different kinds of interactions in the "bar scene." Is that progress? The drink- and smoke-filled room once associated with men's leisure extended to women, they reported, and they knew places where they were not intimidated. Yet they could also tell cautionary legends they heard about the dangers of courtship in bars and single women being out at night. To that, men in the class told versions of a story in which a man hooking up with a woman he met for the first time in a bar wakes up alone the next morning to find "Welcome to the World of AIDS" written in lipstick on the mirror (see Fine 1987a). It admonishes listeners to know their partners in an age of AIDS, but is it also a cautionary tale about aggressive or revengeful women in the new bar scene?

The symbolism of this bar lore, told in gendered narratives, led to a questioning of the separation of behaviors found in an exceptional setting from the workaday world. The setting of the bar as a location for gendered play needed accounting for its diversity, they understood, and I could point to ethnography efforts toward this end, such as *The World from Brown's Lounge* (Bell 1983), about an African American bar scene, or "Fantasy Island" (Caceres and Cortinas 1996), concerning a Latino gay bar. In this volume, Ronald Baker and I examine the frequently collected folk poem "Lady Lil" as being understood within the manly setting of a "bar-room recitation." This and other settings suggest an accounting, too, for not only the sources—biological, psychological, and social—for behavior men exhibit with one another, but for the influences of the material environment as well as implied sexuality in the scene. There is a realization that men think not only of what it means to be a man, appropriate to various situations and settings, but also what it means *not* to be a woman, and all the normative expectations that come with that.

Toward this end, ethnographic studies of settings once considered women's scenes are instructive about notions of appropriate men's behaviors. Frida Kerner Furman's ethnography of beauty shop culture as a ritual of affirmation for older women maintaining confidence through beauty and gossip draws questions, for example, in a "salon" landscape now frequented by men as well as women (Furman 1997). Often men in those settings are self-conscious about being in a women's "beauty" space but compensate by seeking establishments that offer a cosmopolitan atmosphere. Another good example of the dynamic of men negotiating women's behavior is Thomas Adler's query of the commonly reported manly tradition of cooking pancakes on Sunday, whereas women feel obliged to cook other meals (Adler 1981). The manliness of the endeavor is preserved because it is ceremonial and located on a day not associated with work and therefore provision for the family outside the home. Similarly, the question of why many men are willing to barbecue for their families but often consider cooking on the stove to be women's work is answered again by the ceremonial or ritualistic nature of the cooking, particularly with its symbolic association with the primitive outdoors and the capturing of game meat in the act of providing for family.

While the above ethnographic observations were of men in putatively women's roles in America, what of situations in which men's roles are exaggerated to the point of what has been called "hyper-masculinity"? In this volume, events such as African American step shows examined by Tom Mould, Japanese American *taiko* performances investigated by Hideyo Konagaya, or bar-room recitations studied by Ronald Baker and me are examples. Besides lodging in total institutions in prisons, ritual performances of hyper-masculinity can be temporary and are sometimes seen as providing needed outlets for manliness in a feminized society. One may explain such performances with reference to the function of festival which in the face of an oppositional society can create a location to reinforce a suppressed identity and exhibit different behavioral norms, while allowing a return to the oppositional society's expectations after the festival is over.

Some of this need for ritual performances may also be developmental, as indicated in studies of pre-adolescent boys' tendency in America to ritually engage in "contests-in-insults" as a way to separate from the feminine and maternal (Bronner 1978a, 1978b; Dollard 1990; see also Dundes, Leach, and Bora Özkök 1970). The maleness of the contest structure is implied by the etymology of *contest* as *con* (with) *testis* (testicle); ritual combats such as "dozens," therefore, are akin, in Alan Dundes's phraseology, to "games and war . . . to determine who has 'balls,' or in Spanish 'cojones'" (Dundes 1997, 34). Different cultural themes and origins emerge, however, in contests-in-insults as they have been recorded among European American and African American groups (Bronner 1978a, 1978b; Mayer 1951; Dundes 1978, 96–97). Unlike European American "ranking contests," "playing the dozens" in many African American groups exhibits rhymed boasts of aggressive sexual intercourse with the other contestant's mother. Unlike European American contests-in-insults, little reference is made to homosexual activities. In the ritual frame of dozens, the boaster is inviting the other contestant to insult his mother to the delight of an encircling audience. The tradition drew the interpretation from folklorist Roger Abrahams that in separating from the mother to establish his manliness in the adolescent stage, the African American boy enacts such contests to deal with conflicting emotions. As insulter, the boy proclaims his manliness, or separation from the feminine, by bragging of domineering sexual acts, thereby destroying the controlling mother; as insulted, the boy puts himself in the position of defending his mother, with whom he has bonds of affection. "The verbal contests are especially important because they are indulged in by the very ones who are most conscious of their appearance of manliness," Abrahams states. It is also important in a lower-class urban setting associated with the authority of the mother and the absence of the father figure. He points out that the boy seeks to institutionalize a procedure of hyper-masculine humiliation to release aggression and repressed instincts. "Being bested in a verbal battle in front of a group of men has immense potential repercussions," Abrahams observes, because of the terror of disapproval, of being proved ineffectual and therefore effeminate in the eyes of peers" (Abrahams 1970, 56).

While boys' maturation by separation from the mother in verbal dueling is internationally reported, cross-cultural comparison of boys' contests-in-insults shows that particular cultural connections can be drawn to developmental traditions in a society. In this volume, Norma Cantú interprets Pepito joke-telling sessions among Mexican American boys as essentially contests-in-insults dealing with conflicts in the acquisition of *machismo* and finds no equivalent tradition among girls. Alan Dundes has added to cross-cultural interpretation of verbal dueling by pointing out the contrast of dozens, in which the opponent's mother is attacked sexually with Turkish boys' contests-in-insults whereby it is important for Turkish boys to symbolically play the active role in a homosexual relationship as a sign of simultaneous dependence and mistrust in male society (Dundes 1978, 73).

The interpretation of hyper-masculinity often draws on psychoanalytical ideas that the boy's initial identification is with the mother, and there is an imperative, therefore, to separate from her to establish a masculine identity. Further drawing on psychoanalysis, analysts may examine the motives for enacting folk expressions as unconscious and reflective of conflicts and anxieties that need to be resolved through the fantasy and theater of ritual, play, narrative, and festival. Also expressing extreme or distinctly masculine behavior is "manliness" used by many folklorists as a humanistic term, and it carries more of a rhetorical rather than pathological connotation (see Mechling 1987; Abrahams 1970). Jay Mechling, for example, confronts a historical puzzle he calls the "manliness paradox," whereby leaders of youth work revitalizing manly traditions appeared to further the interest of "creating androgynous human beings" (Mechling 1987, 54). The solution, he offers, is to see an evolution in use of "manliness" as a metaphor for desirable human traits in both men and women. He has support from Gail Bederman in *Manliness and Civilization* (1995), who found that manliness for the Victorian middle class comprised "proper characteristics of a man"—in short, being honorable and high-minded in the manner of a gentleman (Bederman 1995, 18). Manliness in rhetorical usage, however, gained through the twentieth century a connotation relative to the ascendancy of a feminine ideal for civil behavior; it represented man in a primitive state without the civilizing influence of women. It suggested for moralists of post-modernity a feral narrative of men's arrogant warmaking, bodybuilding, and social dominance, while some cultural critics saw in it a promising concept to draw sources for the reconstruction of masculinity in a period of gender confusion (Kidd 2004; Bly 1990; Sommers 2000).

In the designation of manliness as a hyper- or ultra-mode of masculinity, there is an implication that a mass cultural masculine norm is fairly static rather than being variable in subcultures and historical periods (see Kimmel 1992). Related to conceptualizations of "hyperactivity" or "hypertension," hyper-masculinity is often approached as a developmental problem, a pathology of having too much masculinity, especially among juvenile delinquents and residents of total institutions (Pleck 1992, 30–34). Intensification of masculinity, for example, is often expressed as dysfunctional social customs among youth gangs, criminal syndicates, penal institutions, military schools, and college fraternities resistant to attempts at domestication rather than a folkloristic consideration of the way that traditions construct a subcultural reality, sometimes in opposition, but typically relative, to mass society. To be sure, ethnographic inquiries into the persistent rituals of all-male groups enacted in the name of male solidarity, sometimes forced underground by disapproving authorities, raise public concerns when they report a growing exaggeration of manly traits of aggression and dominance into extreme violence, gun play, and emotional and physical abuse (Keiser 1969; Vigil 1988; Earley 1995; Bronner 1995, 126–42). Expressions of all-male groups presented as gang models are subject to ethnic, regional, and racial diversity in their expression of competitive manliness, profoundly shown in the intentional intensification of violent rituals by Asian and Chicano gangs to metaphorically enlarge their social presence and body image in relation to black gangs (Vigil 2002; Bing 1992).

Lest one think all men in groups are dangerous, arrogant, and violent, one can also consider accounts of the social construction of pacifism and humility in Amish tradition (Hostetler 1993; Kraybill 1989). The Amish form strictly patriarchal communities emphasizing separation of the sexes in dress and function. Focusing on issues of gender within plain groups, Margaret Reynolds has argued that this arrangement is not coerced; she points out that in exchange for maintaining community order and humility, women grant plain men dominance over the community, and wives voluntarily submit to their husbands and take domestic roles (Reynolds 2001; see also Schmidt, Umble, and Reschly 2002). Amish expression of pacifism does not mean that men abandon the use of guns or competition. In many communities, hunting is avidly pursued, with the biblical justification from Genesis of stewardship of the land and all its creatures. A distinctive all-male Amish game is *mush,* or corner ball, often played at farm sales. The game takes its name from the action of players in corners trying to hit players in the center of a quadrangle. The game has "innings" which are over when each corner player misses a throw or when each center player is hit. In avoiding being hit in the center, players often are forced to the ground, which provides amusement for the spectators. It is a competitive team sport with aggressive actions of hitting players, but one that emphasizes participation of the group since players substitute for those who are "retired." In a symbolic inversion, active competition is used to subordinate aggression, as evident in a tiebreaker significantly called "playing the bully" (Kline 1990).

Both within these subcultures and the presentation of general (or national) societal norms, a common way to approach the problem of revealing unstated core values and beliefs (sometimes stated as "worldview") as part of situated identities is to record expressive texts within various social situations. Repeating and varying, transmitted orally or through customary example and imitation and demonstration, these texts are frequently labeled as folk because they represent the process of tradition. As folklore, they draw attention to themselves as a type of artistic communication in material as well as social and verbal forms. Participants recognize tradition in references to folklore as material with precedent and spread, therefore going beyond the individual to suggest conventional wisdom or social norms. As such, folklore is typically performed and symbolic; in the social interaction of performer and audience, or what has been called a "fictive plane" or "cultural register," analysts interpret the meaning and impact of folkloric forms, or texts, and their contexts. Ironically, such "artistic communication in small groups," the phrase Dan Ben-Amos gave as a definition of folklore, serves in its expression of shared symbols among participants to socially construct reality and convey identity (Ben-Amos 1972; Berger and Luckman 1967). Focusing on the use of symbols expressed in language, gestures, narrative, and play to create a social frame and cultural system, many scholars draw upon an intellectual heritage of pragmatism, symbolic interactionism, and performance theory to arrive at a more particularistic interpretation than psychoanalytical approaches to culture (Sandstrom, Martin, and Fine 2003; Bronner 1988; Abrahams 1985; Charon 2001; Lemert and Branaman 1997; Becker and McCall 1990; Bauman 1977; Geertz 1973; Blumer 1969). In this constellation of related approaches, one finds emphasized the relativity and simultaneity of social situations, the variable, strategic use of symbols, the manipulation and control of identities by individual actors, and the "multivalence" of texts and behaviors—that is, multiple meanings of expressions for participants in the scene. Yet if in a post-modern mode all events are unique, is generalization about gendered expressions and identities possible? Can the generalizations of psychoanalytical interpretation, comparative content analysis, and feminist perspectives be incorporated into a situated interactionist analysis? Several authors in this volume—Jay Mechling, Bill Nicolaisen, Gary Alan Fine, Hideyo Konagaya, Norma Cantú, and I—allude to such methodological questions.

THE TRADITION OF MANLY TRADITIONS

A key that emerges in the essays to venture testable hypotheses about gendered behavior in America is the concept of tradition in "manly traditions." Reference to tradition in folklore and folk groups implies consistencies and continuities "through time and space in human knowledge, thought, belief, and feeling," as folklorists Robert Georges and Michael Owen Jones have underscored, and therefore imply the ability to generate generalizations based on precedents or models (Georges and Jones 1995, 1). Moreover, the reference to tradition carries the connotation of cultural authority or signification, and hence tradition forms patterns that can be identified, compared, and interpreted (Bronner 1998; Williams 1983, 318–20). Tradition as a precedent to guide new enactments is not necessarily fixed; it involves a negotiation between individuals and their various communities, often about alterations to the traditions responding to conditions at the time of the enactment. As traditions, rather than rules, customs and norms are subject to change; individuals often creatively influence or innovate traditions. This malleability also makes traditions vulnerable in a complex, diverse society and puts more pressure on participants to be concerned for outsiders' perceptions raised about the traditions as they are performed by insiders. In this process, as shown by my example of hunting used as a metaphor rather than a practice, symbolizations, or stereotypes, of tradition often arise. Traditions are adapted and renegotiated in various situations, sometimes invented, and therefore the functions of communicated texts may have different functions in a range of settings.

What, one should ask, constitutes a masculine text and setting? For many analysts in this volume using dramaturgical rhetoric, they are the scripts and stages produced by men as social actors. There is also a sense in which such texts and settings are recognized for communicating manly traits, even if the actors are not men or do not come from a male subculture. Women, therefore, can express masculine texts, and often do, as Gary Alan Fine points out in this volume is the case for women operating in formerly male-dominated occupations. And in some cases, as in my essay on narratives and carvings about male corpses sitting up in a coffin, jokesters can alter the performance to mute the masculine voice in the text. Part of the maturation process for children, as contributor Jay Mechling points out, is in fact learning the appropriateness of gendered texts and settings. Some social psychologists believe that separation of expressions into cognitive categories of masculine and feminine begins in infancy, particularly in the differences apparent between mother-raised boys and girls. Shopping for children's bedding is a study, for example, in mass cultural expectations of expressive differences: trucks, athletics, and dogs for boys, usually in shades of blue, versus butterflies, cats, and princesses, typically in pink, for girls. As Mike Ditka's nickname of Iron Mike indicates, metals and metaphors for hardness and endurance often apply to men while flowers and representations of sweetness and softness apply to women.

Studies of the development of gaming in early childhood consistently show that by the time the child enters school, different gendered social patterns occur. Boys tend to run in packs, engage in rough, competitive play, and cover a large amount of ground, while girls tend to play in small groups, enjoy relatively passive cooperative or creative play, and cover a small area (Lever 1976, 1978; Sutton-Smith 1972, 405–15; Sutton-Smith 1979; Hughes 1993; Thorne 1993). Mechling wants to explain these developments in terms of a feminist psychoanalytical theory and extrapolate to adulthood the normative behaviors of childhood (see also Mechling 2001). Other contributors to the volume—Ronald Baker, Norma Cantú, and Tom Mould—question the pivotal role of coming-of-age traditions in the formation of lifelong attitudes toward masculinity, suggesting a kind of "socioanalysis" complementing "psychoanalysis" (see Bourdieu and Wacquant 1992, 62–74). Considering the emphasis on variable performances and texts of identity in this volume, the concept of *habitus* developed by sociologist Pierre Bourdieu, who has written on masculine domination, may be appropriate to summarize the way that *praxis,* or routinized social actions, result from the culturally situated dynamic between individuals and their communities (Bourdieu 1977; Bourdieu 2001). The term denotes the total set of "dispositions," or propensities for specific actions, which shape and constrain social practices, and it implies that meanings are located in the experiences that social actors bring to their interactions rather than in props or objects assumed to have a definite symbolism or value (Bourdieu and Wacquant 1992; Bourdieu 1977). For example, rather than argue

Graphic used in advertising circuit party, featuring its most prominent icon, a full frontal view of a muscular male torso. *Poster by Kevin Mason.*

whether GI Joe or Barbie dolls are toys that are intrinsically "bad" for boys to play with, socioanalysts or interactionists may examine children at play with these toys in relation to traditional practices to observe what meanings they inherit, select, perceive, and conceive in different social situations (Sutton-Smith 1986, 169–216; Best 1998; Thomas 2003). In discussions of diverse possibilities for masculine identity, then, it can be useful to denote the set of experiences, indeed traditions in one's raising, that come to bear on an individual's gendered responses to situations ranging from the family dinner to the hunting camp meal. As every author points out in this volume, men in different situations feel the weight of such propensities and will creatively respond through folk expressions.

Do manly traits necessarily accompany masculine texts and settings? In addressing the behaviors in polysexual "rave" and gay "circuit" scenes, Anthony Avery and Mickey Weems in this volume point out the efforts to organize locations for manly behavior without the associated trait of aggression. Although gay and club cultures are presented as an antithesis to manliness in many studies of masculinity, Avery and Weems show the self-conscious presentation of male muscularity in these contexts and the transformation of dance, often considered a feminine domain, into a showcase for men. Reflecting on the ritualized connection of homosexuality with manliness, and a reconfiguration of cultural expectations in the process, they follow Joseph Goodwin's call for more complex understandings of gay and alternative sexual subcultures through investigations of folklore. Gay folklore, Goodwin found, "calls into question the standards imposed upon society by the straight culture, and in doing so frequently inverts and distorts these values. . . . By twisting the mores of the straight culture, gay people in a very real sense invalidate the heterosexual world, saying not 'gay is as good as,' but 'gay is better than'" (Goodwin 1989, 85). Avery and Weems examine the alternative worlds established through the development of folk events, and their effectiveness in maintaining the subculture, "twisting the mores of the straight culture," outside these events.

Storytelling events are also common locations for manly behavior, particularly joke telling, and several contributors to this volume explore them as social frames in which symbolic communication occurs which could not take place elsewhere (see chapters by McNeil, Baker, Kelley, Bronner, Cantú, Nicolaisen, and Mechling). One macro context for some of these micro-studies is provided in Carol Mitchell's comparison of men's and women's folkloric traditions, drawing on a sample of students at Colorado State University in 1975. Investigating the content and style distinguishing joke telling by men and women, she concluded, "The differences in the male and female joke-telling traditions are similar to and derive from the different roles that men and women have been expected to play in our society. And in turn the joke-telling traditions continue to help in the maintenance of those separate roles" (Mitchell 1985, 166). She therefore hypothesized a reciprocal determinative significance for these texts. She found that men told more openly "aggressive" jokes than women told; they included "more obscene jokes, more racial, ethnic, and religious jokes, and more jokes about death than women told" (166–67). Women, on the other hand, preferred morbid jokes and jokes about authority. Men portrayed stereotypes in their jokes of the "nagging wife, the bitch, and the promiscuous and insatiable female. And often these women are punished in some way by a male character in the joke" (167). Men's joke-telling styles and audiences also differed, she found. Men more than women reported enjoying competitive joke telling in which each man attempts to tell a joke funnier than the last, and they found public settings with more than a few listeners to be appropriate for joke-telling performances. Women preferred telling jokes to small groups of close friends; indeed, they tended to enjoy "personal anecdotes" more than jokes. As a consequence, men appeared to use aggressive jokes to *prevent* friendships from becoming intimate, while women tended to use humorous communication to *invite* intimacy. Jokes to women, Mitchell observed, were a "way of sharing pleasure," of choosing texts that "conciliate opposing views," whereas men select material "to deride someone whom they dislike, while women rarely do this; and men are more likely than women to tell jokes that they think might be offensive to some members of the audience" (167–68).

Such macro-studies raise questions as to how and why men, as men, act in groups and how and why they express themselves. These are primary questions for this volume. The inquiry owes much to the provocation of Lionel Tiger in *Men in Groups* (1969) when he proposed a biological propensity for the formation of relationships in all-male groups which he called "male bonding." Yet there were social consequences, he pointed out, since such bonding did not result in an outcome such as a baby, and further, it risked accusations of homoeroticism. He proposed, for example, that social responses of aggression and violence are outcomes of this tension in male groups. He suggested healthy as well as negative consequences of male bonding, including political loyalty, extension of male membership in groups (compared to the size of women's groups), emotionality of initiations, and ribaldry of anti-female expressions. While aware of skepticism for the universal biological basis for such bonding, Tiger invited ethnographic work on male groups, because "Individuals will presumably react to male-bond symbolic stimuli in terms of their own experience and the canons of their own culture" (Tiger 1984, 197; see also Tiger 1999).

In American culture, questions of relationships of men to one another often center on the maintenance of friendship and its cultural manifestations (see Sherrod 1992; Hammond and Jablow 1992). Drury Sherrod, for example, has observed that men in American groups normatively prefer sharing activities to conversation, and this may be a sign that intimacy is inferred rather than affirmed (Sherrod 1992, 220). A tendency is often displayed, then, for men as friends to "pack" with several other men rather than form intimate relationships with one or two "best" friends by revealing themselves in talk, thought of as a feminine pattern, and they realize their connections by engaging in ritualized events such as sports, hunting camp, playing cards, among other activities. Sherrod hypothesized that change is likely to occur because of shifts in the traditional family structure and the rise of a sexually integrated service and information economy that "will force men to forge new bonds with one another" (238). Indeed, Sherrod advocates for men learning "direct" styles of relating to one another to achieve a kind of closeness he finds in other cultures. Such proposals for a general pattern for American male relationships invite more detailed ethnographic investigation among men's "packs" to understand preferences within the subidentities that naturally arise—for athletic, ethnic, class, and racial divisions, for example—and to uncover the maintenance of such subidentities within a mass culture.

Folklore is valuable as evidence in ethnographic and historical investigations because identities are commonly revealed, and negotiated, through traditional expressions. Yet there has been to date little discussion of masculine genres or metaphors. The founding document of the American Folklore Society in 1888 established an agenda of collecting racial, ethnic, and regional lore; gender is conspicuously absent (Newell 1888). Nonetheless, a bookshelf on women's folklore began forming in the nineteenth century with titles such as *Woman's Share in Primitive Culture* (1894) by Otis Tufton Mason and *Folk-Lore of Women* (1906) by T. F. Thistleton-Dyer. Upon reflection, these titles were less about gendered cultural practice than they were about the evolution of women's roles from the primitive in a natural history of civilization. Even with the wave of feminist calls for women's folklore study as gendered cultural practice from the 1970s to the 1990s, a comparable men's studies movement was slow to develop (see Farrer 1975; Kimmel 1987; Brod 1992). The reason, suggested by Lionel Tiger, is that "whenever social scientists talked generally about 'people,' they really meant males" (Tiger 1984, preface 2nd ed.). As result, women could be conceptualized as a social "other," or subculture, organized as a folk group, but men did not gain a sense of a subculture until they viewed their traditions distinctly from women and from feminized mass society (see Whitehead and Barrett 2001; Carrigan, Connell, and Lee 2002). Ironically, a major impetus for a men's studies discipline based on the realization of folklore came from outside the folklorist fraternity—the best-selling book *Iron John: A Book about Men* (1990) by poet Robert Bly. Inspired by the "wild man" theme of Iron John in the collection of *Märchen* by Jacob and Wilhelm Grimm, he suggested that the tough wild man is part of each man that was once in touch with wilderness and wild animals. Yet in a modern age notable for its unraveling of men's confidence in their own identities, he called for a new archetype in touch with God and sexuality, spirit and earth. In doing so, there is a revisionist agenda of replacing metaphors drawn from folklore of aggression and dominance with ones of virtuous courage and spiritual sensitivity.

CRISES OF MASCULINITY AND THE SOCIOANALYSIS OF AMERICAN DIVERSITY

Related to pleas such as Robert Bly's for reformation of masculine identity was a perceived crisis in the maturation of boys publicized by another best-seller, *Real Boys: Rescuing Our Sons from the Myths of Boyhood* (1998) by clinical psychologist William Pollack (see also Pollack 2000; Sommers 2000). He opened his book with a dire warning:

Boys today are in serious trouble, including many who seem "normal" and to be doing just fine. Confused by society's mixed messages about what's expected of them as boys, and later as men, many feel a sadness and disconnection they cannot even name. New research shows that boys are faring less well in school than they did in the past and in comparison to girls, that many boys have remarkably fragile self-esteem, and that the rates of both depression and suicide in boys are frighteningly on the rise. Many of our sons are currently in desperate crisis. (Pollack 1998, xxi)

The reference to "crisis" implied that therapeutic attention had primarily been given to girls suffering in a patriarchal society, and missed the rise of anxieties for boys relating to their families and communities sometimes hostile to their emerging masculinity. Perhaps, too, observers of crisis questioned the very assumption of instinctual manly oppression and repressive patriarchy underlying much of feminist analysis, or showed concerns for the stigmatization and stereotyping of men's traditions wrought by feminism (Sommers 2000).

Within this broad portrayal of crisis were distinctive ethnic and racial stories, often referred to as tragedies (Franklin 1992; Awkward 2002; Majors and Gordon 1994). Social psychologists bemoaned the "decimation" of ghetto-bound black boys because demographics showed that they spent little time with their biological fathers, engaged in unsafe sex and drug use, and were likely to be incarcerated for crime. While Pollack considered middle-class boys in general to be confused about the proper manly stance to adopt for success in society, sociologists such as Clyde Franklin found an entrenchment in lower-class black youth of a "compulsive masculinity alternative," an extreme "tough guy image" or "violent man" which was oppositional and unrepentant to mass society (Franklin 1992, 157; Oliver 1984; Bryant 2003). Components of this alternative masculinity stressed toughness, sexual conquest, manipulation, and thrill seeking, "all of which inform many black male youth that they must engage in 'deviant' behaviors in order to feel good about themselves," according to Franklin (Franklin 1992, 157). *Ebony*, a popular magazine among blacks, seriously asked its readers, "Is the Black Male an Endangered Species?" (Leavy 1983).

Folkloristic inquiries during the 1960s and 1970s into the male codes of the ghetto streets and the distinctive expressions of this social world such as verbal contests ("dozens"), misogynist "badman" recitations ("toasts"), and "profane" jokes ("preacher" narratives) presaged the crisis, particularly in collections in predominantly black prisons and industrial or reform schools (Roderick J. Roberts 1965; Abrahams 1970; Jackson 1974). The reformist concern that the hyper-masculine "role models" of the black drug dealer and hustler swayed ghetto youth more than teachers and professionals was anticipated by folkloristic explorations of the alternative manly world known colloquially as "The Life" (Wepman, Newman, and Binderman 1976). "The Life," one classic study of black menfolk warned,

African American men gathering on the street for talk in the Mississippi Delta. *Photograph by Simon J. Bronner.*

"provides a highly visible reference group, successful role models whose dash has irresistible appeal for many disaffected black youths. Whether with naturalism or caricature, toasts depict this swagger and dash without apology or defensiveness" (Wepman, Newman, and Binderman 1976). In the folk speech of "dawg" and "bull" used by black men to address each other on the streets is a recognition of this naturalistic connection between men and aggressive animals; their lore often appears hyper-homophobic as the scholarly title *The Greatest Taboo* on the subject indicates (Constantine-Simms 2001). In this volume, Tom Mould examines the inheritance of this black swagger and naturalistic imagery as both positively and negatively perceived traits among mostly middle-class African American collegians, negotiating between the boisterous "gangsta" image of the streets and re-served sophistication of "coolness" within the success model of the college graduate working in feminized mass society. He finds that "step shows," fraternity-organized performances of dance and recitations, figure prominently in this sensitive negotiation.

Latinos have also been a focus of ethnic concern about compulsive masculinities because of the frequent association of hyper-masculinity with terms such as *macho* and *machismo* in Latino cultures. Folklorist Américo Paredes, working with Mexican Americans, calls the *macho* the "superman of the multitude." *Machismo,* he finds, is related to the Argentinean *gaucho* in its characteristic traits: "the outrageous boast, a distinct phallic symbolism, the identification of the man with the male animal, and the ambivalence toward women—varying from an abject and tearful posture to brutal disdain" (Paredes 1993, 215). The folk roots of this masculinity are found in dress (the hat, either the fancy *sombrero* or the wide-brimmed Borsalino), gunplay with the pistol, and elaboration of the horse and automobile (215). They are also apparent in folksongs or distinctive *corridos* in which the man openly admits his frustration and failure and conceals his humiliation or the scorn directed at him by resorting to aggressive or compensatory expressions (216). Paredes worries that while *machismo* appears anachronistic in mass society, it gains strength from a sense of nostalgia by an upwardly aspiring group such as new generations of Mexican Americans. He observes that it is cultivated by "those who feel they have been born too late. The North American *macho* acts as if the Wild West had never come to an end; the Mexican *macho* behaves as if he is still living in the times of Pancho Villa" (Paredes 1993, 234). Ironically, while many Mexican American leaders attempt to reorient the *macho* men for a modern age, *machismo* is being appropriated from Latinos by mass society for "a more perfect realization of the potentialities of man," according to Paredes. Hence, many Chicanos feel mixed messages about the expectations placed on them as men. Noting the public celebration of the Chicana's coming-of-age in *Quinceañera* at fifteen years old, but the absence of an equivalent common ritual for boys, Norma Cantú in her study here of Chicanos in a Texas border community relates this straddling of cultures and its consequent confusion of masculinities as boys mature to manhood. As other contributors have focused on signification of anxieties about manliness in the fictive plane of folklore, Cantú interprets expressions of male bravado in *corridos* and jokes as symbol-laden locations to work through cultural conflicts.

While much of the perceived "crisis" in masculinities is about boys adjusting to the control of their manly traits and traditions, variants of the story are about combating societal prejudice by asserting manliness. Jewish and Asian men in America, for example, frequently complain about being typecast as studious, passive, insecure, weak, and domesticated (see Brod 1988; Gilman 1991, 1996; Eng 2001; Chan 2001). The attribution of superior intelligence to Asian and Jewish men, reinforced in jokes and images, carries an implication of domesticated brains over aggressive brawn, or the absence of muscular masculinity (Gilman 1996). Hideyo Konagaya, in her essay in this volume on Japanese Americans adapting the vigorous Japanese tradition of *taiko,* or traditional drumming, for strenuous displays of manliness, makes reference to motives by a new generation to change ethnic perceptions. She points out that the performed meaning of *taiko* in America as manly display is not one perceived in Japan, where *taiko* carries religious and mythological connotations. Another example of performed meanings different from the country of origin could be the symbolization of aestheticized martial arts as the harnessing of power through discipline associated with Asian masculinity. Whereas martial arts have included participation by boys and girls outside of Asian American communities, *taiko,* Konagaya points out, has been a social experience generally limited to Japanese American male youth.

In the modern esoteric lore of Jews, one compensation for the effeminate image of Jewish smartness is to embrace the "tough Israeli" masculinity. Transnational rituals for observant American Jews introduced in the late twentieth century of spending time on a primitive kibbutz or having coming-of-age experiences in Israel have the intention of adding toughness to the concept of the Jewish *mensch,* a decent, generous man (see Brod 1988). Jewish tradition contains a number of rituals aimed at distinguishing the Jewish man, most notably the *Bris Milah* (ritual circumcision or, literally, "the covenant of circumcision") and *Bar Mitzvah* (coming-of-age ceremony at thirteen years old). Anthropological and psychoanalytical attention to the social responsibilities of the Jewish man to his community has centered on the adaptable symbol of a "covenant" in the *Bris* ceremony and, psychologically, the guilt aroused in the father from submitting his son to symbolic castration (see Dundes 2002, 139–40; Goldberg 2003, 28–76; Schachter-Shalomi 1988; Silverman 2003; Mark 2003). For the Jewish boy, circumcision arouses a deep tradition of jokes that appear to hinge on the self-perception of submission, difference, and weakness from engaging involuntarily in a ritual with implications of castration. One aspect of the ritual that enters into uneasy humor is the fear of being feminized because of the homoerotic overtones of the *metzizah* connected with the rite, in which the *mohel* is expected to stanch the flow of blood from the baby's penis by applying his mouth to it (Telushkin 1992, 95–96). Rabbi Joseph Telushkin, for instance, reports a common riddle circulating among rabbinical students: "What is the worst *mitzvah* (commandment) in Judaism? To have to perform *metzizah* on an adult male convert" (95–96).

Added to this effeminate pressure on the Jewish man is the folkloric image of the overprotective, suffering Jewish mother, who is perceived as a source of the man's guilt, submissiveness, passivity, anxiety, and feminization (Dundes 1985b). The gendered attitude of ultra-orthodox groups differs, since they maintain a pacifist male-centered society and assign honor to the man for piety and study, thereby intentionally encouraging the development of brains over brawn. A *minyan,* or gathering of ten men, is required for worship services to be conducted. Women are not counted toward the *minyan,* and in orthodox congregations the men are separated from women by barriers, with the men's section given a structurally central location in the synagogue. Growing an untrimmed beard, fathering many children, and wearing black hats and distinctive clothing are signs of aspiring to all a pious man can achieve to receive honor—being a *tzaddik,* or righteous man (see Landau 1993; Heilman 1992; Mintz 1992). Yet within other denominational groups moving toward a modern egalitarian ideal,

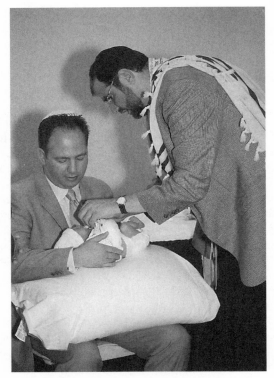

Bris Milah (circumcision) ceremony, New York City. The mohel in this shot is administering a cloth soaked in wine to soothe the baby boy and is holding a tube used in the *metzizah*. *Photograph by Simon J. Bronner.*

ultra-orthodox masculinity is accused of being hierarchical and repressive toward women. While ultra-orthodox groups reject homosexuality and discourage female masculinity in the form of women of wearing pants, reform congregations offer tolerance of such practices (see Stratton 2000). In between, conservative, reconstructionist, and modern orthodox congregations strive to respect traditions while considering adaptations to contemporary society, often making local decisions about worship practices. This brief excursion into the diversity within a single religious group is a reminder of the struggle to avoid an essentialist conclusion about an ethnic group or its masculinity without exploring its varieties of experience.

Some varieties of masculine experience need not be ethnic or racial. More inquiry is aimed at issues of masculinity revolving around identities of region, urbanism, and age. In region, for example, much attention is given to the southern "good old boy" and the hillbilly "mountain man," both of whom are often portrayed as violent, promiscuous, and hell-raising (McNeil 1995; Friend and Glover 2004; Harkins 2004). In a region with a heritage of a racial divide and a cultural ingrained code of honor, many folklorists touch on legends of feuds and folk justice that in one way or another hinged on perceived affronts to honor that men felt an obligation to avenge (see Montell 1986; Wyatt-Brown 1986). Other experiences that figure prominently in a folk history of southern manhood are the Civil War experience, Protestant morality, obsession with hunting and mastery, and plantation manners (Wyatt-Brown 2001; Proctor 2002). The legacy of white southern manhood also has its psychological legacy of a compulsive male submission of black men driven by exoteric folklore exaggerating black sexual and physical prowess (see Fry 2001). Bill McNeil in his contribution to this volume examines the aspect of the southern mountain man as primal man; his wildness is symbolized in unbridled sexual prowess. Jokes that southern mountaineers tell on themselves appear to add to the stereotypes, but often the jokes are on an emasculated cosmopolitan culture.

The rise of cosmopolitan culture, associated with the ascent of urban mass culture, has produced its own set of masculine images from the asexual, addled "city slicker" in McNeil's mountaineer jokes to the cool sophisticate influenced by gay and black culture. The concept of reserved, self-confident "cool" growing out of black urban jazz culture in the twentieth century became adapted as a modern masculine identity—stoic, stylish, and just a little subversive (see Dinerstein 2003). Not outwardly aggressive, this masculinity of urban coolness emphasizes manly self-awareness and difference. During the 1990s, a new, more boisterous brand of urban coolness took on the name of "metrosexual" to refer to absorbing "dispositions" and styles from alternative sexualities to express one's individuality. Popularized by the television show *Queer Eye for the Straight Guy,* the metrosexual male identity, according to many critics, coined a term for a new male narcissism (Safire 2003). *The Metrosexual Guide to Style: A Handbook for the Modern Man* (2003) exudes, above all, a manly self-confidence, even as the man embraces his "feminine side" (Flocker 2003, xi–xv). He is an urban man with a heightened aesthetic sense, and he spends time and money on shopping and enhancing his appearance. As for sexuality, the term's inventor, Mark Simpson, states that "He might be officially gay, straight or bisexual, but this is utterly immaterial, because he has clearly taken himself as his own love object and pleasure as his sexual preference. Particular professions, such as modeling, waiting tables, media, pop music and, nowadays, sport, seem to attract them" (Safire 2003). Usually, the label of "metrosexual" is for a straight man who satisfies his male ego by being up-to-date, setting trends for the twenty-first century, and flattering himself. Besides examining its links to the culture of "cool," metrosexual identity also invites query of its folk roots in the mainstreaming of gay and feminine culture in urban life and the concept of modernity. Wearing of earrings by men and hair dyeing, for example, once considered too gay or feminine by many men, have been incorporated into various masculinities, including supposedly *macho* men's groups such as bikers, professional athletes, and tradesmen.

In a pre-modern mode, much of the attention on the development of masculinity focused on the transition from adolescence to adulthood or the acquisition of gendered behavior in early childhood. Folklorists and social scientists compounded this tendency by rarely dealing with changes over the course of adulthood. Children and senior citizens as marginalized groups drew inquiry about growth and decline of bodies and the transmission of culture in an inevitable process. With the expansion of the life span, adulthood can also be approached culturally and appreciated for its diversity. Stanley Brandes, for example, examined the rise of rituals and beliefs around turning the age of forty, often called the "midlife crisis." He showed its folk roots in beliefs about age forty as a quantity for the end of life and found social factors in America suggesting its special appropriateness for men in a service and information economy (Brandes 1987). This insightful interpretation of an emergent tradition's folk roots raises questions of other milestones in the life course and the way that modern society responds culturally. How is masculinity embodied variously, for example, at eighteen, twenty-one, thirty, fifty, sixty, and at retirement age? With the popularization of cosmetic surgery and drugs such as Viagra to treat erectile dysfunction, we can further understand the association of modern masculinity with youthfulness, especially apparent in humor, beliefs, and narratives about aging. Encouraging this line of inquiry, my exploration of carvings shared among old men in this volume shows that the humor of old age is often in material form and can be examined for its function of displacing thoughts of death.

As a result of the perceived crisis in boyhood and the heightened awareness, and often confusion, of sexual roles in adulthood during the late twentieth century, a distinctive men's studies gained momentum to create a location for clarifying and critiquing the varieties of masculinities in a diverse and rapidly changing culture. A leader of this movement, Michael Kimmel, announced that men's studies did not seek to replace women's studies but, rather, to buttress it and to draw from its scholarship. He insisted, however, that masculinity should not be set up as the negative "whipping boy" or "straw man" for social reform. He sought to avoid caricature of masculinities and replace it with a serious accounting of their complexity, including homosexual and alternative masculinities. Men's studies, he asserted, "responds to the shifting social and intellectual contexts in the study of gender and attempts to treat masculinity not as the normative referent against which standards are assessed but as a problematic gender construct" (Kimmel 1987; see also Brod 1992; Kimmel and Kaufman 1994). This agenda opened opportunities to examine the expressive choices that men make in various cultural situations, the forces of tradition on their formation of identity, and their responses to societal change. Anthologies such as *Men's Lives*, edited by Kimmel, for example, featured contemporary social headings such as "men and work," "men and health," "men in relationships," "male sexualities," and "men in families" (Kimmel 2004), and texts such as *Manhood in America*, also by Kimmel, offered historical sources for this inquiry (Kimmel 1996). The landscape of men's groups in such works is varied as comparisons are made between masculinities in Chinese, African American, southern, gay, and disabled communities, among others. It also opened up space for contemplation on adaptive masculinities for the future, including the recovery of traditional practices and roles.

Since much of the worry about boys and men is about their identities in the face of the "mixed messages" of suppressing manly traditions and at the same time encouraging expression of their masculine responsibilities, ethnographic and folkloristic inquiry often focused on controversial or "troubled" groups such as Boy Scouts, street gangs, immigrants, and ghetto black youth. Folklorist Jay Mechling opened his book-length ethnography of Boy Scouts, for instance, with the declaration, "Americans are worried about their boys. Large numbers of boys roam the streets without much adult supervision or even surveillance. They gather in peer groups and seem to flaunt adult values in their dress and speech. Large numbers of them are foreign-born" (Mechling 2001, xv). He lulls the reader into assuming that this concern is pulled from today's headlines, until he reveals it actually comes from America in 1900. As sociologist Gary Alan Fine accomplished for Little League baseball, so too Mechling offers insight into the ways that boys express their anxieties about becoming men in socially shared lore and construct cultural practices outside the formal guidelines of adult-run institutions (see Fine 1987b). Both Mechling and Fine propose that jokes and other kinds of narrative play an important role in symbolizing many of the anxieties that boys felt. If jokes appear to be a prime vessel for expressing contemporary manly anxieties, some cultural critics have noted the relative absence of other adaptive devices in contemporary America such as rites of passage that have the function of clarifying expected roles in the transition from boyhood to manhood (Raphael 1988). One of the implications, therefore, of considering masculinity in genre studies is to view the developmental uses of forms of folklore as they are enacted on ritual occasions, if not rites of passage, and in daily life.

Is it possible to talk of jokes, or at least some types of jokes, as a masculine *genre*, since men reported knowing more jokes, performing them more often, and appreciating them more than women? Before drawing the lines between the sexes too firmly, it should be emphasized that these are general patterns meant to be tested in observations in situ, and it is not uncommon to find men and women telling some of the same humorous material.

One also needs to be careful in assuming that texts are always mirrors of gendered culture. Some social actors may express texts as distortions rather than reflections of their realities and consciously perform in a manly way or include masculine symbols to communicate manliness. This warning suggests a distinction between *men's folklore,* expressions associated with the group's cultural production, and the *folklore of men,* material circulated as general cultural stereotypes or by women about men. Related to this distinction is William Hugh Jansen's terminology of "esoteric" and "exoteric" lore to represent traditions expressed *by* members of the group to and for themselves and expressed externally *about* the group, respectively, in analyzing themes and images in gender relations and subcultural identities (Jansen 1965).

And to what end is this analysis? For the contemporary moment, it attempts to answer the cultural meaning and expectation of being a man. That suggests all kinds of questions and goals. From whence do these meanings and expectations emerge? What different forms do they take? One thinks of the contextual and social forces of class, race, location, ethnicity, family, and so on. How are they expressed in various situations by individuals, and how do those individuals develop them over the course of their lives? How much control do social actors have over their gendered expressions and identities? How do gendered meanings, or the determinative forces affecting them, persist, change, or cease? And exactly how significant is the cultural meaning and expectation of being a man in the larger scheme of things such as the idea of the self and society?

In one sense, the analysis explains the moment with reference to life's situations and its precedents. In other words, one asks why we do what we do, and in a gendered mode of analysis, how the cultural attributions of masculinity and femininity affect our thought and behavior. This is a "reflective" or inward directed inquiry, aimed at understanding situations as parables to be read for their lessons. By offering interpretations of various situations they encountered in cultural practice, the authors in this volume give broader explanations. Jay Mechling explains the pervasiveness of the penis in men's lore, for example, as more than a sign of biological difference; he views the developmental and cultural implications of family relationships. Answering the question "How could they say that?" Ronald L. Baker and I explain obscene recitations as developmental imperatives of adolescent males to separate from the mother. Externally, then, there is often a *predictive* objective to be able to gain insights from gendered modes of analysis to anticipate cultural developments, nurture alternative models, or instill new ones. It is future, or other, directed in its orientation, often suggesting applications of analysis for the purpose of reform (see Brooks 1998). That is sometimes where the debate on winners and losers occurs, suggesting the corrective path for the future in public policy, therapy, or mass media.

Yet we find that the basis of drawing such paths, the knowledge of masculinity's roots in cultural practice, remain to be charted, for we know woefully little about men as social actors, or "menfolk." Indeed, Jay Mechling in his essay insightfully points out a prevalent folk belief that men are, in fact, somehow easier to understand than women, and this perception borne out in women's lore previously cited, such as the Internet list "Why Men Are Just Happy People," may explain the lag in discerning the complex identities and performances of men. Another reason is similar to the one for children and the elderly being separated for analysis as social actors more than adults. The social position from which observation is made is often imagined to be a metaphor for the society, so that the position is not examined for its cultural dimension within a range of groups.

For that matter, humanities scholarship also tends to generalize the cultural dimension from cultivated intellectual products in popular and elite culture, such as books, art, films, and television, rather than the practices and texts of everyday life and ordinary people that often fit into the purview of folklore and ethnography. We can understand the attraction to such primary evidence because the secondary sources in the training of our scholars normally come from books and visual sources. Yet the practices and texts of everyday life and ordinary people, we argue, get us face to face with what people do, what they say and make, and what they believe. We find a complex array of cultural practices and texts that merit investigation for their revelation of the dynamics of gendered identity, a few of which we present here to inspire a scholarship on menfolk.

MENFOLK AND THE PSYCHOANALYSIS OF TRADITIONS

I have in mind for menfolk an intellectual reference to the analysis of traditions enacted and perceived to be masculine and which contribute to the expression of men's diverse identities. It signals a consciousness of men as social actors whose traditions express their masculinity. More than a study of men, it is an exploration of the meaning of being "one of the guys." In the spirit of referring to everyday practice, "menfolk" is a colloquial rather than academic term that combines meanings of "folk" as group and process (cf. Kalčik 1988). Dictionaries will tell you that its primary reference is to men in groups or men considered as a group. In usage, it often refers to the male members of a community or family who are involved in traditional life. Extending Alan Dundes's idea of the folk group as any group of people with "a linking factor" and some traditions "which it calls its own," presumably to give it a sense of identity, we can show the significance of menfolk as a reference to the many kinds of cultural subidentities expressed by traditions that emerge from social groupings and encounters in men's lives (Dundes 1980, 6–7; see also Dundes 1983; Oring 1994; Del

Negro and Berger 2002; Abrahams 2003). "Menfolk" implies men *creating* as well as *following* tradition.

In his manifesto for a "modern conception of folk," Alan Dundes gave as a primary example the man telling a joke but did not at that point elaborate on the development of masculinity as imperative or style to a group defined by its male members. His point was to emphasize code switching that occurs as individuals move from one group to another. "A man normally wouldn't tell jokes exchanged in a military setting at a Church-sponsored meeting," he offered (Dundes 1980, 9). But unlike some of the other major identity markers he cites—religious, ethnic, or occupational—the appearance of being a man cannot be easily changed or masked. The biological fact of his maleness must be recognized because other men and women will bring cultural expectations of dealing with a man to their encounters with him. The question therefore arises about how the joking behavior exhibited by the man in the military setting or the church is gendered.

Inspired by psychoanalytical theory and cross-cultural anthropology, Dundes in subsequent essays, probably more than any other folklorist, explored forms in games and narratives that were distinctly masculine and provided a set of folklore-centered hypotheses that interpretations of menfolk here and elsewhere necessarily confront (see Fine 1992, 45–58). Although he did not single out men as a folk group in "Who Are the Folk?" he identified male-dominated occupational groups for his examples: baseball players, coal miners, cowboys, fishermen, lumberjacks, and railroadmen (Dundes 1980, 7). Germane to our discussion is his pronouncement of a problem statement for folklore in groups that informs the work of the authors in this volume: "the folklore of such groups provides a socially sanctioned framework for the expression of critical anxiety-producing problems as well as a cherished artistic vehicle for communicating ethos and worldview" (9). As expression and ethos, masculinity in this perspective is a product both of national or mass societal beliefs (i.e., exoteric lore) and the traditions generated by the group for themselves (i.e., esoteric lore).

Dundes's propositions in regard to menfolk can be summarized thus:

1. Because of various status anxieties, including being raised in a maternal-female environment, maturing boys have a need to prove their manhood repeatedly. They need to express their masculinity more than women feel compelled to affirm their femininity. A possible physiological factor contributing to this need is insecurity caused by the temporary nature of the male phallic erection, the "indisputable demonstration of masculinity" (Dundes 1997, 41).

2. Male competitive attempts to feminize one's opponent in games and war is a means of demonstrating masculinity as a reaction to the female-

centered conditioning experience from birth through early childhood until adolescence (Dundes 1997, 42).

3. Manliness is affirmed through ritual homosexuality in which the male guards his buttocks while simultaneously threatening another weaker male. In sport, game, and ritual, men play both male and female parts (Dundes 1980, 209–10).

4. Males attempt to supplant female procreativity through the symbolic creativity of the anus. Excrement therefore is linked with male initiation ritual and is a reference to "pregnancy envy" on the part of males. Initiation rites make boys into men, but they do so by means of feminizing the initiates (Dundes 1980, 193).

5. Particularly relevant to the development of manliness is the meaning of folkloric fantasy, which is unconscious. The symbols created in the fantasy are "projections"—unconscious attributions to another person or to the environment of what is actually within oneself—of internal impulses or feelings which are painful, unacceptable, or taboo (and such projection is not limited to sexuality) (Dundes 1980, 37).

6. A "male bias" or chauvinism is entrenched in American culture because it is inherent in national folklore and is actively transmitted to each new generation (Dundes 1980, 160).

7. It is wrong to try to alter folklore to eliminate the male bias; instead reformers should treat the cause of the disease—society and its attitudes rather than the symptoms of folklore (Dundes 1980, 174–75).

8. "Folk ideas" (also expressed as "cultural axioms" or "cognitive categories") exist as reflections of national "worldview," and in America they may revolve around masculine values such as trichotomy (prevalence of patterns with the number three) and linearity (thinking in linear patterns, manifested in cultural emphases on "straight," "forward," and "upward") (Dundes 1980, 158–59; Dundes 1971).

Among the manly traditions given to his interpretation of American masculinity is the distinctively American sport of football. Indeed, Dundes singles it out as striking the "most responsive chord in the American psyche." Probably because its mass spectacle and the appearance of warrior-players (i.e., exaggerating upper body strength with the padding and the uniform) suggest hyper-masculine image, it is considered a key to success for the identity represented by the team, whether it be the college or municipality. Looking for a source of this manly image, he finds it in adolescent rituals and games such as "Smear the Queer" in which males prove their masculinity by withstanding homosexual attack while feminizing— that is, homosexually attacking—an opponent (Dundes 1987, 178–94). He considers folk speech generated by the sport such as "penetration" into an "endzone" psychologically and culturally significant. He writes, "American football is an adolescent masculinity initiation ritual in which

Boys playing roles of "strongmen." *Photograph courtesy Simon J. Bronner.*

the winner gets into the loser's endzone more times than loser gets into his!" (Dundes 1980, 210). This analysis of masculine development also applies, he argues, to verbal dueling and ritual play in other cultures and to other male-dominated sports in America (Dundes 1987, 187–94).

Dundes suggests yet another connection to a social institution from the roots of manly traditions in the link of the homosexual battle paradigm to the conduct of war, which goes against the view that athletics is a model for control of violent aggression (Dundes 1987, 190; Dundes 1997, 25–45; Cheren 1981). Looking for explanation in male biological difference, Dundes speculates that the temporary nature of the male phallic erection forces males to "feel the need of proving, repeatedly, that they are able to achieve this indisputable demonstration of masculinity. Thus winning one match or one game may not be enough. One has to prove one's ability to feminize/emasculate one's opponent again and again" (Dundes 1997, 41).

The view that men *need* to prove their manhood raises again the questioning stated earlier in this essay as to whether manliness is innate or acquired. Dundes presents the acquisitive idea that in early childhood, boys experience frustrations, and hence anger, because their pleasure drives are socially suppressed. "Superego through parents and the church does its best to inhibit aggressive behavior," he writes (Dundes 1997, 41; see also Carroll 1993, 8–10). The striking feature of his analysis is not only its search for the sport's folk roots for men but also his psychological explanation of its tremendous appeal as a national character trait. Whereas he seeks inner psychological processes for explanation, there have been alter-

Soldier jumping over wall obstacle in boot camp, a sign of manly achievement. *Photograph courtesy Simon J. Bronner.*

native sociological interpretations looking outward at the social structure of patriarchy for their influence on the ritual celebration of violence and property control among men (Dunning 1986).

Structural and psychoanalytical interpretations advocated by Dundes for the interpretation of folklore may themselves be examples of suppressed manly traditions. Although the consideration of gendered behavior, most scholars admit, is indebted to the groundbreaking research on masculinity and folklore in the Freudian movement, Dundes has admitted that most folklorists and anthropologists are not "much inclined to favor explanations based upon structural analysis and psychoanalytic reasoning" (Dundes 1997, 42; Connell 1994). Several explanations can be presented for the skepticism. First, much of the movement was based on the Freudian premise that "human beings consist of men and women and this distinction is the most significant one that exists" (Buhle 1998, 3). Yet the consideration of gender has come relatively late in the folkloristic enterprise after historical emphases on race, ethnicity, and region (see Bronner 1986a, 1998). Second, many "emic" oriented ethnographers (concerned with the native point of view) resist the idea of unconscious functional meaning that must be unpacked by the "etic" analyst (concerned with meanings and categories outside the awareness of participants) (Dundes 1962). The historical and literary approach to folklore as texts tends to dictate literal readings of verbal content, with commentary and explanation from the tradition-bearer, rather than symbolic, structural, and functional interpretation of behavioral rationale often outside the awareness of tradition-bearers. This bias is not restricted to Freudian interpretation alone but can also be found expressed in reluctance to embrace other psychological, philosophical, or cognitive theories not grounded in empirical observation of cultural scenes or literal readings of texts.

Even the socioanalysis I referred to as a major movement in cultural studies may be suspect because of the insistence on inferring identities from symbolic communication in social frames that may not be recognized by participants. The post-modern favoring of situated frame analysis informs a scholarly position that every event is unique and meanings are particular to the social interaction within the frames. There is often less of a comparative and more of a parabolic interpretation; that is, lessons are drawn from the situation as if it were a parable of specific human interrelationships rather than a universal pattern given to structural (or cross-cultural) comparison (see Bronner 1986b, 211–16; Dundes 1989, 57–82). Further, in a "reflexive" check of an ethnographer's findings, post-modern intellectuals are concerned that they cannot be objective, and their studies necessarily reflect their empowered position; applied to psychoanalysis, the position can appear to critics to be male or white middle-class centered (Tavris and Wade 1984, 198–205; Walker 1981; MacCormack 1981; Helen Roberts 1981; Hymes 1974). Coupled with the multicultural fear that findings for one group will necessarily vary according to social forces of race, ethnicity, class, region, and age, and hence not be predictive, particularistic interpretation tends to stress differences rather than unities of social action. That attitude has created some suspicion of the sweeping claims of psychoanalysis for a unity of human development as well as other universalist comparative projects going under labels from various disciplines such as geographical determinism, Marxist or materialist interpretation, and historicism.

Finally, psychoanalytical interpretation has endured critiques for its oppressive "phallocentrism" and uneasy relationship with feminism; many female detractors were especially troubled with Freud's emphasis on penis envy as a motivation for women (Walker 1981; Tavris and Wade 1984, 185–205). Ideas of "womb envy" and "dread of women" have been put forward as feminist answers to penis envy and the castration complex (Tavris and Wade 1984, 185–92; see also Bettelheim 1955 for "vagina envy"). For example, Michael Klein explains the male attraction to sport as a compensation for the inability of men to give birth. He argues, "Since men cannot give birth, they need instruments or weapons to demonstrate their energy and creative power. Because men feel dependent from women and inferior in relation to them, they try to gain collective magnitude by belittling women and to achieve masculine status by surpassing other men" (Klein 1990, 180). Alan Dundes has gone further by suggesting that much of American folklore retains various nonbiblical male creation fantasies such as the male stork delivering babies and Santa Claus coming down the chimney. These fantasies, he asserts, continue the tradition of denying female procreativity while simultaneously asserting male procreativity (Dundes 1980, 173). Implied in the critique is the charge that the "male" self and the social state of inequality are privileged (see Tavris and Wade 1984, 185–92; Hollis et al. 1993; Buhle 1998, 22–52). According to Klein, for instance, the "creative power of man" manifested in "domination, control, command and submission" is contrasted with women's "care and protection" (Klein 1990, 180).

Mari Jo Buhle has argued, however, that rather than being antagonistic to psychoanalysis, feminism and the modern cult of egalitarian sensitivity have been in dialogue with psychoanalysis since its development, resulting in various permutations growing out of the concern for explaining gendered behavior (Buhle 1998; Tavris and Wade 1984, 188–205). Indeed, such permutations include what Jay Mechling and Nancy Chodorow advocate for as a "feminist psychoanalysis," I approach in a "social praxis perspective," and William Doty has referred to as "post-Freudian Mythography," "Psychosociology," and "Psychoanthropology" (Chodorow 1978; Doty 2000, 157–86; Bronner 1986b). They share with one another the connection of culturally symbolic action, often expressed as gendered behavior, to the mind (Cohen 1980; Foster and Brandes 1980; Dundes 1985a; Hudson and Jacot 1991). They draw upon the psychoanalytical and sociological movements, perhaps more than in folklore studies generally, because of the special concern for the development of masculinity. An important project in this intellectual enterprise continues to be finding explanation, and predictive generalization, for the culturally significant materials of folklore, in addition to discerning the dynamics of folk groups that produce them and express the "most significant distinction" of gender. Its imperative is to understand the workings of tradition and masculinity for individuals maneuvering in a complex modern society and address issues, or crises, of identity in our times.

FOLKLORE AS GENDERED PRACTICE, METAPHOR, AND SYMBOL

In this volume, questions of how male groups generate gendered identities in the production of culture are especially important. Folklore is crucial in these identities because it provides symbols, images, and expressions that convey deep-seated, yet often unstated, beliefs and values. Even in communication across the Internet, what could be called "digital culture," we realize folklore is at work, and many have noticed the social formations that go along with a virtual social landscape of online discussion lists, chat rooms, blogs, and buddies—many of which are gendered for types of sexualities—as Anthony Avery and Mickey Weems point out in their chapters (see also Bronner 2002, 58–60; Bronner 1995, 232–46; Kirshenblatt-Gimblett 1995; Ellis 2003; Davies 2003). As I began with folk "rules" for a modern age, I conclude with more gendered humor of rules coming into my "inbox":

> *Rules for Guys* [circulating primarily among women]:
> 1. The female always makes the rules.
> 2. No male can possibly know all the rules.
> 3. If the female suspects the male knows all the rules, she must immediately change some or all of the rules.
> 4. The female is never wrong. (Downloaded 2004)

> *Rules for Gals* [circulating primarily among men]:
> 1. The male makes all the rules.
> 2. If the male fails to make all the rules, his mother will do it for him.
> 3. The male is expected to tell the same golf/fishing/hunting stories at every get-together comprised of more than four people. The female will laugh at the right places and not allow her eyes to glaze over.
> 4. All rules become effective at the onset of the baseball/basketball/football/duck hunting/salmon fishing/snark hunting/Quayle bashing season and continue until the female walks out frustrated and defeated. (Downloaded 2004)

So in noting "the male is expected to tell the same . . . stories at every get-together," the folklore of rules symbolizes folklore itself as gendered behavior. Whether on the Internet or face-to-face, traditions emerge that tell us about attitudes externally expressed about menfolk and womenfolk, and attitudes created by them for themselves. Indeed, these traditions tell much about our search for meaning in folk lives and communities. They may imply a post-modern confusion, since by imposing, even humorously, rules and regulations, they imply a wish fulfillment for clarity, perhaps in imitation of military order or codes of conduct from an earlier era. Unenforceable, the rules call for cultural certainty, especially in relation to gender, in an age of uncertainty.

Drawing upon the evidence of "manly traditions," we aim to identify and interpret the folk roots of American masculinities, if not for imposing cultural certainty, then for encouraging cultural comprehension. We look to explain formation of masculinities in American society by looking not only at cultural practices in diverse groups but also at the metaphors and images they provide for people in mass culture to live by. In addition to identifying distinctive examples of settings, symbols, images, texts, performances, and genres of masculinities, the analyses provided in this volume offer directions that inquiry into these materials can take. The investigation of cultural practice and metaphor, we contend, reveals the influence of gendered symbols for constructions of identity from both within and without groups and situations in which individuals operate. Although authors may variously use historical, textual, contextual, socioanalytical, psychoanalytical, feminist, and other interpretative tools, they agree on the significance of expressive culture in the understanding, and prediction, of gendered traditions.

REFERENCES

Abrahams, Roger D. 1970. *Deep Down in the Jungle: Negro Narrative Folklore from the Streets of Philadelphia.* 2nd ed. Chicago: Aldine.
———. 1985. "Pragmatism and a Folklore of Experience." *Western Folklore* 44: 324–32.
———. 2003. "Identity." In *Eight Words for the Study of Expressive Culture,* ed. Burt Feintuch, 198–222. Urbana: University of Illinois Press.
Adler, Thomas A. 1981. "Making Pancakes on Sunday: The Male Cook in Family Tradition." *Western Folklore* 40: 45–54.
Ames, Kenneth L. 1992. *Death in the Dining Room and Other Tales of Victorian Culture.* Philadelphia: Temple University Press.
Arnold, Allan A. 1986. "The Equator-Crossing Ceremony: Origins and Purpose." In *Literature and Lore of the Sea,* ed. Patricia Ann Carolson, 32–39. Amsterdam: Rodopi.
Awkward, Michael. 2002. "Black Male Trouble: The Challenges of Rethinking Masculine Differences." In *Masculinity Studies and Feminist Theory: New Directions,* ed. Judith Kegan Gardiner, 290–304. New York: Columbia University Press.
Barnes, Earl. 1912. "The Feminizing of Culture." *Atlantic Monthly* 109 (June): 770–76.
Baron-Cohen, Simon. 2003. *The Essential Difference: The Truth about the Male and Female Brain.* New York: Perseus.
Bauman, Richard. 1977. *Verbal Art as Performance.* Prospect Heights, Ill.: Waveland Press.
Becker, Howard S., and Michal M. McCall, eds. 1990. *Symbolic Interaction and Cultural Studies.* Chicago: University of Chicago Press.
Bederman, Gail. 1995. *Manliness and Civilization: A Cultural History of Gender and Race in the United States, 1880–1917.* Chicago: University of Chicago Press.
Bell, Michael J. 1983. *The World from Brown's Lounge: An Ethnography of Middle-Class Black Play.* Urbana: University of Illinois Press.
Ben-Amos, Dan. 1972. "Toward a Definition of Folklore in Context." In *Toward New Perspectives in Folklore,* ed. Richard Bauman and Américo Paredes, 3–15. Austin: University of Texas Press.
Berger, Maurice, Brian Wallis, and Simon Watson, eds. 1995. *Constructing Masculinity.* New York: Routledge.

Berger, Peter, and Thomas Luckmann. 1967. *The Social Construction of Reality: A Treatise in the Sociology of Knowledge.* New York: Anchor.

Best, Joel. 1998. "Too Much Fun: Toys as Social Problems and the Interpretation of Culture." *Symbolic Interaction* 21: 197–212.

Bettelheim, Bruno. 1955. *Symbolic Wounds: Puberty Rites and the Envious Male.* London: Thames and Hudson.

Beynon, John. 2002. *Masculinities and Culture.* Buckingham, UK: Open University Press.

Bing, Leon. 1992. *Do or Die.* New York: Perennial.

Bishop, Julia C., and Mavis Curtis. 2001. *Play Today in the Primary School Playground.* Buckingham, UK: Open University Press.

Blum, Deborah. 1998. *Sex on the Brain: The Biological Differences between Men and Women.* New York: Penguin.

Blumer, Herbert. 1969. *Symbolic Interactionism: Perspective and Method.* Berkeley: University of California Press.

Bly, Robert. 1990. *Iron John: A Book about Men.* Reading, Mass.: Addison-Wesley.

Bourdieu, Pierre. 1977. *Outline of a Theory of Practice.* Cambridge: Cambridge University Press.

———. 1998. *Practical Reason: On the Theory of Action.* Stanford, Calif.: Stanford University Press.

———. 2001. *Masculine Domination.* Stanford, Calif.: Stanford University Press.

Bourdieu, Pierre, and Loïc J. D. Wacquant. 1992. *An Invitation to Reflexive Sociology.* Chicago: University of Chicago Press.

Brandes, Stanley. 1987. *Forty: The Age and the Symbol.* Knoxville: University of Tennessee Press.

Brod, Harry, ed. 1988. *A Mensch among Men: Explorations in Jewish Masculinity.* Freedom, Calif.: Crossing Press.

———, ed. 1992. *The Making of Masculinities: The New Men's Studies.* New York: Routledge.

Bronner, Simon J. 1978a. "'A Re-examination of Dozens among White American Adolescents." *Western Folklore* 37: 118–28.

———. 1978b. "'Who Says?' A Further Investigation of Ritual Insults among White American Adolescents." *Midwestern Journal of Language and Folklore* 4: 53–69.

———. 1986a. *American Folklore Studies: An Intellectual History.* Lawrence: University Press of Kansas.

———. 1986b. *Grasping Things: Folk Material Culture and Mass Society in America.* Lexington: University Press of Kentucky.

———. 1988. "Art, Performance, and Praxis: The Rhetoric of Contemporary Folklore Studies." *Western Folklore* 47: 75–102.

———. 1995. *Piled Higher and Deeper: The Folklore of Student Life.* Little Rock, Ark.: August House.

———. 1998. *Following Tradition: Folklore in the Discourse of American Culture.* Logan: Utah State University Press.

———. 2002. *Folk Nation: Folklore in the Creation of American Tradition.* Wilmington, Del.: SR Books.

Brookes, Crittenden. 1996. "Jungian School: Therapy." In *The Encyclopedia of Psychiatry, Psychology, and Psychoanalysis,* ed. Benjamin B. Wolman, 298–301. New York: Henry Holt.

Brooks, Gary R. 1998. *A New Psychotherapy for Traditional Men.* San Francisco: Jossey-Bass.

Bryant, Jerry H. 2003. *"Born in a Mighty Bad Land": The Violent Man in African American Folklore and Fiction.* Bloomington: Indiana University Press.

Buhle, Mari Jo. 1998. *Feminism and Its Discontents: A Century of Struggle with Psychoanalysis.* Cambridge, Mass.: Harvard University Press.

Caceres, C. F., and J. I. Cortinas. 1996. "Fantasy Island: An Ethnography of Alcohol and Gender Roles in a Latino Gay Bar." *Journal of Drug Issues* 26: 245–60.

Campbell, Gavin James. 2004. *Music and the Making of a New South.* Chapel Hill: University of North Carolina Press.

Carrigan, Tim, Bob Connell, and John Lee. 2002. "Toward a New Sociology of Masculinity." In *The Masculinities Studies Reader,* ed. Rachel Adams and David Savran, 99–118. Malden, Mass.: Blackwell.

Carroll, Michael P. 1993. "Alan Dundes: An Introduction." In *The Psychoanalytic Study of Society: Essays in Honor of Alan Dundes,* ed. L. Bryce Boyer, Ruth M. Boyer, and Stephen M. Sonneberg, 1–22. Hillsdale, N.J.: Analytic Press.

Chafe, William H. 1991. *The Paradox of Change: American Women in the 20th Century.* New York: Oxford University Press.

Chan, Jachinson. 2001. *Chinese American Masculinities: From Fu Manchu to Bruce Lee.* New York: Routledge.

Charon, Joel M. 2001. *Symbolic Interactionism: An Introduction, an Interpretation, an Integration.* 7th ed. Upper Saddle River, N.J.: Prentice-Hall.

Cheren, Stanley. 1981. "The Psychiatric Perspective: Psychological Aspects of Violence in Sports." *Arena Review* 5: 31–36.

Chodorow, Nancy. 1978. *The Reproduction of Mothering: Psychoanalysis and the Sociology of Gender.* Berkeley: University of California Press.

Chudacoff, Howard P. 1999. *The Age of the Bachelor: Creating an American Subculture.* Princeton, N.J.: Princeton University Press.

Cohen, Percy S. 1980. "Psychoanalysis and Cultural Symbolization." In *Symbol as Sense: New Approaches to the Analysis of Meaning,* ed. Mary LeCron Foster and Stanley H. Brandes, 45–70. New York: Academic Press.

Conger-Kaneko, Josephine. 1906. "The 'Effeminization' of the United States." *World's Work* 12 (May): 7521–24.

Connell, R. W. 1994. "Psychoanalysis on Masculinity." In *Theorizing Masculinities,* ed. Harry Brod and Michael Kaufman, 11–38. Newbury Park, Calif.: Sage.

Constantine-Simms, Delroy, ed. 2001. *The Greatest Taboo: Homosexuality in Black Communities.* Los Angeles: Alyson.

Cornwall, Andrea, and Nancy Lindisfarne, eds. 1994. *Dislocating Masculinity: Comparative Ethnographies.* New York: Routledge.

Davies, Christie. 2003. "Jokes That Follow Mass-Mediated Disasters in a Global Electronic Age." In *Of Corpse: Death and Humor in Folklore and Popular Culture,* ed. Peter Narváez, 15–34. Logan: Utah State University Press.

De Angelis, Barbara. 1997. *The Real Rules: How to Find the Real Man for the Real You.* New York: Dell.

Del Negro, Giovanna P., and Harris M. Berger. 2002. "Identity Reconsidered, the World Doubled: Identity as Interpretive Framework in Folklore Research." *Midwestern Folklore* 28: 5–32.

Dinerstein, Joel. 2003. *Swinging the Machine: Modernity, Technology, and African American Culture Between the World Wars.* Amherst: University of Massachusetts Press.

Dollard, John. 1990. "The Dozens: Dialectic of Insult." In *Mother Wit from the Laughing Barrel: Readings in the Interpretation of Afro-American Folklore,* ed. Alan Dundes, 277–94. Jackson: University Press of Mississippi.

Doty, William G. 2000. *Mythography: The Study of Myths and Rituals.* 2nd ed. Tuscaloosa: University of Alabama Press.

Douglas, Ann. 1977. *The Feminization of American Culture.* New York: Avon.

Dundes, Alan. 1962. "From Etic to Emic Units in the Structural Study of Folktales." *Journal of American Folklore* 75: 95–105.

———. 1971. "Folk Ideas as Units of Worldview." *Journal of American Folklore* 84: 93–103.

———. 1978. *Essays in Folkloristics*. Meerut, India: Folklore Institute.

———. 1980. *Interpreting Folklore*. Bloomington: Indiana University Press.

———. 1983. "Defining Identity through Folklore." In *Identity: Personal and Sociocultural: A Symposium*, ed. Anita Jacobson-Widding, 235–61. Atlantic Highlands, N.J.: Humanities Press.

———. 1985a. "The Psychoanalytical Study of Folklore." *Annals of Scholarship* 3: 1–42.

———. 1985b. "The J.A.P. and the J.A.M. in American Jokelore." *Journal of American Folklore* 98: 456–75.

———. 1987. *Parsing through Customs: Essays by a Freudian Folklorist*. Madison: University of Wisconsin Press.

———. 1989. *Folklore Matters*. Knoxville: University of Tennessee Press.

———. 1997. *From Game to War, and Other Psychoanalytical Essays on Folklore*. Lexington: University Press of Kentucky.

———. 2002. *The Shabbat Elevator and Other Sabbath Subterfuges: An Unorthodox Essay on Circumventing Custom and Jewish Character*. Lanham, Md.: Rowman and Littlefield.

Dundes, Alan, and Lauren Dundes. 2002a. "The Elephant Walk and Other Amazing Hazing: Male Fraternity Initiation through Infantilization and Feminization." In *Bloody Mary in the Mirror: Essays in Psychoanalytic Folkloristics* by Alan Dundes, 95–121. Jackson: University Press of Mississippi.

———. 2002b. "The Trident and the Fork: Disney's 'The Little Mermaid' as a Male Construction of an Electral Fantasy." In *Bloody Mary in the Mirror: Essays in Psychoanalytic Folkloristics* by Alan Dundes, 55–75. Jackson: University Press of Mississippi.

Dundes, Alan, and Carl R. Pagter. 1991. *Never Try to Teach a Pig to Sing: Still More Urban Folklore from the Paperwork Empire*. Detroit: Wayne State University Press.

Dundes, Alan, Jerry W. Leach, and Bora Özkök. 1970. "The Strategy of Turkish Boys' Verbal Dueling Rhymes." *Journal of American Folklore* 83: 325–49.

Dunning, Eric. 1986. "Sport as a Male Preserve: Notes on the Social Sources of Masculine Identity and Its Transformations." *Theory, Culture and Society* 3: 79–90.

Earley, Pete. 1995. *The Hot House: Life Inside Leavenworth Prison*. New York: Bantam.

Elllis, Bill. 2003. "Making a Big Apple Crumble: The Role of Humor in Constructing a Global Response to Disaster." In *Of Corpse: Death and Humor in Folklore and Popular Culture*, ed. Peter Narváez, 35–82. Logan: Utah State University Press.

Eng, David L. 2001. *Racial Castration: Managing Masculinity in Asian America*. Durham, N.C.: Duke University Press.

Faludi, Susan. 1999. *Stiffed: The Betrayal of the American Man*. New York: Perennial.

Farrell, Warren. 1994. *The Myth of Male Power: Why Men Are the Disposable Sex*. New York: Berkley.

Farrer, Claire R. 1975. "Women and Folklore: Images and Genres." *Journal of American Folklore* 88: v–xv.

Fein, Ellen, and Sherrie Schneider. 1995. *The Rules: Time-Tested Secrets for Capturing the Heart of Mr. Right*. New York: Warner.

Feirstein, Bruce. 1982. *Real Men Don't Eat Quiche: A Guidebook to All That Is Truly Masculine*. New York: Summit.

Fine, Gary Alan. 1987a. "Welcome to the World of AIDS: Fantasies of Female Revenge." *Western Folklore* 46: 192–97.

———. 1987b. *With the Boys: Little League Baseball and Preadolescent Culture*. Chicago: University of Chicago Press.

————. 1992. *Manufacturing Tales: Sex and Money in Contemporary Legends.* Knoxville: University of Tennessee Press.

Flocker, Michael. 2003. *The Metrosexual Guide to Style: A Handbook for Modern Man.* New York: Da Capo Press.

Foster, Mary LeCron, and Stanley H. Brandes, eds. 1980. *Symbol as Sense: New Approaches to the Analysis of Meaning.* New York: Academic Press.

Franklin, Clyde W. 1992. "Surviving the Institutional Decimation of Black Males: Causes, Consequences, and Intervention." In *The Making of Masculinities: The New Men's Studies,* ed. Harry Brod, 155–69. New York: Routledge.

Friedan, Betty. 1983. *The Feminine Mystique.* 20th Anniversary Edition. New York: Dell.

Friend, Craig Thomas, and Lorri Glover, eds. 2004. *Southern Manhood: Perspectives on Masculinity in the Old South.* Athens: University of Georgia Press.

Fry, Gladys-Marie. 2001. *Night Riders in Black Folk History.* 1975. Reprint, Chapel Hill: University of North Carolina Press.

Furman, Frida Kerner. 1997. *Facing the Mirror: Older Women and Beauty Shop Culture.* New York: Routledge.

Garraty, John A. 1967. *Theodore Roosevelt: The Strenuous Life.* New York: Harper-Collins.

Geertz, Clifford. 1973. *The Interpretation of Cultures.* New York: Basic Books.

Georges, Robert A., and Michael Owen Jones. 1995. *Folkloristics: An Introduction.* Bloomington: Indiana University Press.

Gilman, Sander L. 1991. *The Jew's Body.* New York: Routledge.

————. 1996. *Smart Jews: The Construction of the Image of Jewish Superior Intelligence.* Lincoln: University of Nebraska Press.

Goldberg, Harvey E. 2003. *Jewish Passages: Cycles of Jewish Life.* Berkeley: University of California Press.

Goldberg, Herb. 1976. *The Hazards of Being Male: Surviving the Myth of Masculine Privilege.* Gretna, La.: Wellness Institute.

Goodwin, Joseph P. 1989. *More Man Than You'll Ever Be: Gay Folklore and Acculturation in Middle America.* Bloomington: Indiana University Press.

Halberstam, Judith. 1998. *Female Masculinity.* Durham, N.C.: Duke University Press.

Hall, Nor, and Warren R. Dawson. 1989. *Broodmales: A Psychological Essay on Men in Childbirth.* Putnam, Conn.: Spring Publications.

Hammond, Dorothy, and Alta Jablow. 1992. "Gilgamesh and the Sundance Kid: The Myth of Male Friendship." In *The Making of Masculinities: The New Men's Studies,* ed. Harry Brod, 241–58. New York: Routledge.

Harkins, Anthony. 2004. *Hillbilly: A Cultural History of an American Icon.* New York: Oxford University Press.

Heilman, Samuel. 1992. *Defenders of the Faith: Inside Ultra-Orthodox Jewry.* New York: Schocken.

Hollis, Susan Tower, Linda Pershing, and M. Jane Young, eds. 1993. *Feminist Theory and the Study of Folklore.* Urbana: University of Illinois Press.

Horowitz, Roger, ed. 2001. *Boys and Their Toys: Masculinity, Class, and Technology in America.* New York: Routledge.

Hostetler, John A. 1993. *Amish Society.* 4th ed. Baltimore: Johns Hopkins University Press.

Hudson, Liam, and Bernadine Jacot. 1991. *The Way Men Think: Intellect, Intimacy and the Erotic Imagination.* New Haven, Conn.: Yale University Press.

Huffman, Alan. 1997. *Ten Point: Deer Camp in the Mississippi Delta.* Jackson: University Press of Mississippi.

Hughes, Linda A. 1993. "'You Have to Do It with Style': Girls' Games and Girls'

Gaming." In *Feminist Theory and the Study of Folklore,* ed. Susan Tower Hollis, Linda Pershing, and M. Jane Young, 130–48. Urbana: University of Illinois Press.

Hymes, Dell, ed. 1974. *Reinventing Anthropology.* New York: Vintage.

Jackson, Bruce. 1974. *Get Your Ass in the Water and Swim Like Me: Narrative Poetry from Black Oral Tradition.* Cambridge, Mass.: Harvard University Press.

Jansen, William Hugh. 1965. "The Esoteric-Exoteric Factor in Folklore." In *The Study of Folklore,* ed. Alan Dundes, 43–56. Englewood Cliffs, N.J.: Prentice-Hall.

Jones, Michael Owen. 1989. *Craftsman of the Cumberlands: Tradition and Creativity.* Lexington: University Press of Kentucky.

Jung, C. G. 1989. *Aspects of the Masculine.* Trans. R. F. C. Hull. Princeton, N.J.: Princeton University Press.

Kalčik, Susan. 1988. "Womenfolk." In *100 Years of American Folklore Studies,* ed. William M. Clements, 44–50. Washington, D.C.: American Folklore Society.

Kasson, John F. 1990. *Rudeness and Civility: Manners in Nineteenth Century Urban America.* New York: Hill and Wang.

———. 2001. *Houdini, Tarzan, and the Perfect Man.* New York: Hill and Wang.

Keiser, R. Lincoln. 1969. *The Vice Lords: Warriors of the Streets.* New York: Holt, Rinehart and Winston.

Kidd, Kenneth B. 2004. *Making American Boys: Boyology and the Feral Tale.* Minneapolis: University of Minnesota Press.

Kimmel, Michael S. 1987. "Rethinking 'Masculinity': New Directions for Research." In *Changing Men: New Directions in Research on Men and Masculinity,* ed. Michael S. Kimmel, 9–24. Newbury Park, Calif.: Sage.

———. 1992. "The Contemporary 'Crisis' of Masculinity in Historical Perspective." In *The Making of Masculinities: The New Men's Studies,* ed. Harry Brod, 121–54. New York: Routledge.

———. 1996. *Manhood in America: A Cultural History.* New York: Free Press.

———, ed. 2004. *Men's Lives.* 6th ed. Boston: Pearson.

Kimmel, Michael, and Michael Kaufman. 1994. "Weekend Warriors: The New Men's Movement." In *Theorizing Masculinities,* ed. Harry Brod and Michael Kaufman, 259–88. Newbury Park, Calif.: Sage.

Kirshenblatt-Gimblett, Barbara. 1995. "From the Paperwork Empire to the Paperless Office: Testing the Limits of the 'Science of Tradition.'" In *Folklore Interpreted: Essays in Honor of Alan Dundes,* ed. Regina Bendix and Rosemary Lévy Zumwalt, 69–92. New York: Garland.

Kirsta, Alix. 1994. *Deadlier than the Male: Violence and Aggression in Women.* New York: HarperCollins.

Klein, Michael. 1990. "The Macho World of Sport—A Forgotten Realm? Some Introductory Remarks." *International Review for the Sociology of Sport* 25: 175–83.

Kline, John B. 1990. *Rural Recreation: The Traditional Adult Game of Cornerball Plus Country Schools and Their Recess Games.* Denver, Pa.: Saul Printing.

Kraybill, Donald B. 1989. *The Riddle of Amish Culture.* Baltimore: Johns Hopkins University Press.

Landau, David. 1993. *Piety and Power: The World of Jewish Fundamentalism.* New York: Hill and Wang.

Lears, T. J. Jackson. 1984. "The Concept of Cultural Hegemony: Problems and Possibilities." *American Historical Review* 90: 567–93.

Leavy, Walter. 1983. "Is the Black Male an Endangered Species?" *Ebony* (August), 41–46.

Lemert, Charles, and Ann Branaman, eds. 1997. *The Goffman Reader.* Malden, Mass.: Blackwell.

LeVay, Simon. 1994. *The Sexual Brain*. Cambridge, Mass.: MIT Press.

Lever, Janet. 1976. "Sex Differences in the Games Children Play." *Social Problems* 23: 478–87.

———. 1978. "Sex Differences in the Complexity of Children's Play and Games." *American Sociological Review* 43: 471–83.

Lutze, Faith E., and David W. Murphy. 1999. "Ultramasculine Prison Environments and Inmates' Adjustment: It's Time to Move beyond the 'Boys Will Be Boys' Paradigm." *Justice Quarterly* 16: 709–33.

MacCormack, Carol P. 1981. "Anthropology—A Discipline with a Legacy." In *Men's Studies Modified: The Impact of Feminism on the Academic Disciplines*, ed. Dale Spender, 99–110. Oxford, UK: Pergamon Press.

Mace, Nancy. 2001. *In the Company of Men: A Woman at the Citadel*. New York: Simon & Schuster.

Majors, Richard G., and Jacob U. Gordon, eds. 1994. *The American Black Male: His Present Status and His Future*. Chicago: Nelson-Hall.

Mangan, J. A., and James Walvin, eds. 1987. *Manliness and Morality: Middle-Class Masculinity in Britain and America, 1800–1940*. Manchester: Manchester University Press.

Mark, Elizabeth Wyner, ed. 2003. *The Covenant of Circumcision: New Perspectives on an Ancient Jewish Rite*. Hanover, N.H.: Brandeis University Press (published by University Press of New England).

Mayer, Philip. 1951. "The Joking of 'Pals' in Gusii Age-Sets." *African Studies* 10: 27–41.

McCombs, Michael. 2004. "Pain Is Weakness Leaving the Body: Masculinity, Boyhood, and Rehabilitation in Juvenile Correction Boot Camps." M.A. thesis, Pennsylvania State University at Harrisburg.

McNeil, W. K., ed. 1995. *Appalachian Images in Folk and Popular Culture*. 2nd ed. Knoxville: University of Tennessee Press.

Mechling, Jay. 1987. "The Manliness Paradox in Ernest Thompson Seton's Ideology of Play and Games." In *Meaningful Play, Playful Meaning*, ed. Gary Alan Fine, 45–60. Champaign, Ill.: Human Kinetics.

———. 1993. "On Sharing Folklore and American Identity in a Multicultural Society." *Western Folklore* 52: 271–89.

———. 2001. *On My Honor: Boy Scouts and the Making of American Youth*. Chicago: University of Chicago Press.

Mergen, Bergen. 1995. "Children's Lore in School and Playgrounds." In *Children's Folklore: A Source Book*, ed. Brian Sutton-Smith, Jay Mechling, Thomas W. Johnson, and Felicia R. McMahon, 229–50. Logan: Utah State University Press.

Merwin, Henry Childs. 1897. "On Being Civilized Too Much." *Atlantic Monthly* 79 (June): 838–46.

Miller, Walter. 1958. "Lower-Class Culture as a Generating Milieu for Gang Delinquency." *Journal of Social Issues* 14: 5–19.

Mintz, Jerome R. 1992. *Hasidic People: A Place in the New World*. Cambridge, Mass.: Harvard University Press.

Mitchell, Carol. 1985. "Some Differences in Male and Female Joke-Telling." In *Women's Folklore, Women's Culture*, ed. Rosan A. Jordan and Susan J. Kalčik, 163–86. Philadelphia: University of Pennsylvania Press.

Moir, Anne, and David Jessel. 1992. *Brain Sex: The Real Difference between Men and Women*. New York: Delta.

Montell, Lynwood. 1986. *Killings: Folk Justice in the Upper South*. Lexington: University Press of Kentucky.

Munroe, Robert, and Ruth Munroe. 1971. "Male Pregnancy and Cross-Sex Identity Symptoms." *Journal of Social Psychology* 84:11–25.

———. 1973. "Psychological Interpretation of Male Initiation Rites: The Case of Male Pregnancy Symptoms." *Ethos* 1: 490–98.

Munroe, Robert, Ruth Munroe, and J. W. M. Whiting. 1973. "The Couvade: A Psychological Analysis." *Ethos* 1: 30–74.

Murphy, Peter F. 2001. *Studs, Tools, and the Family Jewels: Metaphors Men Live By.* Madison: University of Wisconsin Press.

Newell, William Wells. 1888. "On the Field and Work of a Journal of American Folk-Lore." *Journal of American Folklore* 1: 1–7.

Niles, John D. 1999. *Homo Narrans: The Poetics and Anthropology of Oral Literature.* Philadelphia: University of Pennsylvania Press.

Nuwer, Hank, ed. 2004. *The Hazing Reader.* Bloomington: Indiana University Press.

Oliver, William. 1984. "Black Males and the Tough Guy Image: A Dysfunctional Compensatory Adaptation." *Western Journal of Black Studies* 8: 199–203.

Oring, Elliott. 1994. "The Arts, Artifacts, and Artifices of Identity." *Journal of American Folklore* 107: 211–32.

Paredes, Américo. 1993. *Folklore and Culture on the Texas-Mexican Border.* Ed. Richard Bauman. Austin: Center for Mexican American Studies, University of Texas.

Pendergast, Tom. 2000. *Creating the Modern Man: American Magazines and Consumer Culture, 1900–1950.* Columbia: University of Missouri Press.

Pittman, Frank. 1993. *Man Enough: Fathers, Sons, and the Search for Masculinity.* New York: Perigree.

Pleck, Joseph H. 1992. "The Theory of Male Sex-Role Identity: Its Rise and Fall, 1936 to the Present." In *The Making of Masculinities: The New Men's Studies,* ed. Harry Brod, 21–38. New York: Routledge.

Pollack, William. 1998. *Real Boys: Rescuing Our Sons from the Myths of Boyhood.* New York: Henry Holt.

———. 2000. *Real Boys' Voices.* New York: Random House.

Porterfield, Nolan. 1996. *Last Cavalier: The Life and Times of John A. Lomax, 1867–1948.* Urbana: University of Illinois Press.

Proctor, Nicolas W. 2002. *Bathed in Blood: Hunting and Mastery in the Old South.* Charlottesville: University Press of Virginia.

Raphael, Ray. 1988. *The Men from the Boys: Rites of Passage in Male America.* Lincoln: University of Nebraska Press.

Reik, Theodor. [1931]. "Couvade and the Psychogenesis of the Fear of Retaliation." In *Ritual: Psycho-Analytical Studies* by Theodor Reik, trans. Douglas Bryan, 27–89. New York: W. W. Norton.

Reynolds, Margaret C. 2001. *Plain Women: Ritual and Gender in the Old Order River Brethren.* University Park: Pennsylvania State University Press.

Richardson, Keith P. 1977. "Polliwogs and Shellbacks: An Analysis of the Equator Crossing Ritual." *Western Folklore* 36: 154–59.

Roberts, Helen. 1981. "Some of the Boys Won't Play Any More: The Impact of Feminism on Sociology." In *Men's Studies Modified: The Impact of Feminism on the Academic Disciplines,* ed. Dale Spender, 73–82. Oxford, UK: Pergamon Press.

Roberts, Roderick J. 1965. "Negro Folklore in a Southwestern Industrial School." M.A. thesis, Indiana University.

Roosevelt, Theodore. 1926. *American Ideals, The Strenuous Life, Realizable Ideals.* New York: Charles Scribner's Sons.

Rotundo, E. Anthony. 1993. *American Manhood.* New York: Basic Books.

Safire, William. 2003. "Metrosexual: New Word for the New Narcissism." *New York Times Magazine,* December 7, 30.

Sandstrom, Kent L., Daniel D. Martin, and Gary Alan Fine. 2003. *Symbols, Selves, and Social Reality: A Symbolic Interactionist Approach to Social Psychology and Sociology.* Los Angeles: Roxbury.

Schachter-Shalomi, Zalman. 1988. "How to Deal with a Jewish Issue: Circumcision." In *A Mensch among Men: Explorations in Jewish Masculinity,* ed. Harry Brod, 79–83. Freedom, Calif.: Crossing Press.

Schmidt, Kimberly D., Diane Zimmerman Umble, and Steven D. Reschly, eds. 2002. *Strangers at Home: Amish and Mennonite Women in History.* Baltimore: Johns Hopkins University Press.

Sexton, Patricia Cayo. 1969. *The Feminized Male: Classrooms, White Collars and the Decline of Manliness.* New York: Random House.

Sherrod, Drury. 1992. "The Bonds of Men: Problems and Possibilities in Close Male Relationships." In *The Making of Masculinities: The New Men's Studies,* ed. Harry Brod, 213–40. New York: Routledge.

Silverman, Eric Kline. 2003. "The Cut of Wholeness: Psychoanalytic Interpretations of Biblical Circumcision." In *The Covenant of Circumcision: New Perspectives on an Ancient Jewish Rite,* ed. Elizabeth Wyner Mark, 43–57. Hanover, N.H.: Brandeis University Press (published by New England University Press).

Simmons, Rachel. 2002. *Odd Girl Out: The Hidden Culture of Aggression in Girls.* New York: Harcourt.

Sommers, Christina Hoff. 2000. *The War against Boys: How Misguided Feminism Is Harming Our Young Men.* New York: Touchstone.

Spradley, James, and Brenda Mann. 1975. *The Cocktail Waitress: Woman's Work in a Man's World.* New York: Alfred A. Knopf.

Sterba, Richard. 1947. "Some Psychological Factors in Negro Race Hatred and in Anti-Negro Riots." In *Psychoanalysis and the Social Sciences,* vol. 1, ed. Géza Róheim, 411–27. New York: International Universities Press.

Stern, Stephen. 1991. "The Influence of Diversity on Folklore Studies in the Decades of the 1980s and 1990s." *Western Folklore* 50: 21–29.

Stratton, Jon. 2000. *Coming Out Jewish.* New York: Routledge.

Strum, Philippa. 2002. *Women in the Barracks: The VMI Case and Equal Rights.* Lawrence: University Press of Kansas.

Sutton-Smith, Brian. 1972. *The Folkgames of Children.* Austin: University of Texas Press.

———. 1979. "The Play of Girls." In *Becoming Female: Perspectives on Development,* ed. Claire B. Kopp and Martha Kirkpatrick, 228–57. New York: Plenum.

———. 1986. *Toys as Culture.* New York: Gardner Press.

Tavris, Carol, and Carolyn Wade. 1984. *The Longest War: Sex Differences in Perspective.* 2nd ed. New York: Harcourt, Brace and Jovanovich.

Telushkin, Rabbi Joseph. 1992. *Jewish Humor: What the Best Jewish Jokes Say about the Jews.* New York: William Morrow.

Thomas, Jeannie Banks. 2003. *Naked Barbies, Warrior Joes, and Other Forms of Visible Gender.* Urbana: University of Illinois Press.

Thorne, Barrie. 1993. *Gender Play: Girls and Boys in School.* New Brunswick, N.J.: Rutgers University Press.

Tiger, Lionel. 1984. *Men in Groups.* 2nd ed. New York: Marion Boyars.

———. 1999. *The Decline of Males: The First Look at an Unexpected New World for Men and Women.* New York: St. Martin's Griffin.

Treadwell, Perry. 1992. "Biologic Influences on Masculinity." In *The Making of Masculinities: The New Men's Studies,* ed. Harry Brod, 259–86. New York: Routledge.

Vigil, James Diego. 1988. *Barrio Gangs: Street Life and Identity in Southern California.* Austin: University of Texas Press.

———. 2002. *A Rainbow of Gangs: Street Cultures in the Mega-City.* Austin: University of Texas Press.

Walker, Beverly M. 1981. "Psychology and Feminism—If You Can't Beat Them,

Join Them." In *Men's Studies Modified: The Impact of Feminism on the Academic Disciplines,* ed. Dale Spender, 111–24. Oxford, UK: Pergamon Press.

Wepman, Dennis, Ronald B. Newman, and Murray B. Binderman. 1976. *The Life: The Lore and Folk Poetry of the Black Hustler.* Philadelphia: University of Pennsylvania Press.

Whitehead, Stephen M., and Frank J. Barrett. 2001. "The Sociology of Masculinity." In *The Masculinities Reader,* ed. Stephen M. Whitehead and Frank J. Barrett, 1–26. Cambridge, UK: Polity Press.

Williams, Raymond. 1983. *Keywords: A Vocabulary of Culture and Society.* Rev. ed. New York: Oxford University Press.

Wyatt-Brown, Bertram. 1986. *Honor and Violence in the Old South.* New York: Oxford University Press.

———. 2001. *The Shaping of Southern Culture: Honor, Grace, and War, 1760s–1890s.* Chapel Hill: University of North Carolina Press.

Part I. Manly Displays and Performances

I

In the Company of Men: Female Accommodation and the Folk Culture of Male Groups

GARY ALAN FINE

Over the past two generations, women have increasingly moved into domains that were once exclusively male: workplaces, private clubs, leisure groups, schools, and colleges. With the exception of certain professional sports franchises and other collegiate and high school sports teams, it is hard to think of a domain that is now entirely male (there remain more domains, including sports, clubs, schools, and colleges, that are entirely female).[1]

This does not mean, of course, that there do not exist numerous social settings that are predominantly male, in which few females choose (or are permitted) to participate. In these settings females are "tokens" or a "minority," and are recognized and defined by their gender. They may be treated well—or poorly—but in either case, their gender serves to define them, even when they are well accepted within the contours of group life. Every group develops a culture—an "idioculture" (Fine 1979)—and the gender composition of the group helps to shape the culture and the boundaries of legitimate behavior and talk.[2]

I argue in this analysis that whether females are accepted in the folk culture of male-dominated groups depends upon their willingness to accept and engage with the sexualized masculine culture of the group.[3] Those women who accept these strictures are likely to succeed, in contrast to those who reject or are unable to fulfill the expectations of their male colleagues. I suggest that males and females have noticeable distinct "folk cultures"—a set of actions and beliefs that are taken for granted within the relevant group, in some cases leading to different gendered pools of knowledge. While the outlines of these folk cultures will necessarily be vague and indistinct, a function of local traditions, structural constraints, and individual abilities, they often include joking patterns, non-verbal communication, sexual knowledge, nicknames, and a wide range of expressive culture, seemingly separate from instrumental tasks, although ultimately, because of their tacit power, influencing the successful completion of those tasks through efficient and pleasant collaborative effort.

SETTINGS

Based on thirty years of ethnographic research, I examine the position and strategies of women in a series of male-dominated groups.[4] These data involve males and females of various ages, including Little League baseball players, fantasy role-play gamers, mushroom collectors, high school debaters, restaurant cooks, and weather forecasters. In each setting, men represented from 65% to 90% of the participants. These were seen as male worlds by participants and by observers. Although I lack the space to present extensive data from each setting, the dynamics evident in each were similar.

Little League Baseball. During a three-year period I observed four Little Leagues in suburban Boston, exurban Rhode Island, and suburban Minneapolis–St. Paul. Little League baseball is organized into teams of twelve to fifteen preadolescents (ages nine to twelve). Girls played on six of these teams, but in small numbers.

Fantasy Role-Play Gaming. For an eighteen-month period I observed fantasy gamers in the community room of a police station in Minneapolis. These games, such as the best-known and widest-selling Dungeons & Dragons, involved players enacting characters under the control of a referee (a dungeon master or game master). Although the participants in the groups changed from week to week, there were three to five young women (mostly late teens and young adults) who participated in the games on a fairly regular basis.

Restaurant Kitchens. I observed in the kitchens of four restaurants in the Twin Cities, spending a month in each kitchen taking notes and interviewing cooks. While the restaurants varied in the style of cuisine served and the status within the local restaurant world, each was well respected. The four restaurants included an haute cuisine restaurant, a continental restaurant, a steak house, and a hotel kitchen. Each of the restaurants had at least one female cook, but no more than two cooks in each restaurant were female.

Mushroom Collectors. For four years I observed a club for amateur mushroom collectors. The club met once a week during the four months of mushroom season in Minnesota and also organized day-long and overnight forays to state parks and other natural sites. Although this social world was more equally divided between men and women, most of the members of the club were males, and during the period that I observed males had the leadership role as club president.

High School Debate Team. During the first half of a school year I examined a debate team at a public high school in suburban St. Paul. The debate team engaged in policy debate, which required teams of two to debate the same debate topic throughout the season (lasting from September until February). The team of fifteen students had three female members, although the coach/teacher was also a woman.[5]

Weather Forecasters. For a year I observed an office of the National Weather Service. This office employed twenty-four people, including three women. One of the three was the office administrative assistant (and receptionist), a second was the port officer, dealing with weather that affected ships and boats, and the third was a meteorological intern. All the forecasters were male, as were the main administrative staff.

While these settings differ quite widely, each is situated within American culture. Although I do not explicitly make the case that these patterns of gendered interaction are directly tied to American culture or social structure, the American emphasis on individualism, personal freedom, and lack of institutional constraint surely influences social relations. American society is certainly not as hierarchically gendered as some cultures, but neither is it as explicitly egalitarian as others. The comparative analysis of the role of women in predominantly male groups deserves further observational analysis.

BEING ONE OF THE BOYS

As noted, the number of social locales from which women are excluded has rapidly diminished. Yet, the mere fact that women have access to a male-dominated setting does not mean they will be fully accepted or treated with respect. Ethnographic research in a variety of social settings suggests that women can be accepted by male colleagues and incorporated into the culture of the group, but this acceptance often comes at a recognizable social cost. Women who wish to be part of male-dominated groups typically must be prepared to accept established patterns of male bonding and must be able successfully to decode male behavior patterns—patterns that take different forms from preadolescence to adulthood.[6] These women must be willing to engage in—or at least tolerate—coarse joking and teasing and must accept the male-based informal structure of the group. While some women find this behavioral pattern congenial, others do not, and as a consequence, they may be treated as outcasts or as marginal to the group. In this analysis I describe the implicit rules and cultural dynamics that influence the acceptance or rejection of women in male groups. As women enter social worlds that are inhabited by men, I ask: How do women adjust? How can women fully enter into group culture? My approach is to examine the informal norms that govern the world of male bonding.

Rosabeth Kanter (1977) in her influential *Men and Women of the Corporation* argues that the numerical composition of a work organization has profound implications for the behaviors of these men and women. As a rule, an organization with a large majority of men and only a few token women has a markedly different culture and set of expectations from an organization that is gender balanced. When women are in the minority, they are more likely to need to adjust their behavior to that of their male co-workers than to push to change that behavior or to behave in their own preferred styles. This is a reality that has proven difficult to alter.

These issues of the micro-politics of gender have been addressed in ethnographic studies of occupations and organizations. Not surprisingly, most of these studies have been conducted by women, and as a result the type of data that could be collected was limited by the gender of the researcher (Easterday, Papademas, Schorr, and Valentine 1977; Hunt 1984; Wax 1979). Gaining access to the informal and hidden activities of the male majority is difficult for the female researcher.

In contrast, I emphasize, based on my field research, how men view those women in their midst and how they treat them. Basically I argue that to be accepted, a woman must choose to be "one of the boys," and this act must be accepted by the men in the group. In general, males have consensual informal arrangements; those women who can and do choose to accept these normative standards are likely to be accepted, whereas those who fail to accept or abide by these informal rules by choice or lack of experience or who choose to challenge the rules are likely to experience rejection and discrimination.

In my six research settings I have found little overt hostility toward women (i.e., little discrimination against women *because of* their gender). In contrast, difficulties arise from the reality that these women did not share the informal work rules and folk culture of men. At times these difficulties derived from unknowing behaviors by the women. In the work setting, men found it often was not "fun" being with women, or at least it was not as emotionally satisfying as being with men. The clubby atmosphere, characteristic of all-male groups, is threatened even—I might suggest especially—with the presence of a solitary woman. Although individual women may have been rejected, and certainly some were not fully accepted in each setting, women were, under some circumstances, able to be accepted if their behavior and attitudes were judged to be situationally appropriate. To describe the ways that women need to adjust their behaviors and accommodate those of their male colleagues, I focus on two core issues, each tied to the folk culture of male-dominated groups: (1) sexualized humor and language and (2) gendered teasing.

SEXUALIZED HUMOR AND LANGUAGE

A common practice when men gather is to trade sexual stories (Fine 1976). Trading stories is a pleasant, expressive diversion from the ongoing, instrumental group tasks. Observations of women in male-dominated environments have recognized the considerable difficulty that many women have in adjusting to this crude humor and rough talk (Valentine 1985). Some women may, in fact, feel that the presence of such talk effectively excludes them from male gatherings (Kirkpatrick 1974, 109). Perhaps for some men this talk is a strategy for excluding women from these male settings, claiming men just would not be "themselves" with a female present—naturalizing this talk and behavior (Easterday et al. 1977, 338). One informant who led fantasy games, after noting that there were few leisure activities in which men and women participate in together, commented:

> I have a feeling that both men and women would be afraid of being with men and women. They would be afraid of embarrassing each other. . . . Any group of men, the pressure is to drift to a sexual nature. . . . People would be afraid of going too far [having their characters acting in sexual or aggressive ways].

In a similar vein, Rosabeth Kanter (1977, 229) suggests in her study of the position of women in a large corporation:

> Indsco women faced constant pressure to allow jokes at the expense of women, to accept "kidding" from the men around them. When a woman objected, the men denied any hostility or unfriendly intention, instead accusing the woman, by inference, of "lacking a sense of humor."

It is plausible that most men felt no unfriendly intent in their joking. They were, after all, only having a good time, and building a social community in the process (see Mechling and Mechling 1985).

Sexualized joking occurred in each site, although, of course, the specific form that it took varied as a function of the age of the participants and the structure and expectations of the group. Simply put, men are endlessly fascinated with sex and its public rendition (the former does not differentiate them much from women, although the latter does in some measure). Younger males are displaying their assertion of maturity (Fine 1976, 1981, 2001); for older males, the test is more subtle, but it is also a judgment of subcultural beliefs and competence to talk fluidly about them. To be sure, different standards for appropriate talk and action exist among groups—not all male groups emphasize "manly" themes (e.g., college professors tend not to have a robust masculine culture).

These comments occurred in each group. For instance:

> A male cook turns to his male co-worker eating a banana and remarks, "I saw my girlfriend sucking on something like that last night." His co-worker grins. On another occasion in a restaurant in which the trout is served with its head on, a cook jokes: "Some people think it's a little gross, but everyone needs a little head once in a while." The men in the kitchen chuckle.

Three male mushroomers are joking with each other. One says to the others: "Someone brought in a nice young specimen." The other jokes, "Did you get her name." The third adds that they should take "her" on the overnight foray next year.

Two fantasy gamers are talking about having their characters find a bar-maid for the night for sexual activities. One comments about his character's sexual prowess, "I'll drown her in my squirt."

One Little Leaguer says to a friend: "I haven't seen you in a long time. Where have you been? Locked in your room with a girl?"

Two meteorologists are joking about attractive female television weather forecasters. One talked about a local reporter who in a story about tornado safety curled up in a bathtub. The other asks, "Was she wearing clothes?" Later when he learned that this channel will be sending someone out to the office to do a story, he jokes, "Are they bringing the blonde in the bathtub?"

Such examples could be multiplied, and they underline a problem with cross-gender interaction. Males enjoy this banter, and yet it is likely that many women would find such remarks to be offensive. Either the sexual joking must be eliminated because of the complaints of women, or the joking remains, and the women must go—or must adjust. In most instances it is the woman who has the choice of exit, voice, or loyalty (Hirschman 1970).

In fact, males do make remarks in the presence of women—remarks that could easily be taken as offensive:

A waitress comes into the kitchen and says to the chef: "A lady would like the tail of an ivory salmon." The chef jokes: "We'll give her some tail."

A female mushroomer asks about how to find chanterelles, and a male mushroomer comments: "I'll go in the woods with you any time." Another male comments: "It's a nice day to take a tramp in the woods. We'll see what pops up."

Playing fantasy games, seated around a table, Andy says to Mark, "Denise turns Bruce on. She walked by and the table moved up three inches."

One weather forecaster says, "It's time to put down some numbers" for the official forecast. Another male forecaster jokes, "36–24–36. All roads lead to Hooters." Then the males joke about going to the opening of a nearby Hooters. With one saying, "The handles [of the door] are soft and firm." One of the females in the office jokes, "I don't think I should be hearing this," and the men joke that this may be "sexual harassment."

One assistant debate coach refers to the author of some evidence as "Ellen, babe," and then adds good-naturedly that he says this "because I'm a sexist asshole."

Such joking could easily lead women to avoid those settings in which such comments regularly occur—lunches, after-hours parties, and the like. These settings, from which women may choose to exile themselves, may represent the heart of group interaction (Epstein 1970; Kirkpatrick 1974).

Some women find such joking to be congenial, and they are successful in integrating themselves into the informal folk culture of the group:

> Bill, a waiter, returns to the kitchen with an order of veal medallions Madeira with morels. The female customer returned them because they were not what she had expected—often customers confuse veal medallions with a veal chop. Bill explains to Don, the sous chef who cooked them, "She's wrong, but I'm not going to argue." This begins a long discussion of the difficulty of pleasing female customers, who are seen as more demanding than men. Bill finally jokes: "She doesn't like it because it's big and fat and pink." Diane, a female cook, adds: "She must have had an awful experience as a child." Don, still annoyed, jokes: "I'd like to go out and give her something that's big and fat and pink." Since they can't use the veal, Don offers it to the others in the kitchen. Diane refuses the veal, at which Don jokes: "I thought you liked things that were big, fat, and pink." Diane jokes back, "I'm trying to quit."

> Some debaters from Randall Park are watching the final round of a debate tournament. The boys comment that one of the finalists up on stage is deliberately exposing her legs to the judges. Brian whispers, "Watch what she does when she sits down." Doree responds, "Good view." Brian responds, "That's why I picked it."

As Rosabeth Kanter notes:

> Some tokens managed to adapt very well. They used the same kind of language as many of the men. . . . A professional woman joined the men on "women hunts," taking part in conversations in which the pros and cons of particular targets were discussed. There were women known to be able to "drink men under the table." (Kanter 1977, 229)

Indicating this adaptation, one forecaster commented to a female colleague about how she is a full member of the largely male group, saying, "You turned macho." She responds significantly, "I lost some of my femininity. I've become one of the guys."

The relationship between men and women depends greatly on the choices and responses of each woman, and her attitudes—perhaps more than on the community of men, where norms are already set and are unlikely to change rapidly, except as they tease each other about "sexual harassment" charges. Yet, this behavior must be interpreted, and as a consequence, it is up to the men to decide what kind of woman their female group member is and how much trust she should be accorded.

The two other women who worked with Diane in the restaurant kitchen both complained about their exclusion from the male subculture, and they both disliked this joking. One reflected, "There's a kind of camaraderie that really hasn't included me since I've been here." When I asked Diane whether she had found any discrimination in the kitchen, she responded:

> I found that I really have to prove myself. There's a period of adjustment for everybody, and they put you through a test that's mostly emotional. They want to see if you have a breaking point; they just want to see how far they can push you.

In a similar vein:

> One male gamer in speaking of a female colleague noted that "She said, 'at first they didn't want me to play' and when they would let her play, they made her play a male character first. Then, after she played a while, she could play whoever she wanted."

> Two assistant coaches were talking about their female debaters. One commented to the other: "I got the girls not to be bitchy. Sweet and kind." Don, thinking back to last year with his male partner, noted: "We didn't have that problem last year."

When I asked the head chef at the restaurant referred to in the earlier quotation what he thought a layperson would be most upset by in his kitchen, he responded:

> I would have to say if they were a woman, probably the behavior that goes on in the kitchen sometimes. Sexism and crude jokes. There's all kinds of things going on. Well, Diane, she's almost like one of the guys. . . . Either she should be detested for it or she's quite admirable because she's always let everybody know that they don't have to tread light steps around here. It's amazing how when you get a woman in the kitchen the attitude changes totally. Everybody clams up a little bit and they are careful about what they say.

A gamer indicated a similar process operates in their leisure that recognizes the special characteristics of women, even if the dynamics of discourse are different:

> *GAF:* Are [women] accepted by the male players?

> *Jack:* Yeah, they're accepted. They're accepted and they're sort of treated special. I mean people make a little joke about them, or talk to them in a kind of kidding way, and it's quite obviously a reflection of our own societal values. You know, they're making sexual remarks to the girl and teasing her about sex and so on: it's considered standard, no big deal.

Women seem likely to attribute deliberate intention to their male co-workers, whereas males appeal to the "atmosphere," "the natural crudeness" of their environment, or they attempt to "naturalize" the joking by suggesting that it is an inevitable part of the male psyche. These relationships remind one of the practice of "binging" (Haas 1972), in which more established workers in the construction industry "test" the new recruits to see how far they can be pushed without cracking: construction work is based on the assumption of trust, an absence of which could prove fatal. Outsiders (in this case, women) especially must be tested to determine whether they can be counted on. Everett Hughes observes:

> In order that men may communicate freely and confidentially, they must be able to take a good deal of each other's sentiments for granted. They must feel easy about their silences as well as about their utterances. These factors conspire to make colleagues, with a large body of unspoken understandings, uncomfortable in the presence of what they consider odd kinds of fellows. (Hughes 1971, 146)

All too often, women with a different sentiment structure can be considered "odd fellows." They are perceived as not really a part of the "team." The more informality and discretion in a setting, the harder it is for men and women to adjust smoothly; formality is, in this sense, easier for women (Epstein 1970). To the extent that males perceive the work environment as "homosocial," it is difficult for a woman to be accepted if she disrupts this atmosphere (Lipman-Blumen 1976). The special characteristics of an environment in which one is associated with like-minded others (e.g., Weston and Rofel 1984) can be threatened by the introduction of those who are presumed not to identify with the basis of community. Since joking is a traditional way by which unofficial, unstated, but crucial values are expressed, the joking culture of a workplace underlies the gender/status character of the group. Elizabeth and Jay Mechling reflect that by eliminating sexual joking, the sense of community that is built by it might diminish as well, with the consequence of making social life less satisfying—at least for male participants (Mechling and Mechling 1985).

CROSS-GENDER TEASING

Men frequently treat women as sexual objects, and often conversation between men and women is sexually charged. Obviously such sexual talk and action is socially situated. Not every woman gets "hustled" by every man every time, and settings differ in the expectations and norms related to cross-gendered humor. These behaviors, also, are responded to and judged in different ways, being variously acceptable or inappropriate. The likelihood of such behavior is related to the personality and status of the male, the physical attractiveness and personality of the woman, the implicit expectations of the setting, the immediate circumstances, and the structural conditions that encourage or prevent such behaviors.

In most instances, it must be admitted, sexual remarks are not designed to make a woman's life unpleasant or to create "a hostile social environment," although, of course, that may be their effect. However, they are aimed typically at those of less status or those who are new in the environment. Some men—recognizing variation in intent, circumstance, and response—may not realize that what they are doing is offensive. There may be a sharp difference between the perspectives of males and females and, of course, differences among women and among men.

Some sexual talk involves the man attempting to establish a sexual relationship with a woman—sexual talk with an instrumental focus. However, I focus upon a milder form of sexual teasing or joshing. This is a form of ostensibly humorous, playful talk in which the female and her body is the target of the remark.

Sexual teasing is a form of public discourse. Because of its accessibility, it can be both easier and harder to handle than the more discreet and private forms of sexual talk, such as "hustling," "pickups," and "come-ons." Its public character means that males will not often push this joking beyond the consensual limits of good taste—at least as defined by the men in the group. Simultaneously, for the woman not to lose face, she must respond so as to present herself as a colleague—enjoyable to be with, and yet not to be treated as a butt of jokes. The woman must learn to give as well as she gets, but always with a smile on her face. The response of the woman is crucial for establishing the tone of her relation with the others in the group, the large majority of whom are men.

Some of these joking sequences are not particularly offensive:

> Phil, the head day cook, notes that Amy, a young pantry worker, is left-handed. He jokes to her: "I finally found out what's the matter with Amy after all this time. She's left-handed. No wonder you can't keep a boyfriend." Amy replies, smiling, "Shut up."

> Doreen, a meteorologist, is wearing two pairs of earrings today, and she tells her male colleagues: "The lower earrings are from my husband." One of the males jokes, "The upper were from your lover?"

> A group of Little League boys come across a preadolescent girls' softball team from a different area of town, sitting around a park picnic table. The boys begin teasing the girls with sexual taunts: "Hey suck me where the sun never shines," "Pluck my hairs," and "You're innocent like my butthole." The girls are not outraged and actually seem to enjoy it—at one point singing to attract the boys' attention. Later the boys return to the picnic table, and throw beer cans at the girls, who giggle and scream. Finally as the boys are leaving, a girl calls out to one of them, "Bye, honey!"

Other examples may be thought to cross a line:

> Once, prior to a debate round, a male coach from a rival school places his hands on a female debater's shoulders, noting pleasantly, "Some of the

guys on the team would like a date with this hot one." Although he was ostensibly complimenting her, he ensured that while she was speaking, she would realize that her body was on display.

One female mushroomer, looking for a particular guidebook, comments, "I'd like to get my hands on Christianson's *Fleshy Fungus.*" A male says, "You can get your hands on mine."

Karen, one of the waitresses, asks Jim, the head chef, for an order of scallops for her lunch, even though waitresses are rarely given such expensive food. Jim makes the scallops, and Phil jokes to him: "You can tell who's sleeping with the chef." Jim jokes back: "You guys are just jealous."

Some joking involves physical contact—although nothing in my observation that would fairly be described as an attack. The touch is of a playful nature, although it is touching that would be inappropriate if done by a male to another male, such as when a cook playfully slapped a waitress's buttocks or a mushroomer rubbed another's back or a debater tickled another. Although most women can handle the situations, the situations are things that do require handling. If the woman can banter in return, interactions flow smoothly:

Ted, a head waiter, rubs the back of Cheri's neck (Cheri is an attractive waitress in her 20s). Later Ted puts his hand around her waist and on her shoulder. Cheri pats Ted's somewhat bulging stomach and asks about his pants size.

Barb, a preadolescent girl, goes up to Rich and says flirtatiously: "Hi, pretty blue eyes." Rich looks extremely embarrassed, and doesn't respond. Later Barb takes Allen's comb, sticks it in chalk (used to mark the base paths), and combs his hair with it. When Allen finally realized what she has done, he says to his teammates with considerable exasperation (but not real hostility), "She's a devil."

Three female mushroomers are joking in front of males about taking a picture of two stinkhorn eggs with a fully extended stinkhorn [*Phallus impudicus*] in the middle (looking like a penis and testicles). One says: "You should send the picture to *Hustler.*" Another comments, "It's a little man." And the third responds: "It's a *big* man."

The male forecasters are joking with the women in the office about baking cakes for them. Later when looking out of the window, they see some "*mammatus* clouds," and someone notes that *mammatus* means breast in Latin, and at this one of the women grabs her own breasts, leading one of the men to comment in surprise, "I can't believe you did that." Later she jokes: "Men. You can't live with them. You can't shoot them."

Each of these settings represents a challenge to which females must respond if they are not to be thought cold and unfriendly. The rules of this engagement are sent within folk understandings, often unstated and un-considered, but easily recognizable when a rule has been broken or an expectation abrogated. Women feel compelled to accept this male sensual play and sexual talk and do so in terms of male norms of group interaction. The rules are set by the majority, and women have little choice if they wish to be accepted. For some women this arrangement is a reasonable bargain, but for others it places obstacles to their acceptance and advancement. It is in this latter sense that "being one of the boys" is not merely a choice that a group enforces, but rather a structural barrier to advancement.

IN THE COMPANY OF MEN

A woman who desires to be accepted in a predominantly male group is compelled to play by the rules of the game that have been set by her male colleagues. Of course, as she is making this choice she has the problem of deciphering their rules. This does not indicate that the game is not winna-ble, but it does suggest that the woman has a set of hurdles to overcome. There are gendered pools of knowledge, grounded in sexual socialization, of which members of the other sex may have only approximate and hazy knowledge. To the extent that masculine and feminine folk cultures do not overlap—and they do not always—the female is be socialized to the stan-dards of the community in which she wishes to play a part.

In general, men do not object to women participating in their groups out of some hostile or mysterious misogynist urge. It is not biology per se that is at issue, but rather the cultural and folk traditions that surround gender in society. Women have the potential to disrupt patterns of male interaction, possibly without even recognizing that they are doing so. Men may feel constrained in their talk and actions in front of women, again perhaps without clear insight as to why this is. This phenomenon is true for all age groups. Joking and cursing may be seen as being outside the legitimate range of proper behavior. Males may be criticized for teasing females in an existing group in ways that are defined as proper in other more sexualized domains. Further, women may be seen as being unable or unwilling to perform all of the tasks that other men share.

These features cause females to be treated as a potentially disruptive influence. The female starts with obstacles that a new male member of the group does not have to face. Although, as I have emphasized, women can and do overcome these barriers, their success is frequently defined as a personal achievement and does not generalize to other women. They are seen as exceptional.

Given current rules, women (and, indeed, by implication, other minori-ties) who wish to be accepted must play by those rules that men (and major-ities) establish. In the short run, informal rules and traditions of the group must be preserved, even when those informal rules and traditions are contrary to women's socialization. The woman in a male-dominated group must reach a modus operandi, without rocking the delicately balanced boat too vigorously.

In doing this, the woman must rapidly acquire a sense of what behaviors and responses are expected of her. These rules are typically unstated by the men of the group and, indeed, may not even be recognized. But these traditions are quite real—their tacit reality transcends the explicit awareness that anyone may have of them. By accidentally breaking the rules surrounding male bonding, women underline the existence of these rules and demonstrate their cultural incompetence.

To understand the folk culture of gender, it is essential to distinguish between the biological and the social. The male orientation that I describe in this chapter can be acquired by women, although whether that decision is desirable is debatable. The underlying argument is that gender roles are socially emergent and grounded in performance. The ability of women to become "one of the boys" demonstrates that these forms of behavior can be learned and are not fixed or immutable. That women can move into male worlds indicates that women are capable of adapting to the behavioral styles practiced by males, although men have typically been less prone to accept the behavioral styles characteristic of female worlds.

This gendered acceptance is accompanied by interpersonal negotiation on a set of sensitive issues. Many of the obstacles that are faced by women of all ages deal in some way with issues of the performance of sexuality. The expressive component of social life can never be disentangled from the instrumental component. No matter how task oriented a group is, its activities can never be completely disentangled from the desires of members to express themselves. Women often find it relatively easy to succeed on the instrumental component of group life, but men's expressive behaviors have proven to be more intractable. Technical integration has not been fully matched with affective integration. Through their behaviors men and women must develop strategies for adjusting to each other with regards to the expressive components of group life. Part of the problem is that neither party may be entirely conscious that there exists this need for negotiation. Something seems to be wrong, but no one is quite certain of what that wrongness consists of and how it might be remedied. Yet, the parties recognize that they feel uncomfortable in each other's presence. This may lead to attributions being made to the new female group members as the "cause" of the problem, rather than to the recognition that it is the contours of the relationship that demand adjustment.

Each gender, like different cultures, has its own standards for comfortable interaction: its own pool of knowledge and experience. Of course, this does not mean that each individual—male or female—needs to share these views, but that these views represent standard expectations. These forms of behavior require little explanation or justification within the group—they are normative standards. For men, these expectations involve a rough and rowdy culture, in which tenderness and the softer emotions are often excised. *Machismo,* while not always present, need not be justified among males. The presence of female equals threatens these standards, changing a relatively unambiguous setting into one fraught with moral ambiguity. If humans desire their expectations fulfilled, it is easy to recognize why the presence of co-workers of the other gender so complicates social life.

While much gender integration has occurred, the fights over admitting women and preserving manly traditions in institutions connected to the military, notably military colleges, such as Virginia Military Institute or the Citadel, remind us that simply opening the door to women does not make gendered issues disappear, especially when an institution itself is firmly committed to backing up masculine prerogatives and folk culture. Successful incorporation of women involves a cultural analysis, as well as one that focuses on instrumental tasks. Some of the rough edges of the male folk culture must be smoothed, while women need to adjust to and understand some of the less noxious, but still distinctive, folk aspects of the work to which they aspire to enter. Tradition is valuable, even while some traditions must be excised. It is this balance between maintaining some masculine traditions, adding some feminine traditions, and creating a blended culture that is a challenge for all participants.

In sum, being "one of the boys" is a position that is completely congruent for some women, whereas for others it is a strain, an offense, or an impossibility. The identical behavior can, in practice, have significantly different meanings. In considering the problem of gender-linked folk cultures, we must avoid the temptation to stereotype the behaviors of either men or women but acknowledge the diversity of responses to informal group standards—expectations based on the culture of the group and not only on the gender of those who participate. These group standards remind us that folk cultures are characteristic of societies as well as interacting units, each with its own particular folk culture.

NOTES

1. In some of these domains, leaders or instructors may be males, as is evident at women's colleges.

2. Here I focus upon the work group, and not upon those domains in which a predominantly female workforce (servers, cocktail waitresses, flight attendants) serves a predominantly male clientele, which sees these workers as sexual embodiments (Spradley and Mann 1975).

3. This analysis builds on arguments made in my essay "One of the Boys: Women in Male-Dominated Settings," in *Changing Men: New Directions in Research on Men and Masculinity* (Fine 1987a).

4. For reasons of space I do not present detailed accounts of each ethnographic setting. For more information readers are directed to the books that describe the research setting (Fine 1983, 1987b, 1996, 1998, 2001).

5. In this research, later in the year I also observed a varsity team in another St. Paul suburb as they prepared for the national debate tournament. However, as this team of two contained one male and one female, I do not discuss them here.

6. Throughout this chapter, in which data span a wide age range, I use the term "women" to refer to women and girls.

REFERENCES

Easterday, L., D. Papademas, L. Schorr, and C. Valentine. 1977. "The Making of a Female Researcher: Role Problems in Field Work." *Urban Life* 6: 333–48.

Epstein, Cynthia. 1970. "Encountering the Male Establishment: Sex-Status Limits on Women's Careers in the Profession." *American Journal of Sociology* 75: 965–82.

Fine, Gary Alan. 1976. "Obscene Joking across Cultures." *Journal of Communication* 26: 134–40.

———. 1979. "Small Groups and Culture Creation: The Idioculture of Little League Baseball Teams." *American Sociological Review* 44: 733–45.

———. 1981. "Friends, Impression Management, and Preadolescent Behavior." In *The Development of Children's Friendships*, ed. Steven Asher and John Gottman, 29–52. Cambridge: Cambridge University Press.

———. 1983. *Shared Fantasy: Role-Playing Games as Social Worlds.* Chicago: University of Chicago Press.

———. 1987a. "One of the Boys: Women in Male-Dominated Settings." In *Changing Men: New Directions in Research on Men and Masculinity*, ed. Michael S. Kimmel, 131–47. Newbury Park, Calif.: Sage.

———. 1987b. *With the Boys: Little League Baseball and Preadolescent Culture.* Chicago: University of Chicago Press.

———. 1996. *Kitchens: The Culture of Restaurant Work.* Berkeley: University of California Press.

———. 1998. *Morel Tales: The Culture of Mushrooming.* Cambridge, Mass.: Harvard University Press.

———. 2001. *Gifted Tongues: High School Debate and Adolescent Culture.* Princeton, N.J.: Princeton University Press.

Haas, Jack. 1972. "Binging: Educational Control among High Steel Workers." *American Behavioral Scientist* 16: 27–34.

Hirschman, Albert O. 1971. *Exit, Voice, and Loyalty: Response to Decline in Firms, Organizations, and States.* Cambridge, Mass.: Harvard University Press.

Hughes, Everett. 1971. "Dilemmas and Contradictions of Status." In *The Sociological Eye*, ed. Everett C. Hughes, 141–50. Chicago: Aldine-Atherton.

Hunt, Jennifer. 1984. "The Development of Rapport through the Negotiation of Gender in Field Word among Police." *Human Organization* 43: 283–96.

Kanter, Rosabeth. 1977. *Men and Women of the Corporation.* New York: Basic.

Kirkpatrick, Jeane J. 1974. *Political Woman.* New York: Basic.

Lipman-Blumen, J. 1976. "Toward a Homosocial Theory of Sex Roles: An Explanation of Sex Segregation of Social Institutions." In *Women and the Workplace*, ed. Martha Blaxall and Barbara Reagan, 15–31. Chicago: University of Chicago Press.

Mechling, Elizabeth, and Jay Mechling. 1985. "Shock Talk: From Consensual to Contractual Joking Relationships in the Bureaucratic Workplace." *Human Organization* 44: 339–43.

Spradley, James P., and Brenda Mann. 1975. *The Cocktail Waitress: Woman's Work in a Man's World.* New York: Wiley.

Valentine, C. G. 1985. "Female Players and Masculine-Typed Instruments: Barriers to Women 'Making It' in the Art Music World." Paper presented at the annual meeting of the American Sociological Association, Washington, D.C.

Wax, Rosalie. 1977. "Gender and Age in Fieldwork and Fieldwork Education: No Good Thing Is Done by Any Male Alone." *Social Problems* 26: 509–22.

Weston, Kathleen M., and Lisa B. Rofel. 1984. "Sexuality, Class, and Conflict in a Lesbian Workplace." *Signs* 9: 623–46.

2

"Running the Yard": The Negotiation of Masculinities in African American Stepping

TOM MOULD

It's the Spring Fling festival at the University of North Carolina at Greensboro, and the Alpha Phi Alphas are hosting a step competition. DJs from the most popular local hip-hop radio station are spinning out the recent favorites, feeding the anticipatory energy of the crowd. The audience is almost entirely African American, almost entirely of college age. Many of the men wear clothing touting various black Greek letter organizations or jerseys from professional ball teams with their favorite players' names on the back. The women are dressed impeccably, hair perfectly coiffed.

By 9:30 P.M., the show is already well under way. During the first hour, the sororities competed. Now the men are about to start. The music abruptly stops, and the crowd murmurs, necks craning around to see where the steppers will enter. Many in the audience pull out video cameras and aim them around the room. One of the DJs steps to the stage: "And now it's time for the oldest, the coldest, the ice cold brothers of Alpha Phi Alpha, Incorporated." He draws out the "in" in "incorporated" just as fraternity and sorority members do. Then, an odd shift in music. Instead of hip-hop, the *Peanuts* cartoon theme music jingles out over the audience as the Alpha Phi Alphas stumble and trip their way through the auditorium. Dressed in ill-fitting plaid shirts and thick glasses, they mimic stereotypical geeks.

A recorded woman's voice booms through the speakers, scolding them for being so lame and unworthy of Alpha Phi Alpha. She then appears on stage and passes a two-liter soda bottle around to each member who pretends to drink from it until he falls to the floor. The woman leaves, and after a moment or two, the men rise up, ripping off their goofy shirts and glasses to reveal black muscle shirts that complement black pants and black combat boots. Their goofy grins have been replaced with exaggerated scowls. The crowd erupts. Greek men and women in the audience give their organizations' calls, skeewee-ing and barking over the cheers. The six Alpha men line up in formation, elbows up, fists together. Then, with a signal from their step leader, the men start stepping. They are in complete unison, each foot stomp, hand beat, and jump timed in perfect sync with the others.

Twenty minutes or so later, the judges are tallying the scores while fraternity and sorority members line and party hop around the auditorium. The Kappa fraternity members are shimmying; the AKA sorority members are doing some of their prissy steps, pinkies extended into the air. Many non-Greeks are dancing in the aisles to the hip-hop music once again being pumped out of the speakers throughout the auditorium. Finally, the winners are announced. The crowd is hardly surprised when the sisters of Delta Sigma Theta win. The crowd response during their performance was twice that of the other sororities. There is more speculation about the men. Only the Alphas and the Kappas competed in this show. Second place goes to the Kappas. The Alphas began calling out and cheering, drowning out the Kappas who storm out down the center aisle, claiming injustice in the various epithets they hurl at the Alphas. Once outside the auditorium, however, any antagonism seems to have dissipated as people discuss their night's plans. The step show is over; the parties are just beginning.

STEPPING IN BLACK FRATERNITY AND SORORITY LIFE

Stepping is an integral part of black fraternity and sorority life and until recently has been confined to black Greek letter organizations. Members step at competition step shows, exhibition shows, probate shows where new members are introduced to the campus community, and, both formally and informally, at parties. "Other people dance," says Jimmie McMillian, Kappa Alpha Psi member at Indiana University, "we step" (1998).

Using the body and the floor as a drum, black men and women clap, stomp, and beat out a series of intricate rhythms while executing physically exhausting moves. Coupled with chants, music, costumes, and themes, stepping is a vibrant and exciting form of entertainment for its audiences. But the social and artistic elements of stepping are often secondary to stepping's major goal: the cultivation and expression of group identity and specifically of superiority over the other organizations. Simply put, "Step shows are a chance for you to profess to the campus that you are the best" (Wheeler 1998).

For most non-black college students, step shows are their first and most frequent encounters with black Greek life. Many black Greeks find this problematic, fearing the reinforcement of racist stereotypes of blacks solely as entertainers as well as a distortion of black Greek life.[1] Stepping has been constructed over the years to portray only a small and idealized part of black Greek identity and therefore presents problems as a means for understanding the complexity of black identity. Studied in its broader social context, however, stepping can provide an understanding of some of the core values underlying various black masculine identities and how those identities are negotiated as very real social power outside the performance context.

Specifically, stepping provides black collegiate men and women with a

Omega Psi Phi fraternity members step at a yard show at Elon University, Elon, N.C., May 7, 2001. *Photograph by Tom Mould.*

vibrant arena for cultivating specific identities that argue for strength and superiority and that hold currency in constructing social hierarchies in daily life. These identities are forcefully gendered for both men and women, often dealing quite explicitly with what it means to be a black man or woman. Further, while the cultivation of fraternity and sorority identities is most explicit, stepping is more clearly a *black* creative tradition for the college setting rather than a Greek one. White Greek organizations do not step. Further, when stepping has moved outside the black Greek system, it has done so primarily within the black community, in black churches, youth organizations, and professional performances such as Step Afrika.[2]

In keeping with the focus of this book, I attend specifically to men's stepping and how images and ideas of masculinity are constructed, reified, and challenged. Ultimately, I argue for one of the volume's basic premises: that folklore often provides the means not merely for expressing values and attitudes about gender, but for defining and challenging them, with implications that extend beyond the performance event and into daily life.

STEPPING IN THE FIELD

This study is based on fieldwork conducted at Indiana University (IU) during the 1997–98 school year and at Elon University and the University of North Carolina at Greensboro (UNCG) from 2002–2004. It includes videotaping of competition step shows, yard shows, probate shows, rehearsals, and black Greek parties, as well as taped interviews with members of black Greek organizations (both male and female, current students and graduates) and non-Greek students who have regularly attended step shows. Further, non-stepping members of an organization frequently videotape their brothers and sisters' step performances, enabling me to study a number of step performances from other schools and time periods in Indiana and North Carolina. This chapter focuses specifically on competition step shows.

The published scholarship on stepping is fairly limited. Elizabeth Fine's recent book *Soulstepping* (2003) is the only book-length study of the genre, joining just a handful of scholarly articles and brief mentions in books (Bronner 1995, 134–36; Davis 1996; Farrar 2001; Fine 1991; Malone 1996; Rouverol 1996; Woodside 1995; Yarger 1996). Like Fine's book, this study relies most heavily on ethnographic fieldwork and interviews and follows the mandate of performance studies with particular attention to the process and construction of performance events, the dynamic interaction between audience and performer, and the importance of contextualization as a means for accessing various referential meanings.[3] However, this study seeks to expand the existing literature by attending specifically to the construction of gendered identities in stepping, one of the dominant arenas for the construction of meaning for this genre. Further, I explore how these identities are translated outside the performance event, both in terms of group and individual identity formation.

I should point out that much of the discussion here can be usefully compared and contrasted to women's stepping. Given the focus of this book, it is not possible to delve fully into women's stepping except in how steppers conceive of it in contrast to men's stepping. Another omission is the specific discussion of class differences that might explain some of the conceptions of black manliness in stepping. None of my informants mentioned class differences as an element of stepping, even when asked specifically. However, scholars have noted the problems of divorcing class from discussions of gender and race in terms of identity (Lemelle 2001; Majors and Gordon 1994, xi; Spraggins 1999). Further study into the relationship between gender, race, and class as embodied in stepping will no doubt prove useful.

THE FUNCTIONS OF STEPPING

Summing up the objectives of the step show, one stepper noted:

> It's all about getting the crowd to respond, and get your name out there, and let people know who you are, and getting remembered. (Calvin Sutton 2003)

Men and women who step often mention entertainment, exercise, and the construction of social bonds between members as relevant functions of stepping. Anyone who has seen a step show can understand how entertaining it is. Anyone who has watched a step show from the front row and has seen the sweat bead up on brows after only the first of five or six full step routines understands the exercise benefits. And anyone who has observed the nightly rehearsals that run for weeks understands how social bonds can be formed and strengthened.

However, far more often, steppers talk about functions of stepping that draw performer and audience into abstract and concrete social interaction. One of the most explicit of these functions is that of the recruitment of new members. As one Alpha Phi Alpha explained,

> People come to step shows, they'd be like, "Dag, did you see those Alphas? You know, I could be that," "I really want to be that, I want to be that," "Man, they were tight up there, know all their moves." That's where you get most of your interest. That's part of the reason you want to have a tight show. (Baskerville 2003)

Fraternities and sororities use step shows as a means of constructing a public image of their organization. That image is, to a great extent, specifically directed to other black students of the same gender. Black men step to attract other black men to their organization, as do black women to theirs. The message is clear: We are the best, and you should want to be part of our organization. What it means to be the best, of course, is contested and constantly being negotiated. One stepper explained,

> Some people compete for the prize money. Some compete for the trophies. I think at the core it's for status. It's mostly, if you win the step show, it's the thing: you're the most popular, the most together, the most unified as an organization. . . . There's a term that's used, "Who runs the yard." That's basically who's the better organization. (Long 2003)

In black college vernacular, one speaks not of Big Man on Campus but of Who Runs the Yard. The yard is the college campus; to run the yard is to be the most popular, most influential, most desirable organization on campus—in other words, to be the best. Step shows are explicit ways for black Greek members to establish their superiority on campus. In fact, being the best step group can translate to being the best organization. Things like service to the community, grade point averages, and leadership in other school activities certainly carry some weight in vying for this title, but it is the step show where organizations most explicitly and most creatively negotiate this hierarchy. Further, because the title of who runs the yard is primarily a social construct, it makes sense that it is the public and social performance of stepping that weighs most heavily in this negotiation.[4] Such performances are all the more efficient and effective since audiences are composed almost entirely of black college students—the exact peer set who grants the title of who runs the yard. While this title is not formal, uncontested, or confined to men, it nonetheless has very real currency for black college students.

Running the yard and constructing an image that will attract other men to one's organization has the important dual function of attracting women. Certainly there can be dramatic differences between what a man thinks women find desirable in a man and what they actually do. The assumption most steppers work from is that the men in the audience have internalized these differences. In other words, a black male in the audience will recognize in the behavior of men stepping on stage the kinds of personas that define not only what is desirable to be as a male but also what is desirable to a female. Both functions can be addressed with a particularly well-constructed step. For example,

> Sweat Me is one a lot of Sigmas do. That one is a bragging step. Don't sweat me. It can have two meanings. Number one, it's focused on the ladies. "Ladies, I know I look great but don't sweat me." The other one is guys can potentially be new members. "You might want to be like me and that's great, but tell me once and that's cool." (Long 2003)

Men present themselves to audiences including prospective dates, constructing personas that they believe will attract women. If an after-party follows the show, some fraternities will add more suggestive moves into their routines with the intention that this public flirting during performance can be developed offstage as well. Many women in the audience admit that stepping is an important part of courtship in college and that a good step show reflects favorably on the individual steppers.

Crucial to interpreting stepping and the masculine identities constructed during it, therefore, is audience approval. Audiences consist primarily of other black students, both from that particular school and nearby colleges and universities. This approval is made concrete by the judging criteria of competition step shows, where audience engagement is a key element of determining a successful performance. The greatest sin of a step performance is to lose the audience's attention. Imprecise and unimaginative steps and routines can disappoint an audience, but nothing bores them faster than a performance that lacks energy. As one student explained,

> You can watch a step show, I don't care who it is, if they don't have energy, if they haven't practiced a lot, you can tell right off the bat, because, I don't know what it is but the whole crowd——I've been at shows where the whole crowd starts talking. They may not be that bad, but they're not energized. It's all about how you present yourself. (Baskerville 2003)

Conversely, nothing engages an audience as fast as steppers who exhibit powerful energy while maintaining precision and unity with their fellow steppers.

The fact that approval is granted by peers, specifically other black college men and women, is of no small importance considering the traditional pressures felt by black men in America. Summarizing the scholarship on black masculinity in America, Ronald L. Jackson II observes: "The black masculine subject is concerned with validation. The question is who validates the black male's masculinity? Is it one or a combination of the following: White males, Black females, other Black males, or some other operating force?" (1997). The answer suggested by many scholars of African American studies is white males, both as validator and model (Connor 1995; Gray 1994; Jackson 1997; Mahalik, Pierre, and Woodland 2001).[5]

Stepping offers black men an arena for the negotiation of identity that is clearly validated within the black community. Whether or not that identity derives from constructions of white masculinity remains debatable, but that this negotiation is being performed by black men to a black audience is a liberating shift from past contexts that have risked being hegemonic and alienating.[6]

THE PROCESS OF PERFORMANCE: CONSTRUCTING THE BLACK FRATERNITY MAN

The image of black masculinity as performed in stepping is most specifically and most explicitly constructed from a set of national stereotypes of each Greek organization. Such formation of group identity would seem to suggest a fairly static and repressive system. Many fraternity members do, in fact, talk about a need to act a certain way during a step show. Much of this obligation is directed abstractly to the national organization, though as often it is directed more concretely to the expectations of people in the audience, including graduate members, members from other chapters, and non-members who have come to see the show. One stepper emphasized:

> A high percentage of the time, we're just feeding the stereotype, wild and out with it, just go with the flow, as long as you're up there hyped. But yeah, people accent those stereotypes all the time in traditional steps. I mean, this goes with sororities, fraternities too. You go with your stereotypes most of the time. (Calvin Sutton 2003)

Every chapter of every organization is different. A Sigma at Elon will be different from a Sigma at UNCG, and both will be different from a Sigma at Indiana University. Yet national ties bind, and each fraternity frequently shares a general national identity—one often, if not always, cultivated by individual chapters across the country. These stereotypes are well known and easily rattled off by any National Pan-Hellenic Council (NPHC) member.[7]

I have summarized these stereotypes below, drawing heavily from interviews with black fraternity and sorority members, retaining the vernacular terms used, such as "cool," "bad," and "nasty." Like many vernacular terms, definitions are fluid. The image of "cool" is one that has dominated academic, literary, and vernacular conceptions of the black male. Generally, to be cool is to maintain emotional self-control. Yet as Joel Dinerstein has pointed out, the concept of cool varies dramatically in different contexts and cultures.[8] For black men today, "cool" derives its meaning partially from its roots in the jazz scene beginning in the 1930s and, before that, from a West African aesthetic that appears throughout black expressive culture (Dinerstein 1999; Thompson 1999). Accordingly, "cool" encompasses the paradoxical notions of control that may mask emotion, with the expectation for personal expressions of power and strength, part of the response to a racist America. "Cool is, in one sense, composed violence" (Dinerstein 1999, 265). Such expressions of composure with an edge are clearly visible in stepping.

"Bad" can be thought of as the more expressive, confrontational version of "cool." In folklore, one finds the character of "the bad nigger" who uses physical force and boasting to establish his autonomy and authority (Abrahams 1970, 61–85; Brearley 1973, 578–85; Dance 1978, 224–46). It was white society who labeled independent, rebellious blacks as "bad," but the very same characteristics led the black community to invest the label with a positive connotation (Brearley 1973, 581, ed. note). That connotation today often includes "strong," "brave," "physically courageous," "aggressive," "fearless," and, more generally, "outstanding" (Claerbaut 1972, 57; Folb 1980, 228; Smitherman 2000, 60). "Nasty" takes "bad" and adds an overt sexual dimension. "Raunchy," "rough," and "bad-assed" are all encompassed by the term (Lewin and Lewin 1994, 262), as well as "sexually attractive" (Lighter 1994, 640).

Alpha Phi Alpha (Alphas or A Phi A's): This was the first organization to be founded, and members pride themselves on their role as "granddaddy" of all other fraternities, frequently chanting "Respect your roots" to the other frats. Typically expressing reserve, they project sophistication and demand respect. They are also "ice cold," the coolest guys around. They pride themselves on being leaders and thinkers, the smart guys on campus. But lest people think they are too refined, they also conceive of themselves as the Alpha males, often howling like apes and performing steps that imitate these primates' movements.

Omega Psi Phi (Ques, Que Psi Phis, Omegas): These guys are the roughest, toughest, "baddest" guys on campus. Often attracting football players and other athletes, the Ques tend to be the biggest men on campus quite literally. They pride themselves on being "nasty"—somewhat rude and

Kappa Alpha Psi member Stephen McCoy stepping with the trademark red and white striped
cane, giving the hand sign of his fraternity. Elon
University, May 7, 2004. *Photograph by Tom Mould.*

domineering. They are the most sexually explicit in their step shows and
often step without shirts. Except that they do not "step"—that is too much
like dance. Instead, they "hop," which means they do less hand clapping
and more hard stomping. With sexual bravado and muscular display, they
claim to be the most manly of all the fraternities, a claim many black college women agree with. Their mascot is the dog, and their call is a dog's
bark, although the Ques' national organization has outlawed any public
references to dogs.[9]

Kappa Alpha Psi (Kappas): These are the ladies' men or pretty boys.
They are smooth and suave and often dress the part in suits as they step.
They almost always step with canes, using them to tap and beat out many
of their rhythms. The canes add to their debonair style, though they can
be used aggressively during a show to establish a harder, rougher image.

Phi Beta Sigma (Sigmas): The Sigmas tend to fight easy categorization.
At Indiana University, they are the party fraternity, the good-time guys who
will do anything. They are funny, fun, raucous, and crazy. It is not uncommon to be mooned by the Sigmas during a show. The Sigmas at Elon

University, however, pride themselves on being gentlemen. They are sometimes "dissed" (disrespected) for being "country"—a little quaint, a little less sophisticated. Their stepping is generally more complicated rhythmically and incorporates more hand clapping than other fraternities. The differences among Sigma chapters are also seen in the social diversity of men within a single chapter, with members varying dramatically on their interest in, for example, partying, religion, and studying.

Iota Phi Theta (Iotas): The Iotas were founded so recently—1963 as compared to the period between 1906 and 1914 for the other fraternities—that their stereotype is marked by the lack of one. The most common diss: "Iota? Who are they?"

These stereotypes depend on explicit constructions of masculinity, of what it is to be an Alpha, Omega, Sigma, Kappa, or Iota man. All the steppers are competing to run the yard, and so all are trying to be the coolest, most manly, most prestigious men on campus. But there is no single identity that will achieve this, no monolithic masculine image. One can run the yard by being the most aggressive and powerful, as the Ques claim, by being the most successful and strongest leaders, as the Alphas claim, by being the most fun and outrageous, as many Sigmas claim, or by being the most appealing to the ladies, the most respectful and gentlemanly, as the Kappas claim.

There are, however, shared norms for the kinds of bragging all fraternities engage in. No Kappa wants to seem weak, no Omega without class, no Alpha luckless with women. What we find, then, are a series of masculine identities constructed upon different major claims but that converge in their totality. Black college men must exhibit elements of all of these characteristics to prove they are the best.

Some fraternities will have certain specific claims they use to support these larger ones that are unique to their organization. The Alphas, for example, frequently brag about their role as the first black fraternity.[10] But to varying degrees, they all share the following:

- We are the best steppers (the only claim confined to the event itself)
- We are the most unified (claims of strong brotherhood)
- We are the most sexually desirable and powerful
- We are the most distinguished, authoritative and self-controlled
- We are the roughest and toughest (often via references to the military)

To enact these stereotypes and images, and to construct these masculine personas, steppers use a variety of material—expressive, gestural and physical, vocal and audio resources, including clothing, props, facial expressions, signs and symbols constructed with the body, movements and steps, chants, songs, and music. Wrapped up in these expressive elements are contextualization cues to the audience, references including previous shows, recent activities on campus, shared organizational knowledge, pop culture, and black traditional culture. By drawing these various contexts into the performance, steppers expand the field of meaning for step shows. More impressive is how economically they do this—with the use of color, a slight hand gesture, a provocative song played in the background, or an oblique reference in a chant. The analysis of some of these strategies, in the context of discussing shared norms of men's stepping, will help illuminate how meaning, specifically in the formation of masculine identities, is constructed in stepping.

PHYSICAL STRENGTH AND THE MILITARY IMAGE

The claims of physical strength and power are inherent in the athleticism of stepping but are often conveyed more explicitly through military symbolism. Fatigues are often worn during shows, whether in full or in part. Unless a group dresses in suits, virtually all organizations wear combat boots to step in. This is important not only symbolically but also practically, as they allow the men to make loud resounding sounds when they stomp. The military influence is also heard in many of the chants and cadence calling. Historically, stepping has close ties to college officer training programs. The Omega Psi Phis, for example, drew many of their members during World War I from officer training camps (Mumford 1998; Ross 2000, 77–78). Today, more than any other fraternity, Omega steppers almost invariably wear fatigues with their gold combat boots, and many of their chants sound like military jodies, both rhythmically and with the heavy dependence on call and response. The call and response chanting also has its roots in traditional black expressive culture, most explicitly in the black church. The dual influence of the drillmaster and the preacher make for a seemingly odd yet powerful resource for steppers.

In addition to the clothing and chants, the steps themselves often imitate marching. The hopping of the Ques is often differentiated from stepping through this more military style, one of more marching than dancing. The Iotas frequently step in military formation with a trademark step that mimics carrying a bow and shield with a fighting stance like that of their national symbol of the centaur.

These references to the military bring with them not only the obvious elements of power, strength, and the warrior persona, but also a very real social reality. Black men and women in America have shouldered a disproportionately large amount of the burden for staffing the U.S. military, something that concerns many black leaders but remains a mark of honor among many young black men (Ricky L. Jones 1997, 81). In this way, references to the military are symbolically and socially relevant.

A more tenuous connection to the military but a clear expression of strength and discipline is embodied in the male stepper's default facial

The stepping "game face" worn by Alpha Phi
Alpha chapter president Justen Baskerville at a
yard show at Elon University, May 7, 2004.
Photograph by Tom Mould.

expression. It is something akin to a scowl. "You have to have your game
face on, and for frats, that's no smiling, no moving or fixing your clothes,"
one student explained (Wheeler 1998). This scowl tends to be exaggerated
far more by the Ques, but all groups use it to convey a hard image, one
that suggests grim determination and often defiance. This is the face worn
by members in between step routines as they gather their breath for the
next step, as well as the face worn most often during the actual stepping.
It is a mask that provides a unified expression of toughness. Such a face fits
the norms for stepping as an arena for dramatic competition, where the
insults are more explicit and more biting than would ever be allowed offstage without a fight. These expressions match that intensified atmosphere.[11]

SEXUAL ELEMENTS

Addressing whether male steppers perform to women in the audience, one
student explained:

In military stance and clothing, Omega Psi Phi chapter president Calvin Sutton steps at a yard show at Elon University, May 7, 2004. *Photograph by Tom Mould.*

And for the females, of course, you really try to have a good show so females notice you on stage or whatever. I didn't really say too much to this, but there's a lot of sex appeal put into most shows. People have, like, dance breaks where they get a little freaky and a little risqué or whatever. But in most shows, there's rules and stuff where you can't get too out there with the sex appeal. I know for Kappas, one of their trademarks, stereotypes— they love to tease women and stuff, thinking like they're about to strip or something like that. Sometimes they even go down as far as their boxers and they'll even like, fake like they're going to go all the way. Sometimes they might even go all the way, but most of the time they get disqualified for that, so it's stupid really. But there's a lot of sex appeal thrown into the show. (Baskerville 2003)

During virtually every show, every fraternity brags about their sexual desirability and prowess. These claims can be declared both subtly and explicitly through chants and steps. The Elon Sigmas' trademark "Sweat Me" step, performed during the 2003 probate show at Elon University, focuses on desirability and the control these men maintain:

It's time to sweat me (4 times)
   [in between each repetition, they strike a different stepping pose]
Sweat.
   [hand-clapping step]
Me.
   [hand-clapping step]
AKAS
off me.
   [They do a trademark Alpha Kappa Alpha sorority step]
Deltas
off me.
   [They do a trademark Delta Sigma Theta sorority step]
Rhos
off me.
   [They do a trademark Sigma Gamma Rho sorority step]
Zetas
we love you.
   [They do a trademark Zeta Phi Beta sorority step. Zeta is their sister
   sorority.]

The Virginia Tech Alphas' chant "Clutch Me, Baby" is more explicit and focuses on the sexual prowess of the members. Each member has his own boast, one of which runs:

Clutch me, baby,
Marcus is my name,
Sex is my fame,
'Cause when my luck is right,
I do it every night,
'Cause it's a smooth roman rocket
That always hits your pocket. (Fine 2003, 71)

Chants such as "Clutch Me, Baby," are more often reserved for the more informal, less regulated, and far rowdier yard shows than the more formal competition shows. At a yard show hosted by the Omega Psi Phis at Elon University, for example, the Kappa Alpha Psis performed a step and chant similar to "Clutch Me, Baby" in which each member bragged of his sexual prowess, using their trademark canes as phalluses. The other fraternities responded in kind, with explicit chants and movements to brag of their own prowess while berating the other groups for the lack of theirs.

During the more formal and structured competition step show, these suggestive steps and interludes are placed after a particularly strenuous step to give the men a chance to cool down and prepare for the next athletic step. Slow, romantic music often accompanies these "breather steps" as they are often called. Justen Baskerville jokes, "Everybody else is going to see it as 'Oh, they trying to get all freaky' [said in higher pitch, imitating women talking], but for you, you're like breathing." (2003).

While virtually every show will include sex appeal/breather steps, references to sexual prowess are conveyed more frequently throughout the
show in smaller ritualized steps, moves stuck in the middle of other steps
to catch the audience off guard and surprise them. Pelvic gyrations are
common, often with both hands placed behind the head. Toward the end
of a particularly athletic step, the Alphas at Indiana University stood erect,
waists thrust forward, shoulders back, arms thrusting up and down as they
chanted "Stroke." It was this climax that earned the loudest crowd reaction, despite the athletic and technically difficult steps that preceded it.

A common variation of the pelvic gyration might be termed "the
roundhouse slap." In this movement, men extend one arm, palm flat and
face down in front of them, as if resting on a table, while the other circles
dramatically overhead to come down as a slap across the table legs. The
imagery is, of course, is not of a table, but rather of a sexual partner on all
fours. During an exhibition step show at Elon University, one of the Ques
dropped to the ground in push-up stance and undulated his hips against
the floor, his tongue hanging out as he stared down the audience. This
move, like the Alpha's stroke, received the loudest cheers of their routine.

While not every movement of the pelvis is intended as sexual, particularly when considering influences of African aesthetics in stepping, many
are, and the audience has little trouble identifying them, regularly responding with the loudest cheers of any part of the show.[12]

The tongue is often used to reinforce sexual imagery. Speaking about
the Ques at Elon University, a female stepper and frequent audience member of step shows notes: "They do different stuff with their mouths and
their tongues. It's really suggestive. It's nothing unusual. No one goes to a
step show and says, 'I can't believe they did that,' because that's what they
do, you know?" (Ashton 2003).

Such explicit sexual imagery risks fueling racist stereotypes of the black
man as hyper-sexed. Ronald Braithwaite, however, argues that such stereotypes ignore the normative sexual socialization patterns of black men that
include a more permissive sexual ethos (1981, 87). Paul Oliver makes a
similar claim about blues music and the stark, unapologetic sexual boasting
of many bluesmen (1963, 131–32). It is clear from crowd response that
these overt sexual innuendos are acceptable in the context of the show.
Such norms and expectations for stepping provide an arena where sexuality, in addition to physical strength, is exaggerated. Even within a cultural
context of a more permissible sexual ethos, the black male stepper is often
constructed as hyper-sexed and therefore hyper-masculine. Such constructions avoid feeding racist stereotypes not only by presenting this construction to a virtually all-black audience but because of the frame of meaning
constructed by the genre of stepping. Exaggeration is expected, even required. Insiders have the liberty of manipulating these stereotypes where
outsiders clearly do not. That said, many black leaders in the NPHC see

the potential damage of these sexual displays and have taken measures to try to eliminate lewd sexual references and other potentially harmful stereotypes, such as the ape calls and steps of the Alphas and the dog imagery of the Ques (see "Omega Psi Phi" 2000; Ross 2000, 427–28). Despite these attempts, many chapters continue to test these boundaries.

STEPPING SPHERES

Perhaps one of the most pervasive if most implicit norms for men's stepping is defined by what it is not—in other words, in contrast to women's stepping. Men's stepping should be bigger, higher, and more athletic than women's stepping. Men's stepping should include more hopping and stomping and less hand clapping than women's. Men can be wild, nasty, aggressive, and sexually suggestive, where many women feel they need to convey a persona of femininity, to be ladylike. While this dyad is not shared by all, many steppers, both men and women, see the two as polar opposites in terms of gendered expression. Men's stepping is manly; women's stepping exudes femininity.[13] The reference to "lady" and the contrast with "manly" ways appear frequently as a sign of femininity in comments from steppers:

> There's a big difference in the way that men and women step. I think that women are more restricted because we have to be ladylike. I mean we just have to be ladies. But the guys, they can do anything they want to. They jump around, they flip, they do a lot of stuff. So I like them both but I really like seeing the guys step. (Shalando Jones 1998)

> The men are more—harder, they are just more stomp versus women, the women pretty much put dance routines in, little sex appeal maybe to get the crowd moving. Where men they just howl, stomp and things like that. (Bentley 1998)

> Men—it's more like, more of a manly thing when we step. We use more muscles, hop around higher, we move around harder. Women's is more sweet, more feminine, stuff like that. It's just like "Wow"; the men's is more like "Wow." The women's is more discreet, being ladylike, things like that. (Nelson 1998)

> I would say for masculine, it would be the hardest step possible. The most difficult, airborne, flipping kind of acrobatic step that you could think of. . . . If you could show your different sides, from a masculine step, show the ultimate masculine that you can through how difficult your step is. (Long 2003)

In performance, men tend to use deliberate head movements from side to side while women may also shake and snap their heads to indicate a no-nonsense attitude. Men often ball their hands into fists particularly when starting and ending a step but also during stepping, while women tend to have their hands open. Men tend to either keep their wrists locked straight or to bend them firmly at right angles toward the elbow. Women tend to bend the wrist the other direction, as with the Alpha Kappa Alpha ivy stance—arms down by the side, hands bent upward at the wrist. Differences in hand usage are particularly noticeable with the high degree of clapping by women compared to men. Some men view hand clapping as reminiscent of girls' playground games and see it as less manly than heavy stomping. It is true that many of the hand clapping routines used by women exactly imitate childhood games. Men tend to have arm movements that extend outside the frames of their bodies more often than women, who often incorporate arm movement within the frame. Men must scowl while women can smile.

For every one of these generalized norms there are a hundred exceptions. It is not unheard of, for example, for sororities to do shows almost entirely comprising steps from their brother fraternity. Women may scowl, wear fatigues, and hop rather than step. Nothing is off-limits.[14] However, audience expectation and approval remain a dominant force and generally encourage adherence to these gendered norms.

BROTHERHOOD

The final shared norm in men's stepping is one that seems to inherently challenge the hyper-masculine image constructed so far. All collegiate fraternities and sororities are based on the idea of brotherhood and sisterhood. The step show itself argues implicitly for strong brotherhood, considering the long hours of practice required. Any successful step show is a testament to brothers working closely together. More specifically, however, a number of chants are shared among fraternities and sororities to proclaim this love and loyalty. One, for example, underscores the devotion members have to their organization and fellow members:

All of my love
My peace and happiness
I give to Que Psi Phi

Each organization modifies the final line, substituting a three-part version of their own organization name, such as A Phi A, Sigma Gamma Rho, and so forth. Many of these chants are sung slowly, with brothers harmonizing the chant in rounds. The uncharacteristically slow and sentimental nature of these chants would seem to undercut the hyper-masculine images derived from national stereotypes.

To some extent, any risk of such "softness" is countered by context. These slow chants often serve as breather steps, chances for the men to cool off after a particularly athletic step and before embarking on another. Like the sex appeal elements of the show that also provide breathers, these slower moments are reserved for expressions of love. In one instance, physical love, in the other, emotional love. The contrast between the two is worth noting. The "softened" image of the man appealing to women is generally disingenuous; the love offered is sexual rather than emotional. Loyalty and faithfulness are not part of this construct, not something granted to women. Yet when men speak of each other, the hyper-masculine mask seems to slip. They avow, often quite adamantly, that it is the deepest of emotional ties that bind them to their brothers. In the same way that the ritual atmosphere of stepping suspends social norms by inviting outrageous bragging, it also suspends interdictions against overt declarations of love for other men.

Even so, love and loyalty are viewed as good while sentimentality and weakness are considered bad. Accordingly, men frequently modify and contextualize their chants with expressions of strength and superiority. In one of the Alpha's versions of the "All of my love" chant, which runs "My heart / And my soul / Belong to A Phi A," one of the members shouts, "I love my A Phi" in between each pause, overlapping the other brothers at the end with "I love my A Phi A" (Black Greek Soundz 2002). The soloist adds an element of hardness to this soft chant, both in volume and tone as well as in its aural reference to military cadence calls.

Other times, the addition of a harder edge is completed through the text of the chant and its subsequent steps. During an exhibition step show at Elon University, the Ques moved from a series of hard steps into the "All of My Love" chant, where they stood motionless, singing. One brother harmonized for the others. Immediately afterward, the Ques shifted into another chant about brotherhood, this one coupled with hard hopping and stomping:

> What's my name?
> Omega Psi Phi.
> Live and die
> For Omega Psi Phi.

Men will almost invariably follow a slow chant with an energetic one. Part of this is due to the function of the breather step: it is intended only as a hiatus, a break until the steppers can get back to the business of hard stepping. But the effect in performance is that any display of love and loyalty is followed by a display of strength and superiority. Not only does this qualify the sentimental connection between brothers, but it also translates that bond into dominance over other men. The stepper implicitly declares that he has brothers who would die for him, whom he can trust implicitly, and because of this loyalty, he has a brotherhood that can dominate any other organization.

Another strategy men use to avoid sentimentality is to convey this bond of brotherhood with steps rather than chants. An especially compelling example of this display of brotherhood and loyalty is the blindfolded step. During a step show at Indiana University during the early 1990s, for example, the Sigmas donned blindfolds for part of the show and stepped in pairs, clapping and moving within the space of the other so that only the most precise timing and movements would allow them to step successfully (Bowling and Harkness 1992). A miscalculation would result in hitting each other. At one particularly dramatic moment during the routine, one brother falls backward, trusting that his other blindfolded brother will catch him. Here, brotherhood is translated from the emotional into the physical.

Considering the initial dichotomy between sexual breather steps as physical and loyalty breather steps as emotional, the physical expression of brotherhood has the potential to suggest a physical dimension of their brotherly love. Other elements of step shows reinforce such an interpretation. Fraternity members frequently line up, as they did during the pledge process, in a "back to belly" formation where the men are lined so closely together that the stomach of one touches the back of the other (Ruffins 1998). When the Alphas performed their trademark step "the Train" during a show at Indiana University, the men lined up in this formation, eventually lowering themselves to the ground, arms hooked into the legs of the brother behind him, rocking side to side while thrusting one leg into the air (Barnett and Mould 1998).

The physicality of the bonds shared by brothers and expressed during step shows feeds, rather than undermines, the powerful male persona being constructed. Yet such expressions must also be viewed as a move away from national stereotypes. The masculine image presented is not emotionally detached but rather engaged quite forcefully in a display of brotherhood.

CRACKING

Employing the preceding norms for performance, fraternity men construct their shared conception of the Alpha, Sigma, Omega, Kappa, or Iota man with two parallel strategies: to argue for one's own group as the best and the others as pale in comparison. Just as organizational stereotypes serve as a base for constructing one's own stereotypes, they are equally useful to other organizations as a source for criticism. There are often two sides to stereotypes, characteristics that can be cast in a positive or negative light. Steppers exploit these to their advantage. Kappas see themselves as ladies' men while other frats deride them as pretty boys. Alphas see themselves as smart, successful, and born leaders, while others diss them for being geeks and stuck up. The Ques see themselves as rowdy, nasty, and the roughest

The brothers of Alpha Phi Alpha at Indiana University displaying brotherhood and synchronization during an end-of-the-year step show, 1998. *Still photograph from video by Tom Mould.*

and toughest guys on campus, while others debase them as crass and animalistic.

"Cracking" is the corollary to bragging. Also known as "mauling" or simply "dissing" (disrespecting), cracking is the act of insulting another organization, putting them down to raise oneself up. Such ritual insulting is common among many black Americans, particularly among black men who may play the "dozens," often exchanging "Your momma" jokes as a means of both competition and social bond formation (see Abrahams 1970; Caponi 1999).[15]

The ritual space of the stepping stage, which provides license to brag more outrageously than normal, allows for even greater violation of social norms in terms of cracking:

> Some of the things I would say on the stage about another organization, I wouldn't say in a meeting, or I wouldn't say it to their faces. Even though it's funny and comical, in that setting, it's funny. If I were to say it when the other president is sitting beside me, that's very offensive. (Long 2003)

Bragging and cracking go hand in hand and are often coupled in chants. Some of these chants are fairly vague in their claims, referencing general perceptions of prestige.

An Alpha is what a Kappa ain't
What a Que wanna be
What a Sigma can't

What a Zeta wants
What a Delta loves
What an AKA can't get enough of. (Black Greek Soundz 2002)

The first stanza simply declares the superiority of Alphas and the desire by other fraternities to be like them. The second stanza, however, brags about their attractiveness to sorority women, a more specific claim tied to the shared claims of masculine identity. The resulting implication is that other fraternities lack this sexual desirability.

The symbols of the fraternities, coupled with organizational stereotypes, become some of the easiest ways to crack on a fraternity.[16] Parodying a trademark step is a common initial keying mechanism for cracking. When the Sigmas, for example, weakly toss up their arms in an inverse Omega, it is as obvious a cue to the audience that they are beginning to disrespect the Ques as "Knock, knock" is to a group of kids to signal a coming joke.

The stereotypes of fraternities also become a resource for the content of the crack, not merely a means of keying it. The manly images constructed by fraternities constitute the most common targets for cracking, the insult being that the men of the other fraternities fall short.

> They may talk about someone's lack of sexual prowess. They may talk about someone's popularity or lack of popularity or that they are drunks or do drugs, which may or may not be true, but it got to be that everyone takes it as fun. It was not meant to be in original mean-spirited, but it was meant to be a kind of tease. (Mumford 1998)

An especially prevalent crack against other fraternities is the accusation of homosexuality. Such an insult seems logical considering the pervasiveness of claims of heterosexual prowess. The inverse of such bragging about oneself is the inverse claim about others. That inverse claim can be framed as a lack of sexual potency or a lack of skill with women, but it is more often cast as a lack of interest in them—an accusation of homosexuality. An Alpha Phi Alpha chant runs:

> I was walking through the jungle Screaming 1–9–0–6
> When a Kappa and a Que was doing the do
> Well, I snapped the Kappa
> And I kicked the Que
> I said, "You no good suckas
> Let the Sigmas join in too."[17]

This tendency to accuse other men of homosexuality more often than of impotence or undesirability to women might be explained by larger social and cultural norms in the black community. Homophobia and a general lack of acceptance of homosexuality are widespread in black culture; arguably no greater insult can be levied against a black man than that of being homosexual.[18]

In a particularly elaborate cracking incident at Indiana University in the early 1990s, the Alphas cracked on each of the other fraternities on campus (Bowling and Harkness 1992). The climax was the accusation of homosexuality among one of the fraternities. The Alpha show started with a prince and princess unconscious in the middle of the stage (in this case, the IU gym floor), after a spell had been placed on them. A man's voice narrated the scene:

> It was very unfortunate. But there was a breath of hope. For the princess could be awakened by a kiss from the most noble Greek. Men from afar came to unleash the spell, hoping to awaken the beautiful princess. There was the first Greek. [Out steps a guy imitating the Ques by imitating a dog. He sniffs around the two people, barking. He then pretends to urinate on the guy and licks the woman, who slaps him].
>
> Then there came the second Greek. [Out steps a guy imitating the party boy Sigma, brown-bagged bottle of booze in his hand. He weaves back and forth, shouting at no one in particular, "You want some of this?" He tries to execute a few steps but fails miserably. He then picks the pocket of the guy and yells at the woman: "You want some of this?" while grabbing his crotch.]
>
> Then came the third Greek. [Out steps the Kappa pretty boy, looking well groomed in black slacks, red sweater and hair combed neatly. He imitates the trademark Kappa shimmy. He sees the woman on the floor and is excited. "Damn, she's beautiful," he repeats, blinking his eyes as if in disbelief, circling her like a shark. But then he sees the man and immediately adopts a flamboyant, stereotypical posture of a gay man. He screams in a high voice, raises his arms and lets his wrists droop, and starts swooning over the man. The crowd erupts. People are jumping up and down in the stands. Eventually, the "Kappa" picks up the man and walks him off stage, squeezing his buttocks as they go.]
>
> And from the east came an army of Nubian knights who came to awaken the princess and protect all the campus ladies. [From a side door, the Alphas, dressed in tuxedos, enter on, and alongside, a white Cadillac. One of the Alphas goes over to the woman, kisses her, and leads her offstage as the others get into formation to step.]

Here we can see some of the range of tools used to construct a good crack. The Alphas signaled the various fraternities they were cracking with the colors of clothing they wore, the trademark steps they attempted, and exaggerated parodies of both national and individual chapter stereotypes. The explosive laughter, taunts, and cheers from the audience made it clear these keying elements and references were understood.

Black Greek men construct their steps whether consciously or unconsciously within a set of standards that are defined partly by what they inherently claim to be via national stereotypes and partly by what they claim not to be—not feminine, dainty, or ladylike. All of the men also engage in brazen self-promotion. The ego is on full display during stepping. Though the content of step shows is changing because of increasing regulation of Greek life on campus, all organizations at one time or another engage in cracking—the brash, often highly insulting criticism of other fraternities. All the men must present an image of the strongest, most in control, most prestigious, most loyal, and most desirable-to-the-women kind of man possible.

Despite these shared themes and identities, however, there is no single black masculinity constructed during step shows. The Sigmas at Elon construct a masculinity based on unity, prestige, and respect, referencing brotherhood more heavily than the military, subtle sexual energy more than explicit sexual promiscuity and prowess. The Ques at Elon, in contrast, more often construct an image of masculinity based on aggressive power and domination, referencing military discipline and roughness more heavily than suavity, sex more heavily than romance. Further, while the national stereotype is a powerful influence, fraternity step groups frequently challenge and redefine the masculine image expected by audiences, breaking away from these stereotypes and subtly undermining them.

PERFORMANCE AS ARENA FOR TRANSFORMATION

The paradoxical nature of performing within a recognized genre is the freedom that restricting the range of creation provides. Recognized keys and structures actually allow the performer to narrow the possibilities for creation, thus uncrippling the imagination that is overrun with options. The paradox is that by restricting creativity, creation is made more accessible.

Yet performance allows for emergent meaning. Genre boundaries are contested and redefined. Expectations are challenged, breathing ever-new life into deeply rooted traditions. Performers within various folk genres often manipulate and negotiate these expectations as an integral part of the genre. This also seems paradoxical. If a person at a festival is expected to break the rules, then breaking them is usual, not unusual—the norm rather than a challenge of that norm. If jokes often challenge the listener in terms of what is appropriate, then jokes about recent, horrific disasters may meet our expectations.

But expectation is vague and opens the door to wide possibility. That something new or disturbing may come does not ensure that it will or in what form it will take. Surprise is still prevalent. It is this surprise that yields paradox but avoids contradiction. It is also this surprise the leads to effective performance. Only by "judicious rule breaking" are these men able to construct persuasive masculine identities and excel in performance.[19]

For black fraternity men, the contestation of proscribed images of masculinity occurs firmly within the genre of stepping, regularly challenging the expectations, assumptions, and stereotypes of what it means to be an Alpha or Sigma, what it means to be in a black Greek organization, and what it means to be a black college man. It is here that fraternity stereotypes are upended, where the "nasty" Ques dress up in tuxedos, where the distinguished Alphas become sexually charged, where the ladies' men Kappas become hard warriors.

There are a number of ways that black fraternity men will challenge these stereotypes. Perhaps the most basic is something that might be called "the change-up." As discussed earlier, no one wins a step show without the involvement of the audience. There are a number of ways to get the audience "hyped" or excited: (1) precise steps, (2) innovative and difficult steps, (3) popular music accompanying the show, (4) humor, (5) sex appeal, and (6) challenging the audience's expectations. This last strategy is most frequently executed by exploiting one of the other stereotypes of the black college man, a stereotype that one's own fraternity generally eschews.

> Omega Psi Phis are the dogs, and we got to be nasty and stuff. One time everybody—they knew we was just coming out in fatigues and our gold boots and no shirts on and tongues hanging out. But we surprised them and came out in tuxes one step show. I thought that was pretty good. Always got to keep the crowd on their toes, and not go always with the expected for your fraternity. (Calvin Sutton 2003)

Despite this challenge to the Que stereotype, negotiation of a black manliness remains fairly restricted. There seems to be a finite combination of images acceptable for the black man to draw upon during step performances. One stereotype gets substituted for another or, more often, added to another, claiming multiple facets of a strong male persona. It is a persona of seeming contradiction: tough but suave, nasty but romantic.

The persona seems to work in terms of audience approval only when the contradictory images are resolved, whether by balancing the two in moderation, or, more often, when the original stereotype is seen to win out. Ques in tuxes can succeed in shocking the audience, but in order to maintain their credibility, they may need to allow the more fundamental stereotype of the nasty dog to dominate. Hard steps in tuxedos work; smooth steps in tuxedos, at least for a Que, generally do not. Many audience members who attended the 2001 Homecoming show were pleased by the effort but generally felt it was not completely successful. The Ques have got to be nasty. They were not, and the crowd responded with lukewarm approval.

From this example, stepping can be seen as fairly conservative in terms of the ability to challenge organizational stereotypes. Yet there are other strategies. One is to strive for more realistic balance in their bold, ego-driven personas. The frame constructed through stepping allows, even en-courages, exaggerated stereotypes and personas. The crowd rewards this over-the-top behavior. But steppers often fight the impulse to merely please the crowd. As a chance to construct identity for the larger public and peti-tion new members, the stakes are too high to allow runaway stereotyping. Steppers refuse to capitulate to ascribed identities, demanding instead the liberty to construct their own. One must be the best, and the best is not a parody but an ideal. Ques have to be nasty but not crude. Kappas have to be suave but not sentimental.

Stepping depends upon unity and precision, with all steppers perform-ing the exact same move at the exact same time. Deviation is not acceptable as it implies either a mistake or a disunified fraternity. There are excep-tions, of course. It is common to choreograph a step where different mem-bers execute different steps to create an overall unified tableaux. Often this occurs in rounds, where a step seems to ripple through the members like "the wave" at a football game. The other exception is also planned but is meant to be viewed as both emergent and unacceptable. This is the "show dog." Here, an individual stepper breaks from the others and seems to go out of control in the frenzy of the moment. The show dog is almost exclusively a male tradition and a common way for steppers to negotiate boundaries.

During the 2002 Elon Homecoming step show, the Alphas performed a step with sex appeal. Each member gazed out into the audience, as if at a specific woman, and shimmied his legs side to side, rubbing his hands provocatively across his chest. Then, while everyone else moved into an-other step, one brother continued shimmying, engrossed in his perform-ance and, seemingly, with a woman in the audience. His moves became bigger and more frenetic as he moved to the front of the stage. The other brothers stopped stepping and stared at him. The crowd laughed and cheered. One of the brothers finally went over to calm him down. Mock-ingly shamefaced, he joined the others and the step continued.

Then the Sigmas took the stage. They performed a slow, romantic step, moving smoothly across the floor and flexing their muscles subtly to the audience. The women cheered. As the rest of the brothers moved into other steps, however, one Sigma continued to slide across the floor, getting caught up in smiling and grinning at the women in the audience. Here again, the other Sigmas stopped stepping until one eventually hauled him back in. The others shouted at him to "Get on with it."

Both show dogs were guilty of getting carried away in their flirtation. However, they parodied this loss of control quite differently. The Alpha is hyper-sexed, the Sigma hyper-sensitive. Both are seen as out of control and exhibiting excessive behavior. Both are admonished for this lack of control. These interludes allow the men in each fraternity to implicitly argue against some of the excesses embodied in their organizational stereo-types.[20]

While the show dog provides for small elements of self-parody, steppers also find more frequent or extensive use of self-parody both an effective way to engage the audience though humor and a way to challenge their organizational stereotypes. In one instance during the 2003 UNCG Spring Fling step show, the Alphas once again parodied the display of hyper-sexuality. They began by performing a series of steps, one of which included the clearly sexual move of raising one leg and turning it outward while slapping the inner thigh and moaning "Ah, ah, ah." However, they proceeded to repeat the entire sequence of steps in slow motion. When they got to this part and slowly moaned "Ahhhhhh, Ahhhhhh, Ahhhhhh," the effect was ridiculous and hilarious, and the crowd erupted with laughter. The Alphas did not discount their sexual prowess, but they critiqued it, suggesting that overt sexual displays were somewhat ridiculous.

In fact, the entire Alpha show was constructed as an extended parody, as described at the beginning of this chapter when the members came out as geeks and slowly became transformed into real Alphas. The parody of the Alpha geek can be interpreted a number of different ways. If we restrict interpretation to the specific performance event, the Alphas seem to be claiming only, "We're not geeks." Nowhere in the show did they remind the audience of their intellectual prowess. Nowhere did they argue that while not geeks, they remain smart. In fact, toward the end of the show, the woman's voice returns over the speakers declaring, "You are playboys, but there's one more test." That test is of their abilities as steppers and as patriarchs of the fraternity system, as they immediately break into their trademark step "the Train" followed by a series of chanted questions and steps:

> Is it how we step?
> [they step]
> Or is it how we————
> [they perform a sexually suggestive move, pumping their pelvises
> slowly].
> Or is it how we 1–9–0–6? [a common chant of their founding year]

In other words, the specific context of the performance suggests an interpretation where the Alphas claim no intellectual superiority over other fraternities and in fact seem to eschew it altogether. Still, the relevant context for step shows is far broader, with meaning relying heavily on past performances.

In talking with audience members after the show, it is clear that the performance was not interpreted as an attempt to undercut their image of being smart, but rather as an attempt to revise the negative corollary to being smart: being geeks. Recognizing the Alphas' frequent claims of intellectual superiority through chants such as: "We party hard / We stay up late / But most of all we graduate" (Baskerville 2003), many viewed the show as a preemptive strike against cracking from other fraternities. Meaning was constructed by synthesizing present performances with previous performances, even without explicit contextualization cues to refer to them. Steppers know their audiences will be able to reference these stereotypes and previous performances, and they exploit expectations accordingly.

GROUP VERSUS INDIVIDUAL IDENTITY

Returning to the primary goal of the step show—to profess to the rest of the campus that your organization is the best—the question arises of how stepping, and its construction of masculine identities, compare and get incorporated into the masculinities enacted off stage by these same men.

During a step show, fraternity members often sit with their sister sorority members although individual members may be friends with both men and women from outside these organizations.[21] Watching the show, one sees these divisions played out quite explicitly. The uninitiated observer might easily conclude that each organization hates the other. The bold insults thrown at each other suggest a campus community torn apart by infighting and rivalries. Generally, this is not the case. The ritual atmosphere of inversion of daily social norms not only allows but encourages such bold bragging and cracking. In most cases, the rivalry and tension is constructed for performance. People see it as "all in good fun" (Nelson 1998). On campuses where rivalries are more imagined than enacted, step shows tend to serve as friendly competition. On campuses where organizational rivalries are intense and the black Greek community divisive, however, step shows often exacerbate rivalries and the potential for violence. Already tense relationships will tend to be made more tense; generally friendly relationships will tend to be made even stronger.[22]

To some extent, the translation of identities offstage in terms of violence remains an issue of group identity. Individual identity, however, is also affected offstage. Stepping has the very real capacity to affect the social drama enacted daily on college campuses. This can be both beneficial and problematic for individual fraternity men. The benefits are perhaps obvious. The coolest, manliest men onstage are often granted similar status offstage. As one sorority woman explained,

> Some girls will be on the guys in an organization no matter what. There are some girls who pretend to be Deltas just to get near the Ques because they're known to be rough and tough and masculine, kind of domineering.[23] So that attracts ladies automatically. I would have to say that girls notice when guys are stepping. (Ashton 2003)

Another benefit of the step show as a means of establishing identity with the potential for offstage negotiation is that step shows generally avoid the problem many black men face outside the college environment. Many scholars have pointed out that socially constructed expectations for black men are often unattainable in contemporary American society. Vestiges of racism, often explicit legacies from slavery, continue to exclude black men (Cuyjet 1997; Ricky L. Jones 1997; Lemelle 2001, 32–33, Mahalik, Pierre, and Woodland 2001; Spraggins 1999, 46). To some extent, the step show avoids this contradiction by being almost exclusively confined to the black college community. Peers rather than an outside job market or a racist society generally measure success in stepping and in constructing powerful masculine identities. Within this context, black men can succeed in translating the social power constructed during step shows into social power offstage.[24]

Nonetheless, stepping retains the potential pitfall of creating dissonance between the persona constructed onstage and both the group persona and the individual persona constructed offstage. Comparing the idealized images during stepping with the idealized images of the fraternity, for example, makes for striking contrasts. Michael Long, president of the Phi Beta Sigmas at Elon University, describes the Sigma man:

> A Sigma man, number one, is different. He's different, as in each chapter. A chapter should be different from one another. Everyone should not be a cookie cutter of the next person. It should be a surprise as to who would be a Sigma. Even though there are stereotypes about us, there is not one chapter that is the same as the next. That's the first thing. A man who is serious about education, because he's there to be a student first, and his first priority is to graduate. Second, one would be one who is very dedicated to his organization, not necessarily for what he's going to get out of the organization, but what he's going to put in. A man who is a gentleman. Who has a background and believes in God, or a god, it doesn't have to be Christian necessarily. A man who does not have to be reminded as to who he is. For example, I know I'm black. But I don't need that to be told to me as I go through life. Who is diverse in his associations. Who is diverse in what he knows and his experiences in life. Who does not let Sigma be his image. That he is a man first. If you find out he's a Sigma, then great. A person who can be a true brother, in or out of the organization. I'm a southerner so a southern gentleman is very chivalrous. He understands that you respect a lady. Regardless if she is the most annoying, rude, not pretty—you still respect her. You have a responsibility to your family. You have a responsibility to yourself. You should not lower yourself to pettiness. (2003)

Certainly not all Sigma men will live up to this ideal.[25] Still, it is significant that this image differs considerably from the representation onstage during a step show. Both are idealized images, but during a step show the Sigma man does not seem particularly interested in school or service to his organization or community. He teases and flirts with women and does not seem particularly religious. And he quite specifically asserts that Sigma *is* his image. The goal is to erase individual identity onstage and present a unified group identity. Accordingly, not only is the identity constructed during a step show disconnected from individual identities enacted off-stage, but it is discordant with other idealized *group* identities. We see quite clearly that the images of manliness enacted during stepping are imaginative and artificial constructions that develop a restricted masculine identity.

The discrepancies in constructed identities become even more explicit when compared to individual identities. We expect the kinds of differences highlighted by the staid businessman who is reserved at work but who curses and violently attacks his opponents during a rugby match. Everyone engages in the code-switching of identity. Presumably both expressions are part of personal identity, simply expressed at different times, each context-appropriate (see Oring 1994). When Michael Long performs a step to stamp out the hateful people on campus, and he becomes carried away, surprising even himself with his anger about such people, he is, he admits, expressing how he truly feels (2003).

But what of those times when group identity demands behavior that is dissonant with one's own personal behavior? The question then becomes, how dissonant? If dramatically, presumably psychic tension and trauma ensue. This has been an overriding concern among many scholars of black masculinity (see Ricky L. Jones 1997 and Mahalik, Pierre, and Woodland 2001 for summaries of this scholarship), beginning as early as W. E. B. DuBois's seminal writings on black identity in America:

> It is a peculiar sensation, this double-consciousness, this sense of always looking at one's self through the eyes of others, of measuring one's soul by the tape of a world that looks on in amused contempt and pity. One ever feels his twoness—an American, a Negro; two warring souls, two thoughts, two unreconciled strivings; two warring ideals in one dark body, whose dogged strength alone keeps it from being torn asunder. (DuBois 1903)

This double consciousness results in a double bind or role strain, the result of which, many have argued, has been for black men to construct masks to deal with these competing expectations and to establish self-respect (see Fleming 1984, 141–43). Richard Majors and Janet Mancini Billson coined the term "cool pose" to articulate one such mask:

> By cool pose we mean the presentation of self many black males use to establish their male identity. Cool pose is a ritualized form of masculinity that entails behaviors, scripts, physical posturing, impression management, and carefully crafted performances that deliver a single, critical message: pride, strength, and control." (1992, 4)[26]

While the cool pose can arguably provide black men with a means of coping with the social injustices of American society and provide men with a strategy for displaying if not necessarily achieving self-esteem, the negative impacts can be dramatic. Scholars have suggested that using the mask of the cool pose can result in misogyny, hindrance in healthy sexual and emotional relationships, increased violence to others and oneself, substance abuse, and the eschewing of "un-cool" activities such as success in school (Connor 1995; Mahalik, Pierre, and Woodland 2001; Majors and Billson 1992). Critics of recent hazing deaths among black fraternities have leveled the blame partly on such masking strategies, particularly when individual identities come into conflict with group identities. Applying his theory that violence is a societal construct to recent hazing deaths among black fraternities, Ricky L. Jones argues:

> Though the *fraternal* self (or any other self) is nothing more than a tributary, many fraternity members mistakenly see it as the *authentic self*. No organization can construct an *authentic self* on its own. If this is not realized and the *fraternal* is seen *as* the *authentic*, insidious behaviors from the larger lifeworld are transferred to the fraternal. Hazing is the result of the illusion that the power of the *authentic* "I" is brought into being and continuously reaffirmed through the dehumanization of the other (in this case, the pledge). (1997, 102)

How do the masculine identities constructed during stepping contribute to the negotiation of various identities, whether conceived as double consciousness, group versus individual, or idealized versus enacted? Are the masculine identities constructed during stepping a series of masks that liberate or further hinder black men when they re-engage in social life offstage?

The sociopsychological studies of black men in America would suggest that the tension involved in negotiating these competing identities is widespread. However, the majority of steppers and audience members I have worked with seem to have a fairly self-aware understanding that the step show is for show. While every member wants that perception of being the best organization on campus to translate offstage in order to recruit members, attract women, and "run the yard," there is a subsequent recognition that the persona constructed onstage is not a persona that must be maintained elsewhere. As one stepper reflected,

> I've done some things on stage that are completely out of character to who I am. It's for the whole show. Some people, if you didn't know me, you'd think I was that way, kind of thing. And I would see that that goes—I can see that correlating. It's like a front almost. And in some cases it's supposedly funny, some of it serious, and then again some of it is very genuine.
>
> If it's the whole, "do it for the ladies" thing, I'm not about that. I'm not a part-time stripper. I'm not going to take my clothes off. Some shows where some people take their shirts off, I'm not going to take my shirt off, I'm not going to do it. But I might have a movement that might be some-

thing sexual, which I wouldn't do normally, unless I was maybe dancing or something. That would be out of character for me. (Long 2003)

Further, while there is a clear recognition that the persona onstage can be dramatically different from individual identity offstage, most men nonetheless retain individual boundaries they will not cross. Coupled with the self-parodying during performance, the potential for these hyper-masculine stereotypes constructed during stepping to perpetuate misogyny, violence, and other antisocial behavior is mitigated. Further, the mask of the cool pose that has been criticized when employed regularly in daily life is here a theatrical mask, one lowered if not completely cast away when the step show is over.

Nonetheless, fraternity members often feel burdened with the stepping persona when meeting people for the first time, assuming, often correctly, that people's impressions of them derive from the personas constructed during stepping. One stepper commented,

> If we had a step show tonight and people didn't know me, and just basically judged me by what I was doing on stage, that would just be, you know, "He's like that all the time," you know, saying stuff like that. And that's entirely not true. (Calvin Sutton 2003)

The manly personas constructed onstage are idealized. While they identify the dominant elements of how black college men should act, they are not scripts to be emulated. When translated to daily life, the social hierarchy offstage is constructed on imagined personas, ones that can be playfully developed in the ritual arena of the step show stage. While those personas do not translate directly to daily life, the social status earned onstage often does. In this way, the step show becomes a place for very real social negotiation with often un-real, hyper-masculine personas as the means for negotiation.

That said, the masculine personas constructed in stepping remain viable and relevant outside the stepping performance. While many steppers will find their expected and performed onstage personas chafe against their individual identities, parallels outweigh discrepancies in terms of social expectations for the black male. Black college men are still expected to be distinguished leaders, physically strong, and sexually potent, simply not to the exaggerated degrees of manliness constructed in stepping.

While conceptions of black masculine identities in stepping are deeply rooted in real social expectations, these identities are negotiated in a ritualized context where exaggeration is the norm. Nonetheless, because of the function of stepping to establish social hierarchies offstage, many male steppers work within these generic boundaries to challenge the fraternity stereotypes that they, and their audiences, often seem to perpetuate. The major claims of the various black masculinities constructed in stepping remain relevant, even when the degrees to which they are constructed are not. While much of the negotiation between these differing expectations occurs offstage, many steppers have found subtle and creative ways to negotiate a more realistic image of the black man onstage as well. Further, by translating these identities into a social system that is directly relevant in daily life, stepping provides black men an important means for self-empowerment within a society that continues to present black men with a double consciousness and a double bind.

NOTES

I am deeply indebted to the skilled men and women who shared their dynamic tradition of stepping with me, during practice, performance, and interview: Bianca Ashton, Lisa Bentley, Raschard Buie, Shawn Howard, Derrick Jackson, Shalando Jones, Jimmie McMillian, Dr. James Mumford, David Nelson, Calvin Sutton, Roderick Wheeler, and Jennie Witt. In particular, I would like to thank Justen Baskerville, who made sure I never missed a nearby show and answered all of my questions, relevant and not, with clarity and patience, and Michael Long, who put up with me tagging along to his organization's meetings, practices, and shows and shared freely his vast experience and love of stepping. Finally, thanks to Brooke and Lily, who indulged my late-night fieldwork forays and encouraged me all along the way.

1. Fraternity members at Indiana University in 1998 recalled being asked by school administrators to be involved in an upcoming campus-wide event where members of Greek organizations across campus would be engaged in various service roles such as staffing booths and guiding visitors. Black fraternity members, however, were asked to step during the event, a request many viewed as racist, casting them as entertainers for a predominantly white audience. As Jacqui Malone notes, because stepping is the most visible element of black Greek life, members constantly battle the assumptions that all their organizations do is sing, dance, and party (1996, 205).

2. The one major exception is the recent adoption of stepping by minority Greek organizations in the United States, predominantly Latino but with some examples among Asian Americans as well (see Fine 2003, 109–15).

3. The process of contextualization and my usage of the concept to interpret expressions of masculinity in stepping follows Richard Bauman's original conception and his recent reformulations of the term "contextualization": the process by which communicative contexts emerge in the negotiation between participants (Bauman and Briggs 1990, 68). Contextualization is, as Bauman and Briggs argue, the key to understanding the transformative power of folkloric performance: "Attempts to identify the meaning of texts, performances, or entire genres in terms of purely symbolic, context-free content disregard the multiplicity of indexical connections that enable verbal art to transform, not simply reflect, social life" (69). Identifying those indexical connections, however, has been problematic, risking either debilitating inclusiveness or false objectivity (Briggs 1988, 13). Bauman and Briggs suggest a solution: contextualization cues (1990, 68). In verbal art, these cues can be recognized textually. In performance, the "text" must be interpreted more broadly, but the cues remain.

4. Parties and other purely social activities are important too, though stepping is often an integral part of these informal gatherings as well.

5. The acceptance of such external validation can be particularly problematic when this European American male ethos is compared to an Afrocentric one, where the former is often defined by power, material acquisition, competitiveness, individualism, hedonism, and a present- and future-time orientation and the latter by ties to the natural world, respect for elders, collectivism, and past-time orientation (Jackson 1997; Mahalik, Pierre, and Woodland 2001, 24).

6. In fact, much of the scholarship on black masculinity has focused on the construction of the black male either by white America, for white America, or in white America (see, for example, Booker 2000; Gibbs 1988; Hearn and Morgan 1990; Stecopolos and Uebel 1997; Whitehead 2002). The result is a view of black masculinity as perpetually under attack, a perspective challenged by Hazel Carby in her book *Race Men* (1998). Stepping seems to provide support for Carby's view by providing a context for black men to construct identities within the black community, presumably avoiding many of these colonizing forces.

7. There is not space here to address the derivation of these stereotypes. Certainly historical influences on blacks in America can shed a great deal of light on why certain qualities have been selected over others to convey appropriate masculine behaviors. Contemporary influences are equally relevant and no doubt involve a variety of available sources, including, but not restricted to, peers, the family, popular culture, and the military (Spraggins 1999, 47), as well as black expressive culture and folklore.

8. According to Dinerstein, for black men in the 1930s–1950s, when the concept of "cool" was being disseminated among jazz and bebop musicians, "cool" was a response to the social roles granted black men in a racist America. Quoting jazz master Lester Young, "They want everybody who is a Negro to be an Uncle Tom or Uncle Remus or Uncle Sam, and I can't make it" (1999, 246). The emotional self-control expected of black men in a racist American society was and remains no small feat. Today, the expression of control through "cool" remains a desirable attribute. (See also Smitherman 1998, 206.)

9. Posted online is a "Statement of Position against Canine Reference" that suggests references to dogs undermines their goals of reaching the "high ideals of manhood, scholarship, perseverance, and uplift to be members of the organization" ("Omega Psi Phi" 2000). It is worth pointing out that dog imagery runs throughout African American stepping, as well as hip-hop (e.g., well-known rapper Calvin Broadus, who adopted the name Snoop Dogg) and more generally among African American male college students. According to Geneva Smitherman in her book *Black Talk*, "dog" is "a form of address and greeting used mainly, but no longer exclusively, by and for males. It can also refer to one's close friend or associate. A symbol of bonding, most likely derived from the African American fraternity tradition of referring to pledges as *dogs*, as in 'Alpha dogs,' pledges of Alpha Phi Alpha" (2000, 111). The question of why the use of "dog" rather than some other image becomes more difficult to address. One might suggest parallel connotations of rough, independent, and loyal, which resonate with other slang terms used among African American men such as "bad" and "nasty," but more concerted research is needed to move beyond such conjecture.

10. Two chants performed regularly at Indiana University provide examples: "We are those granddaddies, make no mistake / From us all others originate / We are the first of the first / 1–9 / The best of the best / 0–6 / The other frats couldn't pass the test / Of an Alpha man, of an Alpha man" (where 1–9–0–6 references the year the group was founded), and "All black people come from Kunte Kinte / But

all black Greeks come from A Phi A / Respect your roots" (Wheeler 1998). These chants are often performed with some of the trademark steps that Alphas have developed to symbolically convey the same message, most notably their trademark step "the broken leg," where they grab one stiffened leg and dramatically limp like an old man. The coda "Respect your roots" is also frequently tacked on to other chants and used as a call during shows to reinforce this paternal image.

11. Fine suggests that the facial expression may have come from the military, as it closely resembles the expression expected of military recruits when standing at attention (2003, 56). Various terms include "game face," "gritt'n" (Dance 2002, 204), and "the grit" (Fine 2003, 56).

12. A sizable portion of the scholarship on stepping has addressed African influences in stepping, including Farrar 2001; Malone 1996; Rouverol 1996; Yarger 1996. This includes the use of African motifs in stepping, generally derived from fraternity symbols and esoteric rituals. The Alphas, for example, have a number of Egyptian symbols, including the sphinx, and frequently mine this cultural heritage during step shows. It is worth pointing out that some scholars writing prescriptively about the troubles facing black men in terms of identity have suggested a more explicit return to an Afrocentric focus.

13. This gendered divide for appropriate steps and moves can be seen in the related dance form of break dancing: "Most girls were heavily discouraged from performing break moves because they were perceived by some male peers as "unsafe" or "unfeminine." Female break dancers sometimes executed these moves in conventionally feminine ways, to highlight individuality and perhaps to deflect male criticism. Again, women who performed these moves were often considered masculine and undesirable or sexually "available" (Rose 1999, 205).

14. Women's stepping seems to negotiate these perceived differences far more actively than men. A study of women's stepping as active negotiation of these gendered expectations would, no doubt, be extremely enlightening.

15. Recently, cracking has come under attack for its divisiveness. Competition step shows uniformly outlaw it, which does not mean step teams do not still try to sneak a subtle crack past the judges. The future of cracking is debatable, but for exhibition step shows and probate shows, it remains an important part of the construction of identity. Both the excessive bragging and cracking permitted in stepping resonates with rap music, a traditionally black American musical style (see Emery 1988, 356–60). Further study of the parallels between these two art forms would be particularly productive.

16. This strategy can usefully be compared to "marking" as discussed by Claudia Mitchell-Kernan (1999), particularly in terms of the strategy of criticism, which "may be more in the nature of parody and caricature than true imitation. But the features selected to overplay are those which are associated with membership in some class" (328).

17. Justen Baskerville, president of Alpha Phi Alpha at Elon University, referred to this chant as an example of a typical crack. He and his fellow Alphas stepped to this chant during a yard show at Elon on May 7, 2004, as a response to similar cracks made about their fraternity by the Kappas and Omegas, who were also present.

18. For discussions of homophobic symbolism in African American culture, see Dollimore 1997, 20–22; Whitehead 2002, 71. For blues music in particular, see Oliver 1963, 135–39. Further, such homophobia can be read as ironic considering the literature analyzing black fraternity pledging as having homoerotic elements (Ruffins 1998).

19. Michael Herzfeld has noted similar expectations in terms of constructions

of masculinities among Cretan men, arguing that role performance is "not just a matter of fulfilled stereotypical expectations. On the contrary, the conventionalized unconventionality of Glendiot male behavior provides virtually limitless opportunities for the display of inventive rebellion against stylistic norms" (1985, 25). The theoretical basis for such conclusions is founded upon Richard Bauman's discussion of rule breaking as an element of effective performance (1977, 34–35).

20. Fine has argued that the show dog allows individual expression in a performance so heavily dominated by the construction of group identity (2003, 67). This is no doubt true. Those members who fill the role of show dog during a performance are generally those men who are just as cocky and outgoing offstage. However, it is important to note that the show dog is almost invariably admonished for his behavior, calmed down, and drawn back into the fold by his fellow steppers.

21. Fraternities and sororities are paired up: the Alpha Phi Alphas and the Alpha Kappa Alphas, the Omega Psi Phis and the Delta Sigma Thetas, the Phi Beta Sigmas and the Zeta Phi Betas, the Kappa Alpha Psis and the Sigma Gamma Rhos. These pairings are often explicitly reinforced during step shows, both onstage through tributes and offstage in terms of who sits with whom.

22. The phenomenon of building social boundaries through insulting play has been studied in various folklore forms. Keith Basso's *Portraits of the "Whiteman"* is particularly lucid in its description of how situational joking can destroy those relationships that are not well established but strengthen those friendships that are (1979). Considering the predominance of scholarship on violence and black male identity, further study of the role of stepping to exacerbate or mitigate violence would be useful.

23. The Deltas are the sister sorority of the Ques. The expectation is that the two organizations will socialize together more frequently than with the other black Greek organizations.

24. I do not intend to dismiss the pressures many black students feel in college, particularly at predominantly white institutions. These pressures and concerns are eloquently conveyed in the comments of black college students surveyed by Edward Taylor and Steven Olswang (1997) as well as in other studies (see, for example, Ellis 2002; Hedegard 1972). It would be interesting to study whether the self-esteem developed during stepping translated into these racially mixed collegiate contexts, providing black men a sense of empowerment outside the black community.

25. Studies have shown that black fraternities have proved effective means for cultivating leadership roles for black men that extend beyond the specific organization. Further, the idealized images of the fraternity have some currency in actual behavior, particularly in terms of service to the community (Kimbrough 1995; Gary 1981, 37–38; Ruffins and Roach 1997; Sutton and Terrell 1997).

26. The cool pose parallels Robert Thompson's application of the West African definition of "cool" to young black men, which demands an external veneer of nonchalance, ease, and disdain, particularly in stressful situations (1974).

REFERENCES

Abrahams, Roger D. 1970. *Deep Down in the Jungle: Negro Narrative Folklore from the Streets of Philadelphia*. Chicago: Aldine.

Ashton, Bianca (member of Delta Sigma Theta sorority, Elon University). 2003. Interview by the author. Elon, N.C., May 13.

Barnett, Brooke, and Tom Mould. 1998. *Stepping.* Video recording. Bloomington, Ind.: WTIU.

Baskerville, Justen (president of Alpha Phi Alpha fraternity, Elon University). 2003. Interview by the author. Elon, N.C., February 13.

Basso, Keith H. 1979. *Portraits of the "Whiteman": Linguistic Play and Cultural Symbols among the Western Apache.* Cambridge: Cambridge University Press.

Bauman, Richard. 1977. *Verbal Art as Performance.* Rowley, Mass.: Newbury House.

Bauman, Richard, and Charles L. Briggs. 1990. "Poetics and Performance as Critical Perspectives on Language and Social Life." *Annual Review of Anthropology* 19: 59–88.

Bentley, Lisa (member of Sigma Gamma Rho sorority, Indiana University at Gary). 1998. Interview by the author. Gary, Ind., May 22.

Black Greek Soundz. 2002. Vol. 1, Alpha Phi Alpha Fraternity. Compact disc recording. Plano, Texas: BGS Enterprises.

Booker, Christopher B. 2000. *"I Will Wear No Chain!" A Social History of African American Males.* Westport, Conn.: Praeger.

Bowling, M. J., and Jerald B. Harkness. 1992. *Steppin'.* Video recording. New York: Cinema Guild.

Braithwaite, Ronald L. 1981. "Interpersonal Relations between Black Males and Black Females." In *Black Men,* ed. Lawrence E. Gary, 83–97. Beverly Hills, Calif.: Sage.

Brearley, H. C. 1973 [1939]. "Ba-ad Nigger." In *Mother Wit from the Laughing Barrel: Readings in the Interpretation of Afro-American Folklore,* ed. Alan Dundes, 578–85. Englewood Cliffs, N.J.: Prentice-Hall.

Briggs, Charles L. 1988. *Competence in Performance: The Creativity of Tradition in Mexicano Verbal Art.* Philadelphia: University of Pennsylvania Press.

Bronner, Simon J. 1995. *Piled Higher and Deeper: The Folklore of Student Life.* Little Rock, Ark.: August House.

Caponi, Gena Dagel. 1999. "The Case for an African American Aesthetic." In *Signifyin(g), Sanctifyin', and Slam Dunking: A Reader in African American Expressive Culture,* ed. Gena Dagel Caponi, 1–41. Amherst: University of Massachusetts Press.

Carby, Hazel. 1998. *Race Men.* Cambridge, Mass.: Harvard University Press.

Claerbaut, David. 1972. *Black Jargon in White America.* Grand Rapids, Mich.: William B. Eerdman.

Connor, Marlene Kim. 1995. *What Is Cool? Understanding Black Manhood in America.* New York: Crowd.

Cuyjet, Michael J. 1997. "African American Men on College Campuses: Their Needs and Their Perceptions." *New Directions for Student Services* 80: 5–16.

Dance, Daryl Cumber. 1978. *Shuckin' and Jivin': Folklore from Contemporary Black Americans.* Bloomington: Indiana University Press.

———. 2002. *From My People. 400 Years of African American Folklore.* New York: W. W. Norton.

Davis, Amy. 1996. "'Deep in My Heart': Competition and the Function of Stepping in an African American Sorority." *North Carolina Folklore Journal* 43(2): 82–95.

Dinerstein, Joel. 1999 [1998]. "Lester Young and the Birth of Cool." In *Signifyin(g), Sanctifyin', and Slam Dunking: A Reader in African American Expressive Culture,* ed. Gena Dagel Caponi, 239–76. Amherst: University of Massachusetts Press.

Dollimore, Jonathan. 1997. "Desire and Difference: Homosexuality, Race, Masculinity." In *Race and the Subject of Masculinities,* ed. Harry Stecopoulos and Michel Uebel, 17–44. Durham, N.C.: Duke University Press.

DuBois, W. E. B. 1903. *The Souls of Black Folk.* Chicago: A. C. McClurg.

Ellis, Cyrus Marcellus. 2002. "Examining the Pitfalls Facing African American Males." In *Making It on Broken Promises: Leading African American Male Scholars Confront the Culture of Higher Education*, ed. Lee Jones, 61–71. Sterling, Va.: Stylus.

Emery, Lynne Fauley. 1988. *Black Dance from 1619 to Today*. Princeton, N.J.: Princeton Books.

Farrar, Hayward. 2001. "The African Roots of Stepping." Paper presented at First National Conference on Stepping, Virginia Polytechnic Institute and State University (Virginia Tech), April 6–7, 2001, Blacksburg, Va. http://www.ipsonet .org/congress/5/papers_pdf/hwf.pdf. Accessed February 5, 2003.

Fine, Elizabeth C. 1991. "Stepping, Saluting, Cracking, and Freaking: The Cultural Politics of African American Step Shows." *Drama Review* 35: 39–59.

———. 2003. *Soulstepping*. Chicago: University of Illinois Press.

Fleming, Jacqueline. 1984. *Blacks in College*. San Francisco: Jossey-Bass.

Folb, Edith A. 1980. *Runnin' Down Some Lines*. Cambridge, Mass.: Harvard University Press.

Gary, Lawrence E., ed. 1981. *Black Men*. Beverly Hills, Calif.: Sage.

Gibbs, Jewelle Taylor, ed. 1988. *Young, Black, and Male in America: An Endangered Species*. Dover, Mass.: Auburn House.

Gray, Herman. 1994. "Black Masculinity and Visual Culture." *Callaloo* 18(2). http://muse.jhu.edu/quick_tour/18.2gray.html. Accessed July 21, 2003.

Hearn, Jeff, and David Morgan. 1990. *Men, Masculinities and Social Theory*. Boston: Unwin Hyman.

Hedegard, James M. 1972. "Experiences of Black College Students at Predominantly White Institutions." In *Black Students in White Schools*, ed. Edgar G. Epps, 43–59. Worthington, Ohio: Charles A. Jones.

Herzfeld, Michael. 1985. *The Poetics of Manhood: Contest and Identity in a Cretan Mountain Village*. Princeton, N.J.: Princeton University Press.

Jackson, Ronald L. 1997. "Black 'Manhood' as Xenophobe: An Ontological Exploration of the Hegelian Dialectic." *Journal of Black Studies* 27(6): 731–50.

Jones, Ricky L. 1997. "Violence and the Politics of Black Male Identity in Post-Modern America." *Journal of African American Men* 3(2): 81–107.

Jones, Shalando (member of Sigma Gamma Rho sorority, Indiana University at Gary). 1998. Interview by the author. Gary, Ind., May 22.

Kimbrough, Walter M. 1995. "Self-Assessment, Participation, and Value of Leadership Skills, Activities, and Experiences for Black Students Relative to Their Membership in Historically Black Fraternities and Sororities." *Journal of Negro Education* 64: 63–74.

Lemelle, Anthony J., Jr. 2001. "Patriarchal Reversals of Black Male Prestige: Effects of the Intersection of Race, Gender and Educational Class." *Journal of African American Men* 6(3): 29–46.

Lewin, Esther, and Albert E. Lewin. 1994. *The Thesaurus of Slang*. New York: Facts on File.

Lighter, J. E., ed. 1994. *Random House Historical Dictionary of American Slang*. New York: Random House.

Long, Michael (president of Phi Beta Sigma fraternity, Elon University). 2003. Interview by the author. Elon, N.C., February 21.

Mahalik, James R., Martin R. Pierre, and Malcolm H. Woodland. 2001. "The Effects of Racism, African Self-Consciousness and Psychological Functioning on Black Masculinity: A Historical and Social Adaptation Framework." *Journal of African American Men* 6(2): 19–39.

Majors, Richard G., and Jacob U. Gordon. 1994. *The American Black Male: His Present Status and His Future*. Chicago: Nelson-Hall.

Majors, Richard, and Janet Mancini Billson. 1992. *Cool Pose: The Dilemmas of Black Manhood in America.* New York: Lexington Books.

Malone, Jacqui. 1996. *Steppin' on the Blues: The Visible Rhythms of African American Dance.* Chicago: University of Illinois Press.

McMillian, Jimmie (member of Kappa Alpha Psi fraternity, Indiana University). 1998. Interview by the author. Bloomington, Ind., April 10.

Mitchell-Kernan, Claudia. 1999 [1972]. "Signifying, Loud-Talking and Marking." In *Signifyin(g), Sanctifyin', and Slam Dunking: A Reader in African American Expressive Culture,* ed. Gena Dagel Caponi, 309–30. Amherst: University of Massachusetts Press.

Mumford, James (graduate member of Omega Psi Phi fraternity). 1998. Interview by the author. Bloomington, Ind., May 22.

Nelson, David (member of Phi Beta Sigma fraternity, Indiana University at Gary). 1998. Interview by the author. Gary, Ind., May 22.

Oliver, Paul. 1963. *The Meaning of the Blues.* Toronto: Collier Books.

"Omega Psi Phi." 2000, June. "Statement of Position against Canine Reference." http://students.washington.edu/aphia/Greek%20Pages/que.html. Accessed May 28, 2003.

Oring, Elliott. 1994. "The Arts, Artifacts, and Artifices of Identity." *Journal of American Folklore* 107(424): 211–47.

Rose, Tricia. 1999 [1994]. "Flow, Layering, and Rupture in Postindustrial New York." In *Signifyin(g), Sanctifyin', and Slam Dunking: A Reader in African American Expressive Culture,* ed. Gena Dagel Caponi, 191–221. Amherst: University of Massachusetts Press.

Ross, Lawrence C., Jr. 2000. *The Divine Nine: The History of African American Fraternities and Sororities.* New York: Kensington Books.

Rouverol, Alicia J. 1996. "'Hot,' 'Cool,' and 'Getting Down': African American Style and Aesthetics in Stepping." *North Carolina Folklore Journal* 43(2): 96–108.

Ruffins, Paul. 1998. "The Persistent Madness of Greek Hazing: Psychologists Provide Insight on Why Hazing Persists among Black Greeks." *Black Issues in Higher Education* 15(9): 14–18.

Ruffins, Paul, and Ronald Roach. 1997. "Fratricide: Are African American Fraternities Beating Themselves to Death?" *Black Issues in Higher Education* 14: 18–25.

Smitherman, Geneva. 1998. "Word from the Hood: The Lexicon of African-American Vernacular English." In *African-American English: Structure, History and Use,* ed. Salikoko S. Mufwene, John R. Rickford, Guy Bailey, and John Baugh, 203–25. New York: Routledge.

———. 2000. *Black Talk: Words and Phrases from the Hood to the Amen Corner.* Boston: Houghton Mifflin.

Spraggins, Johnnie David, Jr. 1999. "African American Masculinity: Power and Expression." *Journal of African American Men* 4(3): 45–72.

Stecopoulos, Harry, and Michel Uebel, eds. 1997. *Race and the Subject of Masculinities.* Durham, N.C.: Duke University Press.

Sutton, Calvin (president of Omega Psi Phi fraternity, Elon University). 2003. Interview by the author. Elon, N.C., February 12.

Sutton, E. Michael, and Melvin C. Terrell. 1997. "Identifying and Developing Leadership Opportunities for African American Men." *New Directions for Student Services* 80: 55–64.

Taylor, Edward, and Steven G. Olswang. 1997. "Crossing the Color Line: African Americans and Predominantly White Universities." *College Student Journal* 31: 11–18.

Thompson, Robert Farris. 1974. *African Art in Motion.* Los Angeles: University of California Press.

————. 1999 [1966]. "An Aesthetic of the Cool: West African Dance." In *Signify-in(g), Sanctifyin', and Slam Dunking: A Reader in African American Expressive Culture*, ed. Gena Dagel Caponi, 72–86. Amherst: University of Massachusetts Press.

Wheeler, Roderick (member of Alpha Phi Alpha fraternity, Indiana University). 1998. Interview by the author. Bloomington, Ind., April 25.

Whitehead, Stephen M. 2002. *Men and Masculinities: Key Themes and New Directions.* Malden, Mass.: Blackwell.

Woodside, Jane Harris. 1995. "'There's a Lot of Pride Wrapped Up in What We Do': Reminiscences of a Fraternity Stepper." In *Communities in Motion*, ed. Susan Eike Spalding and Jane Harris Woodside. Westport, Conn.: Greenwood Press.

Yarger, Lisa J. 1996. "'That's . . . Where Stepping Came From': Afrocentricity and Beliefs about Stepping." *North Carolina Folklore Journal* 43: 109–19.

3

Muy Macho: Traditional Practices in the Formation of Latino Masculinity in South Texas Border Culture

NORMA E. CANTÚ

> To men like my father, being 'macho' meant being strong enough
> to protect and support my mother and us, yet being able to show
> love.
> —Gloria Anzaldúa, "*La conciencia de la mestiza:*
> Towards a New Consciousness"

As a student of cultural practices along the United States–Mexico border, I am often confronted with the apparent contradictions and complexities of cultural performance that is at once gendered in what could be considered traditional Mexican ways while at the same time incorporating elements of U.S. popular culture and even some mainstream Anglo traditions. That such complex cultural structures have evolved along the geopolitical space that is the U.S.–Mexico borderlands might be attributed to what Walter Mignolo (2000) identifies as the geohistorical and geocultural realities of those communities. The very term used to designate those of Mexican descent who inhabit the area points to the complex character of the group. Is it Latino? Or Chicano? Or Mexican American? Or Hispanic? It depends on whom one asks; the factors that determine the self-labeling include age, socioeconomic status, whether the person is an immigrant, or whether his or her ancestors were here before there was a United States. I use the term "Latino" although I can just as easily use Mexican American or Chicano or Chicana.

Cultural geographer Daniel Arreola (2002) has identified the South Texas region as a cultural zone where the blending and adaptation of the two hegemonic cultural forces—the U.S. to the north and Mexico to the south—have created a third cultural zone. Such claims of a distinct border zone are obvious to anyone who participates in or observes any of the myriad of cultural celebrations or feasts in the region, whether religious or secular or whether political or social. For example, the wedding ceremony with its traditional exchange of the *arras* (coins given by the bridegroom to the bride; it is believed to be an old tradition of Arabic origin) and the *lazo* (an over-sized rosary whose "beads" form two large loops that are placed over the couple during the ceremony; it is believed to be a tradition of Aztec origin) will often also include the "dollar dance" and the "something old, something new, something borrowed, something blue" of the customary mainstream U.S. tradition for the bride.[1] In similar fashion, the *quinceañera* celebration, the young Latina's coming-of-age ritual celebrated on her fifteenth birthday, includes the traditional practice of celebrating a mass, now often said in English, and a dance for which the music has shifted from the traditional waltz to hip-hop or another contemporary U.S. musical form. The celebration is sometimes likened to a "sweet sixteen" celebration in American popular culture.[2]

In similar fashion, the way that young boys are socialized by traditional cultural practices exhibits this predictable blending and synergetic overlap of traditional Mexican and contemporary U.S. popular culture found along the U.S.–Mexico borderlands. Although I am more familiar with these practices along the border, we must not ignore the fact that they flourish in the interior of the U.S. where there is a large Chicano or Mexican presence, as I was able to observe when I worked with communities in Tennessee and in Idaho. The complexity of identity formation for young Chicanos is as varied as for any other ethnic group in the U.S. The interactions of religion, class, and, perhaps more importantly, adherence to the root culture follow a complex weaving of various threads that from my perspective remain in many ways still tangled and not smoothly woven into the fabric of American society.[3]

I undertake the writing of this essay with trepidation, for after all, what am I, a Chicana, to say about the masculinities found in my own culture? But I take the challenge in an attempt to understand and to continue what I have done in my creative work, that is, to present the reality of the men in my community, a reality that is often distorted in the mass media and in American imagination generally. In this essay I am focusing on the way that Latino masculinity, shaped by the traditional practices of the Latino community, specifically the more commonly called Chicano or Mexican American community, corresponds to a shifting cultural reality that retains many of the traditional ways while accommodating to a global, technological, post-industrial society in the twenty-first century. While many of the practices found in Chicano communities may be found in the various Latino groups found in the United States, such as Puerto Rican or Central American, I must emphasize that what I am discussing here is not necessarily true for these or even for other Chicano communities in the U.S. such as Nuevo Mejicanos or Californios.

I structure the essay along two continuous tracks: a more academic discussion of what I glean to be the essential elements for formation of masculine identity found in traditional cultural practices and brief sections I am calling "stories/*cuentos*" anecdotes or observations from real life that illustrate, question, or problematize the discussion. These interludes may serve as a trellis for the discussion to cling to and as a means of illustrating the observations.

I. Stories/*Cuentos:* In the mid-1990s the son of my *comadre* (my goddaughter's mother) comes back after his first semester at Harvard and tells his mother that his classmates are afraid of him. One even asked if he carried a knife.

In the fall of 1998, one of my students, a non-traditional thirty-something, writes a moving story of how on his fifteenth birthday his co-workers—all older men in their twenties and thirties—had taken him across the border to Nuevo Laredo to the red-light district for a sexual initiation.

That same year, passing by a shop window in Nuevo Laredo I am stunned to see prominently displayed on some bridal shower cake decorations carefully crafted scenes of domestic violence. In one, the groom holds a rolling pin, and the bride at his feet is drenched in red nail polish; in the other, it is the reverse—the bride holds the "bloody" miniature rolling pin, and the groom lies glue-gunned at her feet with red nail polish on his head.

When I began researching the subject of masculinity, I went to Don Américo Paredes's article on *machismo* (1967), and that led me to one of the first scholarly studies on the topic of *machismo* and folklore by Vicente Mendoza, the preeminent scholar of Mexican popular music, specifically of the *corrido* or ballad tradition (1962). In his work, Paredes uses the lyrics of various *corridos* and folk songs from a century ago to discuss the roots of Mexican manliness. He concludes, *Tanto en Estados Unidos como en México, el machismo a pesar de todas sus lacras ha sido acompañante de todo un complejo de impulsos conducentes a una realización más perfecta de las potencialidades del hombre* (In the United States as in Mexico, *machismo* in spite of all its faults has been accompanied by an array of impulses conducive to the greater realization of man's potential).[4] He especially singles out two classes of *machismo,* much like Anzaldúa (1987) and Mirandé (1982, 1997) identify the false and true *machismo* among Chicanos.[5]

Anzaldúa, for example, in the quotation that began this essay, under-scores the true *macho* who is strong enough to feed and protect his family, an adaptation to oppression, poverty, and low self-esteem (2001, 99). She finds that the false *macho* who puts down women or even brutalizes them does so out of a loss of dignity and respect. The irony she observes is that coexisting with his sexist behavior is a love for his mother, which takes precedence over all others. "Devoted son, macho pig" is all too common, she finds, and in this behavior he is not acting like a woman, or *un macho,* which would appear weak and defective. She offers a psychological explanation for the false *macho's* attraction to fighting, drugs, and alcohol as a way to "wash down the shame of his acts, and to handle the brute in the mirror" (99).

The concern for not appearing weak, for garnering honor and respect, and for showing fidelity to parents is vividly expressed in the classic ethnography by William Madsen of Mexican Americans in South Texas during the late 1950s and early 1960s. He summarized the *machismo* he observed as "manliness" and concluded that "the value of *machismo* governs male behavior in almost every facet of social life but wields its greatest influence in connection with the concept of honor" (Madsen 1973, 20). Madsen found that this concept in border culture meant that the "manly Latin must repay an insult to himself or his family in order to defend the honor with which God endowed him. Revenge is usually achieved by direct physical attack, which may not be immediate but must be inevitable" (21). A location for demonstrating *machismo* is in verbal dueling with his friends while drinking. As Madsen describes the scene, "In this game, it is implicitly understood that hidden accusations and taunts are not serious. They are forgotten on leaving the bar unless some individual has gone too far or is too sensitive. An inebriated male is frequently egged on to make a stand that he cannot defend. His argument is then crushed with a well-turned phrase that is considered a triumph and a moment for hilarity" (21). Yet male virility, he points out, is better proven by direct action than by triumphs in verbal dueling, and that is especially evident in sexual seduction. "Seduction is the best proof of manliness," he asserts. "The true man must demonstrate not only his physical prowess but also his power to lure women into sexual adventures" (22). Further, the true man as strong, virile, proud, and self-reliant appears in Madsen's ethnography to be the perfect counterpart, at least in Madsen's male imagination, to the female who is weak, pure, and submissive. Such images result from a socialization process that sets out "prescribed" and "proscribed" gender behavior (22–23).

Madsen's dated and narrow conclusions aside, few scholars have studied Chicano masculinity. And fewer still have addressed the role that folk practices play in the socialization process, or in providing metaphors to live by, although most point to cultural practices as determining the *macho* or manly performative practices they observe and study (Abalos 2002; Mirandé 1997; Peña 1985; Paredes 1967; Limón 1994; Zinn 2001). The role of folk practices in socialization and metaphorization is especially relevant to musical genres, for the *corrido* with its very male *macho* persona lies emotionally and culturally at the heart of a distinctive Mexican American tradition.

While some scholars like Gutmann (1996) and McDowell (2000) have recently examined masculinity in Mexico, they have not made the transnational connections that must exist for insights into the ways that American culture and the traditional Mexican culture negotiate the shared space that Chicanos and Mejicanos inhabit in the U.S. In Gutmann's work particularly, there is a whole other world of contestation and negotiation of what is "male," or what constitutes the categories as Gutmann found them— *macho, mandilón,* neither *macho* nor *mandilón,* and homosexual.[6] Significantly, the subaltern subject in Mexico occupies the same position in the United States whether he is a recent immigrant or is a descendant of those who lived here before there was a United States. There are differences, of course, but the traditional cultural markers are there in life-cycle rituals such as weddings and funerals.

My discussion, limited to the various practices found especially along the U.S.–Mexico borderlands of Texas and Tamaulipas, includes the folklore and traditional practices of my community in south Texas and the way these practices either shape or reveal a masculine identity. Obviously, there is much more work to be done. For one, it is imperative to look at how gender identity is defined and shaped in the gay, lesbian, and transgendered groups along the border. Transvestite shows, renowned in the border region, are certainly imagined gendered performance.[7] Additionally, the layered cultural display of U.S. and Mexican practices assumes a distinct fusion of both along the border. Yet, some of the practices are uniquely Mexican or Texan and exist as a signifier of such cultural identities.

II. Stories/*Cuentos:* In the mid 1990s after the death of Selena Quintanilla, the Tejano singer who was tragically murdered and who has become a legend and an icon, many gay men choose her as the singer to emulate in their transvestite shows in Nuevo Laredo.

At a popular *discoteca* in Nuevo Laredo, the devil appears and rides the mechanical bull. Men, including one of my brothers, swear that they saw the man and smelled the *azufre* (sulfur) that he traditionally leaves behind.

Texas A&M International University in Laredo holds the first annual T-shirt exhibit to bring attention to the crisis of violence against women.

At Elodia's *quinceañera* all the attendants are boys who dress in black *al estilo contry,* or "country style" with jeans, shirts, and cowboy hats.

Choosing from all the myriad possible configurations, I have chosen to focus on three major areas where I see identity construction played out in more telling ways: oral traditions; coming-of-age rituals and traditional practices; and clothing and body adornment. Considering the oral expressions found in the area, such as sayings, tales, and songs that point decidedly toward a gender specific performance, one can easily see that these oral traditions often refer to an imagined romanticized era of what has been called the "good" *machismo* (Mirandé 1997; Anzladúa 1987). Further, the particular social or familial practices that signal gender and coming-of-age rituals such as hunting, children's games like *piñatas,* marbles, and tops, and rituals that include *quinceañera* celebrations all reveal performance of gender-specific rituals, not always recognized or acknowledged as such by the community itself.

Gender is a marker in terms of the body: clothing worn at festive occasions or during particular age-specific events. Haircuts and particular body tattoos and piercing also indicate gender and mark coming-of-age. They tend to follow fairly traditional patterns of expression, patterns that have crossed class and social barriers at the very interstices of gender. Weddings and funerals are also sites of gendered performance of traditional ritual as certain behaviors are expected of males and females at these rituals. Although most of these behaviors have undergone changes in the last twenty years, many traditional patterns of behavior persist.

While these various areas form the nexus of what I discuss in this essay, it is the more specific patterning that occurs within the community that my project explores, particularly in reference to the oral tradition, to the acting out of expected male behavior, both in relation to the female and in all-male discourse such as what Manuel Peña (1991) studied among Mexican field-workers in California.

In oral tradition, many practices seem to indicate didactic norms that offer gendered structural patterns. While some of these have become anachronistic and have indeed been erased by the current practices, which defy their truth, others remain firmly entrenched in the day-to-day speech and in the ways parents still instruct children in correct behavior for girls and boys. Sayings, tales, and songs are the most common oral expressions whereby such instruction occurs. An analysis of the intersection of folk and traditional practices in the development of a gender identity must therefore explore the role of oral traditions. The sayings (or *dichos*), tales and legends, or myths and songs such as *corridos* convey strong messages of what is appropriate behavior for males. *Dichos,* while not in the particular domain of either male or female speech, appear didactically to signal behavioral expectations. While most *dichos* remain gender neutral, some are of particular use as we look at the way masculinity is performed.

On a recent plane trip, I happened to be sitting next to a man in his fifties who was returning to the lower Rio Grande valley, to Pharr, Texas, specifically, from working in Oakland, California. As we chatted I noticed that when he spoke to his co-workers and *paisanos* (countrymen) his language changed. When speaking with them, he often peppered his discourse with curses in the Spanish slang that is so common in south Texas, beginning most expressions with *chinga* and ending them with *güey* as in *"Chinga, no te la vayas a comer, güey"* (rough translation: "Fuck, don't you dare eat that, asshole") in reference to the rather bland cold snack that we were served. But when he spoke to me, he used the formal form of address that uses the *usted* form; he never uttered a *chinga* or anything even slightly colloquial. He did use *dichos,* traditional sayings or maxims, when speaking with me and with another passenger. Although various factors influence speech acts, this conversation confirmed my previous observations of how we talk in south Texas and what sociolinguists have been studying for some time in Chicano communities.[8] *Dichos* remain standard elements of daily speech: *De tal palo tal astilla* in reference to a child following his parents' footsteps, and *No digas de esa agua no beberé* (never say never). Or one can hear phrases in reference to men, such as *el hombre: feo fuerte y formal* (man: ugly, strong, and serious).

In like fashion certain legends and other folk narratives function didactically in certain situations. I do not think it is a coincidence that still-popular ghost stories of *la Llorona,* the legendary wailing woman, almost always appears to adult males, for she is a vindictive figure symbolizing revenge on males. It is the fury of a woman scorned who finds the male object of her wrath.[9] As a device of gender identity formation the folktale also includes elements from other stories like the one of the hitchhiker who lures young men and the female equivalent for dancing with the devil.[10] All these tales and legends tend to teach men to be "good *machos*" or *caballeros* (men of honor). The lessons are of men who honor women, men who keep their promises, and men who keep their word. The false *machos* whose bravado and lewd drunken behavior includes wife beating, whose word is worthless, and who have the qualities of the "bad" macho, as Mirandé (1997) indicates, are punished in stories of *la Llorona*. While Limón notes the dissolution of many traditional practices and characterizes the "Mexican-American working-class postmodernism . . . that increasingly pervasive, vivid sociocultural condition" he sees linked to "class-determined negations of a historically and seemingly relatively stable cultural past" (1994, 111), in south Texas, he ascertains, "postmodernism may be seen as the gradual decentering, fragmenting transformation of this identity into something else—a difficult version of global culture palpable but difficult to verbalize" (111).

But what Limón (1994) may be missing are the day-to-day interactions where postmodernism is lived and played out as a negotiation of contending belief systems and where no one acknowledges that the shift has occurred. Indeed, people still use the word *compadre* or *comadre* when speaking to their children's godparents. And, yes, some take the role as seriously as ever and continue the traditional gifting practice for the godchildren on their birthdays and at Christmas. At least in the families with whom I am familiar, there are still the notions of *respeto* (respect) and *vergüenza* (shame), albeit translated into twenty-first century terms. A mild example of the way children are socialized into the practices of the region exists in the way a parent or other adult may chastise a child for entering a room and not greeting everyone present. That there has been change in the way such socialization occurs, no one can deny. With the threat of HIV and AIDS, one would think that young boys are not ritually taken to Nuevo

Laredo by their fathers, uncles, or older cousins or siblings anymore. Sadly, that practice still exists, although not as widely as it did forty years ago. So, the folktales take on added value as narratives of vengeance and as didactic instruction of correct behavior. The dances at Casa Blanca Ballroom or in Nuevo Laredo's *discotecas* will continue to draw a clientele that continues the traditions.

Yet another folk genre that points to (in)appropriate manly behavior can be found in traditional Pepito jokes, which typically involve sexual innuendo, foul language, or defiance of authority. Pepito, a young boy, sometimes appears as a comical trickster figure and at other times as a sly and devious, indeed nasty, underdog, but always the joke is gender specific. The jokes often communicate independence in an early coming-of-age into manhood, declared through sexual and social dominance of the mother or teacher, as a manly value. One can read narratives in which the female members of the family often become sexual objects as further distancing of the man from maternal bonds. For example, the following texts can be found in many variations.

Le dice la profesora a sus alumnos: Veamos niños díganme ¿a qué se dedican sus mamás? y le pregunta a Martita:
—a ver, Martita ¿a qué se dedica tu mamá?
—mi mamá es doctora.
—que bien, Martita le dice la profesora. A ver Pepito y tu mamá ¿a qué se dedica?
—Ah, maestra mi mamá es sustituta.
—pero niño, no se dice sustituta, sera prostituta.
—no, maestra mi tía es la prostituta, mi mamá va cuando no va mi tía. . . .

[The teacher tells her students: Let's see, children, tell me, what do your mothers do for a living?
She asks Martita:
—Martita, what does you mother do?
—My mother is a doctor.
—That's good Martita, says the teacher. Pepito, what does your mother do?
—Teacher, my mother is a substitute.
—Now child, you don't mean substitute, you mean prostitute.
—No, teacher, my aunt is the prostitute, my mother only does it when my aunt can't make it.]

Este era que Pepito le escribía la carta al niño dios y le decía:
—Niñito Dios, tengo 3 meses portándome bien y quiero que para esta navidad me traigas una patineta, una bicicleta, un transformer un. . . . Y se oye la voz de la Virgen diciéndole:
—¿Estás seguro Pepito que tienes 3 meses portándote bien?
Pepito rompe la hoja toma otra y escribe:
—Querido niñito Dios tengo un mes portándome bien y quiero que para esta navidad me traigas una patineta, una . . . y le vuelve a hablar la virgen.

—¿Estás seguro Pepito, un mes?
La vuelve a romper, toma otra hoja y vuelve a escribir:
—Dulce niñito Dios, tengo una semana portándome bien y quiero que para esta navidad me traigas una patineta . . .
Y se vuelve a escuchar la voz, entonces Pepito toma la imagen de la virgen que tenía cerca y ya muy enojado escribe . . .
—Mira, Niño Dios, Tengo Secuestrada a Tu Madre, Y Si Quieres Volver a Verla, Quiero Que Para Esta Navidad Me Traigas Una Patineta, Una Bicicleta, Un Transformer . . . !

[Pepito was writing a letter to baby Jesus,
—Baby Jesus, I've been good for three months, and this Christmas I want you to bring me a skateboard, a bicycle, a transformer. . . . Then the voice of the Virgin Mary speaks to him,
—Pepito, are you sure you've been good for three months?
Pepito tears the sheet of paper, takes another one and writes:
—Dear Baby Jesus, I've been good for one month, and this Christmas I want you to bring me a skateboard . . .
Again, the Virgin Mary speaks,
—Are you sure, Pepito? One month?
He again tears the letter, takes another piece of paper and writes:
—Sweet Baby Jesus, I've been good for a week, and this Christmas I want you to bring me a skateboard . . .
And again Mary's voice is heard. Then Pepito takes the image of the Virgin Mary that he had nearby and very angrily writes,
—Look Baby Jesus, I've Taken Your Mother Hostage, and if You Want to See Her Again, this Christmas I Want You to Bring Me a Skateboard, a Bicycle, a Transformer . . . !] (Pepito Jokes 2003)

In yet another narrative I collected in Laredo, the "joke" depends on the language itself. Pepito arrives home and is asked, "¿Qué te enseñó la Maestra?" (What did the teacher teach/show you?), and he answers, "Hoy nada, llevaba los blue jeans" (Nothing today, she was wearing jeans). The play of words is on *enseñó*, which can either be "to teach" or "to show."

In performance, Pepito jokes often emerge in "sessions" engaged in by boys and young men. A boy can start the session by telling a joke, and others feel compelled to add other jokes. The sessions often become competitive, with boys vying for the largest response of laughter from the gathered group. This situation suggests a display of the centrality of the manly sexual theme among the boys. Psychologically, it can be interpreted similarly to "dozens" or contests-in-insults among African American boys in which mothers are intentionally and ritually derided to force maturing boys into a sensitive position of both separating and bonding with the mother (Abrahams 1990). As with dozens, the primary symbol of separation is sexual aggression by the male, particularly when it is aimed at the mother figure. The Pepito joke sessions, however, are distinctive because they emphasize separation more than bonding, especially symbolized by defiling one's *own* mother, in contrast to African American dozens where someone else's mother is objectified.

I do not know of equivalent *Pepita* jokes, although certainly a number of salacious gender-specific female jokes can be heard replete with double-entendre references that are said only among females. In-group joking is a common phenomenon and is rampant during bridal showers as well as bachelor parties. The most recent mode of dissemination of Pepito jokes in Laredo is through the Internet's Laredo Morning Times Reminiscing Room, a sort of chat room where "remmers" can post memories of growing up in Laredo. The seasonal postings render a view of what those who post consider worth remembering. Not surprisingly, many remember Pepito jokes. Songs, both traditional *corridos* and *conjunto,* are also a popular trigger for reminiscing, and many remmers ask for specific memories of locations or events such as the flood in the 1950s or of who lived at which corner. Although the remmers divide equally between male and female, it appears that the male remmers use more code-switching and appear to take on a *chuco* (from *pachuco,* an archetype of 1940s style) persona using the language of the street, but curiously enough that, too, is dated, and they will often use *caló* (the language of the *pachuco* replete with Spanglish and slang expressions), which current youth no longer speak.

In other genres in the oral tradition, one can also find evidence of gendered performance. In *corridos,* from the oldest and most traditional such as *Rosita Alvirez,* about a woman who meets her death after disrespecting a man (and disobeying her mother) at a town dance, or *Delgadina,* with an incest theme, to the contemporary *narcocorridos,* with the glorification of drug trafficking, sexual conduct and correct behavior remain a constant. Here are, for example, the first four stanzas of *Delgadina* from the singing of Lydia Mendoza in San Antonio:

1. Delgadina se paseaba
en su sala bien cuadrada
con su manto de hilo de oro
que en su pecho le brillaba.

2. Levántate, Delgadina,
ponte tu vestido blanco
porque nos vamos a misa
al estado de Durango.

3. Cuando salieron de misa
su papá le platicaba:
Delgadina, hija mía,
yo te quiero para dama.

4. No lo permita Dios
ni la Reina soberana,

es una ofensa para Dios
y también para mi mamá.

[1. Delgadina walked around
in her spaciously squared parlor
with her golden-threaded mantle
shining on her bosom.

2. "Arise, Delgadina,
put on your white dress
because we are going to mass
in the state of Durango."

3. Coming out of mass
her father was saying:
"Delgadina, my daughter,
I want you as my lady."

4. "May the Lord forbid it
and the Heavenly Queen.
That would be an offense to God
and also to my Mamá."] (Corridos 2003)

María Herrera Sobek (1990, 1993), José Limón (1986), and John Mc-
Dowell (2000), among others, have looked at *corridos* in Chicano and Mexican communities and have analyzed the *macho* identity of the hero and
even the manly language in the lyrics. The early *corridos,* they find, glorified
the *macho* and perhaps established the first image of the *macho* as a gun-
slinging, hard-drinking womanizer. Paredes studied the *corrido* as a signifier
of masculine identity in an essay in which he proposes that the reason the
word *macho* occurs so often in *corridos* after Avila Camacho became president of Mexico is that the word rhymes with the president's name (1967).
Herrera Sobek looks at the archetype of the women found in the *corridos*
and notes their submissive victim status even when they are agents on their
own.

The tale of the bad son as related in *El hijo desobediente* (the disobedient
son) is the precursor of many other *corridos* that place the boy or man in
the role of either defying or following the role set for him by society and
the family.

Un domingo estando herrando
se encontraron dos mancebos,
echando mano a sus fierros
como queriendo pelear;
cuando se estaban peleando
pues llegó su padre de uno:
—Hijo de mi corazón,
ya no peleés con ninguno.—

Quítese de aquí mi padre
que estoy más bravo que un león
no vaya a sacar la espada
y la parta el corazón.—
Hijo de mi corazón,
por lo que acabas de hablar
antes de que raye el sol
la vida te han de quitar.—

—Lo que le pido a mi padre
que no me entierre en sagrado,
que me entierre en tierra bruta
donde me trille el ganado,
con una mano de fuera
y un papel sobre-dorado,
con un letrero que diga,
"Felipe fue desdichado."

—La vaquilla colorada,
hace un año que nació.
Ahi se la dejo a mi padre
por la crianza que me dió;
los tres caballos que tengo,
ahi se los dejo a los pobres
para que digan en vida,
"Felipe, Dios te perdone."—

Bajaron el toro prieto,
que nunca lo habían bajado,
pero 'ora si ya bajó
revuelto con el ganado;
ya con ésta me despido
por la estrella del oriente,
y aquí se acaba el corrido
de El Hijo Desobediente. (Lauter 1994, 839–41)

[On a Sunday during branding
Two young cowboys did meet,
Each going for his steel
Each looking to fight;
As they were fighting
The father of one arrived:
—My beloved son
Do not fight with anyone.—

—Get away from here, my father
I feel more fierce than a lion,
For I may draw my knife
To split your heart in two.—
—My beloved son,

Because of what you have said
Before the next sunrise
Your life will be taken away.—

—I only ask of my father
Do not bury me in sacred ground,
Bury me in brute earth
Where the stock may trample me
With one hand out of the grave
And a gilded paper,
With an epitaph that reads
"Felipe was an ill-fated man."

The red yearling
Born a year ago
I leave to my father
My upbringing to him I owe;
My three stallions
I leave to the poor
So that they may say
"May God forgive you, Felipe."

They brought the black bull down,
Never before brought down,
But now the bull has come down
With the rest of the stock;
Now with this I say farewell
Guided by the eastern star
This ends the ballad
Of the disobedient son.]

A contemporary *corrido* by the Hermanos García replaces the language of the traditional "Dos Hermanos" with *caló* and situates the brothers' antics in the region citing the popular Texas grocery store chain, H.E.B. They spoof the brothers in the earlier *corrido* and update the "crime" so that they are carrying cocaine and marijuana in "dos lowriders," a De Soto and a truck. The protagonists of most *corridos*, traditional and contemporary, definitely display a sort of hyper-masculinity, often glorified and embellished.

Taking off from Paredes, Alfredo Mirandé seeks to ascertain the traits of the "good" and the "bad" macho in his book *Hombres and Machos* (1997); it is the latter that populates the oral tradition and in particular the *narcocorridos*. But as in the *corridos*, where dubious heroes often reflect the patriarchal mores as they jealously guard their women, Mirandé like Paredes and others still centers the discussion on the man. I would like to refocus the emphasis for the above discussion, for often the singers of lullabies and *corridos* are women, who are the agents of socialization. As Ana Castillo points out, the women do not hold the authority in the home

(1994, 98–99). She is one more pawn in the capitalist system that perpetuates the patriarchal domination of women, and the onus for change does not fall to the women. They are, after all, not colluding in their own victimization; rather, they are only acting according to the internalized mores of the society. As Anzaldúa points out, "men, even more than women, are fettered by gender roles" (1987, 106).

The *narcocorrido,* the most recent variant form of the traditional ballad, celebrates a constructed manly ethos where patriarchy survives and the violence associated with drug trafficking is glorified. Many folk songs as well as the lyrics of popular music, like *Don Luis el tejano* or *Las nubes,* obviously have a male audience in mind as they admonish the listener and instruct in correct male behavior. The narrator of *Las nubes* advises his friends to stay away from "vice, because it can dominate one's life," and continues, "in this tyrannous life one has to know how to play the game" (my translations). Like the traditional *Rosita Alvirez* and *Juan Charrasqueado* of an earlier epoch, the songs tell stories and celebrate the stereotype of the gun-toting violent men who kill and die defending their property or a woman, or tell of current injustices and cultural heroes like Gabino Barrera or Juan Cortina, who defy the Anglo domination and usurpation of land. Most recently they tell of the events of September 11 and celebrate the heroes—the firefighters and police officers who died saving others. The war in Iraq has spawned several *corridos* in memory of those from the area who have been killed.

Childhood songs and games, as Maria Herrera Sobek shows, have implications for female learned behavior (2002, 81–99). The same holds true for Chicano boys playing tag, mock wrestling, fighting, and playing with action figures and video games, as the appropriate activities that teach boys how to be men. Dolls are taboo; action figures and certain video games, mostly centered on violent or at least competitive strategies, have risen in popularity and have replaced traditional marbles and other toys as preferred forms of diversion. Sports, however, remain as firmly entrenched as ever. Like other children's play practices, Chicano boys engage in sports—soccer, baseball, and, as they grow older, basketball and even tennis and racquetball. Golf is one of the most popular sports for young adults in Laredo belonging to the upper-middle and upper classes. While soccer is gaining popularity in the middle and upper classes, it has been the sport of choice for recent immigrant boys. But there is an even more serious sport that the local population enjoys that is definitely dominated by men and characterized as manly: hunting.

Since Laredo, although fairly urban, has its roots in rural culture, many youth still dream of owning a horse even as they yearn for a car or more probably a truck. Driving marks a coming-of-age and signals that the young boy can now also engage in the widespread sport of hunting. During hunting season in the fall, the *Laredo Morning Times* publishes photos of young boys with their kill. The smiling faces and the celebratory tone of the story, which of course notes if this is the boy's first kill of the season or of his life, indicate that this is indeed a rite of passage into manhood—and manliness. Guns are serious business; while back in the 1950s and 1960s a young boy might have yearned to own his first BB gun, young boys in 2000 expect to own a hunting rifle. The initiation ritual includes killing your first buck. The ranching traditions that often require guns, for protection from rattlesnakes or for hunting, are alive and well in the area.

Letting out *gritos* (exuberant cries), whistling, singing, telling jokes, engaging in verbal arts such as *choteo* (mockery), and applying certain gender-specific linguistic rules (i.e., the use of *chinga* or *güey* as fillers) initiate, mark, or integrate boys and men into the manly domain of Laredo society. Now, not all Chicanos engage in all or even one of these, and over time many practices have changed. Playing the accordion or certain areas of male-only performance such as *mariachi* or dancing with the *matachines* have changed markedly over the last forty years or so. But it seems that even as some things change, others seem to fill in the social need for clear gender markers. Clothes, for example, may signal a growing androgynous teen dress code until hip-hop style comes in with baggy pants, short spiked hair, and pierced ears. While the requisite tattooing is now coupled with earrings, boys usually wear studs but sometimes even small hoop earrings.

Another domain of shifting expectations and behaviors is the family and the roles boys and men play in the traditional structure. These can perhaps best be seen in the performance during specific rituals such as weddings and the accompanying rites. As Juan Castillo, *piñata* maker from Nuevo Laredo, explained during the Smithsonian Festival of American Folklife, *piñatas* are especially ordered for *despedidas* (bachelor parties) with off-color jokes and gender-specific tone. Additionally, the wedding ritual itself is complemented by a series of male-only actions. During the dance, for example, it is not uncommon to have the groomsmen lift the groom and carry him around the dance hall, as if he were dead, as the band plays a funeral march. In many cases the groom is stripped down to his shorts, and his shoes are flung around from one man to the next.

In conclusion, the traditional practices of Chicanos along the U.S.–Mexico borderlands can be said to be a blend of traditional Mexican practices transformed by the inclusion of various U.S. mainstream practices. Some remain more Mexican-identified, such as the Pepito jokes, and others are bound to the region's past history, such as hunting. But, most importantly, I must underscore that the traditions remain essentially the same and have acquired a post-modern tone only as far as the community allows. The various folk genres that persist—*corridos* or ballads, the games young boys play, the *dichos* or sayings, the material cultural products of a community along the border—all point to the fact that as in other cultures, young boys are taught how to be men, and that the *machismo* that is inherent in that teaching remains a site of contestation. The cliché of the *macho* whom William Madsen described in the 1960s is not any truer now than it was back then. The *mandilón* may not admit to being one, but his actions confirm it; the *macho* may not brag about such "bad" *macho* behavior; the "good" *macho* qualities and values are reinforced as the romanticized male behavior remains the ideal—neither *mandilón* nor *macho*.

NOTES

1. I draw here from my own personal observation of the wedding rituals in Laredo, Texas, and from Brenda Gonzalez's presentation on the traditional wedding ceremony in Northern Mexico given at the 1999 American Folklore Society Meeting in Memphis, Tennessee.

2. See Diane Gonzalez Bertrand's young adult novel *Sweet Fifteen;* for a discussion of the tradition as a coming-of-age ritual see Norma E. Cantú (2002).

3. As Manuel Peña (1985) has noted, "despite their increasing absorption into an expanding capitalist economy, *tejanos* remained culturally isolated from the rest of American society, as a result of ethnic prejudice and segregation." But I would add that while the prejudice and segregation certainly played a major role in creating what I call a cultural resistance, it was the people's pride, faith, and even ethnocentrism that resulted in the persistence of cultural practices, both religious and secular.

4. Although I would normally translate *hombre* when used to mean "mankind" as "humankind" or "humanity," in this case it is obvious that Paredes is referring to men's potential.

5. For an excellent tracing of *machismo* to Arabic, Spanish, and indigenous cultural sexist practices, see Castillo (1994, 63–84); for a review of the various uses of the word and its various etymologies and a discussion of machismo from a contemporary anthropological perspective, see Gutmann (1996, 221–42).

6. I first encountered the term *mandilón* in the work of sociologist Maria Elena Ramos Tovar (2001). It is generally believed that the term refers to a "henpecked" husband, and that the term comes from the word for "apron" in Spanish. Gutmann (1996), however, while agreeing with the etymology, found that the meaning of the term was not as harsh as "henpecked." Ramos Tovar's study of the perceptions of men in Cd. Juarez regarding their status as either *macho* or *mandilón* helps explain the apparent discordance between what contemporary Mexican men say and what they do.

7. See José Esteban Muñoz (1999) for an exploration of what he has called "disidentifications." In his study of performance by queers of color he finds that they "disidentify" as a political and survival strategy in order to function in a "counterpublic sphere."

8. See Letticia Galindo and Maria Dolores Gonzáles (1999), Rosaura Sánchez (1983), and Fernando Peñalosa (1980) for a discussion of language and discourse in Chicano communities. Galindo and the other writers of the essays in *Speaking Chicana* explore gendered linguistic codes, while Sánchez provides a valuable sociohistorical framework from a Marxist perspective, and Peñalosa looks at cultural milieu as a determinant of language choice.

9. The story and legend of *la Llorona* has been studied by a number of scholars

along with its implications for both a historical figure of *la Malinche* and as fodder for literary production as in the connection with the Medea story, such as Cherie Moraga's *Hungry Woman the Mexican Medea* and Sandra Cisneros's *Woman Hollering Creek*. For a fuller discussion of the *Llorona* legend in Mexican American communities, see Domino Pérez 2002; José Limón 1986, 1990.

    10. See José Limón (1994).

REFERENCES

Abalos, David. T. 2001. *The Latino Male: A Radical Redefinition.* Boulder, Colo.: Lynne Rienner.

Abrahams, Roger D. 1990. "Playing the Dozens." In *Mother Wit from the Laughing Barrel: Readings in the Interpretation of Afro-American Folklore,* ed. Alan Dundes, 295–309. 1973. Reprint, Jackson: University Press of Mississippi.

Anzaldúa, Gloria. 1987. *Borderlands/La frontera: The New Mestiza.* San Francisco: Aunt Lute Press.

———. 2001. "*La Conciencia de la Mestiza:* Towards a New Consciousness." In *Feminism and "Race,"* ed. Kum-Kum Bhavnani, 93–107. New York: Oxford University Press.

Arreola, Daniel. 2002. *Tejano South Texas: A Mexican American Cultural Province.* Austin: University of Texas Press.

Bertrand, Diane Gonzales. 1995. *Sweet Fifteen.* 2nd ed. Houston: Piñata Books.

Cantú, Norma E. 2002. "Chicana Life-Cycle Rituals." In *Chicana Traditions: Continuity and Change,* ed. Norma E. Cantú and Olga Nájera-Ramírez, 15–34. Urbana: University of Illinois Press.

Castillo, Ana. 1994. *Massacre of the Dreamers: Essays on Xicanisma.* Albuquerque: University of New Mexico Press.

Corridos: Mexican and Mexican American Ballads. University of Texas. http://www.sp.utexas.edu/jrn/corridos. Accessed December 11, 2003.

Galindo, D. Letticia, and María Dolores Gonzáles. 1999. *Speaking Chicana: Voice, Power, and Identity.* Tucson: University of Arizona Press.

Gutmann, Matthew C. 1996. *The Meanings of Macho: Being a Man in Mexico City.* Berkeley: University of California Press.

Herrera Sobek, María. 1990. *The Mexican Corrido: A Feminist Analysis.* Bloomington: Indiana University Press.

———. 1993. *Northward Bound: The Mexican Immigrant Experience in Ballad and Song.* Bloomington: Indiana University Press.

———. 2002. "Danger! Children at Play: Patriarchal Ideology and the Construction of Gender in Spanish-Language Hispanic/Chicano Children's Songs and Games." In *Chicana Traditions: Continuity and Change,* ed. Norma E. Cantú and Olga Nájera-Ramírez, 81–99. Urbana: University of Illinois Press.

Lauter, Paul, ed. 1994. *The Heath Anthology of American Literature.* 2nd ed. Vol. 2. Lexington, Mass.: D. C. Heath.

Limón, José E. 1986. *Mexican Ballads, Chicano Epic: History, Social Dramas, and Poetic Persuasions.* Stanford, Calif.: Stanford Center for Chicano Research.

———. 1990. "La Llorona, the Third Legend of Greater Mexico: Cultural Symbols, Women and the Political Unconscious." In *Between Borders: Essays on Mexicana/Chicana History,* ed Adelaida R. Del Castillo, 399–432. Encino, Calif.: Floricanto Press.

————. 1994. *Dancing with the Devil: Society and Cultural Poetics in Mexican-American South Texas.* Madison: University of Wisconsin Press.

Madsen, William C. 1973. *The Mexican-Americans of South Texas.* 2nd ed. New York: Holt, Rinehart and Winston.

McDowell. John. 2000. *Poetry and Violence: The Ballad Tradition of Mexico's Costa Chica.* Urbana: University of Illinois Press.

Mendoza, Vicente T. 1962. "El machismo en México." *Cuadernos del Instituo Nacional de Investigaciones Folklóricas* (Buenos Aires) 3: 75–86.

Mignolo, Walter. 2000. *Local Histories/Global Designs: Coloniality, Subaltern Knowledges, and Border Thinking.* Princeton, N.J.: Princeton University Press.

Mirandé, Alfredo. 1982. "Machismo: Rucas, chingasos y chingaderas." *De Colores* 6: 17–31.

————. 1988. "Que gacho es ser macho: It's a Drag to Be a Macho Man." *Aztlán* 17, no. 2: 63–89.

————. 1997. *Hombres y machos: Masculinity and Latino Culture.* Boulder, Colo.: Westview Press.

Muñoz, José Esteban. 1999. *Disidentification: Queers of Color and the Performance of Politics.* Minneapolis: University of Minnesota.

Paredes, Américo. 1967. "Estados Unidos, México y el machismo." *Journal of Inter-American Studies* 9: 65–84.

Peña, Manuel. 1985. *The Texas-Mexican Conjunto: A History of a Working-Class Music.* Austin: University of Texas Press.

————. 1991. "Class, Gender, and Machismo: The 'Treacherous-Woman' Folklore of Mexican Male Workers." *Gender and Society* 5: 30–46.

Peñalosa, Fernando. 1980. *Chicano Sociolinguistics: A Brief Introduction.* Rowley, Mass.: Newbury House.

Pepito Jokes. http://www.pepitojokes.com. Accessed December 11, 2003.

Pérez, Domino Renee. 2002. "Caminando con La Llorona: Traditional and Contemporary Narratives." In *Chicana Traditions: Continuity and Change,* ed. Norma E. Cantú and Olga Nájera-Ramírez, 100–113. Urbana: University of Illinois Press.

Ramos Tovar, Maria Elena. 2001. "Women and Men on the Mexican Border: A Mexican Perspective." Paper presented at the University of Texas, San Antonio, November 2001.

Sánchez, Rosaura. 1983. *Chicano Discourse: Socio-historic Perspectives.* Rowley, Mass.: Newbury House.

Zinn, Maxine Baca. 2001. "Chicano Men and Masculinity." In *Men's Lives,* 5th ed., ed. Michael S. Kimmel and Michael A. Messner, 25–34. Boston: Allyn & Bacon.

4

Performing Manliness: Resistance and Harmony in Japanese American *Taiko*

HIDEYO KONAGAYA

At any festival, *taiko* is hard to miss, and that is just the point. Decoratively uniformed Japanese performers vigorously pound varieties of oversized drums in a dazzling display of straining bodies and potent instruments. Your ears cannot miss the loud beating out of rhythms, and your eyes will undoubtedly turn to a mammoth drum dwarfing all the others that is often brought out as an apparent challenge to an especially athletic, if diminutive, drummer. The powerful drum extends the performer and enlarges the performance. *Taiko* as performance provides an ultimate test of mastery for the drummer over the drum—and its expression of manliness.

Taiko as a term refers to both the art of *taiko* drumming and to the *taiko* drums themselves. *Taiko* in Japanese classical arts has a history spanning close to two thousand years, but the performance ensembles of today often are categorized in a modern art called *kumi-daiko*.[1] Translated literally, *taiko* means "fat drum," although there is a vast array of shapes and sizes of *taiko*. Within the last fifty years since *kumi-daiko* became established, it has seen phenomenal growth to the point where there are thousands of *taiko* groups worldwide. Promoters of *taiko* often claim that it is the first native Japanese music to spread through the world, but in places like the United States it has taken distinctive forms and fills functions in response to local and national contexts.

One of those national contexts is the popular American perception of Japanese American men as effeminate, lifeless, small, and weak. In the United States, *taiko* was often the most conspicuous display of Japanese tradition at various festivals in areas with a Japanese American population. It became not only a noticeable sign of Japaneseness, but also of Japanese manliness. Playing the larger drums demands strength and vigor, and bodily animation onstage. In its modern context, it became known as a manly tradition. Notably responding to both the need to build Japanese identity among this assimilating ethnic population and a perception that popular culture portrayed Japanese men as silent, subdued, and studious, *taiko* performances became locations to negotiate between the ethnic and

"Behind the Odaiko." Composed and performed by Bryan Yamami (2003) *Photograph by Robert Meyers. Photograph courtesy the TAIKOPROJECT.*

popular cultures an evolving conveyable sense of masculinity among Japanese American men.

Documents dating to the eighth century recording myths and customs regarding the summoning of the sun goddess mention *taiko* used in sacred rituals among a priestly class. In the myths, the performance of dancing on a drum-like object is described as an occurrence of the divine world. *Taiko* as a folk tradition developed in multiple forms and performance styles among different classes in various regions. Studies by Japanese folklorists, for instance, have described *taiko* in the contexts of a religious ceremony, agricultural rite, and community festival. In pre-modern farming communities, small-sized *taiko* often accompanied a ritual dance or drama that expressed prayer for a good harvest, rain, and reproduction. In a performance called *tabayashi*, costumed performers danced in a rice field, carrying small drums at their waists. In the *samurai* class, the resonance of *taiko* became a symbol of military power on the battlefield. The Japanese *taiko* group that revived group drumming in Nagano, Japan, in the 1960s claimed roots in this tradition.

Taiko was also integrated into everyday life as a signal of time in various communities. It was common at elementary schools for drums to be pounded at the beginning and end of classes. After World War II, many schools switched to bells that seemed more in step with Western modernity and less of a reference to militaristic roots. Because it could be heard over long distances, communities also used *taiko* to signal gatherings and communicate messages. All the expressions that appeared in its historical passage constituted the myriad layers of meanings of *taiko* in Japanese culture. Prior to its revival, then, *taiko* did not have a definite meaning, but some came to be constructed, particularly in its American context.

The group drumming that emerged during the 1960s in Japan emphasized the staged performance of *taiko* as music and entertainment over its ritual uses. The enhancement of musical elements, I presume, was part of the influence of Western music on Japanese culture generally and the importance of youth culture particularly. Tempos, rhythms, and melodies of Western musical traditions, ranging from classical to contemporary, have been replacing traditional Japanese forms since modernization became Japanese public policy in the late nineteenth century, and this displacement accelerated in the post–World War II years. In contrast to classical *taiko*, contemporary performers, both men and women, pound drums with more upbeat, complex, and faster rhythms. *Taiko* once perceived as ritual and custom has become a category of music. It also is associated with festival celebrations in Japanese urban life.

Taiko's introduction in America can be traced to the efforts of a young Japanese man, Seiichi Tanaka, in San Francisco in 1967. Recently arrived on American shores from Japan, he attended the first Cherry Blossom Festival in Japan Town in San Francisco in 1967 and thought it needed a demonstration of *taiko* as a signal Japanese tradition. In interviews, he explained that he was determined to offset the feminine representation of flowers, *kimono*, and sedate dancing at the Cherry Blossom Festival with the vigor of *taiko*. He appeared as a solo drummer in the second festival, and then in 1968 he founded San Francisco Taiko Dojo, the first American *taiko* group (Tanaka 1998, 13).[2] One year after Tanaka's group formed, third-generation Japanese Americans called *sansei* started a *taiko* group in the Senshin Buddhist Temple in Los Angeles. Young *sansei* members of the temple played drums spontaneously one day. The drums were used at the year's *Obon* Festival to demonstrate the Buddhist celebration for the ancestors. They kept beating the drums for about four hours, "until they were sweating, their hands bleeding," and thought they "should do something about this" (Fromartz 1998, 46–47). Their enthusiasm for drumming led to the formation of Kinnara Taiko, the first *taiko* group composed totally of Japanese Americans.

Taiko performance at a community festival, Yaizu Minato Matsuri, located in Shizuoka, Japan, April 2000. *Photograph by Hideyo Konagaya.*

In performance, Tanaka's Taiko Dojo evoked Japaneseness by members holding drumsticks over their heads and striking a large drum with resolute stances and lunges. Tanaka's direction emphasized manly qualities of performance by incorporating the movement and discipline of the martial art of *judo.* When he came to the United States at the age of twenty-four after graduation from a university in Japan, Tanaka's initial aspiration was, in his words, to "venture out into the big country." His rhetoric owes, he says, to film portrayals of American cowboys like "John Wayne or Gary Cooper" (Tanaka 1989, 15). His dream was quickly dashed by the reality of not being able to communicate in his own language and get a job (Tanaka, interview with author, August 2001). He reflected later that *taiko* allowed him to recover his sense of self.

His reverence for *taiko* originated in his boyhood, when he grew up with the tradition of *taiko* in a community festival in Nagano, located in central Japan. Tanaka was inspired by the dynamic performance of the pioneer group of the modern *taiko* movement in Japan, Osuwa Taiko in Nagano, which fashioned the widely imitated style of group drumming.[3] He had strict training in *judo,* which was a way to overcome cowardice and weakness in his path from boyhood to adolescence. Frequently returning to Japan and witnessing *taiko* performances, he affirmed his belief that American Japanese needed *taiko* for revitalization (Tanaka 1989, 13).

"Many Sides." Composed by Masato Baba and performed by the TAIKOPROJECT (2003). *Photograph by Robert Meyers. Photograph courtesy the TAIKOPROJECT.*

Tanaka built relations with the eminent Japanese *taiko* schools of Osuwa Taiko of Nagano and Oedo Sukeroku Taiko of Tokyo. Each of the revival groups claimed continuity with tradition through their familial ties to the historical tradition in Suwa in Nagano and Yushima in Tokyo. Owing to his status as founder of the first *taiko* group in the United States, he has become a legendary figure in the American *taiko* community, respectfully called *sensei* or grand master. He was also recognized nationally in 2001 with a National Heritage Fellowship given for achievement in American folk and traditional arts. With the expressive display of manliness central to Tanaka's *taiko* performances for years, he has recently looked to add self-reflective components to the tradition with the addition of "meditation and the Chinese art of *qigong* to his curriculum" (Watanabe 1999).

The version of *taiko* that emerged on the West Coast in the late 1960s both accommodated and resisted a normative sense of white American masculinity. *Taiko* performances, with their energetic, festive sounds and rhythms, defied images of the domesticated "model minority" associated with Japanese Americans (Okihiro 1994, 144; Uematsu 1971, 10–11). The supposed emotional restraint of Japanese Americans in popular culture was coupled with the view of men as methodically devoted to submissive, routine work. Accordingly, it was common to find feminized images of Asian men in movies and literature as weak, short, shy, and withdrawn (Lee 2001, 232). Tanaka's powerful performances at major festivals, in which

"Hachijo Taiko." Traditional, arranged by Yuta Kato and performed by Yuta Kato and Shoji Kameda (2003). *Photograph by Gabrielle Angeles. Photography courtesy the TAIKOPROJECT.*

he integrated athletic movements of martial arts, showed what he defined as Japanese masculinity (Tachiki 1971, 3). In contrast to depictions of Japanese people as well as technology in a contemplative, inward-looking "compact culture," *taiko* was meant to be arousing, expansive, and sensational.

Taiko also was in part a reaction to the fear of a complete loss of Japaneseness to Westernization. Student movements during the 1960s in Japan protested American influences over postwar Japanese society and global politics (Inoki 2000, 79–80). The countercultural youth movements of both Japan and the United States at the time adapted traditional, rural expressions to recover feelings of natural, communal values in modern urban society (Nishitsunoi 1985, 281–85).[4] In the modern tradition, group drumming implied a synchronous communal connection while privileging physical prowess and demonstration of individual mastery (Nishitsunoi 1990, 118). To be sure, the new tradition of *taiko* allowed women to participate in drumming, but the perception of the skill of drumming, once restricted to men, was still that it was a manly tradition.

Because the origin of American *taiko* was defined by what *sansei* found meaningful in the 1960s, the American and Japanese revivals of *taiko* took different turns (Konagaya 1998). While Japanese performers constructed

"Many Sides." Composed by Masato Baba and performed by the TAIKOPROJECT (2003). *Photograph by Gabrielle Angeles. Photography courtesy the TAIKOPROJECT.*

modern *taiko* to represent the sacredness, indeed the wholeness, of Japanese cultural traditions, *sansei* in America emphasized its display of strength, energy, and power—in short, its manliness.

The display of manly messages in American *taiko* raises the question of the folk roots of Japanese masculinity beyond the American perceptions of it. The gender relations of *issei* (first-generation Japanese Americans) were characterized by the notion of *soto* (outside) and *uchi* (inside). It was applied to differentiate every aspect of life, including the separation of men's sphere from women's, public and private space, and formal and informal settings. The opposition was structured not complementarily, but hierarchically. *Uchi,* the women's sphere, was enclosed and controlled by *soto,* the men's sphere (Yanagisako 1985).

Yet Japanese men felt restricted in their expressions because of their role in a hierarchal chain of command, and this feeling is often translated to values of dependence and submission. Anthropologist S. J. Yanagisako observed that this pattern owes to the gender relations of *issei* in the successor status of a household, which was validated by the *ie* (household) system in the Meiji Civil Code. *Issei* husbands who were designated as successors of the parent household had the authority to exercise firm control over the family economy, and that authority was considered legitimate in the ethnic enclave of *issei* in the husbands' home communities in Japan. Non-successor *issei* husbands did not have any control of the parent household and therefore exercised less dominance in power relations with their wives.

Meanwhile in the United States, Americans constructed the notion of an Asian "yellow peril" threatening American life. Caricatures of Asians as monkeys emphasized the diminutive size and primitiveness of Asian immigrants. After excluding Chinese laborers in the 1880s, anti-Asian forces used rising Japanese militarism to justify expanding the exclusion to *issei* in the early twentieth century. In Alien Land Acts passed in 1913 and 1920, Japanese immigrants were assigned the status of "aliens ineligible for citizenship." The alien status of *issei* forestalled their land ownership, an emblem of American independence and the "good provider" model of effective manhood. The *issei*'s American-born children, *nisei*, were implicated as alien threats in the incarceration of "any person of Japanese ancestry" during World War II. The categorization was indicative of a prevalent view in American society that Japanese Americans were the same as Japanese. The loss of work and property and confinement behind barbed wires was detrimental to values of manhood developed by the *issei*, who had been born and raised in the male-dominant Japanese society of the Meiji Period (1868–1912) (Takezawa 1994, 106).[5]

Incarceration in World War II internment camps resulted in erosion of the *ie* institution in the Japanese American community. In addition to losing economic control, *issei* lost control over their children. Further, the policies of the War Relocation Authority encouraged younger *nisei* to lead the camp population and to subvert *issei* attempts at authority. Although the racial politics of the U.S. government feminized the *issei*, this became a breakthrough for Japanese American women. They gained control over power relations within the family, regardless of the husband's successor or non-successor status. *Nisei* couples who reached marriageable age after the camp and who had positive attitudes toward Americanization tended to follow the marriage pattern common among middle-class white Americans. The even higher intermarriage rate and loss of Japanese language among *sansei* (third-generation Japanese Americans) accelerated the process of assimilation, although it was also evident that the lingering image of the feminized Japanese man in popular culture prevented complete absorption.

For *issei* and *nisei*, "outmarriages" rarely occurred because of anti-miscegenation laws and the community's endorsement of the purity of "in-marriages" caused by the "fear of dilution" (Kikumura and Kitano 1973, 68). After the abolishment of anti-miscegenation laws in California in 1948, the increase of interracial marriage among *sansei* was loosening the hold of Japanese tradition. By the early 1970s nearly 50% of Japanese

Americans were outmarrying, according to a survey in Los Angeles, San Francisco, Fresno, and Hawaii. Outmarriages, according to cultural studies, tended to undermine the hold of values, such as "obedience, responsibility, loyalty, and duty to family and community, respect for authority, and collective behavior" (68).

Generational differences between *issei* and *sansei* in attitudes toward authority are apparent in a lack of protest to the federal government after internment (Maki, Kitano, and Berthold 1999, 64–65). The norms of the peasant class in the feudalistic society of Meiji Japan, from which a large portion of *issei* came, had discouraged direct resistance against authority that required taking a great risk of damaging the unity of the group. One response from the *nisei* creating more of a gulf between the generations was their accelerating assimilation and professional achievement (Iino 2000, 130–31).

The remaking of a new Japanese American community after the dissolution of many Japanese enclaves on the West Coast called for a symbol that could mediate ethnically and culturally stratified layers within its structure. Although *taiko* had been played as a musical or religious instrument in folk rituals and ceremonies in the "Little Tokyo" areas until the 1920s, it did not survive the incarceration, assimilation, and postwar dispersal of the ethnic community to the suburbs (Asai 1985, 163–64).[6] *Taiko* was appealing as a symbol in part because of its reference to social harmony. After all, the spectacular display of *taiko* in the Japanese past was a central feature of *matsuri*, or "festival," where conflicting elements of the community could come together (Yanagawa 1972, 74; Schnell 1999, 142–43). *Taiko*'s provision of spiritual as well as social unity is given in an ancient myth known to many *issei*, in which *miko*, a maiden consecrated to the gods, used *taiko* as a religious instrument to summon up mystical forces.[7] The first reference to *taiko* in *Kojiki* (Records of Ancient Matters) and *Nihonshoki* (Chronicles of Japan), the classical mythological texts that date from the early eighth century, states that *miko* danced on *uke*, which scholars presume to be the original form of *taiko*, pleading with the sun goddess Amaterasu to come out and shine benevolently on the world (Misumi 1990, 109–13; Honda 1990, 105–106). Such references explained in presentations of *taiko* to new generations of Japanese Americans imbued the performances with social and spiritual meanings, and the manly qualities of the performances served to give them added forcefulness.

While I have argued that the constructed emphasis on manliness in American *taiko* was a reaction to popular representations of Japanese men, it also related to other Asian masculinities. The Asian American movement of the 1960s called for solidarity among Asians and awareness to Asian American/Pan-Asian identity, but at the same time, each national group was encouraged to have its own ethnic pride. Koreans and Chinese had drumming traditions similar to *taiko*, but I have observed little if any non-

Japanese participation in *taiko*. Further, the Korean and Chinese immigrant communities have not revitalized traditional drumming as a prime symbol of their modern ethnicity. While the number of people of Asian background has dramatically increased in Hawaii and California since the 1960s, the Japanese also deal with their status as a minority within the Asian American movement. Chinese, Filipino, Vietnamese, Korean, and Asian Indian are the five largest Asian groups in California, followed by the Japanese. Despite some representations of swarms of Japanese businessmen "invading" the West Coast, the Japanese make up only 7.8% of the Asian population of California. In many festivals, therefore, the impact of *taiko* was not only to address a normative view of American masculinity but also to pronounce to other Asian groups a signifier of Japanese tradition.

Language is often a divide between Japanese Americans who tend not to maintain communication in Japanese and Japanese immigrants, or *shin-issei*. Distinctively Japanese cultural traditions such as *taiko* thus became important signifiers of identity to link new immigrants from the home country and third- and fourth-generation Japanese Americans. The common ground for the groups is often in the historic sites of Little Tokyo in Los Angeles and some other West Coast cities. Although not a residential site for a largely suburbanized Japanese population, Little Tokyo emerged as a significant commercial and cultural center, and location for festivals, that united scattered Japanese Americans and *shin-issei*.

Noteworthy is the fact that the founder of American *taiko* is *shin-issei*. In my interview with him, Tanaka cited a proverbial phrase to explain his mediating role between Japaneseness and the development of Japanese American assimilation, and in building this bridge the role of masculinity. This phrase, *choyo no jo*, derives from Confucian teachings and encapsulates the importance of hierarchical social order. It exemplifies this order as senior-junior relationships; *cho* (elderly/head), *yo* (young/infant) *no* (of), and *jo* (order). It was the principle, Tanaka asserted, that he had adhered to his entire life and would never compromise, whereas he had to soften, or modify, his original harsh discipline of *taiko* over his thirty-year experience of teaching *taiko* in the United States.

Choyo no jo refers to one of five virtues, which Confucianism stresses as a construct of fundamental social relations. Although he did not mention the other four virtues regarding parent-child, master-subordinate, husband-wife, and friend-friend relations, these aspects are not irrelevant to his belief and value system.

By administering the vertical orders of social relations, in which the powerful control the weak, Japanese men had constructed masculinity in the feudal system over hundreds of years until the democratization of Japanese society after World War II. The legitimization of manliness called for the maintenance of the social hierarchy and the obedience to and respect for the order by its members. Japanese culture thus defines being manly as being loyal and devoted to one's superior and overarching social structure. David D. Gilmore, discussing the lingering qualities of Bushido or "way of the warrior" in Japanese conceptions of manhood, characterizes it as unquestioned loyalty to constituted authority, unshakable sincerity, self-control, and stoicism (Gilmore 1990, 188–91). In the sharp division of *ie*, this conception represents a category of purity by separation of a homogeneous group and ascetic immersion in a tradition.

In the performance of *taiko* by Japanese drummers, I see the traditional qualities of manhood that Gilmore observes. Tanaka was once known for a severe physical regimen of up to four miles of running, four hundred push-ups, and four hundred sit-ups before every practice and for striking students who did not measure up (Watanabe 1999). The master of the Japanese *taiko* group Ondekoza, later Kodo, was renowned for leading his group in a Spartan lifestyle to master the age-old arts (Kochi 1984). The group's performances were marked by almost totally naked bodily display except for a skimpy loincloth. The appearance not only showed the muscular development and strength of the male group members but also their extreme devotion to the group and their commitment to maintaining their cultural purity.

Tanaka was highly respected by Japanese Americans, but his emphasis on manly traditions of purity was also controversial among some *sansei* performers. Although the public presentation of Tanaka's *taiko* groups countered American popular culture representations of Japanese lack of manliness, some *sansei* also wanted to counter the Japanese image of the warmongering *samurai*. The *samurai* reference could suggest to Americans pre-war images of Japanese who blindly obey authority, follow the emperor, and provide a threat to American democracy. The bind of Japanese American men is to construct a tradition in the American context that neither signifies the eunuch role when they conformed to the model minority type or the barbaric, threatening yellow peril when they act defiantly before American eyes. This sensitivity was especially evident when Japan bashing erupted in the 1980s and 1990s fueled in part by the Hollywood film adaptation of Michael Crichton's best-selling novel *Rising Sun* in 1993, which depicted unflattering images of devious Japanese businessmen who surreptitiously devour American property and white women (Okihiro 1994, 138–39).

Kinnara Taiko was among the first Japanese American groups to depart from the manly tradition that Japanese *taiko* represented, while still striving to show continuity with Japanese folk roots, not choosing American masculinity as their alternative construction. Formed by Masao Kodani, a young minister of the temple, and *sansei* members of the Senshin Buddhist Temple in Los Angeles as the first Japanese American *taiko* group, Kinnara Taiko has supported the growth of the Japanese American Buddhist *taiko* (Hirabayashi and Hirabayashi 1998). The drumming of Kinnara derives from the folk religious ceremony of *horaku*—dharma entertainment with folk songs, staged dramas, and dances, which *issei* members had practiced at the Buddhist temple (Asai 1985, 164). A booklet, titled *Horaku,* in which Kodani wrote about Buddhist teachings, the basics of *taiko,* and making a drum from a wine barrel, has been influential in encouraging the spread of Buddhist *taiko* groups (Tep 1998, 54). Kodani's emphasis is on the wholesome earthy goodness of the peasant roots of the tradition. Kodani claims Kinnara Taiko is inspired by the majority of *issei* who had been from the peasant class (1998, 10). He states, "*Jodoshinshu* denomination of the Senshin Buddhist Temple had been of peasants, in contrast to Zen of *samurai* class" (10). Declaring the distinctiveness of *taiko* as a pre-assimilation Japanese tradition, he comments, "The Asian American movements were mainly led by *sansei* students and activists who belonged to Christian churches, not by those with Buddhist-peasant background" (11). While diverging in the representation of the tradition's folk roots, the two models of *taiko* in America both share the emphasis on the pre-assimilation expression of purity, lending a ritual context to the entertainment on stage.

Taiko spread from the West Coast to the East Coast in the 1970s, including the founding of Denver Taiko in 1976, Midwestern Buddhist Temple Taiko Group in 1977 in Chicago, and Soh Daiko in 1979 in New York (JACCC 1999, 29–62; 2001, 30–54).[8] Japanese American *taiko* flourished as Kinnara and many other groups were sponsored by a Buddhist temple, which has served as a historic center of religious and community life. Often the groups have to deal with a shortage of drums and create new folk adaptations. Beginners beat rubber tires, and leaders commonly make a drum out of a wine barrel (Mori 1998, 18).

The enlargement of the *taiko* movement further paralleled the heightening tension caused by a campaign to seek redemption for Japanese internment, called the Redress Movement. Many *sansei* during the 1970s and 1980s sought to correct injustices done to their parents and grandparents. Finding reluctance among elders in the Japanese American community to take on the federal government, students and activists formed the Japanese American Citizens League to advocate for the cause (Takezawa 1994; Maki, Kitano, and Berthold 1999). More forceful presentations of self such as *taiko* suggested a turn away from submission to a dominant society. In the theory of what James C. Scott calls "everyday resistance," marginalized groups that have a peasant mentality deriving from a feudal system would not risk "collective outright defiance" and "typically avoid any symbolic confrontation with authority or with elite norms" (1985, 29). But these "relatively powerless" groups often take ordinary cultural practices and adapt them as weapons of resistance.

Lon Yuki Kurashige points to an instance of *sansei*'s "everyday resistance" in the annual Nisei Week Festival in Little Tokyo, the largest celebration of Japanese American community. During the 1970s, *sansei* car cruisers and gangsters began to appear as troublemakers in the festival and thus annoyed the *nisei* authority, who had upheld the belief of the model minority and molded themselves into it. *Sansei* youth showed off custom-built cars, which they self-derogatorily called "Buddhaheads," and disturbed the festival traffic. According to one description,

> A Buddhahead car was permanently lowered all around, and while they comprised a wide variety of makes and models often were compact foreign imports, particularly Datsuns or Toyotas. Characteristic of these cars was an even paint job usually without much flash or sparkle, wide tires and rims neatly tucked under the car body's flared wheel wells, and a review "wink" mirror that extended across the top of the front windshield. According to former car cruiser Kevin Quock, the Sansei goal was to have a "clean" car without unnecessary frills, body adornments, or trinkets making it appear unsuitable for racing. While owners cruised their cars slowly to be seen and admired, they built them also for performance. Buddhahead cars were not known ultimately for being fast; they were not patterned after dragsters in a straight line. Rather, Sansei took pride in a vehicle's maneuverability around tight corners and curves, and in so doing appreciated this advantage of Buddhahead cars over more powerful "muscle" cars identified with White youth. (Kurashige 1994, 196)

Another form of resistance in the festival was gang fighting, which indicated the increase of youth delinquency among *sansei*. This drew notice in the popular press because of the unexpected violence of Japanese American youth. It broke the images of the obedient and effeminate Japanese American male.

The connection of the potency of *taiko* with the bold Redress Movement is apparent in developments within the Japanese American community during the 1980s and 1990s. In 1988 President Ronald Reagan signed the Civil Liberties Act, which declared remorse for the incarceration of Japanese Americans in internment camps. Activism continued, and in 1991 redress appropriations were passed (Maki, Kitano, and Berthold 1999, 201). In 1991 *taiko* performances were organized for the first time at two significant commemorations in the Japanese American community. In that year in Los Angeles, home of the largest Japanese American community in the United States, on the Day of Remembrance marking President Franklin D. Roosevelt's 1942 signing of Executive Order 9066 that forced Japanese Americans into camps, a group of *yonsei* (fourth-generation Japanese Americans) performed *taiko* (Maehara 1999, 1). Also in 1991, about three hundred people gathered for a pilgrimage to the Manzanar Camp in the eastern Mojave Desert, California, and according to the *Los Angeles Times*, "A Japanese *taiko* drum boomed over the empty valley, where bulldozers left only broken remains of the Manzanar barracks" (Feron 1991). Drumming historicized the victory of the Redress Movement and aroused recognition of continuity with the past among Japanese Americans. It also signaled a new emboldened ethnic identity symbolized by the manly potency of *taiko*.

The performance by *yonsei* on the Day of Remembrance was a promise that the history of their struggle would be handed down to another generation. In *taiko* performance in this historical event, implicit resistance has been coded. This connotation is simplified in the children's picture book *The Drum of Noto Hanto*, published in 1999. In the story children and adults of a small village in Japan a long time ago "used their wits and their courage to avoid a bloody battle they were sure to lose," and they played the drums of Noto Hanto (James 1999). The story is based on a local folk tale in Noto Hanto (Noto Peninsula) in Japan. The publication of this particular Japanese story expresses the significance of drumming in the United States, since the tale has not been widely known in Japan, because of its localized nature. A *taiko* performance, which the author of the book, J. Alison James, happened to see near her home in Vermont, and the story she heard from the drummers prompted her to visit Noto. The folk narrative in Noto, which James framed in the children's book, reveals that the Japanese tradition had given drumming a symbolic meaning of resistance and redemption for unmanly submission in the postwar years.

The construction of Japanese American masculinity in *taiko* has evolved as a result of challenges by Japanese American women. Women pointed out that men had not dominated *taiko* in Japanese history, since the ancient myths describe *taiko* as a religious instrument of the feminine *miko*. A frequently expressed explanation of the drum's sound by Japanese American performers equates the vibrations of *taiko* with a mother's heartbeats, which an embryo hears in her womb (Tanaka, interview by author, August 2001).[9] The explanation draws on ancient Japanese beliefs that a drum, made from animal skin and tree trunk, contains a life inside (Misumi 1990, 110; Nishitsunoi 2001, 3–5). In a counter-narrative, *taiko*'s roots are connected to the enforcement of Confucianism, particularly in Japan's seventeenth-century feudal system, when men in the ruling class redefined *taiko* as a male domain of *samurai* warriors. They developed the institution of *gungaku*, or "military band," featuring the beating of a drum to stir up courage and fighting spirits on the battlefield. Osuwa Taiko, innovator of the modern style of group drumming, claims it has its origin in *gungaku* in Nagano (Nishitsunoi 1985, 282–85).

Sansei women were involved in the *taiko* movement in the United States as participants and promoters of programs to teach *taiko* to their children (Kodani 1998, 10). Women's participation in leading and supporting *taiko* groups has been essential to the making of a Japanese American *taiko* tradition and to the maintenance of community ties. Increasing women's interest in *taiko* has been illustrated in the participation of women in the biennial Taiko Conference in Little Tokyo, at which performers all over from North America and Hawaii, as well as some professional groups from

Japan, have met since 1997. Women constituted roughly half of the five hundred participants in the past and surpassed the number of the men in the third meeting in 2001.

Thus the enhancement of manliness by Japanese male performers such as Tanaka, Ondekoza, and Kodo was also a reaction to women's empowerment, which had begun to undermine the traditional gender hierarchy of Japanese American society (Nishitsunoi 2001, 6–7).[10] Postwar social changes improved women's social status and removed many of the barriers of restricted spheres between Japanese men and women. There is a sense among leaders of the *taiko* movement that the revival of *taiko* in America required the participation of women if it was to be successful in rallying the whole community around a cultural tradition. The manliness in the performances could be interpreted as emboldening Japaneseness and not just the egos of men. At the 2001 Taiko Conference one female group from Japan called Hono Daiko donned costumes which exposed the exaggerated muscles of their backs as a sign of strength (Aoki et al. 2001, 17–22).

Somewhat to the surprise of early *taiko* organizers, women took up drumming with the idea that it could help break the stereotypes of gentle docility for Japanese women. As a form of resistance, single Japanese American women abandoned taking lessons in so-called womanly practices such as flower arrangement and tea ceremony, which the male dominant society once prescribed as prerequisites for a woman's goal of marriage (Matsumoto 1999, 298–300; Nakano 1990, 33–42). Instead, women intentionally appropriated drumming as an expression of men's culture (Radner and Lanser 1993). Typically in performances of *taiko,* women defiantly hold drumsticks over their head and hit the drums in a wide manly stance, while wearing men's costumes. Adopting the same symbols that embodied men's use of *taiko* for conveying manliness, women acted out a resistance against traditional male dominance and equally expressed social unity for the future of the Japanese American community. Within the *taiko* movement, female performers are known for cultivating the nuances of sounds and drum techniques while men tend to emphasize physical exertion and stamina (Tanaka, interview with author, August 2001).

The participation of women in *taiko* groups appears to be more significant for performances in America than for those in Japan. Japanese American women are more sensitive to the objectification of Asian women as submissive, erotic, and gentle, which have been inscribed in the Orientalist perceptions in Western history (Okihiro 1994, 14–15). There is also a sense that comes out of Asian American literature, however, that Asian American women feel more of a bond with and sympathy for the more socially restricted men and are therefore willing to accept, even encourage, their public construction of manliness (Iwasaki 2000, 21–22; Weiss 1973, 39). One Japanese American woman confesses she was "feeling guilty for not having an Asian boyfriend, feeling that I'm taking unfair advantage of my social and sexual mobility racially when Asian men don't have that mobility" (Kikumura and Kitano 1973, 78). Well aware of the performance of manliness in *taiko,* women typically seek performances alongside men.

One notable mixed group in which women play prominent roles is Ondekoza. The group based in Japan became renowned in their striking debut at the Boston Marathon in 1975 (Hayashi 1992, 201–202). Young members of Ondekoza, after running more than forty-two kilometers at the marathon, gave an impromptu performance at the finish line. The group's charismatic leader, Tagayasu Den, invited young aspirants around the country to the distant island of Sado in the Sea of Japan in the late 1960s. He envisioned launching a movement that directed young generations to save their folk traditions in a local community as well as setting up a university that provided prospective artisans with the teachings of folk arts and performances (Shimazaki 1996, 69–70). But unlike Japanese American groups featuring hyperkinetic bodily displays, this Japanese group was known for its stoic poses. Den conceived this emphasis on stance in response to the casual bodily demeanor encouraged by the Americanization of Japan. As Eitetsu Hayashi, an original member of the group, recalls, "Den was adamantly resolved to overwhelm white men, and his ardor created the uniquely stoic expressions of Ondekoza" (1992, 126). Den introduced the folk art of making the drums from gathered raw materials and the challenge of creating a mammoth drum from a single tree trunk. Den insisted on a severe training regimen and a loss of individualism by living communally in the isolation of Sado. The group's visits to the American West Coast energized Japanese American audiences. A community leader in Little Tokyo described the sensation of Ondekoza in 1978:

> The appreciation for Japanese *taiko* drumming received added impetus last year when the famous Ondekoza group from the Island of Sado electrified three over-flowing houses at the Wilshire Ebell Theater. In spite of the modest publicity campaign, the Ondekoza drummers, with their precision playing of a variety of *taiko,* including a 700-pound giant hollowed out from one huge tree trunk, not only received rave notices from the critics but standing ovations from the audiences which grew so large by word-of-mouth advertising that tickets were impossible to find for the last day's performances. (Kunitsugu 1978, 19)

Ondekoza served to reinforce the virility theme prevalent in American *taiko* groups. After the group's debut performance at the Boston Marathon, members returned annually in a striking display of bodily stamina and power. Den sought to revitalize a Japanese sense of manliness through *taiko* performance. He credited the 1943 film *Muhomatsu no issho* (or *The Rickshaw Man*)," which he had seen in his boyhood, for inspiration. The film, which was based on the popular novel *Tomishima Matsugoro den* (The Story of Tomishima Matsugoro), written by Shunsaku Iwashita in 1939, was re-made in 1958, 1963, and 1965, and the novel has also inspired plays and songs (Yomota 1996, 13). The film climaxes with the performance of *taiko* by the protagonist Muhomatsu. What appealed to Den about the film were class struggles of Meiji Japan, which Muhomatsu internalized in his *taiko* (Hayashi 1992, 69–70; Fujimoto 1996, 19). His occupation of driving rickshaw put him at the lower stratum of hierarchical order of artisanship (Tsukada 2000, 1–6). Not relying on craft skills to earn manly respect, Muhomatsu proved himself through the physical strength that his work required. Yet industrialization shattered the virtues of his strenuous work, and aging diminished his energy (Yomota 1996; Otsuki 1995).[11] In the face of industrialization's growing diminution of his manly role, the protag-onist uses the occasion of the Kokura Gion Festival to climb to the top of the scaffold and pound at the *taiko* drums defiantly in a call to Japanese folk tradition. With this artistic rendering in mind, Tanaka at the Cherry Blossom Festival in San Francisco and Ondekoza at the Boston Marathon invoked the ritual context to underscore the significance of *taiko*. For Ta-naka, the message was primarily intended for Japanese Americans, and for Ondekoza, it was for Americans.

The impetus of Muhomatsu's *taiko* display reached the West Coast dur-ing the 1960s. Johnny Mori, the original *sansei* member of Kinnara Taiko, saw *The Rickshaw Man* in a Los Angeles theater, and according to his recol-lection, he stayed in his seat for three showings (Mori 1998, 17).[12] The opening of the commemorative thirtieth-anniversary concert of Kinnara Taiko in 1999 began with a showing of the scene of Muhomatsu's *taiko* performance. Indeed, the film is mentioned in the concert brochure as inspiration for a new formulation of *taiko:* "Originally, our taiko was brought out once a year to accompany music during Obon, a summer cele-bration remembering those who have passed away. One year, inspired by a film we had recently seen called *Rickshaw Man* starring Toshiro Mifune, we began to beat on the drum rigorously, creating rhythms and patterns quite different from those traditionally played" (Kinnara Taiko 1999).

The pervasive influence of *The Rickshaw Man* in the development of *taiko*'s artisan class imagery is also evident in the widespread costumes of both Japanese and Japanese American *taiko* performers, who commonly put on *happi* (workman's coat or short kimono), *hachimaki* (headband), *momohiki* (workman's long underpants), *jikatabi* (workman's split-toed shoes with rubber soles), and *haragake* (workman's apron) (Hayashi 1992, 111–13; Yomota 1996, 17). The ensemble of these clothes reproduces the typical images of pre-industrial artisans and also typifies the familiar cos-tumes of *matsuri*, of which *taiko* was an important part. The dress shows their admiration for the manliness of artisans, which was proved in their performance of work and maintained in their male union. It also separated the modern symbolism of *taiko* from connections to commanding *samurai* and elite classes. Not only is there a construction of manliness along virtuous artisan lines inspired by the "natural" purity of Japanese pre-industrial tradition, but the dress, especially in the United States, could also use the reference to a victimized class to suggest the lingering subordinate racial position of Asians in America.

Typical of many *taiko* performers is the use of *fundoshi* (loincloths) on a naked body and *hachimaki* around the head. The look has been associated with the popular professional group Kodo on tours of the United States. Kodo was formed by members of Ondekoza, who disagreed with Den's dogmatic leadership and left to form their own version of *taiko* (Oi 1996; Aoki 1996).[13] After Kodo's "three sold-out appearances" at the 1984 Olympic Arts Festival in Los Angeles, *Los Angeles Herald Examiner* music critic Mark Swed took note of their pronounced manly display: "Glistening back muscles of a sweaty loin-clothed drummer are strikingly lit as he strikes the great *o-daiko* [large *taiko*] with massive sticks in a performance as much athletic as it is musical" (Swed 1984). The bodily display with *fundoshi,* often adopted by the Kodo performer, derives from Japanese religious purification rituals, such as *hadaka matsuri* (naked festival) and suggests the attire of ritualistic sumo wrestling as a national sport (Kubota 2000, 363). The use of male nakedness of the *taiko* performer implies that *taiko* is an unadorned natural "essence" of Japanese culture. In a naked festival, with the dissemination of the patriarchal values of the *samurai* class down to the peasant and artisan classes, the exposure of the body itself became the focus of attention, and participants competitively displayed their male virility.[14] *Fundoshi* is a Japanese icon that confirmed a man's sexual maturity in the pre-modern *samurai* class and was given to a boy to wear in rites of passage to manhood (Nagano 2001, 13–184).

Sexual imagery is implicit in many performances of *taiko*. Scott Schnell, for example, observed that in the ritual of *taiko* called *okoshi daiko,* commonly a part of *hadaka matsuri,* the two major male drummers were required to be single and the eldest son in each household:

> The *okoshi daiko* itself is pervaded by phallic symbolism—not surprising in a performance involving hundreds of young men inclined toward demonstrations of their virility. Perhaps the most visible manifestation involves the two young men positioned atop the drum. They are chosen partly based on their physiques, and the semi-naked condition accentuates their bodies. Both hold long sticks in vertical position, striking the drum with a swift downward motion, then raising their sticks slowly back into place in preparation for next strike. They are seated with the great drum positioned squarely between their legs, its thunderous peal emanating from the same locus. (Schnell 1999, 109)

If a drumstick represents the male member, the drum takes on female symbolism, and ritually pounding the revered maternal drum, particularly at spring fertility festivals, designates male-driven intercourse. In the construction of modern *taiko,* Tanaka, Den, and later Kodo declare through bodily display and the mounting of the seemingly insurmountable mammoth drum, virility, sexual power, in performances of group drumming. The sexually suggestive performance reinforces the manly demonstration of dominance, not for the traditional magical reference to fertility but for the projection of a naturally powerful Japanese identity.

Performance in *fundoshi* expresses Japanese male virility more explicitly than in artisan costumes, especially in the context of the 1980s when Americans associated Japanese artifice with technological miniaturization and gadgetry rather than natural bodily power (Okihiro 1994, 47).[15] American music critic Mark Swed displayed an uneasiness in this context when viewing the gyrations of *taiko* on stage. He wrote, "there are contradictions—a physical violence in the drumming that seems dangerously internalized as well as an eroticism of rhythm and performance that is made impersonal by the ritualistic nature of the presentation" (Swed 1984).

To be sure, *sansei* in Kinnara did not apply the virility theme of *taiko* to the degree of the other groups, although it still is concerned with the construction of Japanese American masculinity. The group emphasizes *taiko* as an expression of hybrid culture by invoking cultural roots in the peasant class, not the *samurai* class, and referring to the origin of their performances in the folk religious traditions of *horaku,* not the *gungaku* of warriors in the battlefield. It neither designates a master nor imposes a severe training regimen on their members (Kodani 1998, 12; Mori 1998, 12). The group stresses the egalitarian heritage of the peasant class. It neither recovers Japanese manliness nor appropriates the cowboy image of American masculinity. Since its history has centered on the Buddhist temple in multicultural Los Angeles, it has incorporated elements of African American and Hispanic musical traditions into performances. As the brochure for its thirtieth-anniversary concert states, "Our music draws from traditions in Japan, America and Buddhism. However it is not Japanese, nor is it American. It is a combination of many different musical influences which are part of our daily lives jazz, rock 'n' roll, latin, fusion, hip hop, etc." (Kinnara Taiko 1999).

Arguably, all Japanese American *taiko* groups express hybridity in their construction of manliness. Significantly, the groups recognize that the construction of manliness is the central image in conceptualizing new hybrid formations of Japaneseness (Lowe 1996). Group leaders understand that different perceptions of the appropriate directions for Japanese American practice exist within their community. *Taiko* performances create an imaginary festival, where conflicting forces of the community come together and negotiate their differences. In addition to the symbolic negotiations within the community, it is likely that the modern tradition of *taiko* will evolve as the belittling references to Japanese American masculinity in the larger society change. Whether male or female, *taiko* performers use the imaginary festival to address the clarification of Japaneseness, the bridging of generational differences, and the understanding of modernity. For an assimilating ethnic group within a modernizing nation, *taiko* variously performs a manly tradition to simultaneously convey resistance and harmony.

NOTES

1. Non-Japanese speakers are sometimes confused by the frequent usage of the word *daiko,* which is a suffix used to indicate a type of drum, a *taiko* group, or a style of *taiko* playing, in a compound word. When used in a compound word, the *t* sound in *taiko* changes to a *d* sound.

2. Tanaka borrowed a drum from a local Buddhist temple in the second festival. He formed his first *taiko* group with other newcomers from Japan.

3. Daihachi Oguchi in Nagano formed Osuwa Taiko in the 1950s and popularized the form of group drumming. He led the *taiko* performance in a group of one thousand drummers at the closing ceremony of the Nagano Winter Olympics.

4. Nishitsunoi classifies the form of drumming, which has been preserved in local festivals throughout Japan, by the number and kind of drums, the number of drummers, and the location—whether they are placed on a float, a portable shrine, or the ground. The form that predominated during the 1960s is characterized by use of plural drums and drummers with the drums placed on the ground.

5. Japanese Americans were allowed to have only what they could carry to the temporary assembly center.

6. Regarding folk traditions in temples, Asai states, "in most temples, elaborately staged plays in the Japanese language were presented." Thus, in the decline of the use of Japanese in the community, *taiko* would have replaced the Japanese language as intergenerational communication (Asai 1985, 163–64).

7. In a ritual for the harvest, for example, villagers beat *taiko* to wake up spirits of crops sleeping in the field or to induce raining, mimicking thunder by drumming (Misumi 1990, 111).

8. The website "Rolling Thunder: The Taiko Resource"—http://www.taiko.com/ (accessed September 30, 2004)—provides useful information and knowledge for drummers, such as up-to-date news within the *taiko* community, tips on how to start a *taiko* group, procurement of drums and costumes, and databases of *taiko* groups in North America as well as Asia and Europe.

9. I happened to hear the belief in an interview and a casual conversation with Japanese American informants, including Tanaka. In answer to the mention of this belief, another belief was expressed that if babies accompany their parents to *taiko* lessons, they fall asleep with no problem despite the loudness of drumming.

10. The first female drummer, Kimiko Kawada, began to perform onstage in the early 1960s. Women then joined male groups but were not featured performers until the 1990s. *Taikology,* a popular magazine among Japanese *taiko* performers, frequently carries profiles of female *taiko* "stars."

11. Known as a roughneck in his youth, he got his nickname, Muho-matsu, which combines *muho* (outlaw) with part of his first name, Matsugoro. The story's setting in northern Kyushu is where the Meiji government built the first national steel factory in 1900 to spearhead modernization.

12. Following the awarding in 1951 of the Golden Lion Award to *Rashomon*—directed by Akira Kurosawa—the first Japanese film to be so honored, *The Rickshaw Man,* directed by Hiroshi Inagaki, was the second to receive the award.

13. After Den left Sado, the members of Ondekoza changed the group name to Kodo in 1981 to gain a fresh start. Den used the name Ondekoza later to form his new group and resumed his participation in the Boston Marathon.

14. According to Chizuko Ueno, the Meiji dissolution of the Tokugawa period class system "meant not the 'commoner-ization' of the samurai class but the 'samurai-zation' of the commoners" (Schnell 1999, 195).

15. Okihiro cites *Rising Sun* by Michael Crichton as an example of a depiction of the Japanese as "New warriors, in business suits carrying attaché cases filled with yen, buy[ing] political influence in Washington" (1994, 138–39).

REFERENCES

Aoki, Takao, 1996. "Kodo to iu shudan-ga miru yume" [The dream of the Kodo group]. *Taikology* 14: 20–25.

Aoki, Takao, Akitoshi Asano, Hiroshi Ota, Masahito Ohashi, Masaaki Tsuchida, and Masahiro Nishitunoi. 2001. "Bodaresu jidai no taiko ron" [On drumming in the borderless age]. *Taikology* 18: 12–29.

Asai, Susan. 1985. "*Horaku:* A Buddhist Tradition of Performing Arts and the Development of Taiko Drumming in the United States." *Selected Titles in Ethnomusicology* 6: 163–72.

Feron, Sonni. 1991. "To Manzanar." *Los Angeles Times,* April 28, B1, 12.

Fromartz, Samuel. 1998. "Anything but Quiet." *Natural History* 104, no. 2: 44–48.

Fujimoto, Yoshikazu. 1996. "Oni ga utsu taiko, ningen ga utsu taiko" [Drumming by a demon, drumming by a man]. *Taikology* 14: 15–19.

Gilmore, David D. 1990. *Manhood in the Making: Cultural Concepts of Masculinity.* New Haven: Yale University Press.

Hayashi, Eitetsu. 1992. *Ashita no taiko uchi e* [For the drummer of tomorrow]. Tokyo: Shobunkaku.

Hirabayashi, Roy, and P. J. Hirabayashi. 1998. "Nikkei Beikokujin no supirito wo motomete" [Looking for a Japanese American Spirit]. *Taikology* 16: 22–27.

Honda, Yasuji. 1990. "Geino to taiko" [Performing arts and drumming]. In *Minzoku geino* 2 [Folk performing arts], ed. Masahiro Nishitsunoi, 105–108. Tokyo: Ongaku-no-tomo-sha.

Iino, Masako. 2000. *Mouhitotsu no Nichi-Bei kankeishi: Funso to kyocho no naka no Nikkei Amerikajin* [Another history of Japan–U.S. relations: Japanese Americans in conflict and cooperation]. Tokyo: Yuhikaku.

Inoki, Takenori. 2000. *Keizai seicho no kajitsu 1955–1972* [Achievements of economic growth, 1955–1972]. Tokyo: Chuo Koronsha.

Iwasaki, Naomi. 2000. "Don't Play Yourself." *Gidra* 1, no. 3: 21–22.

James, J. Alison. 1999. *The Drums of Noto Hanto.* Illustrated by Tsukushi. New York: Dorling Kindersley.

Japanese American Cultural and Community Center (JACCC). 1999. *The 1999 Taiko Conference.* Conference booklet.

———. 2001. *The 2001 Taiko Conference.* Conference booklet.

Kikumura, Akemi, and Harry H. L. Kitano. 1973. "Interracial Marriage: A Picture of the Japanese Americans." *Journal of Social Issues* 29, no. 2: 67–81.

Kinnara Taiko. 1999. *Kinnara Kara 2543: 30 Years of Iroiro*. Concert booklet.

Kochi, Georg. 1984. "Kodo Hammers Energy into Art." *Calendar*, June 17, 56.

Kodani, Masao. 1998. "Ego o sutete taiko o enjoi suru" [Cast aside the ego and enjoy drumming]. *Taikology* 16: 10–12.

Konagaya, Hideyo. 2001. "*Taiko* as Performance: Creating Japanese American Traditions." *Japanese Journal of American Studies* 12: 105–24.

Kubota, Hiromichi. 2000. "Hadaka matsuri" [Naked festival]. In *Nihon minzoku daijiten* [Dictionary of Japanese folklore], ed. Ajio Fukuda, Naoki Shintani, Hiroshi Yukawa, Yoriko Kanda, Mutsuko Nakagome, and Yoshio Watanabe, 363. Tokyo: Yoshikawa Kobunkan.

Kunitsugu, Kango. 1978. "Drums of the Festivals." *1978 Nisei Week*. Festival booklet.

Kurashige, Lon Yuki. 1994. "Made in Little Tokyo: Politics of Ethnic Identity and Festival in Southern California, 1934–1994." Ph.D. diss., University of Wisconsin–Madison.

Lee, Steven M. 2001. "'All the Best Cowboys Have Chinese Eyes': The Utilization of the Cowboy-Hero Image in Contemporary Asian-American Literature." In *Across the Great Divide: Cultures of Manhood in the American West*, ed. Matthew Basso, Laura McCall, and Dee Garceau, 231–49. New York: Routledge.

Lowe, Lisa. 1996. *Immigrant Acts: On Asian American Cultural Politics*. Durham, N.C.: Duke University Press.

Machara, G. Akito. 1991. "Commemoration to Focus on Campus." *Rafu shimpo*, February 19.

Maki, Mitchell T., Harry H. L. Kitano, and S. Megan Berthold. 1999. *Achieving the Impossible Dream: How Japanese Americans Obtained Redress*. Urbana: University of Illinois Press.

Matsumoto, Valerie J. 1999. "Japanese American Women and the Creation of Urban Nisei Culture in the 1930s." In *Over the Edge: Remapping the American West*, ed. Valerie J. Matsumoto and Blake Allmendinger, 291–306. Berkeley: University of California Press.

Misumi Haruo. 1990. "Taiko to matsuribayashi" [Taiko and festival music]. In *Minzoku geino* 2 [Folk performing arts], ed. Masahiro Nishitsunoi, 109–13. Tokyo: Ongaku-no-tomo-sha.

Mori, Johnny. 1998. "Tada taiko o tataite-iru Dake-nanada" [I'm just beating a drum]. *Taikology* 16: 17–21.

Nagano, Hiroko. 2001. *Nihon kinsei noson ni okeru masukyuriniti no kochiku to jenda* [Constructions of masculinity and gender in a pre-modern Japanese village: On organization and power relations]. Tokyo: Sanseido.

Nakano, Mei. 1990. *Japanese American Women: Three Generations, 1890–1990*. Berkeley, Calif.: Mina Press.

Nishitsunoi, Masahiro. 1985. *Sairei to furyu* [Festival and folk entertainment]. Tokyo: Iwasaki Bijutsusha.

———. 1990. *Nihon no taiko no bunrui kaisetsu* [A classification and description of Japanese drumming]. In *Minzoku geino* 2, 118–23.

———. 2001. "Onna ga utsu taiko" [Drumming by women]. *Taikology* 18: 2–9.

Oi, Yoshiaki. 1996. "Ondekoza, 1970-nen no tabidachi-kara Kodo-e" [Ondekoza, from its 1970 debut to Kodo]. *Taikology* 14: 8–14.

Okihiro, Gary Y. 1994. *Margins and Mainstreams: Asians in American History and Culture*. Seattle: University of Washington Press.

Otsuki, Takahiro. 1995. *Muhomatsu no kage* [The shadow of Muhomatsu]. Tokyo: Mainichi Shinbunsha.

Radner, Joan N., and Susan S. Lanser. 1993. "Strategies of Coding in Women Cultures." In *Feminist Messages: Coding in Women Folk Culture*, ed. Joan Newlon Radner, 1–29. Urbana: University of Illinois Press.

Schnell, Scott. 1999. *The Rousing Drum: Ritual Practice in a Japanese Community.* Honolulu: University of Hawaii Press.

Scott, James C. 1985. *Weapons of the Weak: Everyday Forms of Peasant Resistance.* New Haven, Conn.: Yale University Press.

Shimazaki, Makoto. 1996. "Hensen: Kyu Ondekoza-kara Kodo-e, Soshite Kodo no Mirai-e" [Transformation: From the Ondekoza of the past to Kodo, and to the future of Kodo]. *Taikology* 14: 69–75.

Swed, Mark. 1984. "Kodo: The Rockettes of Japanese Folk Music." *Los Angeles Herald,* June 28, C1, 7.

Tachiki, Amy. 1971. Introduction to *Roots: An Asian American Reader,* ed. Amy Tachiki, Eddie Wong, Franklin Odo, and Buck Wong, 1–5. Los Angeles: UCLA Asian American Studies Center Press.

Takezawa, Yasuko. 1994. *Nikkei Amerikajin no esunishiti: Kyosei shuyo to hosho undo ni yoru hensen* [The transformation of Japanese American ethnicity: The effects of internment and redress]. Tokyo: Tokyo Daigaku Shuppankai.

Tanaka, Seiichi. 1998. "Hokubei no taiko sanjyunen o furikaeru" [Looking back at thirty years of *taiko* in North America]. *Taikology* 16: 13–16.

Tep, Elsie Okada. 1998. "Kusa no ne kara no taiko no hatten" [The grassroots development of taiko]. *Taikology* 16: 53–57.

Tsukada, Takashi. 2000. *Shokunin, oyakata, nakama* [Artisans, masters, peers]. Tokyo: Yoshikawa Kobunkan.

Uematsu, Amy. 1971. "The Emergence of Yellow Power in America." In *Roots: An Asian American Reader,* ed. Amy Tachiki, Eddie Wong, Franklin Odo, and Buck Wong, 9–13. Los Angeles: UCLA Asian American Studies Center Press.

Watanabe, Teresa. 1999. "A Taiko Tradition: Bang the Drum Loudly." *Los Angeles Times,* July 30, F2, 28.

Weiss, Melford S. 1971. "Selective Acculturation and the Dating Process: The Patterning of Chinese-Caucasian Interracial Dating." In *Roots: An Asian American Reader,* ed. Amy Tachiki, Eddie Wong, Franklin Odo, and Buck Wong, 37–43. Los Angeles: UCLA Asian American Studies Center Press.

Yanagawa, Keiichi. 1972. "Shinwa to taiko no matsuri" [Festivals of affinity and opposition]. *Shiso* 582: 66–77.

Yanagisako, Sylvia J. 1985. *Transforming the Past: Tradition and Kinship among Japanese Americans.* Stanford: Stanford University Press.

Yomota, Inuhiko. 1996. "Yuigon-jo wa okuri todokerareta no ka?" [Was his will sent out?]. *Taikology* 13: 17–23.

5

"I Feel That I'm Freer to Show My Feminine Side": Folklore and Alternative Masculinities in a Rave Scene

ANTHONY P. AVERY

It's around 11:45 P.M., and I am putting my barrettes on. It's Saturday night, and I am going to a rave party called "One" outdoors in the New Mexico desert. This is Family Production's one-year anniversary party. We hop into the car and caravan with my crew of "candy kids." We call ourselves candy kids because of the outrageous costumes we wear and the music we enjoy dancing to: happy hardcore, a techno genre which is really fast (more than 170 beats per minute) with cheesy lyrics like "I need your lovin' like the sunshine." I don oversized pants and bring plastic bracelets and necklaces that we make ourselves to trade and wear. Tonight I am wearing a tight blue shirt and a baby-blue faux fur visor. Lest it not be clear, I should say that I am a man, a young white male raver.

We finally arrive at One and pay a ten-dollar admission fee to help cover the expenses of the DJs and space. As we walk into the "3 Sided Hole" we are surrounded by video loops projected on the cliffs and loud-thumping music. We hug our friends and begin to dance facing the DJ. A dirt floor serves as a dance area. Over three hundred young people of different ages and races are in attendance. I walk over to one set of speakers and put on my white gloves, stretch my arms over my head, and begin to jog in place. This is not just a party—this is part of a rave "scene" and community.

I first began raving in Toronto, Ontario, back in the spring of 1994. I became enthralled with the dancing, the music, and the friendly people. I joined others who took off their shirts and danced until morning. The talk was of gaining release of one's body through dance. The following June I bought a one-way bus ticket from Buffalo, New York, to San Francisco, the rave capital of the United States. Soon after arriving, I went to a New Moon beach rave and an all-day rave at Golden Gate Park. I joined a self-described rave community. The "ravers," as they were called, took me in with open arms and gave me places to stay.

Rave is a dance party with origins in Acid House from Chicago, techno from Detroit, and garage from New York, according to Hillegonda Rietveld

(1993). Rietveld traces the music to material played in mainly black gay clubs, especially the Warehouse in Chicago and Paradise Garage in New York (1993, 41). As a social dance scene, the rave arose from Acid House parties in England, "that heady mix of house 'n' E [Ecstasy, 4-Methylenedi-oxyphetamine or MDMA] dance events in 1988"; these parties were followed by "various moral panics that involved the regulation of body technologies such as loud dancing music and dance drugs" (Rietveld 1998, 254). Raves are also a type of "Temporary Autonomous Zone" (TAZ). A TAZ, according to its proponents, is a guerilla operation which liberates an area (of land, time, imagination) and then dissolves itself to re-form elsewhere before the state can crush it (Bey 1991, 101). The rave folk event is usually a one-night party; moreover, there may be several separate parties in one weekend.

The folk roots of rave reach back to the "happenings" of the 1960s. They were huge gatherings of young people indulging in music and dance (Gore 1997, 54). A continuity with happenings in the "contemporary dance scene" is the attempt to bridge divisions such as gender and race in a mass communal display. Rave is, in part, then, a site for an idealistic political consciousness; reminiscent of the happening scene, it is a politics of peace and pleasure.

The significance of the rave social world for many young men is that they are free to express ecstatic emotions on the dance floor without fear of homophobic harassment. In youth culture, rave men often distinguish themselves from other men engaging in the "macho" world of team sports. That is not to say that rave men do not consider themselves manly. Rave allows young men a location for pursuing alternative paths of masculinity that integrate effeminacy. It is not necessarily a gay identity. Straight men often experience the rave scene as a manly tradition to step, if only temporarily, outside emotional repression and expressed aggression associated with manliness (Gilbert and Pearson 1999, 97). For females, the absence of the heterosexual male gaze means being able to dance freely without being sexually harassed (McRobbie 1994). My thesis is that rave attracts many young men because it is a safe shared space to explore alternative masculinities based on a developed value system of "Peace, Love, Unity, and Respect" (PLUR) at the core of a constructed folk event.

Relying on my own experience in the rave community during the 1990s and afterward in an ethnographic position at rave events in Albuquerque, New Mexico, this essay interprets the attitudes of men in a regional rave scene. My ethnographic observations especially noted uses of the dancing male body to legitimate a feminine masculinity for men. My main research problem is to evaluate change in young men's ideas of masculinity from normative views in popular culture while at rave events. My research objective was to account for the attraction of rave for young men. The men were aware of normative views in popular culture that masculinity involved

Author posing at a Rave in a castle in Pueblo,
Colorado, May 1998.

positions of autonomy, competition, and aggressiveness, and the suppression of intimacy and self-disclosure, which have been traditionally devalued as feminine traits (Philaretou and Allen 2001, 301).

In addition to utilizing participant observation in my research, I also distributed questionnaires and conducted in-person interviews. "Respondents" were young men in either high school or college. I use the term "respondent" because they "determined the data and the direction of the investigation" (Lewis and Ross 1995, 216). In addition to receiving a list of questions, respondents looked at a statement of the above research aims. All agreed to sign a written consent form that assured confidentiality.

Looking at the rave scene ethnographically provided a challenge to event analysis, because of the approach I took to account culturally for men as *men* in contemporary life. While comparative material exists for the role of men as social actors, much less is available on men *as men* and particularly on their attitudes toward manliness. I am motivated by a goal of the critical study of men and masculinities, as stated by Laurence Goldstein, "to recover from history, and from empirically observed behaviors in the present day, that sense of choice and variety in self-definition that so many women have embraced as a means of personal and social liberation" (1994, vii). The tools of folklore studies are significant in this endeavor for interpreting the construction of traditions in emergent groups and the values expressed from cultural practices (Abrahams 1983; Bronner 1988).

At raves, men express emotions often in contradistinction to what many gender theorists call "hegemonic masculinity." Hegemonic masculinity promotes the tough, take-charge, insensitive image of men. It frequently dominates the socialization process in spite of increasing efforts to develop other masculinities and femininities (Disch 2000, 5). An approach to defining hegemonic masculinity is suggested by Deborah David and Robert Brannon, who assign distinctive "manly" traits to folktypes:

- *"The sturdy oak."* Men should be stoic, stable, and independent. A man never shows weakness. Accordingly, boys are not to share pain or grieve openly.
- *"Give 'em hell."* This is the stance of some of our sports coaches, of roles played by John Wayne, Clint Eastwood, and Bruce Lee, a stance based on a false self, of extreme daring, bravado, and attraction to violence. This injunction stems largely from the myth that "boys will be boys" . . . the misconception that somehow boys are biologically wired to act like macho, high-energy, even violent supermen.
- *"The big wheel."* This is the imperative men and boys feel to achieve status, dominance, and power. Or, understood another way, the "big wheel" refers to the way in which boys and men are taught to avoid shame at all costs, to wear the mask of coolness, to act as though everything is going all right, as though everything is under control, even if it isn't . . .
- *"No sissy stuff."* Perhaps the most traumatizing and dangerous injunction thrust on boys and men is the literal gender straitjacket that prohibits boys from expressing feelings or urges seen (mistakenly) as "feminine"—dependence, warmth, empathy. According to the ideal of "no sissy stuff," such feelings and behaviors are taboo. Rather than being allowed to explore these emotional states and activities, boys are prematurely forced to shut them out, to become self-reliant. (Pollack 1998, 23–25; see also Baldwin et al. 1999, 123; Jay Mechling's chapter in this volume)

Compared to this model of normative masculinities, alternative masculinities tend to be based on cooperation and a folk idea of "coolness" defined generally as a cultural sensitivity and social tolerance. In claiming an alternative masculinity, ravers repudiate homophobia, misogyny, and violence. What is important at raves, many respondents claimed, is maintaining "the happy and friendly vibe." A problem of altering perception exists, however, if this maintenance of an alternative masculinity is not to be inexorably linked to homosexuality. After all, open displays of happiness, "auto-erotic" pleasure, "friendliness," and enjoyment of dance are traditionally more closely associated with femininity and gay male culture (Pini 1997).

Addressing the normative perceptions of manliness, ravers offered the following images:

> From society you hear: Get out there and work, bring home the bacon, have a wife barefoot and pregnant in the kitchen. You have to be the tough guy. You gotta be the man, don't show your emotions. (Kid Kinetic 2000)

> I think the image of the American male and masculinity can be different. But lately, there is a trend that men have to be in superb shape (six pack, biceps, etc.) with a deep voice and strong overpowering nature. (SpinDomino 2002)

> Big, strong, tough guy. (Emanon 2001)

> The American Christian soldier. *Sir.* The man who hates "queers," plays football, and dates the captain of the cheerleading squad. Also the guy who plays paintball, and talks about guns. The testosterone drivin' Alpha-Male. (Carl 2002)

In response to these perceptions of manliness in a real-world setting, one form of social construction for rave events is to locate them in settings that lend themselves to cultural transformation. Raves take place largely in post-industrial landscapes, transforming rundown warehouse sites into timeless, de-localized and de-realized spaces, where the obsolete industrial infrastructure is juxtaposed with state-of-the-art technology to create a surreal, almost virtual world—a fun factory (Richard and Kruger 1998, 163). In New Mexico, raves occur at airport hangars, unused warehouses, and esoteric desert landscapes near canyons. The rave event moves between commercial and private settings, and in its private forms, can be illegal (Ward 1997, 4).

While raves attract those who love to dance, they also attract those who prefer to mix dancing with drugs such as Ecstasy, Ketamine, and GHB (Vontz 2001, 2). Non–drug users argue that the rave folk event is conducive for mind expansion without drugs because the sensory overload at raves alters consciousness and notions of everyday reality. Those who choose to ingest drugs often self-identify by wearing drug paraphernalia. For example, they rub a vapor gel under their noses for an additional buzz, bite on pacifiers to stop from grinding their teeth or hang them simply as a fashion accessory, wear dust masks to enhance the effects of the vapor rub—and sometimes just to keep the dance floor dust out of their systems (Brown 2001, 3).

More prevalent than drug paraphernalia on men at raves is young men's frequent adornment with women's fashion accessories. Male ravers could be seen shopping at Claire's in the local mall for feather boas and lip gloss. Is this cross-dressing, and if it is, how is masculinity affected?

What happens at raves is not the kind of cross-dressing present at manly traditions such as fraternity beauty pageants where manliness is enhanced because the idea that men would act feminine is ridiculed (Bronner 1995, 99). It is not the kind of scene described by ethnographers James Spradley and Brenda Mann in a male-dominated bar where men would pretend to order feminine-sounding cocktails from female servers to underscore the silliness of such an act for their identity (Spradley and Mann 1975, 139–41). It is not costuming either of the type at Halloween parties or Mardi Gras, where a carnivalesque atmosphere reigns and gender *reversals* are tolerated. The difference at raves is that men are not ridiculing femininity but are showing their openness to it as a signifier of masculine difference from hegemonic masculinity. Gender *fusions* are encouraged as part of building a new identity through a folk event (Dundes 1983). The festive, magical zone of the raves gives men license to engage in displays of such fashion that would not be appropriate elsewhere. To be sure, men will often take off their shirts in a classic display of muscularity, as a result of the overwhelming heat of collective bodies dancing together. Most male ravers would maintain that their baring their chest was a sign of being "lost in dance" and a symbolic freedom from their previously restricted "self."

Groupness forms at rave events from the mutual awareness of dancers that they are forming a mass social display. Expected to dance, no matter what the skill, participants express solidarity with one another. At a rave I attended in Cleveland, Ohio, participants danced by crisscrossing each other. Spontaneous social dancing in dynamic group formation either through unison movement (hands stretched above the head) or individual free-style movements is a hallmark of the global rave culture. Using Arnold Van Gennep's (1960) model of rites of passage proceeding from social separation to a transition period and finally to incorporation, Lynnette Lewis and Michael Ross have suggested that contemporary dance parties create spaces for alternative gender and sexual roles by giving a sense of moving from a worldly reality to a new social stage in which different values are primary. These social engagements, in their words, "provide the social vehicle for the enactment of social transformation (separation from their everyday reality), for a prescribed period of time (transitory) and re-integration (or incorporation) back into the wider social order" (Lewis and Ross 1995, 136).

A recognized feature of raves is that people of different classes, sexualities, and races dance together and form a new community configuration

(Bradby 1993, 66). Rave events in Albuquerque, New Mexico, typically include a mix of trance dancers from Mexican, Hispanic, Mestizo, African American, American Indian, and Anglo backgrounds found in the region. I asked rave respondents how ethnicity and race figured into their identities. Representative answers were:

> Racial identity is dropped from raving because everyone is loved by everyone, and accepted for who they are. (Mr. E. 1999)

> There are a lot of different ethnic groups, and I have to say that they're pretty mixed in, pretty fine with each other. I don't see anybody having any problems with any ethnic groups at a rave. (Kairo 1999)

> Rave seems to offer an open door policy, where anyone can feel welcome. (Paul 2002)

If ethnicity appeared to be diminished in its importance, then gender loomed large, since men and women were aware of the cultural association of dance with femininity. Angela McRobbie has pointed out, for example, that "dance is where girls were always found in subcultures. It was their only entitlement. Now in rave it becomes the motivating force for the entire subculture. This gives girls a new-found confidence and prominence" (1994, 169). In many responses I received to questions about gender attitudes and behaviors at raves, there was a claim to equality while recognizing differences of identity:

> I like to talk to and meet anyone in rave culture, and try to get to know them, whether they're male, female, gay, bi. Raving is not discrimination. (Elfie 1999)

> Gender is significant but it doesn't bring about a structured power dynamic. I mean there are a lot of people who dress androgynously; there are males who dress machismo, or girls who dress as little girls, or hippychick types. I mean people feel free very much to express their gender, or even exaggerate their own gender in the way they dress. (Adam 1999)

If the dance literature suggests sexual empowerment for girls, the question arises as to what raving does for men. Arguably, men are metonymically transformed into "new men" through the use of Ecstasy; they undergo a conversion to a soft, malleable, and sociable folktype and enter into a different relationship with their bodies that is more tactile, more sensuous, and less focused around sexual gratification (McRobbie 1994, 168). Rave respondents discussed the transformation in rave events on masculinity this way:

> I think it's getting men to think about their bodies. And not necessarily as an object, though, which I think happens at clubs, weight-lifting gyms, and that sort of thing. (Adam 1999)

I guess it helps the males in the scene to be more open-minded. Like I can tell from talking to my friends. I think they are a lot more open-minded and a lot nicer, towards, like, homosexuality. (Skunky Cheese 1999)

It's letting them be themselves. They don't have to put up this front, or act all tough in front of their friends; they can be who they want to be from their heart. They don't have to put up some kind of wall of masculinity. They can just be themselves, whether you're gay or straight; everybody's cool that way. (East 1999)

Rave is teaching men to express more of their feminine side, and be open to new experiences. (Kid Kinetic, 2000)

Rave is connecting them to others, the earth, and their feminine side. (Paul 2002)

It's giving us the opportunity to escape. Whether it's from the stigmas of life, or the troubles of work. One can go to a rave, and act or be however they want, and not be ridiculed. It's a place of acceptance. (Carl 2002)

I think that more males are learning to not worry so much about the macho thing. (Emanon 2001)

The awareness of transformation comes through in references to a rave value system known as PLUR. Like the cant of con men, the jargon of educators, and the slang of youth, it is a means of identification (Richmond 1983, xi).

A source for this value system is in the 1980s when British white youth club culture appropriated the distinctively underground gay African American house music and blended psychedelia and European avant-garde electronic music to form a musical hybrid known tongue-in-cheek as Acid House. De-emphasizing race and sexuality in this hybridity and proclaiming a unity of youth, the music became led by techno-shamanistic DJs. Mostly men, they were associated with male leadership and legitimated male (dance) participation in the scene. Dancers attributed magical powers of transformation to the DJs, and figures such as New Mexican DJ Donovan understand their functions in inciting mass display of unity:

James had an idea to open a record store, but in a place where we could afford. We moved into a 2000 square foot space right smack between two churches. The first night we were there, our friend Christy had already called it the good vibe house, so we dubbed it the House of Vibes. In the months to come, we simply hung about, mixing records, taking drugs, and throwing parties on the weekends to pay the rent. We would get a hundred people. Soon, people were coming to the party and never leaving. I always felt that I've had many roles in the growth of our culture. From DJ to Promoter; I've done it all. For me as a DJ, I always try to get the people moving, get them dancing. Through that pursuit I have developed what I call omni-style. (Donovan)

A dialectical relationship exists between the dancers and DJs at raves. That is to say, the dancers may influence the choice of records the DJ may spin, and the DJ, in turn, may inspire intricate dance patterns from the dancers; the music from the DJ shapes the pace and performance of dancing. The practices of DJ-ing and dancing functionally fit into the definition of folklore, as expressed by Toelken, because "they are mainly learned orally, by imitation, or in performance, and are generally maintained without benefit of formal instruction or institutional direction" (1996, 9). To the ravers, led by the shamanistic DJ, participating in a primal activity of dance, surrounded by the music in an unreal space, the rave scene appears to be an enactment of ritual embodiment.

Notices of rave events are circulated orally through a conduit of friends, materially through distribution of flyers, and electronically through the Internet. In this case the cultural (re)production of rave expands the definition of folklore to include informal communication expressed electronically. The New Mexico rave website has an events calendar, which lists upcoming desert rave parties. One can click on the flyer to retrieve the information telephone line to call for directions to the event. Folks call a few hours before the rave and then will journey to a warehouse, field, or other esoteric places. A person may pay an admission fee and then proceed through a threshold (i.e., curtains), entering the realm of the liminal. The liminal is the boundary-realm of ritual whereby participants are in a "time-out-of-time" realm. Liminality is a cultural manifestation of *communitas* (Turner 1969, 109). *Communitas* is that leveling of all differences in ecstasy that so often characterizes performing (Schechner 1988, 119).

Raves generate a liminal existence, ritually separating, by various means, the ordinary world from the dance environment (Langlois 1992, 236). For instance, when entering the rave, folks are bombarded with mind-altering sensations, including lasers, black lights, smoke, and a thundering bass, of the myriad musical styles of techno. The participants dance as soon as they enter the rave, while hugging their friends. When dancing, folks either emulate each other or develop new dance steps. Dance offers a way of experiencing the music which cannot help but foreground the materiality and physicality of that experience (Gilbert and Pearson 1999, 105). I asked rave respondents about their ritualistic experiences at raves, and here are some representative answers:

> I recall one time when I was dancing to one of the most amazing trance sets I've heard in quite some time, I met eyes with some girl on the dance floor. We locked gazes and we danced from across the dance floor almost in synchronization. We slowly came together, and began dancing within 5 feet of each other. Soon our movements became one, and we danced like the same person. It was an incredible experience, and I will never forget it. (Carl 2002)

At a very critical time in my life, I experienced the magic on the dance floor one night. I was going through a break up at the time, and was just generally down in the dumps in a pretty big way. When the headlining act came on (Dubtribe) I was totally blown away. They make all of their own music, and one of the group members (Moonbeam) was doing some really tribal chants, as well as putting out very positive lyrics through the microphone. Basically the things he said were just what I needed, and I really connected with the music in a special way that night. I've never danced so hard in my life. I also discovered a different way to dance that night. For the first time I was really moving around a lot, doing spins. The movements just flowed out of my body so naturally. Combine the music with the lyrics and my need for the both of them, and you get the magic. (Emanon 2001)

The music is like a drug, when I hear a beat, I resonate with it, sometimes it's hard not to move. Dancing is a way of going into a deep meditative trance state for me. That's when I am closest to god. My most special moments include dancing at sunrise. (Paul 2002)

One of the greatest experiences is dancing with a friend and anticipating each other's moves and dancing in each other's styles and keeping eye contact with each other whole time. It's an amazing feeling. The most important thing for me is to let my body tell me what it is going to do not for me to tell my body what to do. (SpinDomino 2002)

The rhetoric of "trance" is important in the views expressed by ravers. Raves have been described as an ecstatic continuous dance, and the reference to trance offers another unifying strategy between men's and women's roles (Richard 1998, 12). The "trance" denaturalizes the gendered gestures found in exhibition social dance, whereby the man leads the woman. When people trance dance, trance is experienced by the stretching of the arms over the head, shoulder-width apart, palms up, while jogging in place to the repetitive rhythms and loud bass of the sound system, guided by the techno-shaman DJ. Rave trance dance is a synthesis of African and European American dance styles such as the Pentecostal church dances (stretching of the arms) and a hip-hop dance known as the Running Man (jogging in place). Sociologist Herman Gray points out that the Running Man may mime the common experiences of young black men being chased by the police (Rose 1994, 49–50). Additionally, the appropriation by white youth of African American styles—given the disproportionate black role in popular music and athletics—implies loosening of cultural norms suppressing bodily gyrations and self-awareness of one's bodily display (West 1994, 12). The confidence with which male dancers use their body suggests a restoration of manliness within the feminized activity of dance, as this representative response from a raver indicates:

I just let myself go. I used to be afraid to dance but again, the acceptance of the rave scene allowed me to build a lack of caring how others thought I was. So, I began to just let the music take me where it wanted to take me. (Carl 2002)

The rave "trance" emphasizes individual bodily display, for dancers perform ecstatic dance steps usually without a partner. While reducing the binary of masculine and feminine, it also underscores for men the need to be accepting of one's own body, rather than strive for the manly status of conspicuous muscular display.

Compared historically to other dance forms, raves take on a distinctive structure. The waltz brought the sexes together in an intimate movement style; the twist as a rebellious, sexually suggestive form of solo dancing of the 1960s separated the sexes, but dancers still faced one another. Disco dancing was significant during the 1970s for bringing same-sex couples on the dance floor and validating the male dancer in vernacular culture. Ecstatic trance dance uncouples heterosexuality and homosexuality from social dance by encouraging autoerotic free dance styles while facing the DJ.

Unlike the pick-up scene of disco clubs during the 1970s with the DJ securely in the background, raves are curiously asexual, or pre-sexual, environments, with DJs more at the forefront. These features can be linked, at least in part, to concern for AIDS, which provides a "text of anxiety" or of "avoidance" that results in the downplaying of sexual activity (Tomlinson 1998, 200). Sexual aggressiveness is discouraged in males, but sensual dancing is encouraged.

How, then, do male ravers explain their masculinity? There is no precise definition apparent, but coming through in the following responses is the recurrent theme of manly tradition being retained but redefined, refined, softened, and leveled.

> It is a lot more freer, not as hard and structured as in gangsta rap. When masculinity is expressed at raves, it is not as hard and boastful; it's just [expressed] in a soft way. (Jericho 1999)

> There is no need for overbearing masculinity at raves. (Paul 2002)

Noteworthy in this regard are responses to the question of how raving changed conceptions of what it means to be a man.

> Yes, a man means I have the genitalia of a man. Not that I act a certain way. As a man, it doesn't mean that I have to be the way a "man is supposed to be." It just means that I'm a man physically, and I can act how I feel I want to act. (Carl 2002)

> Growing up in our society, all you see about the male image is the whole macho thing. There really is no place for that kind of stuff at a rave. It's taught me to be gentle, and kind to all. (Emanon 2001)

> It changed in a way, showing that you can pretty much act however you want to at raves, no matter what gender you are. You can act feminine and

you won't be laughed at, you won't be excluded, you'll fit right in no matter how you act, gender-wise. (Skunky Cheese 1999)

Before I was a walking beefcake jock. The rave scene has turned that around. I feel that I'm freer to show my feminine side, and have more qualities like taking care of people. (Kid Kinetic 2000)

Such comments suggest that the appeal of rave is bound up with the perceived absence of hegemonic masculinity and invokes folk roots of a primal dancing throng with its egalitarian and emotive connotations. As an outlet for youthful socialization, it provides an alternative to the binary structure of masculine-feminine still evident in most contemporary dance clubs (Pini 1997, 160). The frequently mentioned value system of PLUR (Peace, Love, Unity, and Respect) is a rhetoric of an alternative masculinity whereby emotional, even ecstatic, attainment is manly. As Simon Reynolds has observed, rave culture "constructs its ideal consumer as a biracial androgyny, lost in a swirl of polymorphous sensuality and fantasy glamour, lost for words, and lost to the world" (Reynolds 1990, 154–55).

Arguably, in the blurring of lines between homosexuality and heterosexuality, and what some respondents think of as asexuality, there is a suggestion of polysexuality, or the belief that a polymorphous sensuality allows confidence in and comfort with one's male embodiment in a new, hybrid mode.

REFERENCES

Abrahams, Roger, D. 1983. "Interpreting Folklore Ethnographically and Sociologically." In *Handbook of American Folklore,* ed. Richard M. Dorson, 345–50. Bloomington: Indiana University Press.
Adam. 1999. Interview by author. Albuquerque, New Mexico, June 10.
Baldwin, Elaine, et al., eds. 1999. *Introducing Cultural Studies.* Athens: University of Georgia Press.
Bey, Hakim. 1991. *Temporary Autonomous Zone: Ontological Anarchy: Poetic Terrorism.* Brooklyn: Autonomedia.
Bradby, Barbara. 1993. "Sampling Sexuality: Gender, Technology, and the Body in Dance Music." *Popular Music* 12: 155–76.
Bronner, Simon J. 1988. "Art, Performance, and Praxis: The Rhetoric of Contemporary Folklore Studies." *Western Folklore* 47: 75–101.
———. 1995. *Piled Higher and Deeper: The Folklore of Student Life.* Little Rock, Ark.: August House.
Brown, Janelle. 2001. "Raving Lunacy." *Salon.* http://dir.salon.com/ent/music/feature/2001/06/20/rave_feature/index.html. June 20, 2001. Accessed August 23, 2001.
Carl. 2002. Survey Questionnaire. Albuquerque, New Mexico, February 26.
Disch, Estelle. 2000. *Reconstructing Gender: A Multicultural Anthology.* 2nd ed. Toronto: Mayfield.

Donovan. 2002. Interview Statement. Albuquerque, New Mexico, January 11.

Dundes, Alan. 1983. "Defining Identity through Folklore." In *Identity, Personal and Socio-cultural: A Symposium*, ed. Anita Jacobson-Widding, 235–61. Atlantic Highlands, N.J.: Humanities Press.

East. 1999. Interview by author. Albuquerque, New Mexico, March 11.

Elfie. 1999. Interview by author. Albuquerque, New Mexico, March 23.

Emanon. 2001. Survey Questionnaire. Albuquerque, New Mexico, November 29.

Gilbert, Jeremy, and Ewan Pearson. 1999. *Discographies: Dance Music, Culture, and the Politics of Sound*. New York: Routledge.

Goldstein, Laurence, ed. 1994. *The Male Body*. Ann Arbor: University of Michigan Press.

Gore, Georgianna. 1997. "The Beat Goes On: Trance, Dance, and Tribalism in Rave Culture." In *Dance in the City*, ed. Helen Thomas, 50–67. New York: St. Martin's Press.

Jericho. 1999. Interview by author. Albuquerque, New Mexico, April 13.

Kairo. 1999. Interview by author. Albuquerque, New Mexico, March 23.

Kid Kinetic. 2000. Interview by author. Albuquerque, New Mexico September 8.

Langlois, Tony. 1992. "Can You Feel It? DJs and House Music Culture in the U.K." *Popular Music* 2, no. 2: 229–38.

Lewis, Lynette A., and Michael W. Ross. 1995. *A Select Body: The Gay Dance Party Subculture and the HIV/AIDS Pandemic*. New York: Cassel.

McRobbie, Angela. 1994. *Postmodernism and Popular Culture*. New York: Routledge.

Mr. E. 1999. Interview by author. Albuquerque, New Mexico, February 19.

Paul. 2002. Survey Questionnaire. Albuquerque, New Mexico, January 31.

Philaretou, Andreas G., and Katherine R. Allen. 2001. "Reconstructing Masculinity and Sexuality." *Journal of Men's Studies* 9: 301–21.

Pini, Maria. 1997. "Women and the Early British Rave Scene." In *Back to Reality? Social Experience and Cultural Studies*, ed. Angela McRobbie, 152–69. Manchester: Manchester University Press.

Pollack, William. 1998. *Real Boys: Rescuing Our Sons from the Myths of Boyhood*. New York: Henry Holt.

Reynolds, Simon. 1990. *Blissed Out:The Raptures of Rock*. London: Serpent's Tail.

Richard, Birgit. 1998. "Work Your Body." Icons: *Localizer* 1, no. 3: 7–15.

Richard, Birgit, and Heinz H. Kruger. 1998. "Raver's Paradise? German Youth Cultures in the 1990s." In *Cool Places: Geographies of Youth Cultures*, ed. Tracey Skelton and Gill Valentine, 161–74. New York: Routledge.

Richmond, W. Edson. 1983. Introduction to *Handbook of American Folklore*, ed. Richard M. Dorson, xi–xix. Bloomington: Indiana University Press.

Rietveld, Hillegonda. 1993. "Living the Dream." In *Rave Off: Politics and Deviance in Contemporary Youth Culture*, ed. Steve Redhead, 41–78. Aldershot, UK: Avebury.

———. 1998. "Repetitive Beats: Free Parties, and the Politics of Contemporary DiY Culture in Britain." In *DiY Culture: Party and Protest in Nineties Britain*, ed. George McKay, 208–27. London: Verso.

Rose, Tricia. 1994. *Black Noise: Rap Music and Black Culture in Contemporary America*. Hanover, N.H.: Wesleyan University Press.

Schechner, Richard. 1988. *Performance Theory*. New York: Routledge.

Skunky Cheese. 1999. Interview by author. Albuquerque, New Mexico, June 28.

SpinDomino. 2002. Survey Questionnaire. Albuquerque, New Mexico, March 27.

Spradley, James, and Brenda Mann. 1975. *The Cocktail Waitress: Women's Work in a Man's World*. New York: Knopf.

Toelken, Barre. 1996. *The Dynamics of Folklore*. Rev. ed. Logan: Utah State University Press.

Tomlinson, Lori. 1998. "This Ain't No Disco" . . . or Is It? Youth Culture and the Rave Phenomenon." In *Youth Culture: Identity in a Postmodern World,* ed. Jonathan S. Epstein, 195–211. Oxford: Blackwell.

Turner, Victor. 1969. *The Ritual Process: Structure and Anti-Structure.* New York: Aldine de Gruyter.

Van Gennep, Arnold. 1960 [1909]. *The Rites of Passage.* Trans. M. B. Vizedom and G. L. Caffee. Chicago: University of Chicago Press.

Vontz, Andren. 2001. "The Disneyland Disco." http://archive.salon.com/ent/music/feature/2001/06/18/disney_ravers/. Accessed August 23, 2001.

Ward, Andrew. 1997. "Dancing around Meaning (and the Meaning around Dance)." In *Dance in the City,* ed. Helen Thomas, 3–20. New York: St. Martin's Press.

West, Cornel. 1994. *Race Matters.* New York: Vintage Books.

6

The Circuit: Gay Men's Techniques of Ecstasy

MICKEY WEEMS

"The circuit" is a series of large-scale parties (from 1,000 to as many as 20,000 participants) for gay communities of major cities in the United States. Circuit parties are, on the surface, venues for gay men and their allies across the nation to get together for a weekend and dance. I argue that they are also folk events that serve to construct masculinity through ritualized performance. Having that many men together in one place would in other contexts suggest war or riot. Within the performative frame of circuit parties, however, thousands of shirtless men get intoxicated, flirt, and dance *en masse* without becoming violent. Gayness need not be antithetical to manliness, as popular culture would often suggest, but rather contains a spectrum of masculinities. As one facet of gay identity, circuit masculinity differs especially from conventional assumptions about the American man. Yet it also incorporates normative manly images of muscularity and self-confidence.

I write this essay from the position of a participant-observer who has been to over thirty circuit events across the United States. I have formally spoken with promoters, doctors, law enforcement personnel, and hundreds of participants. The focus of my research has been interviews with circuit DJs. Along with ethnographic observation and interviews, I have worked on production as well. My husband and I were co-chairs of the Columbus Chrome Party 2002.

The idea of circuit masculinity is situated in the history and geography of gay male identity since World War II and the opposing dynamics of normalization and "queering" (undermining standard heteronormative assumptions). A sense of place, historian George Chauncey (1994) and anthropologist Esther Newton (1993) point out, is key to the stability and freedom of expression in gay enclaves such as Manhattan and Fire Island. My research echoes their models; circuit cultural expression has its folk roots in the festivities of those nascent communities. I see circuit parties as contemporary festive enclaves, short in duration but repeated annually as local urban traditions (the oldest have been going on continuously for twenty years). My model differs from theirs because of additional perspectives that I bring as a folklorist of religion and a gay man who loves to dance.

In much of the scholarship on gay constructions of culture, gay male identity is either normalized or queered. I find, however, that the circuit community is both normal and queer. The privileging of the muscular body and standard masculine mannerisms can be seen as a movement in the circuit community to normalize its constituents into adorable, beefy, all-American guys who just happen to have sex with each other. However, the tolerance of drugs, expression of public sensuality, and rejection of violence as a masculine trait undermine standard heteronormative values concerning health, sexual shame, and gender. Deserving analysis for its ritual display of gayness, the circuit as a subject raises ire among several notable "pro-normalist" critics and AIDS activists such as former *New Republic* editor Andrew Sullivan, Michelangelo Signorile, and Gabriel Rotello, who all agree (at least on this one point) that the circuit community is oversexed, overdrugged, and undesirable.

In light of this criticism, the circuit community is a stigmatized community within a stigmatized community, a twofold example of what Erving Goffman calls a "spoiled" public identity (Goffman 1986, 107; Warner 1999, 32). Participants face the possibility of being labeled as "homosexuals" by the general public *and* "substance-abusive narcissists" by the gay community. Although most gay men have heard of the circuit, and many have participated in it at some time or another, the majority of them are either uneasily ambivalent about it or condemn it outright. The circuit is situated at the intersection of sexual desire, illegal drug use, the body beautiful, and public display—all areas of potential anxiety for the average gay man. Because of the circuit community's sensitivity to its own stigmatized image, much of what I report can only be observed firsthand as a trusted insider.

This stigmatization presents me with certain ethical dilemmas that I have resolved in favor of the safety of my collaborators. I say little about actual illegal drug use or unsafe sexual activities and attribute nothing to the actions of an individual, fictional or otherwise. The anonymity of my sources on these topics is assured at all times. However, I refer to the published reports of others who give facts and figures concerning drug use and sex.

As a member of the gay community and the circuit community, I use many terms as an insider, some of which may make readers uncomfortable. I may, for example, refer to other gay men as "fags," a term that is rejected in polite straight society but is a frequently used term of endearment in gay circles. As much as possible, I want to invite the reader into the rich verbal wordplay of circuit expressive culture and use such terms to reveal the typical cultural communication in the circuit scene.

As a scholar of religion, I see the circuit as possessing its own "folk spirituality" as an ecstatic practice without, as Barbara Walker Lloyd puts it, an "institutionally sanctioned and codified doctrine" (Walker 1995, 6). I use, as David Hufford would say, "experience-centered theory" (Hufford 1995, 11) on the premise that the lived experience of the circuit is valid and worthy of study. It is not, however, what Hufford would call a "folk belief" because there is no prerequisite that one believe in non-corporeal spirits (15). Circuit folk spirituality involves the spontaneous transformation of secular social performance into ecstatic communal dance. In this context, "ecstasy" may be defined as "transcendent solidarity," the breaking down of status between participants who share a state of such intense physical pleasure and strong emotional affection that, as a group, they step outside of quotidian reality. Because the community resists any religious codification in the framing and execution of its practice, participants are free to interpret their experiences as ecstatic beings according to the cosmology of their choice.

My position undermines the distinction between the secular and the spiritual, and I mean for it to do so. A remarkable amount of spiritual expression in America is now done in secular settings, from roadside shrines for crash victims to homespun memorials at the former site of the World Trade Center Towers. Scholars refer to "secular spirituality" to encompass the dizzying array of new forms that are both. Circuit folk spirituality is one of those forms. The question I pose in this essay is, "What are the social dynamics behind such a powerful experience, centered in the cultivation of a gay masculine identity, that it results in the expression of masculinity that is almost completely devoid of violence?"

THE CIRCUIT AS ECSTATIC RITUAL

It is important to see the circuit as ritual performance, but ritual with a gay twist. Since gay people come from so many ethnicities, gay performance rituals (such as coming out, pride parades, drag shows, women's music festivals, and AIDS Quilt showings) encourage a broad range of individual expression within an agreed-upon communal frame. The setting, not the script, is codified. The sacredness of self-determination and individual expression is, in fact, a key element in traditional gay rituals.

When we think of rituals, we often imagine them as formal affairs with clearly defined scripts. Catherine Bell, however, feels that formality and routine are not essential prerequisites:

Ritual is never simply or solely a matter of routine, habit, or "the dead weight of tradition" Hence, ritualization can be characterized *in general* only to a rather limited extent since the idiom for its differentiation of acting will be, for the most part, culturally specific. (Bell 1992, 92–93)

By ritual performance, I mean that ritual is staged or framed. Richard Bauman explains, "performance sets up, or represents, an interpretative frame within which the messages being communicated are to be understood, and ... this frame contrasts with at least one other frame, the literal" (Bauman 1984, 9). Performance is recognized and made coherent by its frame, which immediately defines performed acts as non-literal (i.e., symbolic) in content.

Bell observes that linking performance with ritual is problematic because this implies that ritual can be reduced to drama (Bell 1992, 42–43). In order not to limit ritual in this way (but not necessarily to exclude drama as ritual), let us look at another qualifier Bell gives us: ritual "always aligns one within a series of relationship [sic] linked to the ultimate sources of power. . . . It always suggests the ultimate coherence of a cosmos in which one takes a particular place" (141). In other words, it connects us to and defines us within our universe. Through ritual, we seek validation from those ultimate sources of power; we may even tap into them. In ritual, we cosmically situate ourselves. This is the aspect of ritual that makes it sacred.

Ritual also involves real, not fictional, encounter. It brings us face-to-face with something or someone, even if that someone is our own self. When we purposefully encounter something or somebody, such as the state (e.g., a flag-raising ceremony), a deity (e.g., prayer), the dead (e.g., bringing flowers to a grave), or another person (e.g., a handshake), our actions have ritual importance to the degree in which the encounter situates the participants within the universe.

By focusing on encounter, we can see the close relationship between ritual and performance. Goffman defines performance as "all the activity of an individual which occurs during a period marked by his continuous presence before a particular set of observers and which has some influence on the observers" (Goffman 1959, 22). If a performance is non-fictional and cosmic, then it is ritual performance.

Goffman also uses a superbly applicable term: "team," one or more than one performer in a performance (1959, 80). The fluidity of individual and group in Goffman's definition is perfect as a means for describing the complex world of circuit performance in which one may be a solo performer, audience, and teammate, simultaneously or in rapid succession. The circuit is a ritual frame in which all of the participants join together into one multifaceted Goffmanian team, a feat that is accomplished through ecstatic dance.

Ecstatic dance is often associated in folklife with shamanistic trance. In his classic book *Shamanism: Archaic Techniques of Ecstasy,* Mircea Eliade defines "shaman" as a spiritual technician who works outside of the pale of established religions and "is the great master of ecstasy" (Eliade 1964, 4). A traditional shaman is a mystical performer who sings, drums, doses with intoxicants, and dances into "a trance during which his soul is believed to leave his body and ascend to the sky or descend to the underworld" (5). Gay scholars of religion have turned to anthropological discourse on sha- manism to counter the stigma of gay people as morally and spiritually de- prived. They point out that homosexuality is a commonly reported characteristic of shamans around the world. Christian de la Huerta states, for example:

> Another recurrent theme we encounter among third-gender spiritual func- tionaries across culture and time lines is the propensity to use dance and sacred hallucinogenic substances as a means to induce trance or altered states of consciousness. (1999, 37)

De la Huerta goes on to situate the circuit as a contemporary expression of shamanistic performance:

> Oftentimes, dancing at a gay club invokes a sense of real tribal ritual. The constant, rhythmic beat, the theatrical interplay of music, lighting, décor, and the amorphously sensual mass of bodies moving, gyrating, prancing, touching, and cavorting in seemingly wild abandon, can actually induce a trance state or transcendent experience. Needless to say, this is often heightened by many through the use of mind-altering substances. (1999, 37)

The circuit's ecstatic trance, however, does not fit neatly into classical an- thropological definitions of shamanism. Circuit masculinity, with its strong affinity for the "manly" rather than the "girly" or the androgynous, does not fit into gay religious scholarship concerning gender-bending "third- gender spiritual functionaries." In fact, not all circuit participants see the circuit as spiritual. Some would scoff at the notion of comparing the circuit with shamanism.

The circuit is not traditional shamanism, and neither is it neo-shamanis- tic in design. By "neo-shamanism," I refer to various movements since the 1960s for people in the West to re-establish a connection with the spiritual through their own ecstatic rituals, situated within constructions of tribal identity derived from anthropological literature and literary fiction (Noel 1999, 26–188; Pinchbeck 2002, 60–76). It would be misleading for me to say that the circuit is a neo-shamanistic movement; the search for ecstasy need not be the search for spirituality. Nevertheless, the secular dynamics of circuit ecstatic dance culminate in an important neo-shamanistic prac- tice: ritualized construction of communal identity through shared ecstasy. Participants become ecstatic beings—the spirits that they honor are their own.

As I already mentioned, some participants do not feel that the circuit is a site for spiritual expression. They may still, however, experience ecstatic dance regardless of how they feel about it. The magic of the circuit does not lie in a uniform set of beliefs but in the shared celebratory experience of what sociologist Emile Durkheim calls "effervescence" or ecstatic delirium, which he explains "is not without kinship to the religious state" even when it is strictly secular (Durkheim 1995, 386–87). The circuit community produces its own effervescent moment, the moment of mass *ekstasis* or displacement, when the DJ adroitly selects music that transports the dancers into a state of transcendent solidarity. People step out of their egos, merge into the collective, and rejoice in the rapture of the beloved team that they have spontaneously generated. And it is in the crucible of transcendent solidarity that the circuit profoundly confirms what it means to be a man.

THE TRIBE

The circuit community is a loose-knit, transregional association of men and women from many walks of life. There are no membership requirements per se concerning sexual preference, race, age (besides being over the age of eighteen), or appearance. One need not dance well or even walk. I have witnessed people dancing in wheelchairs at circuit events. The circuit is not for everyone, however.

Circuit parties tend to be expensive. Tickets for the weekend events range from $150 to $600. A circuit weekend will cost each participant a minimum of $1,000 after costs of tickets, hotel, travel, and food are tabulated. This gives the circuit community economic clout: businesses cater to it, including hotels, airlines, clothing designers, and CD manufacturers. Considering that the fifteen major parties in the United States and Canada together average about 6,000 participants each, the net community expenditure would be $90,000,000 per year. Taking into account an additional fifteen smaller parties that generate about a third of what the larger ones generate, the total economic impact comes to $120,000,000 per year.

An estimated 200,000 gay men worldwide participate in circuit parties (Nimmons 2002, 157). The average American circuiteer is a white or Hispanic gay male between the ages of twenty-one and fifty-five with some college education. Income level is between $20,000 and $100,000 annually.[1] In terms of physique, most circuiteers are of average height and build, although there is a large and cherished minority of men (around 25%) who have exceptionally muscular physiques.

Most participants attend the events in protective clusters of friends and lovers. Much of the networking in the circuit is interaction between these small groups, forming new friendships and alliances over the weekend. They congregate in specific places between events (usually around the host hotel), transforming these places into safe havens where men may hold hands, kiss, and let down their guard. If these places are already "gay ghettos," they become even more so for the weekend.[2]

Codes for dress and grooming are fairly simple. Most men have short hair and smooth-shaved faces. They eliminate or trim chest, back, and neck hair. Although there can be a broad range in clothing options (many of the parties have themes), a universally accepted outfit is blue jeans and a white sleeveless undershirt (known in the community as a "wife beater"). Boots or athletic shoes are standard footgear. Shirts are removed once dancing starts in earnest.

Preferred intoxicants are recreational drugs, the most popular being MDMA (also known as Ecstasy, X, or E), Ketamine (K), GHB (G), methamphetamine (crystal), tobacco, and alcohol. Due to legal prohibitions against most of these substances, it is impossible to accurately determine how many participants take which drugs.

Although in the minority, straight women, African Americans, Asian Americans, non-European Latinos, men over fifty-five, "drag queens," and "Leathermen" (gay men who mark themselves as sadomasochistic [S&M] participants by wearing black leather clothing) show up regularly at most events.[3] "Bears" (gay men who celebrate being gentler, heavier, and hairier), lesbians, and straight men can be found as well, but usually in fewer numbers. The presence or absence of any minority can be determined in part by geography (more Asian Americans attend parties on the West Coast than the East, for example) and the theme of a particular party.[4] Themes vary, but they often feature fantasy settings and, consequentially, may have folk spiritual references. The theme for the Philadelphia Blue Ball 2004, for example, was "Ascension," and Chicago Fireball 2003 featured a live gospel choir. Perhaps the most moving use of spiritual symbolism was during Montreal's Black and Blue 2000, where participants walked with candles through an arena with a giant red AIDS ribbon in its center.

Participants maintain communal ties by means of circuit-based literature and computer sites that help them keep up with the music, the DJs, and each other between parties. Virtual communities exist by means of online discussion lists and message boards.[5] *Circuit Noize,* a quarterly magazine and Web site dedicated to the circuit, has articles about the scene as well as a calendar of upcoming events. Participants often refer to themselves as a tribe and tend to describe their experiences of transcendental solidarity in neo-shamanistic terms. Human beings, some of them say, have accessed such feelings across the world through intoxication and ecstatic dance since the dawn of time. The circuit is but a recent version of cosmic tribal solidarity. Within this transcendental context, some participants find that the circuit is also a site for the living to bond with the dead, especially when they engage in the folk dance called "flagging" featuring artful waving of brightly colored cloth around the body. Flaggers consider themselves a tribe within the larger circuit tribe.[6]

Male members of the circuit community are often referred to as "circuit boys," a term that is not without derogatory connotations. In the spirit

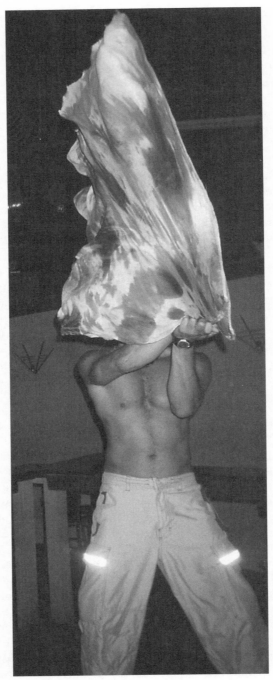

Dancer demonstrating "flagging," an individualistic and deeply introspective dance form. *Photograph by Kevin Mason.*

of playfulness that the community possesses in abundance, participants exaggerate their own stigmatized identity and fondly refer to each other as "crack whores" or "cracked-out circuit queens." Illegal substances are given "girl" names, such as "Stacy" (MDMA or Ecstasy), "Tina" (from "Christina" for crystal methamphetamine), "Katie" (Ketamine), and "Gina" (GHB). The necessity for discretion in obtaining, imbibing, and talking about these substances tends to bond the community even closer.

The circuit community has its share of problems. Members refer to a pervasive attitude of "body fascism" (the obsession with physical perfection and the snobbery that comes with it).[7] Substance abuse plagues the community. Some gay spokespersons call for the end of the circuit, which they see as nothing more than an excuse for taking illegal drugs and engaging in irresponsible sexual behavior (Rotello 1998, 302). Michelangelo Signorile calls the circuit the "Evangelical Church," established upon the "sacraments" of steroids and club drugs, that preaches "the cult of masculinity" (Signorile 1997, 30–132).

In response to these criticisms, concerned members of the community have conducted campaigns for safer sex and intoxicant harm reduction during circuit weekends. There is at least one advocacy organization, the Drug Policy Alliance, that supports the circuit and rave communities. Dr. Chris Mann of Dallas, Texas, leads a volunteer organization (MedEvent) of doctors and nurses who work at events to reduce health risks.[8] Chicago Fireball and Montreal Black and Blue both have held health summits and educational programs during their weekends. Pamphlets and posters are present at many circuit parties that remind participants to party responsibly. Many of the campaigns have considerable marketing savvy, using eye-catching models and outrageous humor to bring home the message.[9]

In addition to safer-sex and harm-reduction campaigns, many parties raise funds for gay causes, especially for AIDS charities. Many of the bigger parties, such as Philadelphia Blue Ball, DC Cherry Party, Miami Winter and White Parties, Chicago Fireball, and Montreal Black and Blue, donate a portion of their revenue to charities. This practice has created some controversy; some critics say that throwing parties that encourage irresponsible sexual behavior and then claiming that these parties are AIDS fund-raisers is the height of hypocrisy (Signorile 118–27).

FOLK HISTORY

Gay scholars consider World War II significant in the formation of gay male identity. The mobilization of men from across the country, separated from the usual constraints of family and friends and exposed to the intimate day-to-day contact that soldiers had with each other, led thousands of homosexual men to join discrete communities in major cities such as San Francisco and New York (Chauncey 1994, 11–12). Homosexual "hot spots" in major

2003 Miami Winter Party held on the beach in South Beach, Florida. The crowd was estimated at 10,000 participants in a dance space the size of two football fields. *Photograph by Kevin Mason.*

urban centers already existed as refuges for sexual outcasts from rural areas; the difference was that these men were recognized as soldiers, already certified by the battlefield as legitimate men. Their struggle was to remain anonymous as homosexuals. The development and expression of a gay male masculinity was severely limited by socially imposed pressures on these men to remain invisible. Notions of being a "real man" were mostly projected onto the straight male as the only manly, and thus desirable, man (Bronski 1998, 103).

The circuit has its beginnings in the Stonewall Rebellion on June 28, 1969, when a routine vice raid on the Stonewall Inn (a seedy homosexual dance bar in New York City's Greenwich Village) was disrupted. Fed up with police harassment of gays, an angry crowd gathered as the police were filling their paddy wagon with Stonewall staff and cross-dressers. Words led to bricks, rocks, bottles, and coins thrown at the officers, who barricaded themselves in the dance bar until reinforcements arrived; a three-day riot ensued.[10] Exactly one year later, the first gay pride parade was held in Greenwich Village, which was followed by a dance party.[11]

"Stonewall," shorthand for the riots and subsequent events, is a pivotal moment in the gay community's folk history, that is, the self-understanding of a heritage. "One of the profound changes wrought by gay liberation," states Michael Bronski, "was the permission granted to gay men to like themselves" (Bronski 1998, 103). Lesbians and gay men quickly went from being socially passive and invisible to politically active and outrageous, a response meant to shake up and undermine popular notions of homosexuality. As a result, pride parades were (and still are) prime sites for displays of self-worth.

The gay male dance scene, however, began to explore a privately constructed rather than publicly responsive gay identity. Clubs were opened that catered exclusively to gay men, who then began developing trademarks of their own expressive culture. The display of the male physique on the dance floor became an in-house activity as men began taking off their shirts while dancing in the new spaces.[12] Drugs other than alcohol became the norm; some clubs did not even serve liquor. DJs would generate a single driving beat over the course of an evening by matching up songs without interruption. In response to these DJs and the popularity of the music they made, record companies produced extended-play versions of dance songs, technicians improved turntables, and clubs invested heavily in lights and sound equipment. Gay club culture quickly spread beyond the gay community with the popularity of disco music. When homophobic backlash resulted in the "death" of disco in the late 1970s and an anti-disco riot at a Chicago White Sox game in 1979 (Brewster and Broughton 2000, 268–70), the first generation of the circuit was hitting its stride.

"The circuit" initially referred to the post-Stonewall pilgrimage of gay partygoers to Fire Island in the summer and the newly legal clubs *du jour* in Manhattan during the off-season (Holleran 1978, 111, 152). Manhattan clubs, such as the Flamingo, 12 West, the Paradise Garage, and the legendary Saint (which featured a planetarium among its special effects), nurtured a new gay dance culture that attracted gay men from across the country and overseas (San Francisco also had its own circuit-style club, the Trocadero).[13] Some of those who had gone to party in New York brought back its dance culture, DJs, and technology to places such as the Warehouse in Chicago. The Red Party in Columbus, Ohio—considered by many to be the first annual circuit party outside New York—branched out from the Manhattan/Fire Island loop in 1977.[14]

At this time, the issue of building an alternative "butch" or manly form of masculinity became important in gay discourse and expression. Gay men made themselves the objects of their desire rather than wistfully lusting after some straight masculine ideal. This ushered in the age of the "gay clone," a mustached, nicely muscled "Macho Man." The deeply internalized stereotypes of homosexuals as "nelly fags" (effeminate men in gay folk speech) or sneaky perverts were challenged on and off the dance floor by the hyper-masculine and highly public manliness of the clone.[15]

The 2001 Red Party in Columbus, Ohio. The Red Party began in 1977 and featured pre-event spiritual rituals and elaborate costumes. The Red Party ended in 2002 after its founder, Corbett Reynolds, died. The party depicted here carried the theme of "Red Fetish" and featured former televangelist Tammy Faye Bakker as the hostess. *Photograph by Kevin Mason.*

AIDS almost brought the club scene to a standstill. The number of sick and dead that had been "circuit queens" was so high that the illness was dubbed "the Saint disease" (Brewster and Broughton 2000, 201). By the late 1980s, many clubs (including the Saint) had to close because their membership had been virtually wiped out. But the community rallied. Speaking from the sadness and despair of those times, Corbett Reynolds, founder of the Red Party, said, "You still have to dance" (interview by author, July 23, 2001).[16] In spite of (or perhaps because of) the fear and depression that AIDS had brought to those fledgling gay communities, people needed a release, a space in which they could communally commemorate their lost ones and celebrate being alive.

At the end of the 1980s, parties were being thrown in many major cities as fund-raisers, and their popularity grew. Successful treatment for remission of the dread illness, along with an underground steroid and marijuana network to help those with AIDS wasting syndrome, led to a resurgence of the dance community and a noticeable number of rather huge (and apparently healthy) men. Born from the pattern set by the original Manhattan/Fire Island circuit, a second-generation transregional circuit of parties catered to a coast-to-coast nomadic community with its own music, DJs, and social calendar.[17] Based on annual weekend festivals rather than clubs requiring year-round upkeep, second-generation circuit parties are now gay traditions in their own right. Major parties are larger than life, with mesmerizing stage shows, fabulous costumes, and nationally renowned DJs. Nevertheless, higher premium has always been placed on the participants on the dance floor than on performers on the stage or in the DJ booth. Continuing the patterns set by the first generation, DJs do not disturb the dancers by talking over the music. Professional performances are tailored to mix in for one song and mix out with the next without skipping a beat—no speeches, no encores. The real action is on the dance floor.

ATTRACTION OVER INTIMIDATION

Three factors have been consistent from generation to generation in channeling aggression away from violent expression in the circuit: physical attraction over physical intimidation, sensuality over sexuality, and us-for-us solidarity over us-against-them separatism.

Masculinity involves modes of appearance and behavior that illustrate and reinforce one's identity as a properly gendered male. It is the outward sign of a man's inner being, learned through observation and validated by the approval of other men. Our environment outside teaches us who we really are inside. As J. H. Van Den Berg states, "[Sexuality] is not in the first place to be found 'in the subject' or 'on' his body, but shows itself as world. Sexuality appears in the other, who is met, in the advertisement, the shop window, the reading matter, the landscape of the twilight, the aspect of the street" (Van Den Berg 1962, 109). Those images of manliness that boys are taught, however, are only occasionally realized. Men rarely become "man enough." As men, we see our role models and then look at ourselves, only to see that we do not measure up one way or another. Nowhere is this more apparent than in front of a full-length mirror.

Many studies of the male body focus on (or rather obsess with) the penis and phallocentrism. For some men, the phallus (either literally or figuratively) is indeed their passport into manliness. But it is one small part of a much larger package. The most obvious form of embodied masculine power is a man's musculature.[18] Dress shirts and ties can hide a pudgy belly somewhat; they do not hide a muscular frame. Regardless of one's status in the office, the factory, or the institution, a muscular body commands respect without even trying. And muscle indicates power, masculinized, irrefutable, casual power, even when that body belongs to a woman.[19]

Traditionally, a big-muscled man is assumed to be more powerful because of the obvious relationship between muscle and physical strength. But this relationship is just one side of the power coin, the other being the relationship between muscle and beauty. A muscular man is also seen as being more beautiful. Two connotations of power exist in muscle: the power to repel and punish (violence), and the power to attract and give pleasure (beauty). These connotations tend to be gendered. Roughly speaking, men are supposed to *respect* a muscular man, while women should *desire* him. The gay male community undermines this distinction by openly celebrating the erotic beauty of the muscular male body.

True to its gay folk roots, the circuit community promotes a masculine ideal of the muscular man without the connotation of violence. This is how it goes: a muscular man who does not behave violently with his body focuses attention instead on his body's beauty. He could become violent if he so chooses but does not because that would make him less attractive. This renders the appearance of physical strength to the status of *accessory*, like a nice pair of shoes or a college degree.[20] By accessorizing muscles, the circuit community trivializes their utilitarian features. When the muscular body is made an accessory, its importance as a means for lifting heavy objects or fighting is made secondary to its aesthetic importance as a means for stimulating the admiration of others.

Outside of the gay community, most men will rarely ever say that another man's body is beautiful because such a statement changes the body from an object of respect to an object of desire. These same men will have no problem saying that a car, dog, or baby is beautiful, which gives us some indication of how severe the problem is for many straight men in defining themselves as violent/active rather than homosexual/passive.

The muscular male body is understood in the circuit to be active and attractive in both penetrator and penetrated sexual roles. According to R. W. Connell, gay relations are marked by their reciprocity. Sex and its inherent roles for dominance and submission are less rigidly constructed for gays than for straights (Connell 1995, 162). Either person can be the penetrator, and there is little to no stigma attached to the receptive partner behaving in a sexually aggressive manner during love-play (what members of the gay community call an "aggressive" or "power bottom").

In terms of wordplay, straight male discourse concerning sex-as-violence does not enjoy the same currency for gay men. The notion of "fucking" another man, either physically or as a verbal imperative (with an insult such as "Fuck you!"), is not intrinsically degrading and does not trigger the same demand for violent response that informs straight masculine social dynamics. The result is that there is not much swearing at circuit parties. When "Suck my dick" is an invitation, it loses much of its power as an insult.

Because men, not women, are the preferred objects of desire in the circuit, the dynamics of sexual competition are radically modified. Rather than being in competition *against* each other, men are in competition *for* each other. The need for a violent response toward a rival is tempered by the fact that he is potentially an object of desire as well. The circuit, with its acceptance of casual physical contact on the dance floor, reduces violence even further.

There are, inevitably, straight women who enjoy circuit events because they are disgusted with the typical straight bar scene. Many women express relief at being able to enjoy the pleasures of dancing close with well-groomed men and not have the hassle of cheap come-ons and the dreaded potential for unwanted groping. It should be pointed out that public harassment of women is often part of the performance of straight, not gay, masculinity. It is done for the benefit of other straight men, who bond with each other by setting up a common enemy in the so-called battle of the sexes.[21]

This is not to say, however, that lack of violence means that there is no aggressive behavior in the circuit. As Lionel Tiger notes, violence is a type of aggression; it is not synonymous with aggression (Tiger 1969, 158). Masculinity for both straight and gay men is based upon a relationship of mutually assured vanity between the individual and the group. Aggression sometimes arises in expressions of disdain from "hot" men for those who are less built and less beautiful.[22]

The dance floor is an exhibition, a highly competitive arena for the display of the body and the performance of self for all to see. This leads to a preoccupation with being seen only with those who are attractive enough to merit one's attention. Selective male bonding with only the right kind of men leads to aggressive behavior toward those who do not make the grade, a confirmation of Tiger's hypothesis that male bonding goes hand-in-hand with male aggression (1969, 190). Occasionally, nasty misogynist echoes from the straight world can be heard, not against women, but against non-muscular effeminate men and drag queens who do not embody the circuit ideal.[23] At its worst, the circuit can be an ego-crushing snub-fest when body fascism takes over.

Body fascism tends to have a racist edge—not all muscular bodies are equal. The white man's body is privileged, although some leeway is given to the Latino body if it is not too far from the white ideal. This is par for the course for American culture in general, which, as Richard Dryer notes, "constructs the white man as physically superior, yet also an everyman" (2002, 269). The muscular white male body (especially the front of the torso) is the most common icon in advertisements for circuit events. When people of color are shown, they are among white models, and rarely is a non-white model the central figure.[24] Absence of violence does not include the absence of racism and subtle forms of aggression and alienation that come with it. It can be a greater challenge for men of color to feel accepted, especially as desirable bodies.[25]

On the other hand, body fascism also undermines discrimination based solely on age. Since muscle is the marker for both masculinity and desire, an older muscular man (popularly known as a "daddy") is a legitimate object of desire. The appreciation for a shaved head or a crew cut in the gay community helps older men significantly.

SENSUAL OVER SEXUAL

José Torrealba, the creator and director of the circuit documentary *Got 2 B There,* describes the circuit as a place where gay men can touch each other without having sex (interview by author, October 2000).[26] In order to understand the import of this statement, one must realize that the gay male community is tolerant of behaviors that the general public would consider excessive, especially sexual behaviors. Since sex is such a casual part of gay male life, it would seem a paradox that the circuit, a gathering of shirtless, intoxicated, flirty men, would not degenerate into one big orgy on the dance floor.

One reason it does not is due to the abundant number of gay male venues that cater to orgiastic gatherings. Most gay communities have bathhouses, sex clubs, and "back rooms" for this purpose.[27] The PnP (Party n Play) community uses the Internet to hook up, do drugs, and have sex, completely bypassing the club and circuit scenes.[28] Circuit parties, even notoriously sexual ones like the New York City Black Party (which features live sex shows and a big dark "back room" for group sex), are primarily about the pleasures of dance. Sexual activity is, for the most part, restricted to things that men can do with their pants on while moving to the beat.

A different range of pleasures is generated in the circuit. Orgies are rather impersonal affairs, almost mechanical in preparation and execution. Gaiety is not the hallmark of bathhouses and sex clubs, which typically feature somber-faced clientele who prowl around with grim intensity. The aesthetics of an orgy tend to be limited to those things that can accommodate the immediate need for the sexual over anything else. The circuit involves many more pleasures and levels of social interaction than the raw expression of orgasmic heat. Sexiness takes on new dimensions with a dancing body as opposed to a stationary body or a rutting body. Close dancing, while highly erotic, is disciplined by the beat of the music and the critical gaze of others. Since the circuit is held in public space, a body that obeys its own sexual rhythm rather than the beat appears disjointed, out of sync with the communal flow, and basically kind of silly.

One important factor that keeps affairs sensual rather than sexual is a collective sense of public propriety. Attractiveness is a most desirable quality, and anything that reduces one's beauty is to be studiously avoided. Lack of control is not attractive. Although many participants feel the need to drink alcohol or do recreational drugs before they feel comfortable enough to dance and be sensual, being overly intoxicated or over-sexed can cost one status on the dance floor. Not everything goes.

Propriety restricting the expression of sensuality by couples with outsiders, however, is lowered to a degree that would be scandalous to those outside the circuit scene. The need to mark, survey, and protect one's sexual property is relaxed.[29] Men involved in serious relationships can dance with other men quite intimately and still consider themselves in a monogamous relationship. This in turn reduces the need for hyper-masculine displays of violence "in defense of one's honor."

Couples just entering the circuit scene may find themselves both enthusiastic and anxiety-ridden about the prospect of engaging in public displays of sensuality with other men. Elaborate rules concerning who may dance with whom and in what fashion are often set until the couple becomes comfortable with the scene and with themselves. Many people in the circuit community consider the acceptance of casual dance floor contact to be a healthy expression of sexuality that can strengthen, not weaken, the bonds of commitment.[30] Proof of this can be seen in the abundance of boyfriends and happily married men who attend circuit parties with their partners; I have met "circuit couples" who have been together fifteen years or longer.[31]

The biggest reason that sensual dancing is preferred over sexual acts is, interestingly enough, pleasure. Overtly sexual expression tends to isolate those who engage in it, which undermines communal solidarity. The combination of sensuality and dance can be wonderfully erotic precisely because it implies but does not actualize the sexual act. I remember a friend of mine describing an incident when his newfound love wanted him to leave the dance floor and go back to his hotel room for sex. His response was, "And quit dancing? You must be out of your mind!"

SOLIDARITY

Whether culturally inculcated or biologically hard-wired, there are some pleasures that men can feel only when they bond with other men. This includes the deep social pleasure of feeling like "one of the boys." To be sure, folk views of male bonding differ in straight and gay worlds, and in traditionalizing male bonding, circuit parties symbolize gay values. Masculine solidarity at the circuit takes on certain characteristics that differentiate it from other kinds of male bonding.

People do not go to large public gatherings simply to see a game, watch a movie, hear music, or listen to an evangelist. A large part of the pleasure that drives these events is derived from the experience of coming together in large numbers. Because of ingrained distrust of strangers and respect for the personal space of other people, however, participants need a reason (an excuse, really) for these gatherings to take place, typically a performance staged for an audience.

Riots and uprisings, on the other hand, undermine the audience/performer distinction in the zone of conflict. The participants are the stars.

The relaxation of propriety can be intoxicating, both between the rioters and their targets and between the rioters and each other. There are great pleasures to be felt while participating in communal violence, and certainly not the least is a profound feeling of collective belonging, often with strong spiritual implications. The overwhelming majority of combatants in the world, be they rioters, warriors, or athletes, are men. I submit that this is true precisely because of pleasures, at times ecstatic, that come with male bonding and the expression of masculinity through the performance of violence. But combatants cannot bond by themselves. They are dependent on their targets, real and imagined, for team identity. *We* are defined by *them.*

Communal dances, like riots, are events in which the crowd is the show, and the line between spectator and performer is undermined significantly. Unlike riots, however, most communal dance is not dependent upon an "other" for participant identity. This does not, however, mean that there is no competition. In many heterosexual dance settings, competition between men is easily observable. Tiger theorizes that male bonding inevitably leads to aggression (1969, 190). Although violence is officially forbidden, popular rules of behavior for masculinity and intoxication regularly result in violence, often because men who bond together while drinking behave aggressively to those outside the group. Attempts to limit male violence through dress codes (no sports caps, tank tops, athletic wear) are futile. They cannot eliminate what is understood as *natural* masculine behavior.

Communal dance in the circuit has rules for masculinity and intoxication that do not naturalize violent behavior. There is a sense of security in that the circuit is a safe space for gay men to flirt and dance with each other with no fear of violent reprisal from straight men. It should be noted that gay circuit identity is not defined against the immorality and violence of its straight oppressors.[32] There is no sense of "us" against "them," only "us."[33] The result is a crowd whose major competitive goal is favorable attention from as many people as possible. Everyone performs for everyone else.

In general, gay men tend to respond to dance with much more enthusiasm than straight men (Nimmons 2002, 165–66), reflecting a significant facet of gendered body perception. The expressive male body is admired for its beauty, something that straight men are not supposed to do (or at least admit).[34] The athletic male body gives the straight male observer the necessary excuse to admire it. In the worldview of the straight community, the athletic body appears to reinforce the value of dominance rather than solidarity, however, because it is typically described as a utility, even a machine, for victory over other men.[35] The gay male gaze, in contradistinction, looks at a man's body as more than just a competitive machine.

Nevertheless, few gay men are raised gay. Many men suffer from the cultural notion (notorious among white Americans) that the only appropriate time for a man to dance is when he is "three sheets to the wind" or "higher than God." Add to these insecurities the highly intimidating environment of the circuit, and it is no surprise that intoxicants play such an important role, regardless of participants' ethnic or racial background.

Alcohol is usually not the intoxicant of choice. The culture of alcohol that we have in this country encourages men to flex their "beer muscles." It allows them to feel, in folk terms, "ten feet tall and bulletproof," thus drastically lowering the threshold for acceptable violence. There are other substances that retard motor skills less severely than alcohol and make the imbiber feel sexy and full of energy. For these reasons, MDMA is a preferred intoxicant of circuit participants.[36] The sense of communal empathy, internal spiritual integration, relaxation of personal space barriers, infusion of vigor, intensification of music, and sheer physical joy of dancing while doing Ecstasy are important factors in the redefinition of masculinity in both the circuit and the rave scene.

The prevalence of drugs in the circuit scene does not have a corresponding increase in violent crime that one might expect to accompany a market for banned substances. Few people involved in the distribution system identify as "drug dealers"—they consider themselves to be friends who help out other friends. Instead of viewing drug distributors as shadowy, dangerous figures, members of the circuit community usually hold them in high regard. In their study of the gay party scene in Sydney, Australia (home of the circuit party known as Sydney Mardi Gras), Lynnette Lewis and Michael Ross state:

> The drug dealers were also significant persons for dance party patrons. They were responsible for the dispensing of conscious-changing substances, caretakers and healers if necessary, a role similar to that of a shaman or some contemporary medical practitioners. (1995, 148)

The most important shamanistic figures in the circuit, however, are the DJs, those almost legendary characters who unite the community through music. They play a pivotal role in helping bring about the communal solidarity that shapes and certifies circuit masculinity. According to Lewis and Ross, DJs carry the highest status as sacred persons in the eyes of participants, higher than that of promoters and drug distributors (149). The DJ is the coach who, in the course of a few hours, brings individual performers together as a team and leads them to victory over their own collective hangups and anxieties.

In standard American masculine discourse, one's status as a man is greatly increased by being a member of elite masculine teams, most of which are military or paramilitary in design. Men who are soldiers, police, firefighters, lifeguards, and athletes in contact sports enjoy a heightened sense of masculinity because they are members of their respective teams. Each of these teams has its moments of ecstatic expression through exhibition of the *corps,* a performance in which teammates merge into one body, be it during a parade, a victory, a party, or a funeral for a fallen comrade. During these moments, each participant's identity is writ large, and if they are men, their masculine identity is confirmed by their fellows.

The paramilitary model does not fit the circuit community. For all of its "clone" tendencies, there is no set circuit uniform, and neither are there standardized rules of engagement for the no-nonsense fulfillment of one's duty. Duty, in fact, is not an issue. The circuit community is a spectacle put on by performers for performers. Participants are not immediately a "team" in either the male-bonding or Goffmanian sense of the word until they have been molded into one under the charismatic leadership of the DJ. The greatest pleasures of the circuit are only possible when the DJ coaxes the crowd into becoming a *corps.*

LOVER AND GUIDE

The two most popular metaphors for what DJs say they do are sex and a journey. The sex metaphor is particularly interesting when we take into account that, in 2003, six of the top forty DJs were lesbians.[37] In fact, I first heard the sex metaphor from DJ Susan Morabito.[38] DJs must be extremely sensitive to the temperament of the crowd and can only pre-plan an evening to a certain extent. Since the places and people change constantly, it is important for the DJs to be flexible in their program of music. What works in one city on a Friday night may not work in another city on a Saturday night. By watching and "feeling" their crowd, DJs fine-tune their selection so that it is specifically designed for that group on that date. DJ art is all about creating the moment according to needs of the moment. Like good lovers, DJs react to the immediate desires of the beloved.

The DJ must behave like a sensitive lover, gently stripping the participant of awkward self-consciousness. All of this is done without word— circuit DJs touch participants through their musical selection. This creates a *simpatico* between the chooser of the music, the music itself, and the recipient. The greatest ecstasy for both the DJ and the dancer is when the music saturates and penetrates them both, body and soul, and they see this rapture in each other. Nevertheless, the DJ is always dominant in the "sex act." According to DJ Ra (b. Wade Maggert), the DJ "fucks the crowd on a good night" (interview by author, April 18, 2001). Since the gay masculine body can be sexually penetrated without losing its masculinity, sexual descriptions of the DJ-dancer relationship are not problematic, even when the DJ is a woman or a straight man.[39] This, in fact, adds to the hilarity when a DJ is told "You worked my pussy!" by a male admirer.

A good evening begins with "foreplay," when the DJ stimulates each individual until participants make their way onto the floor. The truly talented DJ can place a song at just the right time and instigate a rush of energy from the crowd. DJ Don Bishop calls this "tickling the prostate."[40] Once the crowd reaches critical mass, and most of the dancers take off their shirts, the DJ then shifts musical gears to make them "climax," typically marked by shouts, hands in the air, and smiles. Expressing the intensity of climax for the DJ and the dancer, DJ Joe Bermudez compares the pivotal climactic song to ejaculation (literally, "the cum shot," an interesting choice of words for Bermudez, a straight DJ, to use when referring to his relationship with a predominantly gay crowd).[41] At the end of the set, the DJ-as-lover will ease up the intensity of the rhythms and "cuddle" with the dancers until it is time for them to leave.

In a community that favors the sensual over the sexual on the dance floor, it may seem a paradox that sexual language is used to describe the DJ-participant experience, especially since the DJ is removed from the crowd and does not actually touch the participants. This use of sexual imagery can be seen as a fondness for exaggerated and hyperbolic wordplay in the community's verbal performance. It also reflects the profoundly sublime pleasure felt by the DJ and the participants and resembles the use of sex metaphors by mystics to describe their own experiences of ecstatic joy.

The journey metaphor is best understood in the context of crowd dynamics. The circuit gathering is not just a large group. It must literally be a crowd, bodies close to each other for no other reason than the closeness, as if proximity overrides all other considerations. There should be just enough room on the dance floor for the dancers to move, or the venue will be considered too large. It is also preferable that the crowd be visible in its entirety, numerous and spatially close-knit. When seen from a few feet up, the crowd should resemble a sea of people.

In this required closeness, the crowd takes on the characteristics of wayfarers who swim in the communal sea and travel together under the guidance of the DJ. The journey is more properly an individual and communal *quest,* which is one reason why the DJs and the community often resort to neo-shamanistic language in describing the circuit experience. Each traveler may go through any number of adventures, defeats, and triumphs in a constantly changing milieu of interpersonal vignettes. The dance floor is an arena for any number of contests for attention. Guys will flirt, snub, and bond with others outside their immediate circle of friends. If somebody is found to be sufficiently attractive, he may later be sent on his way as his erstwhile suitor makes a bid to "trade up" for someone even more desirable. It is a community in constant flux.

Since the participants in the circuit come from a broad range of backgrounds, looks, regions, and musical tastes, it is a challenge for the DJ to bring them together as a team. Circuiteers arrive with their own cliques, inhibitions, and prejudices. Like a shaman, the DJ utilizes specific techniques for generating ecstasy. A good DJ first generates a communal heart-beat that demands everyone's participation. The music in a circuit party is usually within 125–135 BPM (beats per minute), about the same rate as a human heartbeat during a brisk walk. Continuous flow is key—there are few times when it is acceptable to noticeably stop, slow down, or speed up the BPM past this narrow range. The DJ will not use speech to encourage the crowd because that would disturb the flow and displace the crowd as the center of attention. Through adroit musical selection, a good DJ pro-gressively raises the level of excitement. The crowd exhibits its own *esprit de corps* and moves together as a team to reach the common goal of shared rapture.

DJs live for the moment when they lead the crowd through the maze of potentially devastating trials and tribulations to a "place" where all preten-sions and hang-ups shatter in the shimmering ecstasy of the living commu-nal pulse.[42] These moments are marked by their irresistibleness and hilarity—nobody remains outside the shared joy—sometimes even the bar-tenders and party staff are dancing.

COMMUNITAS

Participants in the circuit often narrate moments when the sexiness, the music, the dancing, and the sheer joy of showing off for each other will catapult the crowd into a state of hyper-awareness that some participants consider to be spiritual.[43] A party with no such moments is a failure.

Anthropologist Victor Turner calls similar forms of sympathetic sharing *communitas*. Defined as "humankindness," Turner describes it as "an essen-tial and generic human bond, without which there could be *no* society" (1969, 97; emphasis in original). *Communitas* is most apparent during rit-ual moments of "liminality," when people are neither one thing nor another and without status. Turner sees *communitas* as a universal phenom-enon, "a transformative experience that goes to the root of each person's being and finds in that root something profoundly communal and shared" (138).

Normative *communitas*, bonding for the purpose of explicit social engi-neering, is specifically utilized by male initiations designed to change a boy into a proper man. Initiations routinely force the production of *communitas* by reducing initiates to a status-less state through suffering, fear, awe, and the elimination of all possible distinctions. In this state of communal degra-dation, initiates can bond with each other. Spontaneous *communitas*, how-ever, is not forced. It is "a phase, a moment, not a permanent condition," that occurs on its own with the free consent of those who enjoy it (Turner 1969, 140). Turner calls it "ecstasy" that is "richly charged with affect, mainly pleasurable ones" (139).

Bonding in the circuit reaches its grandest expression when the DJ and dancers enter into a state of transcendent solidarity, when all distinctions crumble in the face of shared joy. This phenomenon appears to be spontaneous *communitas*. In the circuit, however, transcendent solidarity is fostered in a community that is obsessed with beauty and status. Can we truly consider *communitas* and transcendent solidarity to be the same if the latter is situated in a social setting marked by body fascism and illegal drugs?

The circuit community's preoccupation with beauty and status is a source of anxiety and humiliation, even for those who consider themselves to be "A-list" (specimens of physical perfection). One cannot be at the pinnacle without the constant fear of falling off. Nobody, no matter how good-looking, well connected, or wealthy, is above devastating ridicule by the ugliest, skinniest (or fattest), queeniest participant. Everyone feels the pressures of competition, which is why many gay men refuse to attend circuit parties, and why most go with friends for moral support. All it takes is a single eye-roll or sarcastic remark from the object of one's desire to utterly wreck one's ego.

These pressures shape the way the circuit community performs as a tribe. Unlike sports teams or political units, "tribe" is imagined to be a self-regulating entity without the need for impersonal bureaucracies, institutions, or enemies. The circuit community is self-regulating—random acts of kindness are the rule, not the exception. There is likewise a code of etiquette for regulating aggression that punishes excessively rude behavior with ridicule. In the land of the circuit, positive attention is the coin of the realm, and ridicule is to be avoided like bankruptcy. There is little need for bouncers in this world; sharp tongues tend to regulate behavior much more effectively than dress codes, metal detectors, or billy clubs.

Ridicule is a vital performance genre intrinsic to the community's internal regulatory mechanisms. Anyone who attempts to solemnize the neo-shamanistic elements of circuit ecstatic dance is, whether they deserve it or not, a candidate for spoof and ridicule. There have been normative movements, such as Soul Dance, to channel circuit spirituality as a means for group psychic healing by reducing or eliminating drug use and having dancers follow a script (Lennox, Kammon, and Maris 2000, 38–40). So far, these movements have been unsuccessful. Arguably, such admirable efforts have not caught on because of the importance of masculinized excess in circuit expressive culture (see Bataille 1986). Getting intoxicated, having a body with more muscles than it needs, and humorous exaggeration of stigmas and solemnities are all treasured features of circuit male bonding.

Perhaps it is because the circuit community is so competitive and anxiety-ridden that it prizes the moments when the barriers fall, when fierce ridicule transforms into all-inclusive hilarity and acceptance. Instead of a paralyzing fear of being seen as foolish, everyone is welcome to act a fool, to clown around, to laugh. These moments are perhaps the least sexually charged because participants interact in a state of innocence. It is during such moments that, interestingly enough, gay men can forget that they are gay and enjoy being men.

Circuit *communitas* is not like the normative *communitas* I experienced when being initiated as a marine on Parris Island or a Candomblé *ogã* ("patron") in Bahia, Brazil. Normative *communitas* is the result of manipulative directives for *reducing* participants as a means of eliminating status. The spontaneous *communitas* of the circuit is, using Turner's word, "invoked," not forced (Turner 1969, 138). All are invited to *rise* to the heights of transcendent solidarity together. The more that participants are raised up, the greater the joy is for all concerned. *Communitas* is a priceless gift that the dancers give to each other without coercion. To achieve it, the circuit must remain a frame in which the creative expression of the participants is paramount.

THE PROBLEM OF TRADITION

Distinctions are made in the circuit community regarding different kinds of transcendental solidarity. Many claim that the current state of the circuit is woefully inferior compared to its pre-AIDS antecedents, that the ecstatic bonding between men in past times was much more real and intense. The circuit today, they say, is messier, less personable, and less sophisticated.

"The central problem of tradition," Simon Bronner declares, "is explaining the ways that people rely on one another, with reference to precedent, for their wisdom, their expression, their identity" (Bronner 1998, 9). In the circuit, the problem concerns how people *dispute with* one another in what is an intergenerational conflict. Those who survived the devastation of AIDS during the formative years of the community often speak wistfully of the closeness and intimacy of earlier times. They tend to prefer the lush musical productions of the disco era over the sharp synthesizer "stabs," heavier percussion, and "noisiness" of contemporary circuit music. The circuit has become unwieldy, they say, too large and too impersonal.

The common referential point for this dispute is the Saint, which closed in 1988 due to the death of most of its clientele. The Saint has taken on the aura of myth and, to a degree, sanctity, which is not entirely undeserved. One Saint member said that the experience of dancing there was " 'liberating, spiritually uplifting. That's where I learned to love my brothers" (Brewster and Broughton 2000, 196). In narrative, one can hear in the gay community that there never has been a club as beautiful as the Saint. The etiquette at the Saint did not allow for drink glasses or cigarettes on the dance floor. After being doused and burned a number of times by fellow dancers, I have a degree of sympathy for the complaints of the "traditionalists" on this issue. The Saint community was not inflicted with GHB, a drug that leads to dance-floor convulsions and even respiratory failure. Although "Gina fall-outs" have recently decreased from what had been alarmingly high ambulance runs per party, they still happen with depressing regularity. Indeed, the larger, less regulated circuit community of today appears to be messier and less couth.

But, as with real-life idols, the halo around the Saint is not without tarnish. Body fascism and its implicit racism were perfected to a fine art there. With a balcony for sexual trysts right above the dance floor and no awareness for years that acting on the spur of the moment could lead to a life-threatening illness, the Saint was a prime site for HIV seroconversion. The popularity of PCP or "angel dust" during the Saint years created its own problems, with inevitable drug-induced paranoia. The Saint was sexist, initially not allowing women in at all, and then modifying its rule somewhat until it was forced by rapidly dwindling numbers to drop all restrictions and cultivate a straight clientele.

The "good old days" for any community tend to take on the fuzzy beauty of nostalgia over present-day grit and grime. The problem of tradition is exacerbated in the circuit, however, by the loss of almost an entire generation due to AIDS. If the expressive culture of the community has changed for the worst, and if the performance of masculinity has an unpleasant edge that was not found in the Saint, it could be due to the lack of mentors. Until recently, gays frequently mentioned that they had few older men to teach the younger men "how to do things right."

PARALLEL UNIVERSES

In American culture, the manly traditions of Promise Keepers and ravers may be compared to the alternative masculinity of the circuit community. The first time I saw the Promise Keepers was during a news program that showed thousands of men in a stadium, hugging each other affectionately (it was outdoors and hot, and many of the men were shirtless). I realized that this was the nearest thing that heterosexual Christian men could get to the circuit experience.[44] The Promise Keepers community (also known as "PK") was founded in 1990 by Bill McCartney (affectionately known as "Coach Mac") and Dave Wardell (PK website).[45] PK is demographically similar to the circuit in that it is primarily made up of European Americans. Its vision of masculinity is one in which violence is not an appropriate expression outside of sports or the military.[46] They are told, subtly and overtly, that racism is unacceptable. Violence in any form against wives and children is seen as cowardly and unmanly.

In order to achieve a more normative rather than spontaneous form of *communitas,* PK uses music, theatrical productions, and personal testimonies to break down its participants with an onslaught of highly emotional stories from coaches, ministers, and members of the military. Team membership is constantly referenced, and the audience is addressed as "men," just as a coach would address athletes or a general would address troops. The seductive power behind such discourse should not be underestimated. Many of the participants may never have belonged to a sports team or the military but may wish that they had so that they could feel more manly. Those who have belonged to a team in the past may miss the camaraderie and identity. The word usage unifies the participants and confirms their masculinity in a world where such confirmation may be scarce.

A big part of the PK bonding process comes through testimonials. Some stories have to do with failure to be the best father or husband. Others deal with family tragedies. The relationship between Jesus, the Divine Son, and His Heavenly Father is constantly invoked. Grandfathers, fathers, and sons often travel together with their friends and fellow church members to PK events, which are held in sports stadiums and arenas in order to accommodate large crowds that can number in the tens of thousands.[47] After listening to the testimonials, participants will no doubt share their own stories more openly. They are encouraged to express their own regret and sorrow (and sing!) in the company of other men. Counselors go through the crowd, ready to assist those who need individual attention. After a weekend of sessions, soul searching, and sharing, participants feel euphoric, freed from the demons of their past, and are better able to bond with their fellow men in PK's own brand of communal ecstasy.

There is no body fascism evident among PK participants. Space is reserved in front for those with physical handicaps, including the deaf, who sign-sing along with everyone else. Nevertheless, there is definitely a bias for the athletic type in speaker and performer selection. For example, one of the most popular performer-witnesses in the PK lineup is Joe White, a former coach for Texas A&M, who would carry a fourteen-foot log on his shoulder to the stage and then build a cross with twelve-inch spikes. The sheer strength of the man (who was in his fifties) and his masculine credentials as a coach, hunter, and motorcycle enthusiast make him an icon in the PK community.

PK events are very much men-only spaces. Women enthusiastically attend these conferences, but only as support staff. They do not go beyond the periphery of the stadium onto the main area because, as one female staff worker told me, "Men need to settle their problems by themselves. A woman's presence would only embarrass them." The biggest complaint of PK critics is that wives are expected to be helpers of their husbands, not leaders or co-leaders of the family. Variations in masculine and feminine expression, such as Leathermen and drag queens, are unacceptable. Homosexual men are welcome to attend if they do not "flaunt" their homosexuality. Heterosexual love and affection between men is encouraged—Joe White's newsletter is about the importance of "bear hugs" (PK website). Men will hug, sing, and cry together over the weekend in a veritable love feast of physical, emotional, and spiritual bonding.

The rave community is similar to PK in that it does not tolerate violence as an acceptable option in the performance of masculinity. Structurally, rave culture and the circuit are closer because both are based on secular dance leading to ecstatic experiences, while faith-based PK promotes ecstatic bonding through prayer and singing. Team performance, an essential role for participants of the circuit and raves, is less pronounced in PK in that its participants make up, for the most part, a clearly distinguishable audience that watches a staged performance. Military and sports, so dear to PK, are important in the rave and circuit scenes only as clothing accessories.[48] The tolerance of intoxicants (forbidden at PK events) also marks raves and circuit parties as kindred phenomena. Raves differ from PK and the circuit in the large number of female participants who attend them. Acceptance of diversity is much more pronounced in the rave scene than either the circuit or PK. More than a few circuit boys and girls began their dancing careers as ravers.[49]

The DJ culture that spawned both raves and circuit parties began in gay clubs in 1970s Manhattan. The rave community was formed when New York–transplanted Chicago house music (along with Detroit techno) and MDMA traveled overseas to England and the Spanish island of Ibiza in the late 1980s. The scene jelled there and quickly spread to New York, San Francisco, and eventually every major city in the United States and Canada (Silcott 1999, 17–46).

The average age of ravers is younger than that of circuiteers (twenty-two compared to thirty-three years). Like circuiteers, ravers tend to see themselves as a tribe. DJs are stars, perhaps even more so than in the circuit. Music can go from very slow grooves in the "chill room" (a lounge with its own DJ where the volume and room temperature tend to be lower) to fast-paced music as high as 170 BPM on the dance floor. Raves tend to have faster dance beats on average than the circuit (perhaps attributable to the exuberance of a younger crowd). This in turn necessitates the presence of chill rooms, rarely found at circuit parties, to give exhausted and overheated dancers a place to rest and recuperate.

Masculinity in raves is understood differently than in the circuit. A truce exists in the battle between the sexes that extends to relations among men. Rave sensuality is much less sexually explicit than circuit sensuality. Men learn quickly not to treat women the same way as they would in the alcohol-based dance culture of the typical club scene. There is more free expression—one may dance by oneself, with men, with women, with friends. The unwritten code that insists upon one-on-one dancing between a man and a woman is null and void. Men can learn to peacefully bond with *people* through the performance of rave ecstatic dance.

This is not to say that a man cannot be sexy at a rave. But it is a radically different kind of sexiness for straight men: "beer muscles" will draw ridicule rather than respect. There is also less emphasis on muscle and physical perfection. Clothing is looser and shirts do not come off as a matter of course. In general, men in raves tend to use their bodies to show off how well they can dance, while men in circuit parties use dance to show off how good their bodies look.

THE FUTURE OF THE TRIBE

Over the years, circuit parties have grown in size, extravagance, and expense. Since 2001, however, there have been indications that the scene is downsizing. Numbers have been lower at most of the parties. Some events are disappearing altogether.

The circuit world managed to avoid public scrutiny until 2001 when two articles about excessive drug use and sexual behavior during circuit parties were published in professional journals (Mattison et al. 2001, 119–26; Mansergh et al. 2001, 953–58).[50] The reports sparked a series of investigations by health officials, law enforcement personnel, gay media, and evangelical Christians. On June 20, 2002, the national newspaper *USA Today* had an article about the circuit and rampant drug abuse (Leinward 2002, 11). Four days later, *The O'Reilly Factor* television show featured a live debate concerning the same issue.[51]

Even before 2001, the federal government has been waging an aggressive campaign to eradicate the rave scene.[52] Since the rationale behind this campaign has been to save the youth of America from drugs, the older, gayer circuit community has not been targeted with the same vehemence. It is only a matter of time, however, before the circuit faces the same pressures as the rave community. As more attention is focused on the gay community with TV shows, movies, and gay media darlings, the more the public will be exposed to the glamorous and controversial world of the circuit. Scandals lead to crackdowns. Reduction in the availability of MDMA and other substances could possibly result in a more physically aggressive scene if participants go back to alcohol. This is doubtful, however, because there are other options for intoxication that skirt the law and are quickly passed along throughout the community, which is well versed and up-to-date on its own folkways. Psychoactive prescription drugs are already making their way onto the dance floor, and no doubt new chemical alternatives will be found that are not yet illegal. After all, MDMA club use started that way (Silcott 1999, 29–30).

One unexpected ally, the police force in cities that host the parties, may help keep the scene alive.[53] Since the police must deal with the violence of some straight crowds at certain concerts and sporting events, the refreshingly well behaved gay circuit parties have inspired law enforcement officers for years to overlook all but the most blatant displays of drug use. The presence of openly gay police officers allows for better communication between circuit promoters and officers to determine what problems in the circuit truly deserve investigation. Officers may continue to be tolerant and perhaps even supportive of the circuit, which often hires off-duty officers to act as security at events.[54] Unlike the federal government, local law enforcement personnel have everything to gain by coordinating their efforts with, not against, the circuit.[55]

Signs are that most circuit parties will continue to diminish. Yet their historical importance as ritual displays of gay masculinity is still significant. To justify their existence, circuit parties will have to be more than just parties. Those that are not fund-raisers will be more vulnerable to negative portrayals and crackdowns, as are parties not situated in week-long community-based festivals. Many people feel that the heyday of the mega-party with 15,000 to 20,000 participants has passed. Smaller, more intimate parties may be the wave of the future. The privileged stereotypical white circuit body will become less ubiquitous as more non-whites enter the scene, and physical desires merge with demographics. DJs are slowly but surely moving away from vinyl records to compact discs. They are also becoming better versed in the production of music, making more of their own remixes of songs and personalizing their sets even further.

With the advent of gay-based comedy shows, "reality TV," a gay cable channel, and gay issues in the mainstream press, Americans are becoming more familiar with the gay community. There is talk about the "new" urban man, dubbed by British writer Mark Simpson as "the metrosexual," who dresses with care and affects a "gay" look regardless of his sexual proclivity. The "newness" of copying gay sensibilities in dress, manner, and physique for straight male consumers is highly questionable, however. Susan Bordo traces its origins back to 1974 when Calvin Klein visited the Flamingo, one of the original Manhattan/Fire Island circuit clubs:

> Sex, as Calvin Klein knew, sells. He also knew that gay sex wouldn't sell to straight men. But the rock-hard athletic gay male bodies that Klein admired in the Flamingo did not advertise their sexual preference through the feminine codes—limp wrists, raised pinky finger, swishy walk—which the straight world then identified with homosexuality. Rather, they embodied a highly masculine aesthetic that—although definitely exciting for gay men—would scream "heterosexual" to (clueless) straights." (Bordo 1999, 401)

The biggest change since Klein's "discovery" and commodification of early circuit sensibilities into designer jeans is that people now realize that a rock-hard masculine body is no longer the sole domain of straight men. It is becoming commonplace for people to assume that a man who looks *too* good *must* be gay. With this realization in mind, one does not imagine the typical gay-mimicking metrosexual to be physically out of shape any more than he would be underdressed. I would imagine that more than a few metrosexuals have adapted other "hip" gay male attitudes and activities, such as going to circuit parties. In fact, I know some that do.

Circuit masculinity, with its privileging of muscle and macho, is a continuation of the club tradition witnessed by Klein in 1974 and is becoming as commercially exploitable for stylish straights as it is currently for gay male consumers. The circuit and the metrosexual "movement" are blurring gay and straight boundaries, but with a notable difference. Their novelty lies not so much in the blending of sensibilities but in the reduction of stigma attached to trendy urban homosexuality. As barriers between straight men and gay men fall, interaction between the two will become less difficult, and both will feel free to experiment with their sexual and social identities. Because the circuit is so unabashedly masculine, and because young straight men increasingly question the violence-tinged standards of heteronormative masculinity, I expect to see more straight men at circuit parties. Like gay men, they, too, can enjoy ecstatic male-bonding camaraderie without having to worry about violence.

We can also expect a better-educated and more mature circuit community. As mentioned earlier, one of the things that hurt the circuit was the death of almost the entire first circuit generation because of the AIDS epidemic. There is now an older generation in sufficient numbers to serve as examples to the younger ones. The eroticized masculinity of the circuit already privileges muscle daddies as legitimate objects of desire. This older generation is learning to stay physically fit (and sexually attractive) well into its forties and beyond, a phenomenon that impresses upon the younger generation that the party does not have to end if one takes proper care of oneself and one's friends.

N O T E S

1. Averages are based on my own observations of the circuit and conversations with promoters and are similar to those of Mansergh et al. and Mattison et al. The Mansergh survey (295 participants in San Francisco) is more restricted in age range (78% between 25 and 39 years of age) but concurs with me in that 70% are white, 91% have an education past high school, and 79% have an annual income between $20,000 and $100,000 (955). The Mattison survey (1,169 participants from across the country) differs somewhat from Mansergh in terms of categories: 76% Caucasian, 68% with a BA or higher, and 50% with an annual income of $50,000 or more (122). Both give an almost identical median age: 32 years (Mansergh) and 33.5 years (Mattison).

2. It is an interesting phenomenon to see these gay havens come into being. Usually a protective social bubble envelops these areas, and most homophobes tend to avoid them. Lately, however, the Christian Fundamentalist Right has been invading some of these spaces (such as Gay Days at Disney World in Orlando and New Orleans Southern Decadence in 2003) in order to protest the moral laxity that comes with the revival of Sodom.

3. There has been a significant rise in the number of Asian and Latino men

joining the circuit community. In some areas of the country, these groups may no longer be properly called minorities.

4. Four events draw both circuiteers and Leathermen: Southern Decadence in New Orleans, IML (International Male Leather) in Chicago, Folsom Street Fair in San Francisco, and the notorious Black Party in New York. For IML, Folsom, and the Black, the majority of participants will be Leathermen. As a rule of thumb, Leather parties tend to be more overtly sexual than circuit parties. Some circuit weekends include one night dedicated to Leather or, more commonly, military fetish.

5. Party List, Just Circuit, the Circuit Dog, Circuit Party Insanity, and Circuit Life are some of the more popular online discussion lists and Web sources of information.

6. "Flaggers" are dancers who artfully wave large pieces of colorful cloth. Flagging (considered by many to be the most spiritual side of the circuit) is usually an individual activity. It often puts the flagger into deeply introspective states. More than once I have heard flaggers recount experiences that they have had with the dearly departed while flagging.

7. "Body fascism" is a term members of the circuit community use.

8. MedEvent personnel are all licensed in the medical field as doctors, nurses, or EMTs who have been in the circuit scene and are familiar with the ever-expanding range of intoxicants and combinations that gay men concoct. MedEvent has state-of-the-art protocols for dealing with partiers that are, in many cases, superior to the standard practices of local health care workers. Local EMS personnel have been known to misdiagnose problems of patients, be it GHB-caused seizures or HIV medication complications. In 2003, MedEvent sponsored its first hepatitis vaccine parties in Dallas and Montreal.

9. Three parties of note in the production of harm reduction advertisements are Philadelphia Blue Ball, Chicago Fireball, and Montreal Black and Blue.

10. The Stonewall Rebellion was a lesson in successful violence management. It should be noted that the three-day uprising did not lead to a single fatality. Humor played an important role in keeping things in hand, which included an impromptu chorus line of drag queens that sang songs to the riot police, much to the amusement of the rioters. (Kaiser 1997, 197–202).

11. At least three gay pride weekends are also full-fledged circuit parties: the San Diego Zoo Party, Toronto Pride, and New York Pride.

12. The Saint (opened in 1980, closed in 1988) is a topic of gay men's folklore that borders on the mythical. DJ Warren Gluck said that the Saint was all about creating a rich aesthetic and transcendental experience. "When you stepped onto the dance floor, you walked into the music," he told me (interview, December 30, 2002). On certain weekends the Saint's crowd would dance from Saturday night to Monday morning. By 1980, the pattern for the then-embryonic circuit had been set: "The Saint's dancefloor would be a mass of bodies, each sculpted to perfection, moving in tribal unison. To the strains of the club's ornate music, these beautiful men would proceed to get utterly trashed—on angel dust [PCP], Quaaludes, ecstasy, cocaine, amphetamines. They were Greek gods with drug habits" (Brewster and Broughton 2000, 197).

13. Others argue that the modern circuit began when men began traveling coast to coast between clubs in LA/San Francisco and Manhattan.

14. DJ Robbie Leslie said that the custom of taking shirts off began in the late 1970s in the big dancehalls of New York and Fire Island (personal communication, October 26, 2002).

15. See "The Life and Death of Gay Clones" by Martin Levine (1998). He says

"the circuit" included the bars, clubs, barbershops, coffee shops, bathhouses, etc., that the "clones" would frequent in Manhattan.

16. Reynolds was also instrumental in raising awareness of and money for people with AIDS in Columbus.

17. Costs for the Black and Blue 2002 Main Event ("Humanité") were approximately $225,000 (Fondation BBCM 2002, 74).

18. In the modern West, the muscular male body began to be celebrated as the masculine ideal in the middle of the nineteenth century (Budd 1997, xi). At the end of that century, it had its first superstar, Eugen Sandow (b. Ernst Müller). Famous both for his physique and his strength, Sandow promoted what was then called "physical culture" and linked his own training regimen to athletic and military training (37–44).

19. In interviews with female bodybuilders, Maria Lowe says, "Most [female] bodybuilders gave examples of strangers making unsolicited remarks about their physiques, some of which were imbued with threats of physical violence" (Lowe 1998, 44). Bias against them is also present in competition: "Many in the sport, particularly officials and judges, consider it extremely inappropriate for women to take steroids [as opposed to men taking steroids] because they become too muscular and thus less feminine, whereas in male bodybuilders muscularity and masculinity are seen as compatible" (75).

20. The most fascinating aspect of the Stonewall Rebellion is that violence was initiated to alert the police and the city authorities that the gay community did indeed have "muscle" but would use it only when sorely provoked. It was a necessary accessory, so to speak, donned so that the message of gay pride would be taken seriously. Unlike other riots, there was never any deep-seated hatred or stigmatization of a target group. No call was issued for the death of anyone.

21. Michael Kaufman says, "boys [who were harassing girls] weren't doing it primarily to have an impact on the girls. They were doing it for the other boys. They were proving to the other boys and, presumably, to themselves, that they were real men" (Kaufman 2000, 220). Compare this with Maria Lowe on mistreatment of female bodybuilders: "Most of those [men] who felt compelled to make negative comments about the women's muscular physiques were men in groups while the female was by herself" (Lowe 1998, 44). Muscular gay men must occasionally bear the same group taunts and threats when they, as couples, "threaten" straight men by holding hands or kissing in public.

22. Alan M. Klein speaks of the vanity of bodybuilders: "It is true the narcissist craves attention. He or she thirsts for admiration, but, ironically, tends to disdain those who give it" (1993, 206). Nowhere is this more apparent than in the circuit in its not-so-stellar moments.

23. Folklorist Joseph Goodwin states, "A reluctance to accept female impersonators and flaming queens is also common in the [gay] subculture, since many gays feel that such people are 'politically incorrect,' reinforcing straights' stereotypes of gays and thereby hindering the cause of liberation" (1989, 61). This is true in the circuit as well, since many of the muscular "circuit boys" see themselves as the antithesis of the "faggy" stereotype. Nevertheless, most circuit weekends will have at least one performance by drag performance artists, many of whom are African American. Besides, muscularity does not guarantee masculine bearing. Some of the biggest muscle men in the circuit (popularly known as "muscle marys") can be quite nelly at times.

24. Racially inclusive advertisements have been produced by circuit parties that are situated in week-long community festivals, such as Chicago Fireball, Miami Winter Party, and Montreal Black and Blue.

25. This may change in the very near future, however. The demographics of the circuit population are shifting with the increase of non-European Latinos and Asian Americans. I predict that we will eventually see a broadening in what is perceived as the masculine ideal. Nevertheless, I do not see any change concerning the privileging of the muscular body.

26. In 1999, José Torrealba produced *Got 2 B There* (175 BPM Productions), a documentary on the circuit in which he interviewed DJs. producers, activists, scholars, participants, and critics of the circuit.

27. Nimmons states that "[Gay men] have arguably the most complex, flourishing, nuanced sexual culture the planet has ever known. No other population alive today enjoys a sexual milieu so elaborated and robust, so richly creative, as ours" (2002, 81).

28. The problem of drug addiction in the gay community is far from being limited to the circuit. Scott Van Tussenbrook, writer for *Circuit Noize,* described PnP: "A whole lexicon of terms has grown up around this 'scene,' and most seem to downplay what's happening or at least avoid using scary words. 'Chem friendly' in somebody's profile is a nice way of saying 'drug user.' But spend any time with these guys and you find that 'Chem friendly' really means, 'I can't have sex without crystal [methamphetamine].' The whole thing is so out of control they might as well cut to the chase. 'Looking to party n play. U?' as an opening line might as well be, 'I've bumped [snorted drugs] myself silly. Why don't you come over here and just drive your car up my ass?' " (personal communication, August 28, 2003).

29. Michael Warner describes the intricate gay male social network: "Try standing at a party of queer friends and charting the histories, sexual and nonsexual, among the people in the room. You will realize that only a fine and rapidly shifting line separates sexual culture from many other relations of durability and care. The impoverished vocabulary of straight culture tells us that people should be either husbands and wives or (nonsexual) friends. Marriage marks the line. It is not the way many queers live. If there is such a thing as a gay way of life, it consists in these relations, a welter of intimacies outside of the framework of professions and institutions and ordinary social obligations" (1999, 116).

30. Monogamy for gay men often does not include total sexual exclusivity. Most couples, in fact, do not expect it. Pointing out this fact about gay society, Nimmons adds, "When a clear majority of stable, successful long-term gay couples redraw the rules to include outside sex, and still about a quarter don't, it says that we *have clearly elaborated a parallel set of acceptable cultural norms*" (2002, 85; emphasis in original).

31. Mansergh reports that 46% of participants have a "primary partner" (2001, 955), while Mattison gives 49% (2001, 122). It is uncommon to meet somebody in a committed relationship at a party without his partner, and rarer still without his partner's knowledge or consent.

32. Goodwin says, "When gays use their folklore to cope with such pressures [tension caused by straight oppression], it serves to invalidate the straight world. In doing so, it validates the gay culture. It is this defiance that is the essence of much gay folklore" (1989, 63). The circuit, however, carries on without demonizing or even lampooning straight culture as much as it simply ignores it for the weekend. Nevertheless, modes of behavior that occur when so many gay men gather in one part of town tend to shock more than a few straight people.

33. This point was brought home to me in an interview I conducted with DJ Tom McBride. I asked him what the difference was between the solidarity of the circuit and the solidarity of the Nuremberg rallies of Nazi Germany. He said that the circuit is not unified *against* anyone (interview by author, June 16, 2003).

34. The following statement by somatics scholar Seymour Kleinman sums up the prevalent straight male understanding of the masculine body: "It appears that in our pursuit of and subservience to game and sport, the body almost acts as an obstacle which must be overcome. The body and its movement is viewed as the means to attain the ends of a game. We seek neither significance nor meaning to human movement" (1964, 123).

35. Susan Hatty states that "Organized sports generally involves spectacular contests, in which fit and muscular bodies are pitted against each other. Such contact between bodies is inherently physical; however, it is often violent. [It involves] the hardening of the body into a potential instrument of harm" (2000, 126).

36. There seems to be a shift to crystal methamphetamine over MDMA in some circles, possibly because crystal is so readily available and easily produced. Some participants complain that the prevalence of crystal has led to a more aggressive crowd.

37. Susan Morabito, Lydia Prim, Wendy Hunt, Kimberly S., Allison Calagna, and Tracy Young. All of these women are lesbians; I cannot think of a single nationally known DJ who is a straight woman, although three are straight men: Victor Calderone, Chris Cox, and Joe Bermudez.

38. Morabito stated that the sex metaphor is just that, only a metaphor. It is the best way she knows to convey the experience of DJ-ing and connecting with the crowd. "Sex is the analogy I use because everybody can relate to it," she said. "It's pretty impossible for people to *really* relate to DJing if they have never done it." Morabito also sees no difference between the sex and the journey metaphors. "Sex *is* a journey," she said (personal communication, November 4, 2002).

39. Lydia Prim said that circuit parties, particularly the Leather-based events, have an overpowering sense of sexual masculinity to them that she found appealing (interview by author, February 3, 2003).

40. Bishop, interview by author, November 6, 2002. Bishop listed three requirements for DJ-ing: count to thirty-two, drive a car (adjust the speed), and have a thorough understanding of anal sex to place songs in the set that have similar qualities of a sexual orgasm. "If you are a good top or bottom," he says, "you know just when the feeling is just right. If you get this while DJing, you place your songs to build and build until you pop" (personal communication, July 25, 2003).

41. Bermudez feels that the sex metaphor adroitly conveys the depth of pleasure possible for both sides in the DJ-dancer experience, adding, "When you're really fucking somebody, you don't have to ask if they're having a great time" (interview by author, July 25, 2003).

42. DJ Julian Marsh mentioned that the pleasure of the circuit in its transcendence, solidarity, etc., is felt by the DJ as well as the crowd. What many people do not realize is that the journey can be every bit as intense and desirable for the DJ as it is for the dancers. To interrupt a DJ with conversation, even when between songs, is to deprive the DJ of the pleasure, just as if someone interrupts a person dancing.

43. In an interview with DJ Barry Harris (May 26, 2003), I asked him if he had ever felt a total bonding with the crowd. His eyes lit up, and he spoke of it as an experience without equal, as if he and the crowd were, for that moment, telepathically bonded. When I asked him if he would consider that experience spiritual, he agreed. Most DJs I have interviewed have had similar experiences.

44. I attended a Promise Keepers weekend in July 2001 at the Nationwide Arena in Columbus, Ohio.

45. It is interesting to note that the circuit (outside of New York), PK, and the

rave scene all formed and grew at about the same time in the late 1980s to early 1990s.

46. Sports and military metaphors are used almost as frequently as biblical references.

47. Messner reports that 600,000 men attended PK events in thirteen cities in 1995 (2000, 401). Recent numbers are much lower: approximately 160,000 in 2003 (PK Web site).

48. Julie Ruckel of the Drug Policy Alliance and a rave aficionada, says that camouflage pants are worn to raves because they are comfortable to dance in and have plenty of pockets for holding water bottles, candy, etc. (interview by author, July 29, 2003). Both the military and athlete image are valued (and trivialized) in the circuit for their erotic appeal.

49. DJ Bob Ganem, who made the switch from the rave scene to the circuit scene, said that body fascism is not a problem in the rave scene because "Raves began as places where misfits could go and be accepted. There is a rejection of surface values" (personal communication, October 24, 2002).

50. The Mansergh et al. article indicates that there is substantial drug use and sex during circuit weekends. The abstract concludes that "Intensive, targeted health promotion efforts are needed" (2001, 953). The Mattison et al. article states, "circuit party attendees are well educated and financially secure. Party drug use is high . . . [party drugs] are associated with various measure of unsafe sex. More comprehensive research on club drug use in gay men is required" (2001, 120).

51. The debate was between two gay men, Richard Elovich (pro-circuit) and Michelangelo Signorile (against), which degenerated into a shouting match between them. O'Reilly, a conservative pundit who is not known to be a supporter of the gay community, appeared to be delighted with the fracas.

52. After an unsuccessful attempt to pass the RAVE (Reduce America's Vulnerability to Ecstasy) Act in 2002, Congress passed the Illicit Drug Anti-Proliferation Act in 2003 by quietly placing it within the Amber Alert Act for missing children.

53. See Nimmons (2002, 13–39) about police reports concerning lower levels of violence in gay bars as opposed to straight bars. The same trends can be found when one compares circuit parties with large-scale straight events.

54. Van Tussenbrook described the following conversation he had with police at a circuit party: "While attending the White Party in Palm Springs, I found myself standing next to a couple of off-duty cops who were hired as security. I asked them what they were thinking. The woman officer replied, 'Oh, this is our favorite party of the year!' and the (presumably) straight male officer with her nodded. The man said that at most straight parties and sporting events they have to prepare for lots of 'incidents'—fights, drunkenness, drama. 'But we never get any of that at the White Party,' the woman added. 'You guys just show up, take off your shirts, look pretty, and dance. It's fun!'" (personal communication, November 3, 2002).

55. There is an overwhelming silence and erasure in government discourse concerning the social benefits of a drug culture that reduces violent public behavior by men. Perhaps the government fears the consequences of such a culture on the young, especially those who are expected to continue American military campaigns. Homosexuals are still not admitted openly into the military or in many male contact sports because they are not considered real men, due, in part, to their distaste for violence. Rave masculinity undermines this in that straight men can be nonviolent like homosexuals. Circuit masculinity undermines it in that homosexuals can be considered as masculine as straight men.

REFERENCES

Bataille, Georges. 1986 [1962]. *Erotism: Death and Sensuality*. San Francisco: City Lights.
Bauman, Richard. 1984 [1977]. *Verbal Art as Performance*. Prospect Heights, Ill.: Waveland.
Bell, Catherine. 1992. *Ritual Theory, Ritual Practice*. New York: Oxford University Press.
Bordo, Susan. 1999. *The Male Body: A New Look at Men in Public and Private*. New York: Farrar, Straus and Giroux.
Brewster, Bill, and Frank Broughton. 2000. *Last Night the DJ Saved My Life*. New York: Grove.
Bronner, Simon. 1998. *Following Tradition: Folklore in the Discourse of American Culture*. Logan: Utah State University Press.
Bronski, Michael. 1998. *The Pleasure Principle: Sex, Backlash, and the Struggle for Gay Freedom*. New York: St. Martin's Press.
Budd, Michael Anton. 1997. *The Sculpture Machine: Physical Culture and Body Politics in the Age of Empire*. New York: New York University Press.
Chauncey, George. 1994. *Gay New York: Gender, Urban Culture, and the Making of the Gay Male World, 1890–1940*. New York: HarperCollins.
Circuit Noize website. 2003. http://www.circuitnoize.com. Accessed December 29, 2003.
Connell, R. W. 1995. *Masculinities*. Berkeley: University of California Press, 1995.
De la Huerta, Christian. 1999. *Coming Out Spiritually: The Next Step*. New York: Penguin Putnam.
Dryer, Richard. 2002. "The White Man's Muscles." In *The Masculinity Studies Reader*, ed. Rachel Adams and David Savran, 262–73. Malden, Mass.: Blackwell.
Durkheim, Emile. 1995 [1912]. *The Elementary Forms of Religious Life*. New York: Free Press.
Eliade, Mircea. 1964. *Shamanism: Archaic Techniques of Ecstasy*. Princeton, N.J.: Princeton University Press.
Fondation BBCM. 2002. *Humanité*. Montreal: Fondation BBCM.
Goodwin, Joseph. 1989. *More Man Than You'll Ever Be: Gay Folklore and Acculturation in Middle America*. Bloomington: Indiana University Press.
Goffman, Erving. 1959. *The Presentation of Self in Everyday Life*. New York: Doubleday
———. 1986 [1963]. *Stigma: Notes on the Management of Spoiled Identity*. New York: Touchstone.
Hatty, Suzanne E. 2000. *Masculinities, Violence, and Culture*. Thousand Oaks, Calif.: Sage.
Holleran, Andrew. 1978. *Dancer from the Dance*. New York: William Morrow.
Hufford, David. 1995. "Beings without Bodies: An Experience-Centered Theory of the Belief in Spirits." In *Out of the Ordinary: Folklore and the Supernatural*, ed. Barbara Walker, 11–45. Logan: Utah State University Press.
Kaiser, Charles. 1997. *The Gay Metropolis*. New York: Harcourt Brace.
Kaufman, Michael. 2000. "Working with Men and Boys to Challenge Sexism and End Men's Violence." In *Male Roles, Masculinities and Violence*, ed. Ingeborg Breines, Robert Connell, and Ingrid Eide, 213–22. Paris: UNESCO.
Klein, Alan M. 1993. *Little Big Men: Bodybuilding Subculture and Gender Construction*. Albany: State University of New York Press.
Kleinman, Seymour. 1964. "The Significance of Human Movement: A Phenomenological Approach." In *NAPECW Report*, 123–28. Interlochen, Mich.: National Association for Physical Education of College Women.

Leinward, Donna. 2002. "Worries Crash 'Circuit Parties.'" *USA Today,* June 20.

Lennox, Michael, Steve Kammon, and Pamela Maris. 2000. "Dance of the Passionate Heart." *Circuit Noize* 25 (Fall): 38–40.

Levine, Martin P. 1998. "The Life and Death of Gay Clones." In *Men's Lives,* 4th ed., ed. Michael Kimmel and Michael Messer, 55–67. Needham Heights, Mass.: Allyn and Bacon.

Lewis, Lynnette A., and Michael W. Ross. 1995. *A Select Body: The Gay Dance Party Subculture and the HIV/AIDS Pandemic.* London: Cassel.

Lowe, Maria R. 1998. *Women of Steel: Female Bodybuilders and the Struggle for Self-Definition.* New York: New York University Press.

Mansergh, Gordon, et al. 2001. "The Circuit Party Men's Health Survey: Findings and Implications for Gay and Bisexual Men." *American Journal of Public Health* 91: 953–58.

Mattison, Andrew M., et al. 2001. "Circuit Party Attendance, Club Drug Use, and Unsafe Sex in Gay Men." *Journal of Substance Abuse* 13: 119–26.

Messner, Michael. 2000. "Essentialist Retreats: The Mythopoetic Men's Movement and the Christian Promise Keepers." In *Men and Masculinity: A Text Reader,* ed. Theodore F. Cohen, 397–408. Stamford, Conn.: Wadsworth.

Newton, Esther. 1993. *Cherry Grove, Fire Island: Sixty Years in America's First Gay and Lesbian Town.* Boston: Beacon Press.

Nimmons, David. 2002. *The Soul beneath the Skin.* New York: St. Martin's Press.

Noel, Daniel C. 1999. *The Soul of the Shaman: Western Fantasies, Imaginal Realities.* New York: Continuum.

Pinchbeck, Daniel. 2002. *Breaking Open the Head: A Psychedelic Journey into the Heart of Contemporary Shamanism.* New York: Broadway Books.

Promise Keepers website. 2003. http://www.promisekeepers.org. Accessed November 3, 2003.

Rotello, Gabriel. 1998. *Sexual Ecology: AIDS and the Destiny of Gay Men.* New York: Penguin.

Signorile, Michelangelo. 1997. *Life Outside: The Signorile Report.* New York: Harper-Collins.

Silcott, Mireille. 1999. *Rave America: New School Danscescapes.* Toronto: ECW.

Tiger, Lionel. 1969. *Men in Groups.* New York: Random House.

Turner, Victor. 1969. *The Ritual Process.* New York: Aldine.

Van Den Berg, J. H. 1962. "The Human Body and the Significance of Human Movement: A Phenomenological Study." In *Psychoanalysis and Existential Philosophy,* ed. H. Rirstenbeek, 90–129. New York: E. P. Dutton.

Walker, Barbara, ed. 1995. *Out of the Ordinary: Folklore and the Supernatural.* Logan: Utah State University Press.

Warner, Michael. 1999. *The Trouble with Normal.* New York: Free Press.

Part II. Manly Expressions and Texts

7

The Folklore of Mother-Raised Boys and Men

What do we make of the commonly expressed folk belief that men are a great deal easier to understand than are women? Granted, men are far more likely to hold this view than are women, but even many women voice this idea. Perhaps because being male was the last "unmarked," taken-for-granted category in our study of Western cultures, women seemed to male scholars to be another sort of "exotic other," mysterious creatures that men strive to understand. In contrast, men tend to believe that males are rather simple, straightforward beings. For their part, women usually understand at some level that living within the patriarchy requires the ability to "decipher" men, to understand how these more powerful members of society see the world, if for no other reason than as a defense mechanism necessary to maximize a woman's happiness.

The scholarship on men's folklore generally adopts this folk view that men are rather more easy to understand than are women. Put differently, most folklorists writing about the folk cultures of men have not felt the need to resort to theory in order to understand the meanings of men's folklore. The one exception might be Freudian-leaning psychoanalytic theory, which in the hands of Gershon Legman (1968), Alan Dundes (1978), and a few others unpacks men's jokes, verbal duels, and games as symbolic thrusts and parries in the ultimate contest of "who has the larger penis?"

In contrast, the scholarship on women's folklore has been more eager to embrace theory. If the women's movement of the 1960s and 1970s was the impetus for folklorists' seeing women's cultures as suitable subjects for dissertations, articles, and books, the rise of feminist theories as tools for understanding how gender codes construct reality brought increased analytical sophistication to the project. Some folklorists studying women's folklore have been more friendly toward theory than have others, but the ongoing body of work (e.g., Farrer 1975; Jordan and Kalčik 1985; Hollis, Pershing, and Young 1993; Radner 1993) suggests that an active exploration of the complexities of women's folklore is underway, as women invent and adopt ways to make their lives more meaningful within a society and within organizations that assign them certain restricted roles and that limit their access to agency and power.

This large body of feminist scholarship in folklore studies is, almost without exception, by women and about women. Men appear in this work, but the complex players in the scenarios are the women, not the men. Men are still the simpler folk, easy to understand. What strikes me as odd about this situation is that feminist theory fulfills only half its promise for folklore studies if it restricts itself to the study of women. A theory of gender should be able to account for the social construction of masculinity as convincingly as it does the social construction of femininity. And, in fact, we have such theories. The rise of masculinity studies in the 1990s can be understood as a reaction to a great many forces—including a felt "crisis" of white, heterosexual masculinity in the public discourse—but it is also true that feminist theory had to reach a mature stage of articulation and critical practice before the theory could be turned on masculinities as its subject matter. Most of the scholarship on masculinities in the past ten years, including my own (Mechling 2001), has relied on feminist theory to explain men's varied performances of their masculinities (purposely plural).

Unfortunately, folklorists have been slow to appropriate this theory for their own study of men's lives in folk groups. The scholarship on men's folklore has done its work well by the usual expectations we have. That is, folklorists have studied complex, multi-textual folklore events in their full contexts, showing how men fashion their folk performances in response to individual personalities, family relationships, invented traditions, and inherited traditional forms. Thus, folklorists have been pretty good at answering most of what I take to be the fundamental folklorist's question—namely, "Who performed what traditional item for what audience, how, on what occasion, for what motives, and with what outcome?" The essays published in Elliott Oring's *Humor and the Individual* (1984b, a special issue of *Western Folklore*), for example, do an excellent job of answering the folklorist's questions (see also Fine 1987b, a study of boys' folklore in a Little League baseball setting, and Goodwin 1989, an extended study of the folklore of gay men). What gets shortchanged in most of this scholarship, however, is the "motives" question. Talk of motives drives folklorists to talk of the functions of folklore (see Oring 1976) and, occasionally, to draw upon depth psychology to say something meaningful about motives. Unfortunately, the probing of deep motives usually begins and ends with traditional Freudian thinking or its functional equivalent.

That men think quite often about sex and about their penises is no great news. Attributing these thoughts, including anxieties about penis size and sexual performance, as a motive for a folk performance seems almost circular in its reasoning. The story of why men have these thoughts and anxieties is the deeper story of motive that we need to explore, and fortunately feminist theory has a story to make this all much clearer. Men only appear to be easy to understand; in some respects, their gender and sexual identities are a great deal more complex than those of women.

My goal in this chapter, then, is to lay out the "story" that current, feminist-based theories of masculinity tell about the social construction and performance of masculinities. *Manly Traditions* seeks both to sum up where we are in understanding the folk roots of masculinities and to suggest some future directions for studying manly traditions. In that spirit, I want to steer new explorers of masculinities toward a whole body of theory and critical practice that may help bring us closer to a full understanding of the ways men use folklore to construct, maintain, and repair their masculine identities.

To illustrate my point, I focus briefly on penis jokes as a folk genre. In truth, the theory I outline here can illuminate any aspect of the folklore of boys and men, a point I make in my work on the folk culture of a Boy Scout troop (Mechling 2001). A focus on penis jokes, though, goes right to the root of the matter. So, after a brief excursion into penis lore, I pull back and show how feminist theory helps make sense of this obsession.

THE PENIS IS NO JOKE

"The phallus," writes feminist critic Susan Bordo, referring to the symbol of masculine authority and power, "haunts the penis," creating impossible expectations of potency. "Paradoxically, at the same time the penis— capable of being soft as well as hard, helpless as well as proud, emotionally needy as well as a masterful sexual performer—also haunts phallic authority, threatens its undoing" (1999, 95). Sometimes a cigar is just a cigar, as Freud is said to have quipped, just as sometimes the phallus is just a penis.

Even brief reflection reveals the pervasive presence of the penis in male folklore. I confine my comments here to male folk cultures in the United States, but a comparative perspective reveals much of the same obsession with the penis in male folklore through time and space. The folklorist could march through a list of traditional folklore genres and find endless references to the penis. Some men give their penises nicknames, and that name might become dyadic folklore between the man and his lover (Oring 1984a). Men play pranks and practical jokes (e.g., Ben Gay ointment in the jockstrap) involving penises, and fraternities and other male folk groups (e.g., the military) create elaborate hazing and initiation rituals focusing on the penis. In my fieldwork with a troop of Boy Scouts (Mechling 2001), I saw boys perform campfire skits about the length of penises, and a traditional way of tormenting a particular member of the troop was to ask him, "Do you have a pencil, Dick?" ("pencil dick" is a derogatory term for a thin penis) or to call someone "penis breath" (implying the target of the insult had just performed fellatio). Traditional and newly invented limericks often involve penises of some unusual length. And on it goes.

I narrow my inquiry here to jokes about the penis, in large part because the genre embodies so well one of the most important functions of folklore. Freud (1960) devoted an entire volume to the joke, which has been elaborated by psychologists, anthropologists, folklorists, and other scholars taking a psychoanalytic approach to humor (e.g., Wolfenstein 1978; Legman 1968; Dundes 1987; Oring 1992). Jokes often accomplish the functions and goals we attribute to all folklore, often expressing forbidden thoughts and feelings in a coded way or within the safety and license of a "joke frame," an agreement between two or more people that their immediate communications are to be taken as playful, as "just joking," and not as serious commentary. Jokes help decrease anxiety about a psychological or social situation. Jokes can be aggressive, as Freud said, but within the joke frame joking can signal relationships and group identity.

There is no end to penis jokes. A great many men and numerous women have an available repertoire of at least some penis jokes, and folders in folklore archives at universities bulge with many examples of such jokes. Printed versions show up in all sorts of books, and there are entire books (e.g., Cohen 1999; Paley 1999; Friedman 2001) and websites (e.g., www.the-penis.com, www.penisarchives.com, www.penisowner.com) devoted to the organ, with some attention in these books and websites to jokes about the penis and penis-related topics (e.g., masturbation). In some jokes (like their tall-tale cousins) men enjoy or endure enormous penises, while in other jokes the penises are miniscule. Circumcision, castration, and masturbation are other common topics of these jokes.

I do not seek here to gather and survey a collection of penis jokes, nor am I much interested in creating a typology of male jokes—which would be an exhausting task, in any case. Rather, I want to show how current theories of masculinity help make sense of the penis-centeredness of so much male folklore, and I also want to join others in steering the study of jokes away from the collecting, text-based approach and toward the more time-consuming, but much more instructive, ethnographic approach to the ways contexts make the meanings of these jokes.

Turning to theory might seem to some readers to take all the fun out of penis jokes. The study of folklore is fun, to be sure, and folklorists enjoy as much as anyone sitting in a bar at a convention hotel and telling jokes to one another. But without theory, our understanding of penis jokes (for example) is thin. Just about every man and woman knows that men have anxieties about their penises, and it does not take Freud (though it does take the pop Freudian understandings so familiar to everyone) to see that men joke about their penises as a way of addressing this anxiety. These anxieties also slip into mass-mediated, popular culture representations of the male body (Lehman 1993). Theory opens for us an understanding of the origins and depth of these anxieties, and the developing theories of masculinity go far in explaining the sometimes puzzling ways in which men behave. So, risking turning a lively topic dull, I first explain at some length the emerging theory of the social construction of masculinities and return, finally, to issues of joking about the penis.

MASCULINITIES AND PENIS JOKES

Jokes about penises, especially the size of penises, address men's real anxieties. Men rarely express these anxieties to anyone, but the anonymity of surveys (especially now with online surveys providing specific instructions on how to measure the length of one's penis) provides men the opportunity to report both their genital size and their images of their own bodies. These surveys (e.g., see the surveys available on www.jackinworld.com) consistently report average erect penis length to be in the vicinity of five and one-half to six inches. The surveys also report that one in four men thinks his penis is too small, and among these are many men whose penises are of average size.

Doubtless there are many reasons why men fixate on penis size, just as many women fixate on breast size. Folklore and popular culture narratives contribute to the notion that larger penises and larger breasts are better. Even the sociobiological literature on penises takes the view that "bigger is better" (within limits), reasoning that there are evolutionary advantages to the male's being able to deposit his semen deep in the female's vagina, as close to the cervix as possible, especially if (as some of these scientists argue) the male's sperm is competing with the sperm of other males who recently copulated with the female (Friedman 2001, 219–20).

My argument is that feminist theory—especially feminist psychoanalytic theory—contributes best to our understanding of the construction and maintenance of masculinities. Initially, feminist theory concentrated its attention on women. Eventually—and probably for reasons having to do with the "post-Vietnam syndrome" and other signs of a "crisis" in white, heterosexual masculinity in the 1980s—feminist scholars (including pro-feminist men using feminist theory) began applying their theories to the social construction of masculinities.

The fundamental project of feminist studies is to understand how the learned gender code in society affects the other ways people see the world and interact. Psychoanalytic theory, especially as revised by feminist scholars, provides powerful insights and tools for understanding the role of folklore in the everyday construction of masculinities. Freud's androcentric and nineteenth-century bourgeois Viennese biases notwithstanding, many feminist theorists, and the theories of masculinities derived from feminist theory, find psychoanalytic theory and method the most sophisticated tools we have for understanding patriarchy, capitalist society, and the psychologies of both men and women within society; the point is to discover how *both* men and women internalize and consent to patriarchal arrangements (e.g., Mitchell 1974). Although there are some feminist theorists who still work with Freud's basic ideas, feminist critics more often rely upon the later elaborations and corrections of Freud's initial insights, relying on such theorists and practitioners as Karen Horney (1967), D. W. Winnicut (1965), and others.

In much of this theory, the Oedipus complex and its solution in American society are at the root of patriarchy as it operates in the United States. This "complex" emerges in middle childhood as the developing boy must "solve" somehow his attachment to his mother and his jealousy of his father's access to the mother. Fearing punishment (i.e., castration) by the father, said Freud, the boy typically solves this crisis by identifying with the father and by distancing himself from the mother and, more broadly, from the feminine. Psychoanalyst Karen Horney (1932) elaborated this point, arguing that the boy's narcissistic withdrawal from the feminine creates "a dread" of women possibly stronger than the fear of castration. The boy's "solution" to the Oedipus complex, therefore, creates a rather shaky foundation—certainly an emotionally conflicted one—for the subsequent construction of male heterosexuality. The gender arrangement of the typical American family, in which women do most of the mothering under intensely emotional conditions, helps cement the power of the patriarchy and its "othering" of the feminine (Chodorow 1978, 1994; see also Connell 1995). Let us break this argument into its constituent steps.

First, the theory insists that humans are by nature bisexual. This was Freud's view. The flexibility and world-openness of human beings makes it possible for them to respond sexually to male or female. Society's project is to turn male infants into heterosexual male adults and female infants into heterosexual female adults, but a range of in-between possibilities testifies to the plasticity of human sexuality (Garber 1995).

Second, the theory notes that generally in patriarchal culture, women mother. Feminists and pro-feminist men aim to fundamentally rearrange traditional domestic roles so that fathers take an equal part in the early nurturance of children.

Third, it follows from "women's mothering" that in the pre-Oedipal stage the mother-son and the mother-daughter attachments are strong. The primacy and intensity of this attachment creates ambivalence (Mitchell 1974, 57). In the object-relations theories developed by Winnicott, Chodorow, and others (see Greenberg and Mitchell 1983), these attachments and the infant's gradual distinction between itself and the mother are powerful moments in the infant's development.

Fourth, the mother is the figure who introduces the pre-Oedipal child to the joys and humiliations of being and having a body. The mother is also the figure who introduces the child to the domination of the will.

Thus, it is in the pre-Oedipal period that the cultural creation of gender differences begins. The bisexuality of the child must be repressed in favor of identification with the culturally "appropriate" role model.

Fifth, the male and female Oedipus complexes are asymmetrical. The developmental projects for the male child and for the female child are different. The male child must separate himself from his mother and identify with the father. The female child also must separate herself from the mother, but she must then identify with the mother as the "appropriate" model for adult gender performances and sexuality.

Masculinity, therefore, is created by repressing the feminine side of the self. This is the key insight in this feminist theorizing about the social construction of masculinities. As Frosh puts it,

> Masculinity has the appearance of being defined by something positive— that which the male has and the female lacks. However, emphasizing this, as Freud did and as Lacan appears to do, is a masculine strategy employed to deny the implications of the converse, that masculinity is defined negatively, as that which is not feminine. . . . [T]he Oedipus complex operates as a division between child and mother: the boy only becomes a boy through renunciation of the feminine, not just as object of desire but also as subject of identification, and incorporation into the very general, very "other" paternal law. (1994, 79)

That "masculinity is defined negatively," as a "lack," has enormous consequences, many of which show up in men's folklore. One cost of patriarchal society's "solution" to the Oedipus complex, for example, is a misogyny felt and expressed by men and often internalized and expressed by women. Another cost of this "solution" to the Oedipal complex is a homophobia based on the repudiation of anything feminine.

Chodorow is quick to say that for both boys and girls "mothers represent regression and lack of autonomy," but it is also true, she adds, that masculinity "becomes an issue in a way that femininity does not" (1978, 181). Whereas a girl's "negative feelings" toward her mother tend to be fear and hostility, the boy's negative feelings are much more likely to be experienced and performed as "contempt and devaluation" (1978, 182). Building on Karen Horney's (1932) notion that men "dread" women's omnipotence and intimacy in early child rearing, Chodorow connects this phenomenon with the concerns of folklorists. Dread of the mother is "ambivalent":

> Although a boy fears her, he also finds her seductive and attractive. He cannot simply dismiss and ignore her. Boys and men develop psychological and cultural/ideological mechanisms to cope with their fears without giving up women altogether. They create folk legends, beliefs, and poems that ward off the dread by externalizing and objectifying women. . . . They deny

dread at the expense of realistic views of women. On the one hand, they glorify and adore. . . . On the other, they disparage. (Chodorow 1978, 183)

Sixth, because masculinity is founded on a negative ("not female") rather than a positive, this social solution to the Oedipus complex is extremely fragile, despite the seeming strength and permanence of hegemonic, heterosexual masculinity. The boy defines his masculinity as that which is not feminine, not the mother. Becoming masculine, therefore, is experienced as moving beyond maternal intimacy and dependence. In his best-selling book, *Real Boys,* William Pollack (1998) draws upon work by Deborah David and Robert Bannon to delineate what Pollack calls the "Boy Code." The "four imperatives" Pollack sees as central to the Boy Code are these:

- The "sturdy oak." Men should be stoic, stable, and independent. A man never shows weakness. . . .
- "Give 'em hell." This is . . . a stance based on a false self, of extreme daring, bravado, and attraction to violence. . . .
- The "big wheel." This is the imperative men and boys feel to achieve status, dominance, and power. . . . [B]oys and men are taught to avoid shame at all costs, to wear the mask of coolness, to act as though everything is going all right, as though everything is under control, even if it isn't. . . .
- "No sissy stuff." Perhaps the most traumatizing and dangerous injunction thrust on boys and men is the literal gender straightjacket that prohibits boys from expressing feelings or urges seen (mistakenly) as "feminine"—dependence, warmth, empathy. (1998, 23–24)

The small group cultures of boys (with plenty of reinforcement from adults and popular culture) enforce the Boy Code through a culture of shame. What is "shameful," in brief, is to think and act like a female.

Seventh, the fragility of the construction, maintenance, and constant repair of masculinity means that the boy and adult male must constantly "prove" their masculinity. This never-ending "test" might even lead to what Beneke (1997) calls "compulsive masculinity," by which he means "the compulsion or need to relate to, and at times create, stress or distress as a means of both proving manhood and conferring on boys and men superiority over women and other men" (1997, 36). Masculinity is never a state comfortably obtained and occupied; each day sees a new onslaught of assaults and tests. Masculinity is a project never complete.

Eighth, the creation and constant maintenance of this fragile masculinity has direct consequences for male sexuality. Men's attitudes toward sex are fraught with fears of intimacy and dependence, feelings that threaten to return them to the pre-Oedipal stage (Frosh 1994, 102, 112). "To the extent that sex is absorption in the body," writes Frosh, "involving giving up self control and overcoming inhibitions of desire . . . it represents the return of the repressed—of nature and all its feminine flows" (105). Fearing sexual desire as a potential loss of mastery, the boy converts sexual experiences and fantasies of sexual experiences into ones of "conquest and performance" (112). Against these feelings, true male sexuality tends to require activity rather than passivity, independence rather than dependence, detachment rather than engagement, and the status of penetrator rather than penetrated.

Several of these qualities require an erect penis, and therein lies some of the vulnerability of a masculine identity based on erections, penetration, and performance. Adolescent boys get erections when they do not want them, and men of all ages can fail to get erections when they do want them (see Friedman, 2001, esp. chapter 6, "The Punctureproof Balloon," on the erectile dysfunction industry). More important, perhaps, are the ways men tend to objectify their own bodies and body parts (e.g., Messner 1992, 62–67, 121–25). Male athletes develop an exaggerated instrumental view of the body, but most men do this to some extent. Once again, folklore provides some clues to this. Previously I mentioned that men are known to give nicknames to their penises, and it is worth noting that in doing this they often talk about "it" in the third person, as if it had an independent existence. Friedman's choice of title for his book on the history of the penis, *A Mind of Its Own*, merely reflects the folklore drawing a parallel between a man's actual head and the "little head" at the end of his penis. Consider this joke commenting further on the independent existence of the penis:

> God says to Adam, "Adam, I have some good news and some bad news. The good news is that I've given you both a brain and a penis. The bad news is that I haven't given you enough blood volume to use both at the same time."

Other examples of folklore reinforce the ways men detach themselves symbolically from their penises, while simultaneously strongly identifying with them. "Tool" is a common slang for the penis, as is "meat." More sinister, perhaps, is the penis as a metaphorical weapon—the condom as a "sheath," the army marching cadence, "This is my rifle [touching rifle], this is my gun [grabbing crotch], This [rifle] is for shooting, this [penis] is for fun," or the saying that a vasectomized man "is shooting blanks." One way to remain detached and autonomous during coitus is for the male to view his penis as separate from himself, as a surrogate entering the dangerous place. Male folklore, from the "AIDS Mary" and *vagina dentata* legends to various castration jokes and stories (e.g., jokes about Lorena Bobbitt's cutting off John Bobbitt's penis) play on male distrust of women (closer to Karen Horney's [1932] "dread of women") and what they will do to a man's penis, given half a chance:

This guy picked up a girl at a bar and took her to his apartment, and the next morning she was gone. He went into his bathroom and written in red lipstick on his mirror was "Welcome to the world of AIDS." At first he thought it was a prank, but he called the police who told him, "We didn't want to worry people but that's the seventh time that happened this year, and one of them tested positively." (Fine 1987a, 194)

Female Viet Cong would put broken pieces of glass or razor blades in the vaginas and then allow a G.I. to have intercourse with them. The result would have to be excruciatingly painful, physically disastrous, a fate worse than death. (Gulzow and Mitchell 1980, 308)

What did John say to Lorena after the deed was done? No hard feelings. What did Lorena say to John after the deed was done? I have the matter well in hand. (Collected 1994)

If women are not exacting revenge in many jokes, they may be denying men pleasure, as in this joke with many variations discussed by G. Legman:

A boy masturbating in a tree is reprimanded by an old lady who tells him that this wastes a possible president, baseball player, aviator, or similar. The boy continues anyhow, and the ejaculate lands at the old lady's feet. "I guess you're right," he says. "There goes an acrobat." (Legman 1968, I, 86)

Indeed, a great deal of penis humor involves masturbation, and we can learn a great deal about the penis and male sexuality by listening to how men joke about masturbation. In talking about "the male sexual script" in American culture, Fracher and Kimmel (1992) speculate on what masturbation teaches boys and men. The privacy of masturbation affirms sex as secret, covert, and hidden, and the focus on the penis teaches the boy to detach the pleasure of sex from emotions. The boy and man may fantasize during masturbation, but the fantasies tend to objectify everyone involved; the masturbator objectifies himself as well as the object of his imagined penetration. "The essence of pornography," argues Beneke (1997, 84), "is to offer men arousal and gratification without vulnerability, without risk to the self." Pornography, he continues, "is a kind of prop that attempts to offer training in the emotion work of attaining sexual arousal and gratification while feeling proud and feeling little identification with women" (85). Masturbation ironically encourages a radical separation of the self from the body. In reading Kimmel's (1990) collection of essays by men about their relationships to pornography, Susan Bordo expresses surprise to discover

a felt powerlessness at the heart of the psychology of male porn-consumption. This felt powerlessness is the deep belief that women are in control of male sexuality and thus "manhood" itself, through our [women's] power to intrude on male subjectivity and arouse desire and then to reject that desire, leaving the man humiliated, shamed, frustrated—and, often, enraged. (Bordo 1999)

Timothy Beneke (1982) found the same themes in the interviews he had with convicted rapists, who reported feelings of powerlessness in the face of female control of male sexuality. In fact, if the theory is correct, most men harbor some version of this "male rage" in the face of the dangerous intimacy and dependence sexual relations with women seems to entail.

Not surprisingly, many critics note that gay masculinities often merely reproduce the heterosexual script and the leading role of the penis in the drama. Beneke (1997: 156–70) devotes an entire chapter to "Gay Sexism," pointing to (among other things) the easy way some gay men denigrate "the feminine" in other gay men. As part of an hour-long radio documentary on "Sissies," for example, *This American Life* (WBEZ, Chicago, December 13, 1996, episode 46; see www.thislife.org) included a segment on gay men who take out personal ads seeking potential dates and mates who "act masculine."

Finally, what the cumulative theory presented here says about the social construction of masculinities seems to retain its explanatory power across social class, race, and ethnicity in the United States. In a society in which "women mother," all sorts of men experience similar socialization, a similar "solution" to the Oedipal complex. The "cool pose" that Majors and Billson (1993) identify as a common African American style of performing masculinity has its roots in the common need for the male to detach himself from the female, to keep his emotional distance precisely because the foundation of the masculinity is so tenuous (see also, Harper 1996). Latino men in the United States struggle with traditions of *machismo,* a conceptualization of masculinity a good deal more complex than outsiders imagine, but still one bearing similarities arising from defining the masculine as "not female" (see the essays in González 1996). Asian American (Eng 2001) and Native American masculinities have their own complexities, but (again) they seem as capable of misogyny and homophobia as do other stylized performances of masculinity. The brotherhood of the penis knows neither class nor race.

The theory I outline here describes the developmental, psychological dynamics underlying men's complex relations with their penises. In the psychoanalytical model, the deep dread and lesser anxieties are displaced in the unconscious and emerge as "symptoms," understanding that term very broadly to include a range of human expressions, including folklore, popular culture, and high culture. The folklore of boys and men is filled with these symptoms, so it is time to return to penis jokes.

PENIS JOKES VERSUS JOKING ABOUT THE PENIS

Folklore archives and published collections of joke texts help folklorists survey the topics and formula traditions of penis jokes. Collections of texts and their variations across time and space tell us something about the collective, changing themes that jokes might reflect, such as Clinton/Monica jokes (including references to Bill Clinton inserting his cigar as a penis substitute, as in the joke "How does Bill Clinton practice safe sex? He doesn't light his cigar") and Viagra (a prescribed medicine to cure impotence; its introduction sparked jokes based on traditional formulas such as "What do you call a snake on Viagra? Rod") jokes during the 1990s and into the new century.

By far the more desirable approach to understanding the role of penis jokes and other folklore in the social construction of masculinities is to use fieldwork (ethnography) to record and analyze the entire frame for the joking event. Again, who performed what traditional folklore, how, for what audience, under what circumstances, for what motives, and with what outcome? Who, what, where, when, for whom, why, and so what?

Unfortunately, there are not many examples of contextual analysis of male joking. We do have a few examples to build on. *Humor and the Individual*, edited by Elliott Oring (1984b), has three excellent essays (Leary 1984; Bronner 1984; Burns 1984) showing how a full contextual analysis can detect the multiple meanings of a joke in the teller's social and psychological contexts. Goodwin's (1989, 29–42) path-breaking book on gay men's folklore pays some attention to jokes, as do other ethnographic studies of boys in natural settings (Fine 1987b; Mechling 2001). It is far more important to understand the actual uses of a penis joke in its full performance context than to endlessly chronicle context-less penis jokes.

One night around the staff campfire at the summer encampment of the Boy Scout troop I studied for several years, one of the adult men told this joke:

> There's this guy in the army who's caught beating off [i.e., masturbating] in the shower, and when the officer confronts him and says, "Stop that, soldier," the guy just says, "Sir, it's my soap and it's part of my body, and I'll wash it as fast as I want to."

This version was close to the one I heard and incorporated into my own joke-telling repertoire at my boyhood Scout camp when I was about fifteen (around 1960). Part of the context for this joke is that the Senior Scouts (aged 14–17) developed a tradition of singing masturbation songs before camp staff meetings (see Mechling 2001, 30, 100, 192, 248). One of these songs has deep folk roots (see Cray 1992, 339–41):

> (Tune: "Finiculi, Funicula"—traditional Italian song)
> Last night I stayed at home
> And masturbated,
> It felt so good, I knew it would.
> Last night, I stayed at home
> And masturbated,
> It felt so nice, I did it twice.

Chorus
Whomp it, stomp it, beat it on the floor,
Wrap it around the bedpost, make it come some more
Some more, some more, some more, some more,
Some people go for intercourse
But me, I beat my meat. Hey!

Masturbation humor and insults (e.g., "penis breath") were much more common among the boys than were jokes involving the heterosexual uses of the penis, at least within my earshot. But that makes sense. The adolescent boys were experiencing considerable anxiety over a number of things. Their detachment from everyday life, especially from women, created intensified performances of the misogyny and homophobia the feminist theory predicts these young men will feel as they work on distancing themselves from the feminine. At the same time, a crucial marker of manhood is the ability to ejaculate (the only marker at all parallel to the girls' onset of menstruation). Most boys masturbate when they can, or at least know about masturbation and "wet dreams" (nocturnal emissions). At the same time, the "shame culture" of boyhood and adolescence often equates (through jokes and ritual insults) the masturbating boy with the "loser" who cannot get his sexual experiences from girls. Add to these complications the difficulty of a boy's masturbating at camp, where he is almost always in the company of one or more other boys, and one can see the psychological and social tensions concerning this topic in a summer camp full of adolescent boys.

Individuals and groups have available to them various possible strategies for dealing with situations creating ambivalence (Babcock-Abrahams 1975). In this case, the adolescent (ages 14–17) boys in the Senior Patrol took masturbation—which, in another frame, would be the cause for shame and teasing—and turned it into the centerpiece of a collective folk performance. The song "Last Night I Masturbated" tamed the personal anxieties felt by individual boys by making the personal threat impersonal (Abrahams 1968). Singing together a traditional, humorous song both tames the anxiety and works to signal the friendship bond of the boys.

I see in the song precisely the penis-centered obsession the theory expects to find in men's folklore. It also reinforces the separateness of the penis, the fact that it is a tool to be used and enjoyed.

The adult male's masturbation joke easily could have been told by one of the boys. Masturbation is as highly charged an issue for these men (many of them married or in monogamous heterosexual relationships) as for the boys, and the joke's content has the added enjoyment that the masturbator flaunts normal lines of authority, making personal rights claims in the face of an officer's otherwise lawful order to cease engaging in a genital act. This rebuff to military authority takes on even more meaning when we recognize that a prevalent feature of the socialization of enlisted men in basic training is the feminization of those men by the drill sergeant (see, for example, Stanley Kubrick's 1987 film *Full Metal Jacket*).

But is this genital act sexual, and what difference does that make?

This joke, like so much penis humor, distances the man from his penis. His penis, in this case, is just a part of his body he happens to be washing, quickly. But there is in this joke still another element—namely, that another man is the accidental audience for the act. The masturbator, rather than being ashamed, both rebuffs authority and presumably continues the act in front of the officer. Still, most men would not consider this a sexual act. It is a paradox of the performance of masculinity that men's nakedness in each other's presence actually reinforces the heterosexual norm. Presumed heterosexual men can be naked together because the frame communicates the metamessage, "This is okay because we do not view each other as sexual objects." The presence of openly gay men in the military disrupts this frame, threatening to cast the aggressive "male gaze" not on women but on other men. Presumed heterosexual men can even masturbate in each other's presence (the legendary "circle jerk") and engage in other genital play (e.g., in military or fraternity hazing) because they do not view masturbation as a sexual act so long as the participants are all heterosexual. This is penis-centered male bonding at its best.

Finally, we should note that women also joke about the penis, sometimes among themselves and sometimes with men. Quite often, these jokes are about size, confirming men's fears that women believe that "size does matter" when it comes to penis length and girth. Here are two examples:

Q: Why are women so bad at math?
A: Because they've been told all their lives that *this* [joker holds her hands about four inches apart] is nine inches.

The second is a joke I witnessed performed by a white woman in her late twenties at a Boy Scout troop "after campfire campfire" (Mechling 2001):

Q: Girls, how do you say "short" in three words?
A: "Is it in?"

In the case of the "Is it in?" joke, one has to understand the entire context of a traditionally male folk event (the Boy Scout leaders' campfire) that, in this one exception, includes women who are the wives or romantic friends of the men at the campfire. The campfire's frame is a complex one, something like adding women to a traditional men's rugby team's party. The folklorist can understand the "meanings" (including ambiguities) of the joke through understanding the frame and the relationships of the people in the event (Mechling 2001).

THE FOLKLORE OF MOTHER-RAISED BOYS

The feminist theory I review here—the theory underlying most contemporary work on the social construction of masculinities—helps make sense of a great many features of folklore in male friendship groups. It explains the misogyny and homophobia in much male lore, for example. It explains the dependence/independence struggle we see in the uses of folklore to "perform" and achieve a status within the male friendship group (Tannen 1990).

Certainly the theory explains the penis-centeredness of so much male humor. Given the central role of the penis in the social construction of masculinities, and given the fragility of that ongoing construction even with the most reliable erections, jokes are a natural folk genre for taming the fears and anxieties by exploring them in a safe, impersonal way. This is Abrahams's (1968) important point about folklore in our everyday lives, that folklore provides impersonal, indirect, safe ways to deal with some very personal, dangerous social and psychological threats to order. Men's folklore might help address men's dread at the "return of the repressed," but the project of "proving manhood" is never complete.

REFERENCES

Abrahams, Roger D. 1968. "A Rhetoric of Everyday Life: Traditional Conversational Genres." *Southern Folklore Quarterly* 32: 44–59.

Babcock-Abrahams, Barbara. 1975. "Why Frogs Are Good to Think and Dirt Is Good to Reflect On." *Soundings* 58: 167–81.

Beneke, Timothy. 1982. *Men on Rape.* New York: St. Martin's Press.

———. 1997. *Proving Manhood: Reflections on Men and Sexism.* Berkeley: University of California Press.

Bordo, Susan. 1999. *The Male Body: A New Look at Men in Pubic and in Private.* New York: Farrar, Straus and Giroux.

Bronner, Simon J. 1984. "'Let Me Tell It My Way': Joke Telling by a Father and Son." *Western Folklore* 43: 18–36.

Burns, Thomas A. 1984. "Doing the Wash: Cycle Two." *Western Folklore* 43: 122–26.

Chodorow, Nancy. 1978. *The Reproduction of Mothering: Psychoanalysis and the Sociology of Gender.* Berkeley: University of California Press.

———. 1994. *Femininities, Masculinities, Sexualities: Freud and Beyond.* Lexington: University Press of Kentucky.

Cohen, Joseph. 1999. *The Penis Book.* Cologne, Germany: Könemann.

Connell, R. W. 1995. *Masculinities.* Berkeley: University of California Press.

Cray, Ed. 1992. *The Erotic Muse: American Bawdy Songs.* Urbana: University of Illinois Press.

Dundes, Alan. 1978. "Into the Endzone for a Touchdown: A Psychoanalytic Consideration of American Football." *Western Folklore* 37: 75–88.

———. 1987. *Cracking Jokes: Studies of Sick Humor Cycles and Stereotypes.* Berkeley, Calif.: Ten Speed Press.

Eng, David L. 2001. *Racial Castration: Managing Masculinity in Asian America.* Durham, N.C.: Duke University Press.

Farrer, Claire R., ed. 1975. *Women and Folklore.* Austin: University of Texas Press.

Fine, Gary Alan. 1987a. "Welcome to the World of AIDS: Fantasies of Female Revenge." *Western Folklore* 46, no. 3: 192–97.

————. 1987b. *With the Boys: Little League Baseball and Preadolescent Culture.* Chicago: University of Chicago Press.

Fracher, Jeffrey, and Michael Kimmel. 1992. "Hard Issues and Soft Spots: Counseling Men about Sexuality." In *Men's Lives,* ed. Michael S. Kimmel and Michael A. Messner, 438–50. New York: Macmillan.

Freud, Sigmund. 1960 [1905]. "Jokes and Their Relation to the Unconscious." In *The Standard Edition,* vol. 8, ed. and trans. James Strachey. London: Hogarth Press.

Friedman, David. 2001. *A Mind of Its Own: A Cultural History of the Penis.* New York: Free Press.

Frosh, Stephen. 1994. *Sexual Difference: Masculinity and Psychoanalysis.* London: Routledge.

Garber, Marjorie. 1995. *Vice Versa: Bisexuality and the Eroticism of Everyday Life.* New York: Simon & Schuster.

González, Ray, ed. 1996. *Muy Macho: Latino Men Confront Their Manhood.* New York: Anchor/Doubleday.

Goodwin, Joseph P. 1989. *More Man Than You'll Ever Be: Gay Folklore and Acculturation in Middle America.* Bloomington: Indiana University Press.

Greenberg, Jay R., and Stephen A. Mitchell. 1983. *Object Relations in Psychoanalytic Theory.* Cambridge, Mass.: Harvard University Press.

Gulzow, Monte, and Carol Mitchell. 1980. "'Vagina Dentata' and 'Incurable Venereal Disease' Legends from the Viet Nam War." *Western Folklore* 39: 306–16.

Harper, Phillip Brian. 1996. *Are We Not Men? Masculine Anxiety and the Problem of African-American Identity.* New York: Oxford University Press.

Hollis, Susan Tower; Linda Pershing, and M. Jane Young, eds. 1993. *Feminist Theory and the Study of Folklore.* Urbana: University of Illinois Press.

Horney, Karen. 1932. "The Dread of Women." *International Journal of Psycho-Analysis* 13: 348–60.

————. 1967. *Feminine Psychology.* New York: W. W. Norton.

JackinWorld: The Ultimate Male Masturbation Resource. http://www.jackinworld .com. Accessed September 11, 2004.

Jordan, Rosan A., and Susan J. Kalčik, eds. 1985. *Women's Folklore, Women's Cultures.* Philadelphia: University of Pennsylvania Press.

Kimmel, Michael S., ed. 1990. *Men Confront Pornography.* New York: Penguin.

Leary, James P. 1984. "The Favorite Jokes of Max Trzebiatowski." *Western Folklore* 43: 1–17.

Legman, G. 1968. *The Rationale of the Dirty Joke: An Analysis of Sexual Humor.* New York: Grove Press. Reprint, Bloomington: Indiana University Press. 2 vols.

Lehman, Peter. 1993. *Running Scared: Masculinity and the Representation of the Male Body.* Philadelphia: Temple University Press.

Majors, Richard, and Janet Mancini Billson. 1993. *Cool Pose: The Dilemmas of Black Manhood in America.* New York: Simon & Schuster.

Mechling, Jay. 2001. *On My Honor: Boy Scouts and the Making of American Youth.* Chicago: University of Chicago Press.

Messner, Michael A. 1992. *Power at Play: Sports and the Problem of Masculinity.* Boston: Beacon.

Mitchell, Juliet. 1974. *Psychoanalysis and Feminism.* New York: Vintage/Random House.

Oring, Elliott. 1976. "Three Functions of Folklore: Traditional Functionalism as Explanation in Folkloristics." *Journal of American Folklore* 89: 67–80.

———. 1984a. "Dyadic Traditions." *Journal of Folklore Research* 21: 19–28.

———, ed. 1984b. *Humor and the Individual.* Special issue of *Western Folklore.* Los Angeles: California Folklore Society.

———. 1992. *Jokes and Their Relations.* Lexington: University Press of Kentucky.

Paley, Maggie. 1999. *The Book of the Penis.* New York: Grove Press.

Penis Humor Archives. http://www.penisarchives.com. Accessed September 11, 2004.

The Penis Owners Club. http://www.penisowner.com. Accessed September 11, 2004.

Radner, Joan Newlon, ed. 1993. *Feminist Messages: Coding in Women's Folk Culture.* Urbana: University of Illinois Press.

"Sissies." 2000. *This American Life,* WBEZ, Chicago, December 13, 1996, episode 46. http://www.thislife.org. Accessed November 20, 2004.

Tannen, Deborah. 1990. *You Just Don't Understand: Women and Men in Conversation.* New York: Morrow.

The-penis.com: A Website About the Penis and Male Sexuality. http://www.the-penis.com. Accessed September 11, 2004.

Winnicott, D. W. 1965. *The Maturational Processes and the Facilitating Environment.* New York: International Universities Press.

Wolfenstein, Martha. 1978. *Children's Humor: A Psychological Analysis.* 1954. Reprint, Bloomington: Indiana University Press.

8

Be Careful What You Wish For: Images of Masculinity in Tragedies of Wish Fulfillment

GREG KELLEY

Susan K. Langer once observed that fairytales, with their typical endings of resolution and restoration, become the narrative embodiment of wishful thinking. The folktale, she noted, "is frankly imaginary, and its purpose is to gratify wishes" (1957). Other scholars have termed the folktale *Wunsch-dictung,* that is, "wishful fiction" (see Rohrich 1991, 24). Moreover, with respect to psychoanalytical perspectives, wishful thinking and wish fulfill-ment can be regarded as one of the "principal characteristics" of folklore generally (Dundes 1971, 34). Without question, there are plenty of stories in European-American folk cultures about wish fulfillment, from prototypi-cal folktales to more contemporary renderings in American jokes. We can accept the spirit of these scholarly premises, while noting that there are narratives in which individuals are granted wishes, and the fulfillment of the wishes proves to be something less than what the recipient expects. Sometimes the result is overt disaster. No matter what the outcome, it is noticeable that the wisher in European-American folktales is typically a man.

In all the material collected here from oral sources and folk literature, the tragic wishes reveal the dispositions of men—in the reflections of them-selves, in their dealings with women, in their dealings with other men. As it turns out, folklore shows us that there is a dark side to getting what you ask for, and the examples provide a sort of construction of masculinity—a gauge of typical male anxieties, phallocentric rivalries, and aggression. This essay is organized into several subsections, each outlining a different man-ner in which wishes can be tragically fulfilled and the ways in which men are essentially victimized (by themselves or by others) as a result:

(1) ambition destroys the good luck of the granted wish;
(2) two wishes are used foolishly, and the third wish must be spent in re-pairing the damage;
(3) tragic wish fulfillment results from shortsightedness or some sort of misunderstanding; and
(4) fulfilled wishes are manipulated in order to inflict harm on others.

The representative texts that I have gathered exemplify a range of traditional and contemporary narratives, beginning with European oral and literary examples of medieval vintage and ending with contemporary American adaptations of the manly tradition of wishful thinking. In various ways, these narratives qualify, re-define, or confuse conventional notions of wish fulfillment—and they show men who, for better or worse, fall victim to their own wishing or the wishes of others. Wishing, in this way, demonstrates patterns of manly traditions, a glimpse into men's fears and foibles.

Narratives of wish fulfillment often involve some measure of upward movement, a transition from what might be considered an inferior position to one of higher social significance (Glazer 1979, 75). "The Fisher and His Wife," tale 19 from the Grimms' *Kinder und Hausmärchen,* is perhaps the best-known example. The folktale is about a fisher who one day hooks a talking fish that is actually an enchanted prince. The fisher releases the fish, and upon telling his wife of the magical fish, she urges him to ask the fish for favors. The fish grants the wishes of the fisher's wife, each one more avaricious than the one before. The wife requests a larger cottage, a stone castle, and then she asks to be king, emperor, and then pope. Even with all her wishes granted, the wife remains dissatisfied and grows progressively more desirous, finally insisting that the fish make her to be like God himself. This last arrogant demand is denied, and instantly she finds herself returned to the dirty hovel where she began. It seems at first that the wishes will be granted without limit, but the good fortune is reversed finally because of the temperament of the wife, who is appropriately punished, it seems, for her unreasonable requests that overstep moderation. In the end, it is her implacable ambition that nullifies the magic.

Antony Landon (1984) has argued that some early oral version of "The Fisher and His Wife" stored away in Shakespeare's memory may have become an impressionistic prototype for *Macbeth.* Shakespeare presumably would have found in the tale a ready-made narrative model for his drama—a man, perhaps well intentioned but weak in spirit, is seduced by mystical forces of nature and easily manipulated by his controlling, power-hungry wife, whose inexorable ambition ultimately undoes them both. Whether or not Shakespeare consciously recollected a told variant of "The Fisher and His Wife," the play's psychological backdrop of aggression as masculinity is an instructive model for reading the gender dynamics of the tale and its framework of overly ambitious wishing. To the point here, for Lady Macbeth, masculinity finds its natural expression in terms of political aspiration (effected, she believes, in exploits of cruelty and violence). She pushes her husband to acts of murder (and therefore to manhood [see Greene 1984])—and all the while her own realization of political power and personal malevolence emanates from a conscious program of de-sexualizing herself. The reversal is apparent in her solitary supplication to the darker spirits:

Come, you Spirits
That tend on mortal thoughts, unsex me here,
And fill me, from the crown to the toe topful
Of direst cruelty! Make thick my blood,
Stop up th' access and passage to remorse,
That no compunctious visitings of nature
Shake my fell purpose, nor keep peace between
Th' effect and [it]! Come to my woman's breasts,
And take my milk for gall, you murth'ring ministers,
Wherever in your sightless substances
You wait on nature's mischief! (1.5.41–50)

"Lady Macbeth has so internalized the stereotypes of her society," Carolyn Asp observes, "that she is convinced that she must divest herself of her femininity if she is to have any effect on the public life of her husband." Similarly, we can see the ambitions of the fisher's wife as a "desire to take on a male psyche" (Asp 1981, 160).

She demonstrates a rapacious appetite for material wealth and status, what might be regarded as a desire for masculinity with all its appurtenances: "wealth, power, prestige, and influence, together with independence, aggressiveness, competitiveness, and success." These are seen as trappings of male dominance, and "social dominance in males *is* masculinity" (Franklin 1988, 22; emphasis in original). In fact, social dominance in the manner that the fisher's wife and Lady Macbeth embrace it is an appropriated masculinity. The wife is granted her wishes to occupy escalating positions of political power typically associated with men. And thus the fisher, in a classic folktale role of the weakling husband, may appear symbolically emasculated in the face of her successive "manly" aspirations. These shifts in expected gender roles reverberate patterns of later American jokes, as noted by Carol Mitchell, in which male aggressiveness is deemed acceptable, while aggression marks a female stereotypically as "the nagging wife, the bitch" (1985, 167). Lady Macbeth and the fisher's wife circumvent those associations by taking on the mien of masculinity. We might impugn the fisher for his lack of fortitude (Mitchell observes that under-aggressive males in American jokes are often depicted as fools); but he garners our sympathies through it all, as perhaps Macbeth does, because he negotiates a bit of dignity amid his wife's relentless self-promotion. Still, sadly for him, circumstances unfold to their mutual detriment. That is, even though the wife's offense is considerably more egregious, the fisher suffers as much as she does when all the wishing is done.

In this way, the tale suggests a pattern by which we might consider other narratives about wish fulfillment. They often punctuate existing tensions in the relationships between men and their wives, who are in the wishing together, for better or worse. And more often than not, matters for them turn out worse rather than better. Even when material circumstances seem to end exactly where they had begun, as in this tale, the couples find themselves marred, for the process of adulterating the wishes instills in them a heightened awareness of loss and failing. Notably, among all the characters who are granted wishes in the stories gathered here, none recognizes the magnitude of the opportunity more than the fisher's wife does. But, as said, both she and her weak husband are undone because the possibilities are over-exploited.

More commonly, the wishes are squandered foolishly. Aarne-Thompson (1961) tale type 750, titled simply "The Wishes," outlines the characteristic features of one subcategory whose operative trope involves the imprudent use of two wishes—so that the third (and final) wish must be spent repairing the damage of the previous two. For example, in "The Rich Man and the Poor Man," another tale from the Grimm collection, a poor man is granted three modest and honorable wishes when he shows hospitality to the Lord. The rich neighbor looking on coerces the Lord for three wishes as well, but the result is quite different. On the way home, the rich man's horse stumbles, so he wishes its neck broken. After the horse drops dead, the man is walking along carrying the heavy saddle on his own back, thinking of his wife at home relaxing and having a good meal. At that thought, he wishes the saddle off of his back and his wife attached to the saddle, unable to free herself. When he finally returns home, he finds the woman in that uncomfortable position. And as much, then, as he wants to wish for great riches, he cannot ignore her emphatic protests: "You wished me up here," she says, "now you better get me off!" And so he does. All wishes gone.

As before, the wishing turns tragic for the rich couple only because of problems that exist between them in the first place. The tale gives no details of their marital past, but that is hardly necessary. It can be assumed to be a long history rife with fury and resentment, apparent enough as it percolates to the surface in the prospect of wishing. In some sense, the events of the tale are fated by the rich man's irascible anger. His exasperation at having imprudently wasted a wish by cursing the horse only increases as he plods along under the weight of the saddle. From there he falls naturally into an ill humor that will prevent him from ever realizing anything constructive from the wishes. Regardless of how fervently he ponders ways to exploit the remaining two wishes to his advantage, no good can come of it because his petulance colors everything (the tale describes his "hot and surly" temperament). It isn't surprising that his compulsive anger surfaces again along the way, this time leveled against his wife (simply because she is comfortably alone at home). Thus, he formulates the wishes unwisely, but for him true to character, as attacks. The final paragraph delineates the disparity of the wishing outcomes:

> Whether he liked it or not, he had to use the third wish to get her off the saddle and rid of it. His wish was fulfilled at once, and so he got nothing

but irritation, trouble, and abuse from the wishes and lost a horse in the bargain. On the other hand, the poor people spent their lives happily, peacefully, and devoutly until they reached their blissful end.

So we can see that moments of wishing are neither inherently positive (as might be expected) nor necessarily negative. Rather, they are fortuitous opportunities that point up the established state of affairs in relationships. Emotionally healthy enough couples like the poor man and his wife find their rewards. Dysfunctional types, like the rich couple, do not fare so well.

Other familiar variants have the husband wishing foolishly for only a sausage. He answers his wife's complaints by wishing the sausage attached to her nose—and the final wish is spent in removing the sausage. In one twentieth-century version collected by Vance Randolph in the Ozark Mountains in the United States, the wife wishes for a home-cured ham. The angry husband responds with a wish that lodges the ham in the woman's throat. "The ham was stuck in the old woman's goozle," the tale continues,

> She rolled on the floor, and kicked like a steer, and turned plumb black in the face. It looked like she was dying, and the old man was scared out of his wits. The only thing he could do was wish the ham out again, and so he did it. WHOOMP, and there it was back on the table. The old woman was cured quick as a flash, and she and the old man just sat there looking at each other. (1952, 140)

Notably in these stories, regardless of how or by whom the first wish is squandered, it is most often the husband who angrily expends the second wish in some malicious act against the wife. In some sense the wife cannot win in either case. She is punished by the husband for misusing the first wish herself, as in the Ozark tale, or for impugning his first wish, as in the following variant collected in Scranton, Pennsylvania, in 1934, whose cruelty is even more extreme:

> An old man and woman do a favor for the Fairy Queen, who tells them they can have any three wishes they want. As they cannot imagine what to wish for, living in the woods as they do, they decide to go to the nearby town and look in all the store windows. After looking all day, and not being able to find anything worth wasting a precious wish on, just at evening they pass the five-and-ten-cent store, and the woman sees a rotary egg-beater in the window. "Oh, look at that!" she says, never having seen one before; "I wish I had something like that for beating eggs." And there it is in her hand. The man is furious. "You could have wished for millions!" he shouts at her, "millions! billions! You could have wished for three more wishes. And instead you wished for *that*! I wish it were up the farthest corner of your ass!" And there it was. So they spent the last wish getting it out again, and lived happily ever after. (Legman 1975, 2:621)

We do not have to analyze very far to find phallic meaning in the eggbeater, shown first by the woman wanting it as her superlative wish and then in the fact that her getting it infuriates the man. But the most convincing suggestion is the man's use of the object against the woman in a symbolic sodomistic rape (see Legman 1975, 2:621). The joke articulates one type of masculinity, expressed as violence and sexual aggression. In Freudian terms, it is a conflict of the forceful id against its weaker counterpart, the ego. Ultimately, the extroverted sexual aggression is a show of power to subdue the woman; in this realm, efforts of repression are never fully successful because the male libido "is always straining to express itself in whatever way it can" (Brittan 1989, 48). Given that profile, it seems doubtful that the wishing couple could truly live happily ever after under any circumstances.

Moreover, it should not surprise us that in bringing together men and wishes, these narratives outline all sorts of phallic anxieties, sometimes represented symbolically—sometimes overtly. For example, *The Arabian Nights* includes a short tale of a holy man granted a series of wishes on the night of miracles. Reasoning that the larger a man's "zebb," the greater his manhood, the man requests of the benefactor: "enlarge my zebb even to magnificence!" The apprehensions of phallic compensation and castration are anything but subtle as this story unfolds (almost literally):

> This wish was no sooner expressed than granted. At once the saint saw his zebb swell and magnify until it looked like a calabash lying between two mighty pumpkins. And the weight of it was so considerable that he had to sit down again when he would rise. . . .
> His wife was so terrified by what she saw that she fled away each time that the holy man brought his new treasure to the business.

After some deliberation, the man uses his second wish to reduce the burden. The story continues:

> Even as he framed the words, his belly became quite smooth, with no more sign of zebb and eggs than if it had been the belly of a little girl.
> Needless to say, this complete disappearance did not satisfy the good man and was even more distasteful to his wife, who began to curse him and accuse him of cheating her. (Mardus 1923, 43–45)

Of course, the familiar pattern presents itself once again as he uses the third and final wish to restore that which he had in the beginning.

These variants of tale type 750 portray an array of wasted wishes, misused because of carelessness, anger, or ignorance. But the phallic associations, these archetypal male fears and fantasies, lead naturally into another category—wishes turned tragic because of some misunderstanding or seemingly innocent oversight. There is a fairy story about a prince who gains a horse-sized penis when he is given three wishes by a fairy. When the king hears about this, he goes out and finds the fairy and does her another service; then asks for the same reward, "To be hung like his horse." On the way back to the castle he suddenly realizes he was riding a mare [rather than a stud]. So the king and the prince get married and live happily ever after. (Legman 1975, 2:619)

The narrator added the tag punch line, "I told you this was a fairy story." What begins as a male fantasy of equine proportions becomes a sad story of castration. Certainly, the king gets much more—or less, rather—than he bargained for.

The castration anxieties are even more pronounced in another variant from Ronald Baker's *Jokelore*, in which a cowboy, riding through the desert, comes upon a rattlesnake and pulls out his six-shooter in order to kill the snake. But the snake begins to speak, saying that it will grant the cowboy three wishes provided its life is spared. The cowboy wishes for a new ranch house, he wishes for Brigitte Bardot to be lying naked in his bed, and finally, he asks, "I want to be hung like the horse I'm riding." Sure enough, he rides off to find a new split-level ranch house and a naked Brigitte Bardot waiting for him. At that, he jerks down his pants, looks down at himself and screams, "Oh, hell, I was riding Maude instead of Claude" (Baker 1986, 100; the teller is a seventy-year-old retired male construction worker).

Even before the joke's denouement of emasculation, in his wishing the cowboy may be telegraphing signals of compromised masculinity, according to familiar tropes of the Hollywood Western. "Westerns have always made an absolute and value-laden division between the male and female spheres, have always valued the one over the other," argues Martin Pumphrey. Whereas cowboy masculinity is connected with outdoor living, mobility, and emotional restraint, femininity is linked with romance and domestic containment. All traits feminine are seen as a threat to male independence and are generally viewed as "the negative against which masculinity is measured." The thinking is that men too closely associated with femininity—that is, men who willingly express emotion, who idealistically embrace notions of romance, or who commit to domestic pursuits—are rendered incompetent in some measure (Pumphrey 1989, 82–83). In light of these cinematic conventions, the cowboy in the joke can hardly be considered as the ideal image of manliness, for he appears too anxious to obtain the trappings of romance and domesticity.

Another variant, appearing in Richard Dorson's *American Negro Folktales* (1956), shows a different cowboy with his own particular wishes and his own set of accompanying anxieties. Appropriately guiding us into considerations of masculinity, the story begins, "This was a cowboy, and he wanted to be a strong man. So he saddled his horse and went down the street riding along." As with his counterpart in Baker's version, the cowboy happens upon a magical snake that offers him wishes in exchange for sparing its life. The list of preferences is very specific: "I wisht I had muscles like Joe Louis. And I'd like to have features like Clark Gable. I'd like to be as strong as this stud I'm riding." The consequences are discovered the next morning when the cowboy awakens:

> He throwed his bathrobe back; he says, "I got the muscles like Joe Louis."
> He looked in the mirror, and he says, "I got the features like Clark Gable."
> Then he pulled his bathrobe back again and looks down. He says, "Well,
> I'll be durned; I forgot I was riding a mare." (1959, 344)

The punch line of the blundered third wish is essentially the same as the earlier joke; but the preceding two wishes, which are realized according to expectations, are notably different and offer us another insight. The critical issue here, it seems, is the gendered coding with respect to the cowboy's gazing at others. The scopophilic (or voyeuristic) male gaze directed at women (e.g., in advertising, film, and pornography) has been seen as an assertion of heterosexual male power; the look is regarded as masculine and active while the object of the look is passive and feminine. On the other hand, "the male figure cannot bear the burden of [such] sexual objectification" because heterocentric imperatives discourage men from gazing at other men (Mulvey 1975, 12). That is to say, presenting the male body as an object to be looked at is, as Pumphrey puts it, "to locate it in a feminine position and thus inevitably feminise it" (Pumphrey 1989, 85). Within this frame, the Hollywood Western, with its "heterosexually normative discourse of masculinity," provides a contrastive model, as before, by which we might interpret the joke. The Western prescribes strict codes about how men, namely cowboys, are to negotiate the acts of looking and being looked at. The cowboy in the joke violates the generic expectations when, in effect, his admiring gaze objectifies and fetishizes the athlete and the movie star, transforming them essentially into models, or male pinups. It is a feminine and feminizing maneuver, and in that construction the cowboy, Joe Louis, and Clark Gable all lose something of their masculine credibility.

This reading fits with the emasculating conclusions of the jokes. As the cowboys ready themselves to exterminate the phallic snakes in the beginning, we are symbolically prepared for the literal castration that will occur in the end. But neither narrative takes us beyond the cowboy's discovery; we are left at the moment of castration (and, in the first joke, a disappointing occasion of terminal coitus interruptus). On the surface the king and the cowboy jokes seem the same, but the former one provides some latitude in its expression of sexuality. In fact, the king's castration might be considered disastrous only from a heterocentric perspective, for the joke incorporates presumably the deepest fantasy of male homosexuality—father-son incest. Nevertheless, the fact remains that the wishers in these stories, through their oversights or imprecise language, bring on the final cut themselves as instances of auto-castration.

The prospects are only slightly better for the wish victim in the following joke, collected from a colleague at the University of Georgia in 1989:

> This woman went to her magic mirror and said, "Mirror, mirror, on the wall, give me long, beautiful blond hair." The next day she woke up with a full head of gorgeous blond hair. Then she said to the mirror, "Mirror, mirror on the wall, make my breasts larger." The next morning she woke up with the most voluptuous breasts you've ever seen. Well, her husband was watching all this and he decided to get in on the act. He went over to the mirror and said, "Mirror, mirror on the wall, make it so my penis drags the ground when I walk." The next morning he woke up and his legs were two inches long. (Collected from a male University professor in his mid-fifties)

It is refreshing to see in this case that the wish granter, the mirror, has a genuinely feminist allegiance—and the husband is rightly rebuffed for subscribing to the common but erroneous male assumption that size is everything. That assumption is often projected onto the woman as a matter of female preference, as in the related joke about the man whose penis has grown so long that it "darn near drags the floor." When the doctor suggests that they operate and remove part of it, the wife speaks up, saying, "Hey, Doc, can't you just stretch his legs" (Legman 1975, 618).

Misunderstandings and misstatements of the wishers notwithstanding, sometimes the wishes are compromised because the supposed benefactors, for whatever reason, prove to be duplicitous or malicious.

> A fellow is having a few beers in a local pub on a Saturday afternoon when he is approached by a man dressed all in green. "Know what?" the man in green asked confidingly. "I'm a leprechaun, and I'm feeling extremely generous. So generous, in fact, that I'm willing to grant you any three wishes you'd like."
>
> "No kidding! Gee, that's great," blurted the lucky fellow. "I could sure use some extra cash.
>
> "No problem," said the leprechaun with a gracious wave. "The trunk of your car is now crammed with hundred-dollar bills. What's next?"
>
> "Well, I wouldn't mind moving to a nicer house."
>
> "Consider it done," announced the leprechaun grandly. "Four bedrooms, three-and-a-half-baths, up on Society Hill. And your third wish?"
>
> "Well, uh, how about a gorgeous blonde?" suggested the fellow, blushing a bit.
>
> "She's in your new house, waiting for you in a flimsy negligee."
>
> "This is really great," said the lucky guy, getting down from his stool and starting for the door. "I wish there were some way to thank you."

"Oh, but there is," spoke up the man in green. "I'd like a blow job."

"A blow job?" The man wasn't sure he'd heard right.

"Yup. And after all I've given you, it doesn't seem like much to ask, now does it?"

The lucky fellow had to admit that this was true, so in a dark corner of the bar he obliged his benefactor. As he pulled on his jacket and turned away, the man in green stopped him.

"Just one question," he asked. "How old are you?"

"Thirty-four."

"And you still believe in leprechauns?" (Knott 1989, 113–14)

Judging from his wishes, the man at the bar is not exactly innocent, but he is too trusting, and his credulity is exploited. The world of this joke is wholly cynical, for the unsuspecting man is penalized for his romantic willingness to believe in the realm of fairy tale magic. None of that magic exists here. Misfortune transpires not because of the man's ill-conceived wishing but because of his erroneous assumption that wishes can be granted in the first place; that is, the driving force of the joke is not his wish disappointment, per se, but rather the secret homoerotic designs of the counterfeit leprechaun, who, through self-serving trickery, ultimately finds his own sexual wishes fulfilled. It is important to keep in mind that we are not subscribing to some universal notion of masculinity but rather pondering a variety of masculinities, defined and re-defined by social and cultural context. The requests of the wisher in this joke—for all the trappings of material and heterosexual success—reflect conventional sensibilities of the urban male (though the very same sorts of requests might seem questionable within the expected codes of masculinity of the Hollywood Western, for example). His optimism is quashed and his wishes prove futile, because he fails to see the deeper (non-magical) insinuations of the exchange. In actuality, the leprechaun orchestrates the presumed symbiotic encounter into an antagonistic battle of differing masculinities. The wisher's willingness to engage the leprechaun homoerotically, even if only as a projected means to more traditional heterocentric goals, demonstrates that he has internalized the conflict into himself. We can note here, as R. W. Connell has generally, that one brand of masculinity "is constituted in relation to other masculinities and to the structure of gender relations as a whole" (1995, 154). It is difficult to challenge openly the "social authority" of hegemonic, heterosexual masculinity; therefore, homosexuality often finds its expression furtively, as it does here in the dark corner of the bar.

One general point with the stories of wish fulfillment is that the granter of the wishes, whether it is God, a fairy queen, a genie, magic mirror, or a leprechaun, holds all the cards. I have noted only one exception to the typical pattern, collected during an extended hand-clapping rhyme session between two girls, one eleven years old and the other fourteen:

There once was a genie with a ten-foot weenie
And he showed it to the woman next door [giggle].
She thought it was a snake
She cut it with a rake
And now it's only 5-foot-4.

The rhyme is obviously more compressed and stylized than the jokes and longer narratives, a simple function of its being a different genre. But the social context tells us something about why this text presents such a divergent message in its content. It appears in a playground repertoire that is almost exclusively the domain of adolescent girls. They may understand that genies typically possess the magical power of granting wishes, but that is not an imperative component of this genie's profile. He has traded the more familiar domicile of a lamp or bottle for a house in suburbia, complete with next-door neighbors. And there his magical powers diminish. What is vital is the fact that he is male, emphatically so. The genie sports a weenie for more than just poetic license in the rhyme. Exposing himself to the lady next door, he is inappropriately sexually aggressive—and because of that, in the end he finds his prodigious maleness de-emphasized, as it were. So we see the same sorts of characters and images that appear in the narratives—genies and phallic snakes—but the rhyme privileges real-life assertive female power over ethereal magical (male) power. Perhaps the girls find themselves already wary of the phallic snake from their previous experience with other playground folklore:

Cinderella, dressed in yellow,
Went upstairs to kiss a fellow.
Made a mistake and kissed a snake,
Came downstairs with a bellyache.
How many doctors did it take?
One, two, three.

Overtly, this popular jumping rhyme leads Cinderella into the world of sexuality as she is preparing to kiss the boy. That theme resonates with the tone of the familiar fairytale, which concerns a young woman's sexual awakening. The latent ramifications of her "kissing the snake" instead are more symbolically graphic, resulting in her pregnancy (i.e., bellyache) and inevitably calling for a doctor's care (see Mechling 1986, 101–2). With each turn of the rope the jumper adds another doctor to the list. One woman reminiscing about her childhood practice with "Cinderella Dressed in Yellow" recalled thinking, as did other neighborhood girls, that the doctors were required not for a conventional delivery but rather to perform a necessary abortion. The rhetoric of the rhyme, from the initial "mistake" and beyond, suggests an unwanted pregnancy. In her adult recollection the informant viewed the rhyme as a "scary indoctrination into womanhood." Another contemporary rhyme takes the girls into an intergalactic environment: "There's a place called Mars where the women smoke cigars / Every puff they take is enough to kill a snake." The long tradition of playful references to Freudian cigars notwithstanding, the sexual implications of women smoking cigars can be likened to Cinderella's kissing the snake. Here, the typically masculine behavior of smoking cigars is appropriated by the women and given a particular sexual energy, but that is coupled at the same time with a sort of sexual ambivalence, even repulsion, as their actions lead also to the death of the phallic snake. So in their folk culture, adolescent girls come honestly by their aversion to (the veiled suggestions of) snakes. It is not surprising, then, that in the genie rhyme they may find some unspoken satisfaction in the next-door neighbor's violent actions against the genie's disproportionate phallic presence.

The wish-granting genies are almost always male, and we might assume that a different sort of encounter would ensue with the typically gendered roles reversed. One salient example from American television culture is the popular sitcom *I Dream of Jeannie,* which ran for five seasons beginning in 1964. A thinly disguised male fantasy about sexual servitude, the program featured an alluring Barbara Eden as the female genie. She is contractually bound—according to the seemingly incontrovertible imperative of genie jurisprudence—to fulfill the wishes her master (played by Larry Hagman) because he had freed her from her bottle. Jeannie was sexual aggressor to the unwilling Hagman, who, improbably, discouraged her advances and insisted always on a platonic relationship, to Jeannie's apparent frustration (and to the general frustration of millions of adolescent male viewers). Similarly, the following joke—the only one I collected from folk tradition inverting the usual gender roles—places the female genie and the male wisher in sexual tension with one another.

A guy walks into a bar and he sits down on a stool in front of the bartender. He looks normal, his body size and all, but he has this tiny head. About the size of a peanut. You know, like Beetlejuice, remember, very little head that seems real little on top of his shoulders. The bartender says, "What the hell happened to you?" And the guy says, "Well, it's a long story, but anyway I was clearing out some land, you know, and I found this bottle. I didn't know what it was at first, what it could be, and I rubbed it and this genie came out, and the genie was a woman. A total babe. I mean, this genie was hot! And she was wearing one of those thin little tops, you know, and anyway, she says I can have any three wishes—whatever I want. So I said that I'd like to be the richest man in the world. And she said, "All right, you got it. What else?" Well, I said, I said I want to be the most powerful man in the world. And she said, "All right. You're the most powerful man in the world. One more." And I thought and thought and couldn't really think what else would do it for me. I mean, you know, all that money, all that power. What else is there? And all the time I was looking at this genie, you know, that little top and all and she was standing there with her hand on her hip, and I said, okay, baby, how about a little head? (Collected from a male graduate student in his early thirties)

As indicated, typically in the wish narratives even the most carefully thought-out wish can backfire if the powers that be, justified or not, are leveled against the individual making the request. In fact, the wish granters in some of these stories, it turns out, can be as sexist, racist, or malicious as the next person.

A black guy knew he had it made when an old brass bottle he found in the back yard turned out to have a genie in it. Any three wishes he had would be granted, the genie informed him.

"I wanna be rich," said the black man. The back yard filled with chests of gold coins and jewels in the blinking of an eye.

"I'm no fool," said the black. "I wanna be white." And there he stood, white, blond-haired and blue-eyed.

"Thirdly, I never want to work a day in my life."

And he was black again. (Knott 1982, 30)

Since the genie apparently subscribes to old racial stereotypes, chances are diminished that this black man will really profit abundantly from the wishes, regardless of how industrious or lazy he may, in fact, be. The joke does appear to be on him since he squanders one of his wishes, but his lot is better than when he began. After all, he remains rich in the end. With that in mind, we might question why he would still want to be white anyway. The implications are graver for another black man wandering down the beach who comes upon a tarnished old lamp protruding from the sand. He picks up the lamp and rubs it a few times. A genie appears out of nowhere and tells the man that he can have any three wishes. The black man thinks for a moment and then says to the genie: "I'd like to be white, up tight, and outta sight." So the genie turns him into a tampon (collected from a twenty-year-old male university student). The moral of this story, it appears, is that you shouldn't accept anything from a genie—because there are always strings attached. Perhaps the black man's heart is not really in the right place, because in wishing to be white he is compromising his own identity. But, clearly, he does not deserve to be penalized to this degree. Alas, as in our real world, sometimes the folktale world of wishing does not operate with much compassion—and a black man's wish submitted to an unsympathetic genie cannot turn out well in any case. But the nature of the misunderstanding is particularly telling here. When Stevie Wonder sang "Ev'rything is all right, uptight, outta sight" in the popular song "Uptight (Everything's Alright)" (Motown, 1966) it was understood that "uptight" and "outta sight" denoted something positive (see entries in Major 1994). The familiar lyrical phrase from the song is exploited for the purposes of the joke. First of all, the black man makes his request of the genie in what might be regarded as some dated version of ebonics. Perhaps the essence of the request is lost in the linguistic register of the presumably white, presumably racist genie—who insidiously literalizes the black man's metaphorical, vernacular diction. From that communicative confusion the gender issues once again present themselves; that is, his being transformed into an object that iconographically symbolizes menstruation is a quintessential feminization. In the request, the black man may have held fantasies of time spent inside women, but certainly not in the literalized, emasculating manner that his wish eventuates. In another version that more overtly recapitulates some of the phallocentric attitudes, the black man asks the genie, "I want to be white, I want to be hard all the time, and want to get lots of ass." So the genie turns him into a toilet seat.

Both jokes reverberate deep racist implications in their stereotyped notions of black manhood. Bigoted thinking has traditionally held images of black men as primitive, virile, and dangerously violent—a sexual exoticization that created distance and that was historically manipulated in order to rationalize subjugation. In lynchings between 1885 and 1900, for example, black men were only occasionally accused of having raped white women as the punishable offense, but almost always the acts of torture were justified in general as a way to protect white womanhood from the perceived bestial sexuality of the black man (see Carby 1986, 307). The fearful mindset of the oppressors was clear enough in the fact that lynchings commonly concluded with literal castrations. (At the same time, but more sublimated, there was a sort of idealization of the black man's sexual potency [see Segal 1990, 181].) Of course, these notions found different expression from a black perspective, especially later during the social climate of the 1960s. Black Panther activist Eldridge Cleaver conceived of the racial dichotomy in terms that empowered the black man with regard to the body, what he termed "the Supermasculine Menial." Strength, brute power, force, and virility became the touchstone attributes. Conversely, the white man, as "The Omnipotent Administrator," privileged the mind and was associated with weakness, frailty, cowardice, and effeminacy (1968, 180).

In their way of wishing, the men in these jokes seem to want it all. They conform to one part of the stereotype by seeking out a heightened sexual potency stereotypically attributed to the black male. But neither of them wants the blackness that goes along with it. They desire instead an accompanying social status and (non-sexual) social power; hence their respective wishes to be white. Essentially, they are endeavoring to become what Cleaver, and white administrators, for that matter, would regard as an impossible conflation of omnipotent social power and hypermasculine sexual potency. Much is at stake for them as they articulate such a request. In other wish tragedy jokes and tales, ill-fated recipients are castrated, blinded, deformed, or trapped in a compromising or inferior social position.

But only in the jokes that deal with black masculinity are the victims ultimately transformed into objects. It seems that their aspirations to contravene expected racial roles are read (by the genies at least) as a challenge, as a sort of arrogant affront to social mores. And the cruel requital is that the wishers in the end lose their humanity altogether.

Shortsighted wishers, although usually getting exactly what they ask for, cannot see beyond their immediate circumstances in order to make the most of the opportunities available to them in the proffered wishes. In the classic tradition of numskulls, these characters are destined to sabotage themselves because of their absurd ignorance or lack of discernment, and their antics often become satirical comments against a particular ethnicity or nationality (see Baker 1986, 93), as in the following text:

> A Pole, an Italian and a Jew are marooned on an island. While walking along the beach, one of them comes across an old bottle. He rubs it and out comes a genie, who is empowered to grant each of them their dearest wish.
>
> "Ah," says the Italian, "let me go back to the Old Country, where the wine is sweet and the women are beautiful." Poof!—he vanishes.
>
> "For me," says the Jew, "I want to go to the Holy Land and live out the rest of my days with my people." Poof!—he vanishes.
>
> "Gee," says the Pole, "it's kind of lonely here. I wish I had my friends back." (Knott, 1982, 42)

Another version groups together an Englishman, an American, and a Pole. The Englishman wishes himself returned to Piccadilly Circus, the American back in New York City, and the Pole, again the butt of the joke, wishes his friends returned to him on the island. In its varied permutations, the joke does indeed poke fun at imagined or real ethnic stereotypes or national cultural traditions, but it addresses as well notions of the fraternity of men. It resonates a pattern of joking noted by Christie Davies, that ethnic jokes stereotyping a particular group as stupid tend to exaggerate the group's fixation on leisure time and their place in the world as "social beings" (1990, 36–38). In this case, the Pole is marked as stupid because he is myopic in that arena, projecting a hyperbolic picture of male bonding—at the cost of all else, every luxury and even freedom itself. Perhaps we could admire the Pole because his wish is not purely self-serving; he makes his request based on sociability and a desire for restored camaraderie with his fellows. But his stupidity undoes the good fortune of his (more selfish) compatriots—and, sadly for the Pole, upon their return they will probably not consider him a *mensch*, or good person, nor are they likely to form a drumming circle to celebrate their masculinity (see Bly 1990). The Pole's wishing violates codes of male bonding, which allow for companionship and sociable esprit de corps but which generally prescribe a guarded stance against intimacy or mutual dependence.

Stories of wishes gone bad appear in another permutation, as the Aarne-Thompson tale type called "The Covetous and the Envious" (number 1331). Perhaps the oldest extant written variant comes from Jacques de Vitry's collection of medieval exempla:

> An avaricious man and an envious man were allowed to ask whatever they desired, on the condition that the one who asked last should be given twice as much. Each was unwilling that the other should receive more, and hesitated to proffer his request. At length the envious man said, "I wish one of my eyes to be torn out," and it was done, and the avaricious man lost both of his eyes according to the agreement. (Crane 1890, 212)

Although this text is classified under a separate tale type, it deals with the same sorts of anxieties as the other stories, since eyes, in psychoanalytical terms, are often seen as upwardly displaced symbols of the testicles, and dismemberments of whatever ilk are suggestive of castration. But we do not have to rely on speculative psychoanalytic readings in order to arrive at that conclusion. The folk mind has already done the interpretive work for us in this more recent joking version:

> There is this guy who absolutely hated his neighbor. One day he found this magic lamp, he rubbed it, and a genie appeared and told him that he could have whatever three wishes he wanted, but whatever he wished for his neighbor would get double the wish. So the man wishes for 100 million dollars. And he looks over and his neighbor gets 200 million dollars. And then he wishes for a twenty-room mansion; the neighbor gets a forty-room mansion. Seeing all this, the man gets really frustrated, and so he says to the genie. "For my last wish, cut off one of my balls." The neighbor lost 'em both. (Collected from a thirty-four-year-old male travel executive; cf. a similar version, "The Jew's Wishes," in Baker 1986, 150, told by a seventy-one-year-old male retired supermarket owner and operator)

Perhaps the wisher here is happy with the final result, but we must conclude that only in a demented, overly competitive world can his partial castration be regarded as a positive outcome; it is positive to him, of course, only in comparison to the more severe damage done to the hated neighbor. It leaves him as the Alpha male, at least in this neighborhood, but that is hardly a wish well spent. As in the other tales, the great possibilities of a granted wish are needlessly and senselessly squandered.

These stories and jokes are gathered from a variety of text sources and from my own field collection. It is notable that nearly all of the documented tellers from the written texts are male, as are the informants generating these jokes from their working oral repertoire.[1] This fundamental pattern in the present corpus of material bears out findings from other ethnographic studies showing the ways in which perceptions of masculinity can be reinforced, questioned, and even modified through the joking exchanges of men. Peter Lyman, for example, drawing upon the work of Max Weber, conducted case research on joking among males and found that their intra-gender jokes form a sort of structure of validation (and conformity) for societal notions of manliness. Functioning beyond simply recreation or as a means of stress negotiation, certain types of jokes, he observed, become "a reflection of the emotional foundations of organizational life for men" (1987, 157). In the context of telling, men's jokes are often competitive and aggressive, tending toward ridicule and humiliation and containing predominantly sexual themes, in marked distinction to jokes told among women, which favor "social or intellectual functions" (Ziv 1984, 158; see also Murphy 1999, 66–68). These more recent suggestions corroborate some of Freud's foundational psychoanalytic findings regarding joking and gender: men's jokes directed toward women tend to be erotic in nature and canny in form (turning on verbal maneuvers like double entendre), and to function in the realm of seduction. Jokes that men tell in the exclusive company of other men, on the other hand, are more aggressively sexual (rather than erotic), less clever in their form, and often openly hostile (1960, 99, 102ff.) These are attestations of what Gloria Kaufman regards as "mainstream masculinist attack humor" (1991, ix).

We should keep in mind that there is no single disposition that might be called *the* dominant masculinist perspective. As Michael Kimmel notes, "masculinity is a constantly changing collection of meanings. Manhood is not the manifestation of an inner essence; it is socially constructed. Manhood does not bubble up to consciousness from our biological makeup; it is created in culture" (1994, 120). The stories of wish fulfillment demonstrate as much, that narratively constructed images of masculinity are themselves contextually variable. We see a range of masculinities emerge in opposition to generalizations concerning the constitution of the so-called "hegemonic male"—in relation to sexual minorities, racial minorities, and women.

In that light, my analysis of this narrative complex is not proposed as an assertion of *the* meaning, but at least as a consideration of possible meanings. The corpus of narratives here presents a world of wishes in which as many things go wrong as go right; some of the basic assumptions about wishful thinking and wish fulfillment are undone, with the usual expectations parodied and inverted. Taken together, these stories of wish mishaps, or the more serious wish disasters, form a montage of masculine sensibilities. They dramatize men's existential dilemmas regarding the tensions in their relationships with women, homoerotic anxieties, male bonding, and a miscellany of phallic obsessions and fears—prompting us to reconsider what we may mean by masculinity in the first place. Ultimately, the tales and jokes suggest that men are vulnerable to and often victimized by their own deepest desires.

N O T E

1. As observed, only the jumping rhymes were proffered by females, and the core rhyme about the genie, with the male wish granter falling victim to a female assailant, is markedly divergent from the typical patterns in male-narrated texts.

R E F E R E N C E S

Aarne, Antti, and Stith Thompson. 1961. *The Types of the Folktale*. Helsinki: Suoma- lainen Tiedeakatemia.

Asp, Carolyn. 1981. "'Be Bloody, Bold and Resolute': Tragic Action and Sexual Stereotyping in *Macbeth*." *Studies in Philology* 78, no. 2: 153–69.

Baker, Ronald L. 1986. *Jokelore: Humorous Folktales from Indiana*. Bloomington: Indi- ana University Press.

Bly, Robert. 1990. *Iron John: A Book about Men*. Reading, Mass.: Addison-Wesley.

Brittan, Arthur. 1989. *Masculinity and Power*. New York: Basil Blackwell.

Carby, Hazel. 1986. "'On the Threshold of Women's Era': Lynching, Empire, and Sexuality in Black Feminist Theory." In *"Race," Writing, and Difference,* ed. Louis Gates Jr., 301–16. Chicago: University of Chicago Press.

Cleaver, Eldridge. 1968. *Soul on Ice*. New York: Delta.

Connell, R. W. 1995. *Masculinities*. Berkeley: University of California Press.

Crane, Thomas Frederick, ed. 1890. *The Exempla of Jacques De Vitry*. London: D. Nutt.

Davies, Christie. 1990. *Ethnic Humor around the World: A Comparative Analysis*. Bloomington: Indiana University Press.

Dorson, Richard M. 1956. *American Negro Folktales*. New York: Fawcett.

Dundes, Alan. 1971. "On the Psychology of Legend." In *American Folk Legend*, ed. Wayland Hand, 21–36. Berkeley: University of California Press.

Franklin, Clyde W., III. 1988. *Men and Society*. Chicago: Nelson-Hall.

Freud, Sigmund. 1960. *Jokes and Their Relation to the Unconscious*. Trans. and ed. James Strachey. New York: Norton.

Glazer, Mark. 1979. "The Role of Wish Fulfillment in Märchen: An Adlerian Ap- proach." *New York Folklore* 5: 63–77.

Greene, James J. 1984. "Macbeth: Masculinity as Murder." *American Imago* 41: 155–80.

Kaufman, Gloria. 1991. *In Stitches: A Patchwork of Feminist Humor and Satire*. Bloomington: Indiana University Press.

Kimmel, Michael S. 1994. "Masculinity as Homophobia: Fear, Shame, and Silence in the Construction of Gender Identity." In *Theorizing Masculinities*, ed. Harry Brod and Michael Kaufman, 119–41. Thousand Oaks, Calif.: Sage.

Knott, Blanche. 1982. *Truly Tasteless Jokes*. New York: Ballantine.

———. 1989. *Truly Tasteless Jokes, IX*. New York: St. Martin's.

Landon, Antony. 1984. "*Macbeth* and the Folktale The Fisherman and His Wife." In *Proceedings from the Second Nordic Conference for English Studies*, ed. Hakan Ring- bom and Matti Rissanan, 423–35. Åbo, Finland: Åbo Akademi Foundation.

Langer, Susan K. 1957. *Philosophy in a New Key*. Cambridge, Mass.: Harvard Univer- sity Press.

Legman, G. 1975. *No Laughing Matter: An Analysis of Sexual Humor.* 2 vols. Bloomington: Indiana University Press.

Lyman, Peter. 1987. "The Fraternal Bond as a Joking Relationship: A Case Study of the Role of Sexist Jokes in Male Group Bonding." In *Changing Men: New Directions in Research on Men and Masculinity,* ed. Michael S, Kimmel, 148–63. Newbury Park, Calif.: Sage.

Major, Clarence. 1994. *Juba to Jive: A Dictionary of African-American Slang.* New York: Penguin Books.

Mardus, J. C. 1923. *The Book of the Thousand Nights and One Night.* Trans. E. Powys Mathers. London: Casanova Society.

Mechling, Jay. 1986. "Children's Folklore." In *Folk Groups and Folk Genres: An Introduction,* ed. Elliott Oring, 91–120. Logan: Utah State University Press.

Mitchell, Carol. 1985. "Some Differences in Male and Female Joke-Telling." In *Women's Folklore, Women's Culture,* ed. Rosan A. Jordan and Susan J. Kalčik, 163–86. Philadelphia: University of Pennsylvania Press.

Mulvey, Laura. 1975. "Visual Pleasure and Narrative Cinema." *Screen* 16 (Autumn): 6–18.

Murphy, Peter. 1999. "Insidious Humor and the Construction of Masculinity." *Mattoid* 54: 61–73.

Pumphrey, Martin. 1989. "Why Do Cowboys Wear Hats in the Bath? Style Politics for the Older Man." *Critical Quarterly* 31: 78–100.

Randolph, Vance. 1952. *Who Blowed Up the Church House.* New York: Columbia University Press.

Rohrich, Lutz. 1991. *Folktales and Reality.* Trans. Peter Tokofsky. Bloomington: Indiana University Press.

Segal, Lynne. 1990. *Slow Motion: Changing Masculinities, Changing Men.* New Brunswick, N.J.: Rutgers University Press.

Ziv, Avner. 1984. *Personality and Sense of Humor.* New York: Springer.

9

Manly Characters in Contemporary Legends: A Preliminary Survey

W. F. H. NICOLAISEN

A quest for the folk roots of American masculinities, such as the one under-taken in this volume, cannot be convincing in its findings if it ignores the evidence provided by folk-narrative sources. What do the stories told in the folk-cultural register have to say about the perception of the American man by tale tellers and their audiences? While this is perhaps a net cast too far, a somewhat less ambitious inquiry may limit a similar investigation into the role and image of manly characters—not necessarily protagonists—in a particular folk-narrative genre such as, let us say, the comparatively short, and therefore also relatively manageable and accessible, stories which have received various scholarly labels, among them urban myths, modern myths, urban legends, modern legends, and contemporary legends. The fact that they have, in the essay which follows, been chosen for special scrutiny is not accidental because I have, over the past two decades, been involved in the study of a number of facets of that genre (Nicolaisen 1984, 1985, 1987, 1988, 1990, 1992, 2001) and have, in the course of these investigations, observed with passing interest, though never presented these thoughts in print, the kind of treatment that the notion of masculinity and its represen-tatives receive in the world it opens up, or takes for granted, for its tellers, listeners, and readers.

While recognizing the frequent usage by other scholars of some of the other labels already referred to, I prefer, and therefore use throughout this essay, the term "contemporary legend," not because it is ideal, but because it eliminates the special emphasis on modernity, removes the stories from an exclusively urban environment, and frees the narratives in this genre from any misleading association with a mythical time before our time or, worse, with any denigrating suggestions as to the credibility of their tellers and the gullibility of their audiences. The epithet "contemporary" is used here to indicate that these stories always have, in their temporal and spatial settings, close links with the times in, and of, which they are or were told; and the term "legend," once removed from its exclusive traditional con-nections with stories about saints and other religious figures, seems to be the closest we can get to in an attempt to define the narratives in question as residing on the edge of believability (not truth!) and in the vicinity of actuality, and therefore capable both of being told in the first person and, even more commonly, of having therapeutic effects as first-person stories told in the third person.

The corpus of "contemporary legends" to be examined in the following pages are solely drawn from a systematic cull of Jan Harold Brunvand's five volumes of "urban legends" (Brunvand 1981, 1984, 1986, 1989, 1993), excluding any instances or parallels adduced from non–North American countries. As the arguments put forward, on the whole, are not based on the significance of variants, references to other published collections will be limited to cases in which a special point is to be made. This also applies to Brunvand's more recent books on the genre (1999 and 2001) since these do not notably increase the number of types contained in the first five volumes.

The idea for the scope of this essay was prompted by a comment which Brunvand makes in connection with "modern legends about sex" (*CD* 147). "First," he says, "the urban legends about sex seem most typically to be told from a male heterosexual point of view. . . . Another side of this male dominance in the sex-legends is shown by the insulting way that certain male characters in the stories treat women." Without wishing to doubt the fundamental veracity of this statement or to reexamine the evidence for it, it seems a worthwhile undertaking to discover whether this supposed "male dominance" extends to the whole relevant inventory of contemporary legends, or at least to most of it. This essay therefore concentrates on stories in which men play significant roles, although the function of women will sometimes be alluded to, especially if it turns out to be an adversarial one, or if the characters of men and women are interchangeable.

In this preliminary survey, it is probably worth looking first at what might be called the "winners" among the male personnel of the relevant contemporary legends from a point of view both of actual gain and of moral qualities, in order to determine with what kind of characters listeners and transmitters of these stories can be said to be siding or even identifying. For example, there is never any doubt (how could it be otherwise?) about any satisfaction with the helpful veterinarian who, as a professional healer of animals, prevents the death of a faithful dog by successfully removing a burglar's two fingers from its throat, in the popular story of "The Choking Doberman" (see *CD* 3–18).

> A woman came home from a shopping trip, loaded with parcels, and she found her Doberman pinscher lying in the hall gagging and choking. She dropped her packages and tried to clear the dog's throat, but without success; so she picked up her pet, rushed back to her car, and sped to the veterinarian.
> The vet took one look at the wheezing watchdog and said that he'd

probably have to operate in order to remove whatever was blocking the dog's windpipe. He said that the owner should go home and wait for his call. The Doberman continued to choke and gag in a most pitiful manner, growing weaker by the minute.

The woman drove directly back home, and as soon as she got out of her car she heard her telephone ringing ["ringing off the hook!" people say when they tell this story]. She opened her front door and grabbed the phone; it was the vet, highly excited. "Listen carefully," he said in a tone of great urgency. "I want you to hang up the phone when I tell you to; then don't say a word, but turn around and run straight out of the door again. Go to a neighbor's and wait for the police to arrive; I've called them. Now! Don't say a word and don't hesitate, just get right out of there!"

The woman was greatly alarmed at the vet's message and his manner, but she was also very impressed. So she wasted no time in following the orders, and in a few minutes a police car came screaming up. The police explained that the vet had found two fingers stuck in her dog's throat ["two *human* fingers," storytellers often say], and he figured that someone must have been trying to break into her home when the Doberman caught him. He might still be there. The police searched the place and found a man in her bedroom closet, cowering back in a corner in a state of shock. He was trying desperately to stop the flow of blood from his right hand, from which two fingers had been neatly nipped off. (*MP* 41–42)

Similarly, in this era of frayed nerves and "road rages" in the world of car travel, there is apparently full approval for resourceful and compassionate drivers who, sometimes by unorthodox means, stop a potential "Killer in the Back Seat"—always a man in the narratives—from carrying out his plans (*VH* 52–53; *MP* 58–59), give a ride to a young lady in distress who turns out to be a phantom hitchhiker (*VH* 29–40; *CBA* 108–10), or come to the aid of a woman driver in trouble (*MP* 60–61) or of a celebrity whose car has broken down (*CBA* 114–16). And who would not applaud, though with envy in his heart and purse, a keen-eyed bargain hunter who manages to acquire, for ridiculously little money, an expensive sports car, often a Porsche (*VH* 22–23; *CBA* 123–24), or a 1953 Panhead Harley-Davidson motorcycle (*BT* 210)?

One's own parsimony, not to say miserliness, may, however, not prevent genuine admiration of generosity in others as, for example, when a sports celebrity (e.g., Reggie Jackson, Larry Holmes, Wilt Chamberlain, "Magic" Johnson), after inadvertently frightening a couple of "little old ladies" in an elevator because of his size and the size of his dog, makes good by surreptitiously paying for the ladies' dinner in a restaurant (*CD* 18–28; see also Beck 1984). Another positive trait looked for in celebrities or other persons who have reached a certain status in the world is humility, perhaps mixed with a sense of humor, as when another tall, black athlete (e.g., Karl Malone) plays along with being mistaken for a skycap, or a famous politician (e.g., Jesse Jackson) is mistakenly tipped by a woman who takes him to be a bellhop (*BT* 171–73). It is less easy to estimate the approval rate for the Mafia boss who, by dint of a phone call, arranges the return of stolen goods to his neighbor (*MP* 147), since the stereotypical notion of the "kind-hearted crook" receives here a less admirable, though thoroughly effective, admixture of powerful criminal muscle. On the other hand, there is likely to be much support for the manly "roughneck" who takes his revenge on his employer, who has just sacked him, by dropping a hammer or some other tool down an oil-drilling hole from which it has just been recovered at great expense (*BT* 163).

Bikers, especially in "gangs," are sometimes seen as destructive bullies who, after harassing a trucker in a diner, get their comeuppance when the trucker runs his truck over a whole row of motorcycles, crushing them flat in the process (*BT* 213–14). In another biker legend, the dictum that people are not always what they are thought to be is confirmed when at a large rally a group of manly bikers make their purchases in a store, frightening the storekeeper through their very presence although not actually doing any harm. The storekeeper therefore heaves a sigh of relief when they leave and welcomes his next customers, a group of college boys—who proceed to hold up the store and steal all the money which the bikers have just spent (*BT* 211). The story plays upon the cognitive connection of the threatening biker as primal giant man with aggressiveness and danger and makes commentary on the perception of manly appearance in modern society. A contrastive pair is established with the brawn of the biker, depicted as a burly operator of dangerous, greasy machinery, against the brains of the student, often depicted as slight of build and of poor eyesight, sometimes with upper-class associations—feminized in demeanor and occupation.

The troublemakers in student lore, however, are cast as men (Bronner 1995, 27–70). In the intramural ambience of academe, tellers of contemporary legends and their audiences, mostly students and other academics presumably, divide their sympathies between students and crusty, decrepit male professors, in the context of the all-important stepping-stone of examinations, sometimes sharing the success of an ingenious student who manages to beat the system (*MP* 196–99; *CBA* 275) and at other times giving credit to professors who fool students by giving unannounced tests or varying their expected questions (*MP* 191–95; *CBA* 284; *BT* 296). Fraudulent behavior and hoodwinking also occur outside the college classroom and seem, in some instances, to receive approval from tellers of, and listeners to, contemporary legends. After all, why tell stories about them otherwise? Cases in point are the "dishonest note" which a driver writes instead of giving his name and address after accidentally damaging a parked vehicle (*CBA* 118–20) and the ruse employed by a manly bricklayer to collect full payment for his work (*BA* 260). Perhaps more problematic might be the behavior of a criminal—again the threatening man—who takes a dog's place under a girl's bed and licks her hand during the night in order to remain undetected (*CD* 73–77; see also Baker 1982, 209), and several men who, hiding under cars, slash the ankles or Achilles tendons of passersby (*BT* 134–38), although the fact that they apparently avoid arrest may be regarded as a kind of "success."

In spite of these ambivalent examples, there are obviously certain legends (some of them in a number of variants) in which men and their masculinities are endowed with positive traits: helpful veterinarians, resourceful and compassionate drivers, lucky bargain hunters, generous or humble celebrities, even neighborly Mafia bosses, certain revengeful employees, well-behaved bikers, fraudulent students, and sneaky professors. Their laudable characteristics—helpfulness, resourcefulness, compassion, generosity, among others—reflect some of the qualities which most members of the general public might well approve of and are indicative of some of the kinds of positive traits associated with masculine behavior in North America.

Much larger, however, is the group of contemporary legends in which men play anything but praiseworthy roles, throwing a curiously oblique light on the whole concept of what may popularly be regarded as masculinity and casting considerable doubt on the idea of so-called male dominance. At this point, it is, however, worth remembering that the inventory of contemporary legends with which we are concerned in this essay is largely culled from written sources with only limited reference to actual storytelling situations and is therefore somewhat short of the kind of data usually collected from oral tradition. Nevertheless, it is more than likely that they mirror extra-legendary contexts and attitudes, similar to the ways in which they are narrative responses to people's anxieties, ambitions, fears, desires, suppressed feelings, and the like. Perhaps they might also have affinities to these insofar as one of their functions can be understood to be as therapeutic aids in inter-personal relationships.

A keynote to many of this larger group of legends may be expressed in terms such as male incompetence, failure, inadequacy, inexperience, and vulnerability in connection with their jobs, chosen activities, or roles in their relationship to women. Thus we come across an incompetent carpet layer who kills the house owner's pet canary, parakeet, or hamster by flattening a bump in a new carpet he has just laid (*CD* 94); two careless welders who are killed when a spark ignites their butane lighters (*MP* 164–65); a novice driver who sets the cruise control of his recreational vehicle at sixty miles per hour and then steps back to fix himself a drink (*CD* 64); a young man, anxious to please, who, while waiting for his girlfriend in her apartment on the fortieth floor of a New York City high-rise, tosses a ball to be retrieved by her dog, but the ball bounces out the open window, and the dog jumps after it (*CD* 97); a scuba diver who, during a forest fire, is scooped up from a nearby lake by a fire-fighting plane and then dumped on the blaze, ending up tangled in the branches of a blackened tree (*CBA* 47); a mortuary employee who, discovering that the corpse of a woman he is transporting in his hearse is still alive, radios for an ambulance with which he collides in his excitement, thus killing the woman (*CBA* 67); a patient who dies from a bad reaction to an anesthesia while his dentist is attempting to put another patient under gas, who also dies (*CPA* 68–69); a frustrated bank robber who inserts a slip of paper into a bank's ATM, saying "Give me all your money or I'll shoot" (he is arrested after shooting the machine full of holes) (*CBA* 189); an insecure professor who is "trained" by his student audience to lecture while standing on a waste basket (*CBA* 311); an older man who is mistaken by a young female hairdresser for a sexual deviant when he is polishing his glasses under the covering sheet and who is knocked unconscious by her (*BT* 44); a doting father, dressed up as Santa Claus, who gets stuck in a chimney and dies of asphyxiation (*BY* 74); a dimwitted burglar fooled by a "quick-thinking woman" (*BT* 113–14); a woman on a Manhattan subway who tears a much more valuable gold chain off the neck of an attacker who has just stolen hers (*BT* 125); a fraudulent blackjack dealer in Nevada who is beaten by his own ruse of dropping money into his boot tops (*BT* 129); credulous criminals who confess to their crimes by the police use of a colander as a "lie detector" (*BT* 139); a car thief who is killed when the car he has stolen is destroyed on the I-880 freeway as the result of an earthquake (*BT* 146–47); an examiner who meets his death when he jumps out in front of the wrong motorcycle to test the driver's reactions (*BT* 214); a young motorcyclist who is run over by an oncoming truck when he mistakes the truck's headlights for those of his two cyclist friends (*BT* 215–16); an arrogant young man who is outwitted by an older woman in a dispute over a parking space (*MP* 67); various disguised potential killers in back seats of cars who are unsuccessful because of the vigilance of others (*VH* 52–53; *MP* 58–59, 157); and similarly, a "Hairy-Armed Hitchhiker" exposed and caught (*CD* 52–55). Also in this category are a would-be burglar attacked and mauled by a watchful dog (*CD* 6–17; *MP* 41); another male burglar dressed as a woman outwitted by a ruse by the lady of the house (*MP* 121); and a criminal with a hook on one arm failing in his attempt to enter the car of a courting couple (VH 48–52).

A cluster of stories relates the revenge or other actions by women in which men are the hapless or deserved victims or men show by their own behavior that they are "losers" in their relationship with the opposite sex: at the top of the list is probably the "Philanderer's Porsche" (or expensive sports car or motorcycle) which is sold extremely cheaply by a betrayed woman to take revenge on her unfaithful husband (*VH* 22–23; *CBA* 123–24; *BT* 210). Then there is the husband who is trapped with his lover and uncomfortably driven by his wife around the country in a recreational vehicle (*CD* 66–67); another husband's erect penis is superglued to his abdomen by his wife in punishment of his infidelity (*CD* 146); a business-man intending to enjoy an escapade on a train journey is robbed of his wallet and left stranded by a woman of considerable charm (*VH* 136–38); a young man discovers that the father of a young girl whom he looks for-ward to dating is the pharmacist from whom he has earlier bought con-doms (*MP* 126); a jealous husband shoots the wrong milkman, taken by him to be the one with whom his wife has had an affair (*MP* 132); a hus-band's affair with a neighbor comes to light when the dog instinctively takes his wife to his lady friend's house on a morning walk (*MP* 132–33); and a would-be bride slaps the bridegroom at a wedding ceremony in pun-ishment for his infidelity with the maid of honor the night before (*MP* 134–35). Some variants of the widespread "Welcome to the World of AIDS" legends attribute the deliberate infection of a male partner with the disease to an enraged, recently divorced wife (*CBA* 195–202); a live-in girlfriend dumped by her boyfriend takes her revenge by dialing a weather number in Tokyo and then leaving the phone off the hook for a week (*CBA* 216–17); a husband dressing up as Batman in a sex session with another woman hurts himself when he is jumping down onto her from a dresser (*BT* 39–40); businessmen who have on several occasions gone on flights with other women are caught when an airline employee phones one of the wives with a query about the tickets (*BT* 116–18).

Closely linked to this cluster of stories is another group of legends to which the precarious relationship of men and women also provides the context or background, with women usually causing the discomfiture of men or, at the very least, acting as foils to it. Among these are the accounts of the thirsty lover who swallows his girl friend's contact lenses in the mid-dle of the night (*MP* 85); the jealous husband who fills solidly with cement a luxury convertible (usually a Cadillac), which he sees parked in his drive-way, only to discover that it was his wife's birthday present for him (*VH* 125–32); the nude husband who is left to wander the roads when his wife accidentally drives off without him (*VH* 132–36) or, in contrast, the hus-band who leaves his scantily dressed wife behind when she, like him in the previous legends, momentarily steps out of the trailer in which she has been sleeping (*CBA* 126); a surprise birthday party gone wrong because a manager misinterprets his secretary's intentions, only to find himself in the nude (except for his socks) in front of his whole family and many friends (*VA* 140–46; also *CD* 221–22); the husband who blows himself off a toilet by igniting with a burning cigarette some hairspray or paint which his wife has just squirted into the bowl (*VH* 18; *MP* 13–14); the man whose wife drives off when he has tied a rope around his waist at one end, thrown it over the roof of his house, and tied it to the car's rear bumper on the other side, in order to do some kind of work (*VH* 181); a male skier who, seeing a bare-bottomed woman skier who had tried to relieve herself behind a tree but slid down the slope, laughs so hard that he collides with a ski-lift tower (*VH* 181; *MP* 117); the couple (often not husband and wife) who suffer a case of *penis captivus* during intercourse (often in a car) as the result of the woman's *vaginismus* (*CD* 192–95); a male student who, not realizing that it is Visitors' Day in his men's dormitory, exposes himself to his parents and girlfriend in an embarrassing prank (*BT* 305); and, on the periphery of this theme, the male driver who, misunderstanding a woman's warning, runs over a pig in the street (*CBA* 127), a gullible young man who is duped into paying an enormous bill in a supermarket because of his misplaced sympathy for an older woman (*CBA* 247–48; this story is also told of gullible girls), and a woman who, thinking that she is doing a good deed, throws an expensive leather glove out of a closing subway door, only to discover that it really belongs to a surprised male passenger continuing his journey on the train (*BT* 125).

The last group of legends relevant to my theme is best classified as "miscellaneous" although it is still concerned with the discomfiture of American men, albeit under a variety of unconnected circumstances: the buyer of a seeming bargain discovers that there is an irradicable nasty smell in the car he has bought because somebody has died in it (*VH* 20–22; *MP* 12–13; see also Baker 1982, 196); an ominous rattle in a Cadillac, when finally detected, is traced to a disgruntled factory worker (*CD* 62–63); a man wrapped only in a towel steps outside his apartment door, which closes after him (*CD* 66); a jogger is locked into a walk-in refrigerator while changing his clothes and is revived by being "placed in a special oven in a hospital and given piping hot blood transfusions" (*CD* 71–72); a wounded coyote gets its revenge on a cruel camper, who had tied a stick of dynamite to it, by blowing itself and the camping vehicle to bits (*CD* 678); a variant is told of farmers' rabbits and a pickup truck (*MP* 36); boys are abducted or mutilated in a department store or shopping mall restroom or some such location (*CD* 79–92; Baker 1982, 213–14); ingested snake eggs hatch and grow into a ten-foot snake in a boy's stomach (*CD* 108); succumbing to an occupational hazard, a barber dies of hairballs (*MP* 77–78); a golfer who has got into the habit of putting the tee into his mouth after he has teed off dies because the course had been sprayed heavily with insecticides (*CBA* 66); three brothers die by successively wearing shoes containing venom from a snake's broken tooth (*CBA* 76–77); a jogger in Central Park accuses another jogger of having stolen his billfold and retrieves it from him, only to discover later that it is still lying on his dresser (*CD* 188; variants in *BT* 264–66); an amateur hunter wrongly thinks that the deer he has shot is dead, but when he is just about to pose for a photograph with it, the animal revives and runs away with his expensive rifle across its antlers (*MP* 24–25), while another amateur hunter, shooting a deer, is under the impression that he has shot a farmer's prize bull and writes him a substantial check (*CBA* 138); a jubilant lottery prize winner proudly displays his ticket, passing it around the room, but when it is returned to him it is a different ticket (*MP* 142); a Mormon missionary accidentally kills a cat (*BT* 276–77); a frustrated golfer, who throws his bag into the water and storms off the course, returns a quarter of an hour later, removes his car keys from a zippered pocket, and returns his bag to the water (*BT* 203).

(Drunken) male drivers doing stupid things figure in several contemporary legends: a drunken driver is stopped by the police, but while they are busy with an accident nearby he hops by mistake into the police car and drives home (*CBA* 101); a car owner secures his car in such a way that it is practically unstealable, but would-be thieves nevertheless break through his security arrangements, leaving a note to that effect without stealing the car (*CBA* 105); a New York City driver whose car has broken down is mistaken by a car thief for a fellow "stripper" and is offered half the takings (*CBA* 111–12); a butcher's prank of concealing a wiener in his pants goes wrong when a friend dies of a heart attack seeing what looks like a penis sticking out of his trousers be chopped off by the butcher with a cleaver (*BT* 47); a grandfather is wrongfully arrested when a photo-processing company reports him for having taken pornographic pictures which are really photos taken by his grandchildren for fun (*BT* 53); a former Mafia member turned informer who has been given a new identity finds in his mail box a soliciting letter from the alumni organization of his university, addressed to him by his new name (*BT* 128); duped by a woman, a young man is kidnapped and has his kidney removed (*BT* 149–53); a bragging American tourist is effectively silenced by an Italian tourist guide who claims that Milan cathedral appears to have been built overnight (*BT* 195).

Among the most memorable of legends telling of the incompetence or incapability of seemingly competent or capable men are those relating chains of interlinked events: the legend of the exploding toilet, for example, sometimes has a sequel in which, on learning what has happened, the paramedics who are about to take the victim to the hospital laugh so hard that they let go of the stretcher, and then the man falls off and breaks his leg:

> There was a guy I heard about that had to be in the hospital for something. [Often it is to recover from an earlier hilarious accident.] And while he was in there his wife decided to paint the bathroom. Well, when she finished painting, she cleaned the brushes and dumped the paint thinner in the toilet; but before she could flush it down, her husband arrived home from the hospital. The first thing he happened to want to do was to use the bathroom, so he sat down on the toilet; and he had a cigarette in his hand, so he just dropped it into the toilet at the same time. He blew himself right off the pot! So the paramedics came—or maybe it was the ambulance guys that had just brought him home—and they had to load him on the stretcher face down. Then one of the ambulance guys asked him what in the world had happened, and when he told them, they started to laugh so

hard that one of them let go of the corner of the stretcher, and fell off and broke his leg. (*MP* 13–14)

The same coda is often attached to the legend of a man who, with a towel draped round him, tries to catch a snake which has slithered out from among the leaves of a potted palm; he drops the towel, gets down on his hands and knees, is startled by his dog putting its cold nose against his bare rear end, bangs his head, and knocks himself out. The paramedics, when hearing the story, "laugh so hard that one man loses hold of a corner of the stretcher. Her husband is dropped to the floor and breaks his leg [arm, neck, collarbone, etc.]" (*MP* 114). A water skier gets caught in barbed wire and falls onto a nest of snakes from whose bites he dies (*MP* 29). A woman driver throws herself out of a car because she notices a garter snake crawling out of her pants leg; a passing driver stops and runs over to her to find out what is wrong; another driver, seeing him bending over her, thinks he is attacking her and punches him in the face (*MP* 60–61). And that's not all!

So much for the evidence which, in its severely summarized or abbreviated form and shorn of its narrative structure, stylistic features, and storytelling qualities, gives the general impression of an overwhelming but boring litany of denunciations of male characters, destined to bumble their ways through life. Surely it cannot be that bad! Well, the purveyors and consumers of contemporary legends are, as we have already seen, aware of, and sometimes highlight, certain redeeming features in men, although not necessarily those which men themselves, or even a conditioned general public, would choose to associate with what they expect to be the hallmarks of manliness or personifications of the "stronger sex."

Even bearing in mind the essential purpose of contemporary legends—to entertain, startle, and engage through a selective emphasis on events bordering on believability and therefore also on eyebrow-raising accounts of the unusual and bizarre—the picture which emerges from the corpus of folk narratives briefly alluded to in the foregoing is essentially one of astonishing failure to succeed, even of a lack of resources to make potential success a possibility. The fact that these are demonstrable exceptions and that, in some instances, the same stories are told about women does not alter this picture to any significant degree. After all, it would be surprising if there were not indications of a shared humanity (or vulnerability at the top of the evolutionary pyramid) in some of these accounts, creating a limited gender balance. Nevertheless, while in a certain number of legends both male "winners" and "losers" make a joint appearance (the buyer and seller of an expensive sports car, the trucker and the biker, the "roughneck" and his employer, the veterinarian and the burglar, the writer of a "dishonest note" and the owner of the damaged car, and so on), accounts of women's victories over men do not seem to have counterweights in men's victorious actions over women, when any kind of gender competition is involved.

What kind of men are given this pejorative treatment in American contemporary legends? Looking at the evidence presented above, it is hard to establish any discernible patterns, although three distinct groups of characters are referred to more often than others: road users (drivers, either drunk or sober, truckers, bikers, motorcyclists, husbands, wives, buyers of cars, drivers of a hearse, car thieves); philandering husbands and bridegrooms, lovers, courting young men, recent divorcées; and criminals (bank robbers, burglars, subway attackers, car thieves, potential killers, disguised killers, escapees). I have deliberately included various categories of criminals in this listing for, although "they had it coming to them" because of their anti-social behavior, they are nevertheless "failed professionals" and just as dimwitted or incompetent as, for instance, some carpet layers, welders, scuba divers, dentists, professors, barbers, fathers, examiners, businessmen, skiers and water-skiers, students, paramedics, butcher's customers, grandfathers, golfers, joggers, farmers, hunters, lottery prizewinners, Mormon missionaries, former Mafia members, and tourists. Though these characters may not represent the whole spectrum of male members of society, they nevertheless include a large and varied number of male persons, not least sportspersons, tradespersons, hunters (whose particularly male domain and manly aspirations seems to be singled out for special ridicule), and academics.

Despite the richness and the obvious underlying biases of the evidence, it is not clear whether we find in the telling and transmission of contemporary legends any particularly female participation or shaping. Admittedly, the fundamental attitude in many of these stories appears on the surface to be anti-masculine and therefore undoubtedly boosts a feeling of feminine superiority. On the other hand, the often painful and humiliating treatment men undergo from women in these stories may well have a therapeutic effect on the relationship between the sexes insofar as the vicarious suffering and denigration of other men in these narratives, while confirming to both men and women what they have probably known all along and what for the former has been a constant subconscious threat, and may well lead to improved personal gender relations for both tellers and listeners as individuals and to a genuinely liberated, redefined masculinity in concert with a strengthened sense of positive femininity, in place of an uncomfortable feeling of "male dominance." Men may well frequently be regarded as incompetent poltroons, but this recognition may also release the (re)discovery of other values which had lain covered, even dormant, under artificially mulched layers of stereotypical opinion and opinionatedness.

I have already occasionally alluded to the fundamental intentions of this chapter as a preliminary survey, that is, as an initial attempt to make available examples of the action and depiction of male characters in American contemporary legends, mainly as a means toward illustrating what over many years of involvement in the study of this genre had, for this writer, become an increasing recognition of rather unexpected patterns in manly behavior. As a means to this end, Brunvand's corpus of stories has served us well in its typological richness and the wide scope of its collective inventory. This is where its strength and usefulness for our purposes lies. What is much less easy to accomplish is the exploration of some other issues which would obviously be relevant if one were to go beyond the information that his five volumes can offer, mainly with regard to contextual matters; the reason for this is to be found in the nature of his sources and the format of his presentation.

It is self-evident in that respect that my quest would, for instance, have greatly benefited from a close scrutiny of the tellers and audiences involved: who tells what kind of legend to whom under what circumstances? Even some minimal consideration of these aspects might throw considerable light on the peculiar roles played by men in the legends which I have surveyed. Is it possible, for example, on the basis of a more informed overview and its individual components to test Gary Alan Fine's contention that for women who tell the AIDS story ("Welcome to the World of AIDS") the narrative may represent "a subtle revenge against men" and that men telling the legend perhaps reveal "collective paranoia toward women" (Fine, 1987; quoted in *CBA* 201–02)? It is in the discussion of this story, derived from his newspaper column of August 31, 1987, that Brunvand (*CBA* 199–202) gives us some of the most detailed insights into the social and performance contexts of the tellings of what is, after all, a dramatic and harrowing theme closely concerning both men and women.

In Brunvand's five cases in which the sequence of transmission appears to be clear, he speaks of a letter from a male correspondent, and the sequences male>male>female, male>female>female, male>male, and female>female. The personnel involved in these channels of transmission are a "young man"; a woman, her husband, and a convention member; male>sister>female roommate; boss>student; and hairdresser>client (*CBA* 199–202). No gender-related pattern in the teller versus listener relationship seems to emerge from this admittedly small sample, except for the absence of a woman telling it to a man, which may hint at the possibility that women are least likely to tell this kind of story to a man. A quick glance at some other legend types, for which several variants are available, reveals that in the fourteen versions of the "Vanishing Hitchhikers" and related stories (*VH* 24–40) only one "teenager" and a nineteen-year-old man are identified as tellers, while all the others are anonymous and unspecified as to gender and age, mostly in a written environment. One newspaper version retells the legend of "The Choking Doberman" (*CD* 6–18) as told by a woman to a man at a dinner party; in another variant "a Salt Lake City man told [it] to a woman in his bowling league"; all other references lack specificity as to the gender and age of the teller and the occasion of the telling. The teller of "The Licked Hand" (*CD* 73–77) is sometimes male, but the story is also remembered by two older women. The named tellers of two versions of "The Clever Babysitter" (*CD* 78–79) are both male. No particular patterns emerge from these examples, and the quest for this kind of contextual information is often hampered by the filtering of the stories through newspapers and other media and the summarizing retellings of the author (see also Nicolaisen 1992).

A much more encompassing trawl of collections of contemporary legends, preferably from recorded or transcribed tellings, would be required to comment adequately on Fine's observation, both specifically and generally. Undoubtedly some, or even many, tellings may be motivated in the ways he suggests, but without the record of spontaneous renderings in natural settings, which are extremely hard to obtain, a convincing set of explanations may be beyond our reach. Nevertheless, even a basic record of the personnel involved (teller, audience, gender, age) in a performance will provide us with the fundamental evidence needed to reach sound conclusions, but even such a limited exercise must—like, for example, a valid assessment of the relative popularity of certain legend types—be outside the aims of a preliminary survey such as this and be assigned to a much fuller investigation.

Let me conclude with a representative contemporary legend which has close affinities with the numbskull stories of traditional tale-telling in the folk-cultural register and which also displays many aspects of what I have been trying to convey in this essay. After all, storytellers are always at least one step ahead of their critics or interpreters. This version (note the first-person narrative) was first heard in Louisiana in 1945:

> A man operated a band saw in our woodworking mill, and one time he accidentally severed two fingers on one hand. After recovering, since the loss of fingers did not affect his performance, he returned to work on the same machine and was there for many years without another accident.
>
> One day the manager brought some family friends on a tour of the mill, and one of the visitors was an attractive woman. She oohed and aahed at everything she saw.
>
> When the visitors came to the bandsaw station the blonde moved in for a closer look, and she noticed the missing fingers.
>
> She asked the man how his accident had happened. "Like this," he replied, and he promptly cut off two more fingers. (*BT* 178)

REFERENCES

Baker, Ronald L. 1976. "The Influence of Mass Culture on Modern Legends." *Southern Folklore Quarterly* 40: 367–76.

————. 1982. *Hoosier Folk Legends*. Bloomington: Indiana University Press.

Beck, Ervin. 1984. "Reggie Jackson among the Mennonites." *Mennonite Quarterly Review* 58: 147–67.

Bronner, Simon J. 1995. *Piled Higher and Deeper: The Folklore of Student Life*. Little Rock, Ark.: August House.

Brunvand, Jan Harold. 1981. *The Vanishing Hitchhiker: American Urban Legends and Their Meaning*. New York: W. W. Norton (cited as *VH*).

————. 1984. *The Choking Doberman: And Other "New" Urban Legends*. New York: W. W. Norton (cited as *CD*).

————. 1986. *The Mexican Pet: More "New" Urban Legends and Some Old Favorites*. New York: W. W. Norton (cited as *MP*).

————. 1989. *Curses! Broiled Again! The Hottest Urban Legends Going*. New York: W. W. Norton (cited as *CBA*).

————. 1993. *The Baby Train: And Other Lusty Urban Legends*. New York: W. W. Norton (cited as *BT*).

————. 1999. *Too Good to Be True: The Colossal Book of Urban Legends*. New York: W. W. Norton.

————. 2001. *The Truth Never Stands in the Way of a Good Story*. Urbana: University of Illinois Press.

Fine, Gary Alan. 1987. "Welcome to the World of AIDS: Fantasies of Female Revenge." *Western Folklore* 46: 192–97.

Nicolaisen, W. F. H. 1984. "Legends as Narrative Response." In *Perspectives on Contemporary Legend, Sheffield, July 1982,* ed. Paul Smith, 167–78. CECTAL [Centre for English Cultural Tradition and Language] Conference Paper series, 4, 167–78. Sheffield, UK: CECTAL.

————. 1985. "Perspectives on Contemporary Legend." *Fabula* 26: 213–18.

————. 1987. "The Linguistic Structure of Legends." In *Perspectives on Contemporary Legend, II,* ed. Gillian Bennett, Paul Smith, and J. D. A. Widdowson, 61–76. CECTAL Conference Paper series, 5. Sheffield, UK: Sheffield Academic Press/CECTAL.

————. 1988. "German Sage and English Legend." In *Monsters with Iron Teeth: Perspectives on Contemporary Legend, III,* ed. Gillian Bennett and Paul Smith, 79–87. Sheffield, UK: Sheffield Academic Press.

————. 1990. "Linguistic Aspects of the Vanishing Hitchhiker." In *Dona Folcloristica,* ed. Leander Petzoldt and Stefaan Top, 187–99. Bern, Switzerland: Peter Lang.

————. 1992. "Contemporary Legends: Narrative Texts versus Summaries." *Contemporary Legend* 2: 71–91.

————. 2001. "Burglars and Burglaries in Contemporary Legends." *Folklore* 112: 137–46.

10

Mountain Masculinity: Jokes Southern Mountain Men Tell on Themselves

W . K . M C N E I L

During the past one hundred years, few Americans have been so often stereotyped in so many popular media as the southern mountaineer. In widely circulating jokebooks (e.g., *On a Slow Train through Arkansaw* [1903] by Thomas W. Jackson and *Three Years in Arkansaw* [1905] by Marion Hughes), popular novels (e.g., *Shepherd of the Hills* [1907] by Harold Bell Wright and *Trail of the Lonesome Pine* [1908] by John Fox Jr.), syndicated comic strips (e.g., *Snuffy Smith* created by Billy DeBeck and Fred Lasswell, first appearing in 1934), popular songs (e.g., *Martins and the Coys* written by Ted Weems and Al Cameron in 1936 and recorded by Gene Autry and many others; adapted for a Disney animated film in 1946), mass-market movies (e.g., eleven *Ma and Pa Kettle* films between 1947 and 1957, including *Feudin', Fussin' and A-Fightin'* [1948] *and The Kettles in the Ozarks* [1956]), and hit television shows (e.g., *The Beverly Hillbillies* on network television between 1962 and 1971), residents of the Appalachians and the Ozarks have been frequently labeled as either humorous, shiftless, dumb, illiterate, fertile, or in other ways generally out of touch with modern civilization (Jackson 1985; Otto 1986; Blevins 2002; Harkins 2004). In some cases, the comic strip *L'il Abner* (created by Al Capp, first appearing in 1934; adapted for Broadway theater in 1956 and a Hollywood movie in 1959) being the best known instance, all the stereotypes were combined in the gendered image of the primitive "mountain man" or "hillbilly." Indeed, the image even permeated scholarly circles, as attested by those writers who followed in the footsteps of William Goodell Frost to discuss our "contemporary ancestors" in the southern mountains (Frost 1899; Mc-Neil 1995, 91–106).

To elucidate the traditions of the southern mountaineer, scholarly studies typically concentrated on "proper" materials, primarily those in printed sources (see Harkins 2004; Shapiro 1978; Caudill 1963; Weller 1966; Eller 1982). Only a few dealt with oral traditions, and most were concerned primarily with the outsider's image of the mountain man (see McNeil 1987, 1995). But stereotypes generally do not work just one way; usually there are self-effacing views that are also held by members of the group. So it is in regard to southern mountain men who, particularly in their privately expressed folk narratives of sex, provide a sharply etched picture of themselves. Aware of the way that southern mountaineers are ridiculed in media as being ignorant, backward, and shiftless, many jokesters from the region have used the caricature as well as adding one of the easily duped city slicker in their narrative repertoire as a source of reserved regional and manly bravado.

I am not claiming that a monolithic image can be delineated or a uniformity easily charted between Appalachian or Ozark cultures in the sense of specific traits found throughout the two regions and possessed by all residents.[1] Nonetheless, some dramatic features of living in the mountains, often presented as being in conflict, drive the urge to express folk narratives about sex. On the one hand, there is a self-awareness of the isolation and often harsh conditions of mountain living, and the mountain man expresses pride in possessing hardy physical attributes or sexual prowess resulting from an environment that outsiders might find undesirable. One can hear reference to the mountain man as a kind of primal man close to nature—wild, rough, strong, and potent—whose powers for living and sex are heightened by his mountain experience. On the other hand, the isolation can breed ignorance and a lack of economic opportunity, as well as social marginalization. Humor channels some of this negative awareness by tempering the primal man's potency with a lack of realization of what he can really accomplish. The result is a complex form of manliness expressed in humor, one that appears to resolve the conflict between the unbridled sensual primitiveness of mountain identity with the genteel cosmopolitanism of mass society.

As told by mountain men, humorous narratives about mountain manliness simultaneously caricature the mountain man's earthiness, at odds with the "sacred" dictates of cleanliness and tact in cosmopolitanism outside the mountains, while normalizing his natural urges as part of a culture in synchrony with the natural mountain environment. Mountain men doing what "comes naturally" is apparently denied, the narratives imply, in emasculating—if ascendant—urban culture. The symbolism of sex and excrement—natural, normal events repressed by cosmopolitanism—highlighted in what mountaineers keep in oral tradition as "obscene" narratives serves to draw attention, then, to mountain manliness as cultural identity.

Certain characteristics crop up with enough frequency in mountaineers' folk narratives about sex that they can be accurately designated part of this overall mountain manliness, an internal view perpetuated by natives of the Ozarks and the Appalachians. One of the most persistent attributes of the mountain man in bawdy narratives is that he is endowed with an enormous penis, and it serves as a reminder of his primitive power. Implied in these narratives is the idea that "domesticated" men in mass society have been emasculated, since tellers often relate a sense of the ample size as normative in the mountains. Even in a relatively small collection like *Pissing in the Snow* (1976) by renowned folklore collector Vance Randolph, there are eight accounts of men with extraordinarily big penises. One text from Farmington, Arkansas, tells of Tom Burdick, who was endowed with such an enormous organ that it was impossible to close his casket until it was cut off and placed up his anus (Randolph 1976, 93–95).[2] In the community of Retreat, North Carolina, people tell of a certain man who had a prick so long he could tie it in three knots and still have plenty left over for any necessary business.[3] At Galena, Missouri, the story was told as an understated truth of a man known as "twelve-dollar Jack," because he could knock twelve silver dollars off a counter top with his penis (Randolph 1976, 90–92). This feat was topped by the citizen of Jefferson City, Tennessee, who reportedly could easily remove thirteen silver dollars without "even having a hard-on."[4]

In narratives told by mountaineers *about* mountaineers, a mountaineer's huge penis automatically makes him a super lover. While sexologists would deny validity to this claim, it is universally recognized by all the characters in off-color stories. This is the point of the following story I first heard in the fifth grade of a North Carolina mountain town:

> A couple was on their honeymoon and they were fixing to get ready to go at it. The man got undressed and turned to his wife and beating his chest said: "Look, honey, two hundred pounds of pure dynamite."
>
> His wife looked at his prick and ran out of the room screaming. She called the fire department and told them to come over there. "There's two hundred pounds of dynamite over here with a two-inch fuse."[5]

Men with a short supply, presumably a distinctive minority in the mountains, to listen to the narratives, recognize their lack makes them less desirable. Thus, in one yarn a "hillbilly" from eastern Oklahoma hires a local pastor with "a tool pretty near a foot long" to stand in for him in a "dick-measuring contest" in which, if he wins, his wife will not divorce him (Randolph 1976, 111–13). Perhaps none was so embarrassingly inadequate as the Arkansas peckerwood who had a two-inch penis that caused the deaths of three wives who broke their backs trying "to get a little fucking out of the poor boy" (see Randolph 1976, 121–22).[6]

Whatever the mountaineers' equipment, though, the feature of disinterest in sex comes into play in humor that highlights the missed opportunities of isolated mountaineers. In a "yarn" identified as "The Tire Change" in collections, a farm boy helps out a pretty girl whose automobile has had a flat tire. After he changes the tire, the girl tries every method she can think of to get him to accept sexual intercourse as payment for his help. Finally, she undresses, and he runs his fingers over her panties and says, "Them flimsy things ain't no good. Why don't you just give me twenty-five cents and we'll call it even" (see Randolph 1976, 144–45; Legman

1968, 93).[7] Rather than expressing backwardness, the disinterest theme implies manly strength because the man is not lured by women's sexual powers. He may be shown seducing, but he will not be seduced.

While the mountaineer finds a large penis desirable, he doesn't have the same feelings for a large, loose vagina, probably as an indication of the superordinate position of the man and the implication of the woman as wizened from hard mountain living. This manly preference is clearly expressed in two jokes, one from Poplar Bluff, Missouri, and the other from Gravette, Arkansas. In the first, a farmer complains to a friend that he has lost his best heifer, a real prize because she "had a cunt just like a woman." His friend tries to placate him by offering the services of his wife who, he says, "has a cunt just like a cow" (Randolph 1976, 107).[8] The linkage of woman and cow as serving the instrumental needs of the man cause the structural incongruity at the heart of the humor, as perceived by mountaineers in the narrative, but it also fits in with the distinctive symbolic theme in the mountaineer narratives of continuity in the natural domain.

In the second tale, a farmer's daughter hides her father's gold coins from robbers who get away with the man's horse and wagon. The father asks her where she hid them, to which the girl replies, "Between my legs inside me." The father responds, "Too bad your mother wasn't here; we could have saved the horse and wagon, too!" (See Shumaker 1983, 62–63).[9] While the tall tale appears to praise the mother for her prodigious cavity, it also is interpreted as a plaint of the effects of mountain life on the woman's sexuality, while the man's potency remains strong to the end.

Coincidental with the ability to be a good lover is the lack of concern about to whom one makes love, a rejection of cosmopolitan expectations. Anyone is an eligible target, for, in stereotype, the mountaineer is, in the words of one Farmington, Arkansas, informant, "none too particular where he puts it" (Randolph 1976, 94). Often his sexual partner in humor is a member of his own family—another symbolic representation of isolation. True, there are texts such as the account of a country boy who asked to trade "twitchets" with a city fellow at a dance because he had mistakenly mounted his own sister (Randolph 1976, 54). Far more common, though, are stories such as that related by J. H. McGee of Joplin, Missouri, who told of a young boy who tells his sister she is a much better lay than his mother. To this compliment the sister replies, "That's what Paw always says" (Randolph 1976, 18–19; see also Legman 1968, 96).

In one widespread story a mountaineer applauds his son's decision not to marry a girl who is a virgin because "if that girl ain't good enough for her own kinfolks, she ain't good enough for us, neither!" (Randolph 1976, 80). In another narrative a farmer threatens to shoot a city slicker who has sexual intercourse with his wife and daughter. The father explains that he does not object to the stranger shagging his wife, but the girl "is just a innocent child, and never screwed nobody but me in her whole life" (Randolph 1976, 147).

Of all mountaineers, the most incestuous and sexually active in humor are preachers, a statement of humanizing, and mountainizing, lofty social figures. Although the mountain man appears profane in many jokes, the apparently sacred preacher, at least publicly, ultimately shares the mountaineer's private sexual attributes. It is said that a revival at a backwoods church near Aurora, Missouri, broke up because of an argument that resulted when the two pastors involved got into a contest boasting of their sexual conquests. Whenever a woman they bedded came by, they would say "Amen." The winner would be the one who could say "Amen" most often. This worked fine until one preacher's fourteen-year-old daughter and wife came by. The father and husband indicated he had engaged in sexual intercourse with both women; but when the other minister indicated the same, a fistfight broke out between the two men, and the meeting was disrupted (Randolph 1976, 29–30).[10]

But sex is not the only thing the preacher of stereotype has a large appetite for, as is indicated in a story told throughout the southern mountains. The conspicuous consumption of food is often connected in humor to a compulsion for sex. A youth tells his neighbors that he plans to be a preacher and knows he will be a good one because he has "the biggest prick in the neighborhood and a terrible craving for fried chicken" (Randolph 1976, 77). But usually the minister in bawdy narratives is after only one thing, as is made clear in an ancient tale in which a man of God visits a woman with a promiscuous reputation. Upon returning to his car where a driver is waiting, the preacher says he does not understand why people tell so many bad stories about the woman—to which the driver replies, "All right, Pastor. Just zip up your pants and we'll go home" (Randolph 1976, 83–84).[11]

Sometimes the preacher's sexual appetite leads to embarrassing moments for him, as in the case of a Holy Roller minister who tells a young female of his congregation that his penis is a glory-pole and proceeds to give her a hands-on lesson in its main function. Later, at the church the girl starts to feel the spirit and blurts out loudly in the service, "There's blessings on my soul! Whoopee, he stuck the glory-pole up my piss-hole, and squirted salvation all over my ass-hole! Praise the Lord" (Randolph 1976, 113–14).[12] Occasionally, it is just the preacher's sexual endowment that leads to embarrassment, as in the story of the minister with a foot-long penis who is a substitute for one of several men standing behind a wall in a "dick-measuring contest." The intended deception comes to naught when one of the ladies from his church walks by and says, "That's not old Joe Duncan; that's Preacher Hickok's pecker. I would recognize it anywhere" (see also Randolph 1976, 111–12).[13]

Embarrassing situations are only one way to humanize and mountainize preachers. Another is represented by the story of the boy who wants a dose of venereal disease ("the clap" in narrative) so he can give it to his sister, who can give it to his father, who can give it to his mother, who will give it to the preacher, who is "the son-of-a-bitch I'm after" (Randolph 1976, 61–62).[14] Perhaps the ultimate insult differentiating the image of the lofty preacher and cosmopolitan lawyer from the "down-to-earth" mountain man, though, is found in a story from Floral, Arkansas, that involves a discussion between two men. One says that he had an extraordinarily large supply of manure on his farm, and so he made a lawyer. When asked why he didn't make a preacher, he replied, "I didn't have that much shit."[15]

While preachers are categorically maligned in the bawdy folk narratives of southern highlanders (the only occupational group frequently mentioned), their attributes are similar to those of other Appalachian or Ozark residents. Most of the traits possessed by the ministers are also found in other mountaineers mentioned in the "dirty" stories. Besides the already mentioned large penis, sexual abilities, and predilection for incestuous relationships, these characteristics include crudeness and a general lack of tact. The countrymen of these fictions waste little time in getting directly to the point, as is shown in the following yarn told throughout the southern mountains:

> There was this old hillbilly who came into Batesville one day and saw this pretty young thing who actually was a prostitute.
> He hadn't been around much but he knew what he wanted. So he walks right up to her and says, "Hey, honey, let's fuck."
> "Why you smooth-talking devil, you talked me into it."[16]

Although this narrative can be interpreted as a sign of lack of refinement from a cosmopolitan viewpoint, it can also from a native mountaineer's perspective be representative of a mountaineer form of pragmatism—the direct and immediate acquisition of needed goals. To be sure, sometimes this directness backfires in narrative, as in the yarn of the young mountaineer who, striding up to a young lady, asks, "Darling, what do you say to a little fuck?"—to which she replies by waving her hand and remarking, "Hi, little fuck."[17] But more often the lack of concern with proprieties, characteristic of a community in which people are familiar to one another, is successful.

The repressed "other" of cosmopolitans draws ridicule from mountaineers in a variety of manly narratives expressing little interest in tact or niceties. In one story a girl from the city of Raleigh and a boy from the country are riding a bus when they pass through Canton, North Carolina, a paper mill town. Both immediately become aware of the terrible stench emanating from the paper mill. The girl says, "What is that awful odor?" The boy replies, "I don't know; I guess the driver's been eating some bad beans and let a fart." The girl becomes indignant and says, "I didn't get on this bus to be insulted." The boy says, "Neither did I; if he farts again I'm going to get up and knock hell out of him."[18]

The crudity, and ignorance, of the isolated mountaineer as a "different sort" also comes through in the story of the mountain parents who decide that their thirteen-year-old will have to start wearing pants because he has been climbing on the table and dragging his pecker through the butter too often (Randolph 1976, 57–58).[19] Again contrasting the primitive, unrepressed mountaineer against the educated cosmopolitan, there is the case of the mountain man who bursts into a doctor's office and blurts out, "There's something wrong with my prick." The doctor takes him aside and, after giving him some medicine for venereal disease, condescendingly tells him to use the euphemism "arm" rather than "prick." A week later he appears in the doctor's office and, when asked about his arm, says, "It's so damn sore I can't hardly piss through it" (Randolph 1976, 30–31).[20]

Coinciding with the mountaineer's lack of tact is an indifference to cleanliness, consistent with the view of the mountain man's lack of concern for boundaries of sacred and profane which would hamper his expressive freedom. Often yarns like this deal with situations in which the protagonist expresses great concern for being sanitary when clearly the narrator intends just the opposite. This is evident in the following yarn about guests at a dinner on an Ozark farm. Dinner is interrupted when a baby enters: "You could see where he has shit all over himself. The kid's mother didn't pay no attention, but the man spoke right up. 'Marthy,' says he, 'fetch the dishrag, and wipe that youngun's ass! If there's one thing I can't stand, it's nastiness'" (Randolph 1976, 134–35).

Occasionally, the mountaineer's symbolic "unclean" position is exaggerated even by the characters in the story. There is the common joke about the farmer who calls a veterinarian to correct the vision of a cross-eyed bull. The vet produces a glass tube and tells the farmer, "Run this up his ass and blow real hard. His eyes'll come back just like new." Yet, after several tries the farmer achieves no results. The vet then offers to try and proceeds to pull the glass tube out, turn it around, and run it back up the bull's rectum. Just as he leans over to blow, the farmer asks him what he's doing—to which the reply is given, "You don't think I'm going to blow on the same end you did, do you? That's nasty."[21]

Another character trait of the southern mountaineer depicted in obscene narratives is an inclination to deceive concerning sexual matters. Often there is good reason for the deception, as in the case, told as true, regarding a Joplin, Missouri, native, who, after coming down with a case of bullhead clap, tries to conceal the true source of his discomfort from his wife. With the help of a doctor, also male, he succeeds in convincing her that he has been bitten by a spider and will have to abstain from sexual relations with her until he is cured (Randolph 1976, 125–26). In another tale, an old husband keeps his young wife from engaging in extramarital relations by convincing her that every man in the neighborhood is cut like a steer. He also spreads the erroneous story that she is insane and carries a little sharp knife with which she emasculates a man every time she gets a chance (Randolph 1976, 36–37).[22] A different type of ruse is involved in the story of "The Romping Party," in which a boy sneaks in on a party where several girls are using bananas as dildoes. He grabs the biggest girl and gives "her a real fucking so that she squealed and farted like a mare." A short time later the girl learns she is pregnant and marries a local boy to save face, never realizing the true cause of her predicament (Randolph 1976, 50–51).[23] But if the hillbilly in these yarns is devious, he also has a certain cleverness, as is illustrated in a couple of stories from Missouri. In one a country boy who has been shot in the testicles explains to his girl-friend that he did not get shot in the penis because he was thinking about her at the time. "So naturally it was a-standing straight up" (Randolph 1976, 142–43). A North Carolina version of the same tale has the boy reply to the girl's inquiry about where he was wounded: "If it had been you, the bullet would have missed."[24] A second story reported from Missouri has a young fellow leave a note on the bed after making love to a waitress with whom he has been having a clandestine haystack affair. The note contains only the word *Hollyhock,* which is a mystery to the girl until she discovers a seed catalogue. There she finds the word *Hollyhock* marked with a pencil. "Fine behind privies and barns but not very good in beds" (Randolph 1976, 133–34).[25]

Frequently in joke lore and in reality, men of the Ozarks and Appala-chians delight in playing practical jokes, particularly on outsiders. Their wit, sense of humor, and ability to think fast come to the forefront when-ever they can put one over on someone from, say, cosmopolitan Chicago. A tale, related to me as a "naughty," but true, incident sufficiently illus-trates the point:

One of them guys from Chicago came down here once and went out to Ballentine's store [about eight miles from town] and asked old man Ballen-tine where he could get a good fuck. The old man didn't waste any time. He took the man out on the front steps of the store and pointed to his own house. He said, "Now, stranger, anytime I want a good piece of ass I go to that woman who lives over there. She really knows how to fuck. Just tell her you're a stranger here and wanting a good screwing and I'm sure she'll give you more than you can handle. I'm telling you all this because you are a stranger here and likely won't be back here again. Don't tell her I told you about her because she might cut me off if she thinks I am talking too much about her." The stranger took off all excited and went over to the old man's house and old man Ballentine stood there watching him. He knocked on the door and the old woman came out. He could see them a-talking and soon she went back in the house and got a baseball bat and started beating the shit out of the stranger. He lit out a-running and ran plumb out of sight and never has been seen in these parts again. She sure did give him more than he could handle.[26]

With all the interest that the mountaineer of obscene fiction has in sex, it may appear surprising that he is also frequently depicted as naive about sexual matters, except that it is equally a symbol of mountaineer "natural" simplicity and isolation. In one yarn a young mountain man does not know how to make his wife pregnant. To obtain the secret he visits a doctor, who tells him, "All you have to do is stick something long and hard in around close to where she pees." So our hero goes home and sticks a broom handle in the commode.[27] Perhaps more widespread is the yarn about the girl who is worried that her husband-to-be will find out she is not a virgin. She goes to a "granny woman" for advice and is given a little tin snapper that makes a loud click when the top is pushed. The granny woman instructs her: "The first night you and him get in the bed just hold this thing in your right hand. Soon as he gets to going strong, just give a little yell and push the top. When he hears that click, he'll think it is your maidenhead a-popping." Unfortunately, another girl finds out about the snapper and puts a giant powder cap inside that almost blows the house apart. It did, however, have the beneficial effect of making the man forget about maidenheads (Randolph 1976, 8–9).[28]

Where his wife is involved, a mountain man is often naïve, as in the old tale of "The Miller's Prick." A miller marries a twelve-year old girl and explains that his prick is the only one in the county. A few days later the girl sees the postmaster urinating out behind his office and tells her husband that his is not the only prick in the county. The miller responds that he had two of them and gave the postmaster his spare. Eventually the postmaster and the miller's wife have an affair, and one day while the miller is bragging about his enormous tallywhacker, his wife says, "Yours is good, but you gave the best one away." Rather than catching on, the miller merely assumes his wife is too innocent to ever make love to anyone other than himself (Randolph 1976, 98–99).[29]

All the traits discussed here are not the only ones to be found in "dirty" stories told by southern mountain men. In fact, several narratives might be cited that would provide contradictory descriptions, but the characteristics mentioned here seem to me the ones most frequently encountered in such materials.

Since many of these distinctive features are not ones that most people would find desirable, the question needs to be asked: Why do mountaineers tell such yarns about themselves? The answer may be found in the response of a Springfield, Missouri, narrator who was asked this question: "These old stories really aren't about typical Ozarkers. Instead, about the oddballs, the lamebrains, the real exceptions."[30] Another exclaimed, "they ain't no damn documentary!'" To be sure, the scenes are distortions of the every day and thereby suggest symbols and fantastic characterizations that draw attention to themselves. Yet in finding much to mock in these characters, tellers also identify with their plights. The teller may claim a cognitive distance between his reality and the fantasy of the rube character, but it is bridged by the symbolic themes relating to the manly identity of the mountaineer in contrast to ascendant, and therefore emasculating, cosmopolitan culture. As they discern the dynamic between the inherited folk values of the region and modern norms, apparently imposed by cosmopolitan culture, narrators use the fictive plane of the jokes and tales to work through the constructions of new identities. Indeed, in performance, narrators often ask for commentary on these identities, often stereotyped, in the jokes and tales or other narratives that comment through their themes. Many of the narratives have as their distinctive reference, not just the context of mountain living, but the "other" of cosmopolitan culture and its perceived construction of genteel, feminized masculinity. Their obscene content is significant, as a reminder that they remain private in impolite or manly oral tradition and therefore circulate within, and indeed relate to, the folk community of mountain men.

NOTES

1. The fact that there is no uniform culture throughout either region is one of the facts that have frustrated those who would write about such features. For example, John C. Campbell (1867–1919) in *The Southern Highlander and His Homeland* (2004) fretted about his inability to make a coherent volume on the complex subject of Appalachian culture. See Shapiro 1978, 264–65.

2. Although Randolph recorded the story in November 1941, it was heard by his informant about forty years earlier. Variants of this story usually have someone attempting to masturbate the penis down. See, for example, Legman 1968, 346, 655–57.

3. Recalled from my childhood (I grew up about three miles from Retreat, which is about nine miles from Waynesville, North Carolina) as being told on a local character named Ananias Hightower.

4. This was a tale told about Maurice Williams, a native of Lenoir, North Carolina, but a student at Carson-Newman College, Jefferson City, Tennessee, 1958–62. Most of the students at this college were from Appalachia.

5. As nearly as I can recall, this was exactly the way it was told to me by Joseph Woodfin "Woody" Henderson, Canton, North Carolina, 1951.

6. I have heard several versions of this story in the Arkansas Ozarks from informants in Mountain Home, Batesville, and Mountain View. The version quoted here is from a resident of Mountain View who wishes to remain anonymous.

7. Told by Ray Suttles, Rosenwald, Kentucky, 1965. In some versions of the story it is a bicycle rather than a car. Legman (1968, 93) reports a homosexual version of the tale in which the girl offers the man anything he wants, and he takes the car.

8. This is a particularly widely told story, known not only throughout the United States but in Europe as well. A variant from France appears in the journal *Kryptadia* 2: 154–55, which was originally published in the 1880s. This means the tale is at least one hundred years old.

9. Told by an informant, aged twenty-one, from Gravette, Arkansas, who wishes to remain anonymous. Shumaker's version (1983, 62–63) is more literary.

10. I heard a version of this story from several persons in Kentucky during informal joke telling sessions, 1965–66.

11. I have heard several versions of this narrative in North Carolina, Tennessee, Kentucky, Arkansas, and Missouri. Gershon Legman in *No Laughing Matter* (1975, 219–20) states that it dates back at least to the fifteenth-century Talmudic *Pirke Avoth*.

12. This is closely related to Aarne-Thompson type 1425, "Putting the Devil into Hell," and is widely known.

13. Told by Frank Reynolds, Hinkle, Kentucky, December 1965. The tale is quite old and can be traced back at least to the fifteenth century, when it appeared in the volume *One Hundred Merrie and Delightsome Stories*, no. 15.

14. A related yarn appears in Voltaire's *Candide,* but it lacks the revenge motif. The earliest printed form of that motif dates only from 1912.

15. Told by Wayman Evans, Floral, Arkansas, October 12, 1983. Evans has lived in Arkansas for many years but originally is from northern Georgia, an area culturally and geographically quite similar to northern Arkansas. It is also told that the man made a Methodist minister and, when asked why he didn't make a Baptist, gives the same reply as above.

16. I have heard numerous versions of this joke told by men throughout the southern mountains. The text cited here is from Mike Sutter of Mountain View, Arkansas, who says it is one of his favorite jokes. It has become so associated with him locally that other persons now telling the story call it his.

17. Again, a story told by many men throughout the southern mountains. The text quoted here is from C. R. von Kronemann, Mountain View, Arkansas, October 4, 1983.

18. As nearly as I can recall, this was the way it was told to me in 1952 by Gudger Shipman, Canton, North Carolina. I also heard a polite version from my father in which the girl asks the boy, "What did you do?" He replies, "Don't blame me. I think it was the driver." He then adds, "If he does it again I am going to slap him."

19. Randolph cites an article dated January 12, 1939, by May Kennedy McCord in the *Springfield, Missouri, News* that says boys wore shirttails without pants to school and other public places until they were ten or twelve.

20. I also have a "polite" version from G. C. "Bill Sky" Ellis, Batesville, Arkansas, October 4, 1983. In this text a child is asked not to say out loud that he wants to go to the bathroom. He is, instead, to say "I want to whisper." Later, when he says this, someone other than his parent asks him to whisper in their ear. Thus, the protagonist, the child, is not the butt of the joke, as in the text from Randolph.

21. Collected August 20, 1982, from a resident of Ava, Missouri, who chooses to remain anonymous. A more "literary" version appears in Shumaker 1983, 17.

22. This is Aarne-Thompson type 1359 and Thompson motif K1569, "Husband outwits wife and paramour—miscellaneous motifs."

23. Although Randolph did not record this text until April 1950, his informant heard it in the early 1890s.

24. Heard from Joseph Woodfin "Woody" Henderson, Canton, North Carolina, in 1957.

25. A related text is reported in Legman 1968, 675, which he states he heard in

Minnesota in 1946. In Legman's version it is the man's wife who is called "Holly-hock."

26. Collected May 20, 1982, from a resident of Ava, Missouri, who wishes to remain anonymous. The names of individuals have been changed, and the town is not mentioned.

27. Heard from Joseph Woodfin "Woody" Henderson, Canton, North Carolina, in 1952.

28. Legman 1975 notes that this story dates back at least to the sixteenth century, when it appeared in several Italian Renaissance stories.

29. Legman 1968 suggests that the basic form of this story dates back at least to 1451 when it appeared in Poggio's, *Facetiae*, no. 62. He also cites a variant from 1610 in which the unsatisfied wife gives her husband money to buy a better penis. She scolds him when he tells her he threw the old one away because, she says, it would have been just right for her mother.

30. Interview, August 20, 1982, with a resident of Springfield, Missouri, who wishes to remain anonymous.

REFERENCES

Blevins, Brooks. 2002. *Hill Folks: A History of Arkansas Ozarkers and Their Image.* Chapel Hill: University of North Carolina Press.
Campbell, John C. 2004 [1921]. *The Southern Highlander and His Homeland.* Lexington: University Press of Kentucky.
Caudill, Harry. 1963. *Night Comes to the Cumberlands: A Biography of a Depressed Area.* Boston: Little, Brown.
Eller, Ronald D. 1982. *Miners, Millhands, and Mountaineers: The Modernization of the Appalachian South, 1880–1930.* Knoxville: University of Tennessee Press.
Frost, William Goodell. 1899. "Our Contemporary Ancestors in the Southern Mountains." *Atlantic Monthly* 83 (March): 311–19. Reprinted in McNeil 1995, 91–106.
Harkins, Anthony. 2004. *Hillbilly: A Cultural History of an American Icon.* New York: Oxford University Press.
Jackson, Thomas W. 1985. *On a Slow Train through Arkansaw.* Ed. W. K. McNeil. Lexington: University Press of Kentucky.
Legman, G. 1968. *Rationale of the Dirty Joke.* First series. New York: Grove Press.
———. 1975. *No Laughing Matter: An Analysis of Sexual Humor.* Rationale of the Dirty Joke, second series. New York: Breaking Point.
McNeil, W. K. 1987. "The Image of the Southern Mountaineer in Obscene Folk Narratives." *Midwestern Folklore* 13: 27–38.
———, ed. 1995. *Appalachian Images in Folk and Popular Culture.* 2nd ed. Knoxville: University of Tennessee Press.
Otto, John Solomon. 1986. "'On a Slow Train through Arkansaw: Creating an Image for a Mountain State." *Appalachian Journal* 14: 70–74.
Randolph, Vance. 1976. *Pissing in the Snow & Other Ozark Folktales.* Urbana: University of Illinois Press.
Shapiro, Henry D. 1978. *Appalachia on Our Mind: The Southern Mountains and Moun-*

taineers in the American Consciousness, 1870–1920. Chapel Hill: University of North Carolina Press.

Shumaker, David. 1983. *Dirty Dave's 101 X-Rated Jokes.* New York: Bell.

Weller, Jack E. 1966. *Yesterday's People: Life in Contemporary Appalachia.* Lexington: University of Kentucky Press.

11

Secret Erections and Sexual Fabrications: Old Men Crafting Manliness

SIMON J. BRONNER

Well into his seventies, George Blume knew me for several years before he shared his fears of death with me. Before then, he showed me his carvings, related jokes and legends, and advised me on managing my affairs, but he hardly dwelled on the end of life. I had some evidence, though, that he understood this time as the twilight of his years. He would smile broadly as he closed our sessions with a reminder that he would still be around for the next occasion, "I'll be looking for you, if I'm living!" I came back time and again intrigued by his many traditional talents and impressed by his sharp memory. We talked on his porch, where he liked to sit and look out on his neighborhood. People came by, and stopped to talk, and asked him about his latest carving. "What are you working on?" they might say, and he would facetiously reply, "Some kind of darn stuff, that's what it is!"

Raised in rural Siberia, Indiana, and working in industrial Hunting-burg, Indiana, he represented much of the cultural character of the area. Of German Catholic background prevalent in the region, he had experience in farming before turning to one of the region's many furniture factories for work. Promoted as the "Nation's Wood Capital," the region's industrial heritage is in woodworking. Its natural surroundings featured abundant forests, which also inspired lively folk arts of basketry and woodcarving.

George drew wages from a furniture factory, but he gained notice, and social importance, for his identity as a carver. The two were related in that they called for turning the raw materials of timber into products, but in the factory George sat at a gluing table and did not take control of the process of transforming lumber to product. As he neared retirement, his bosses took him off the table and relegated him to menial tasks around the factory. George responded by carving elaborate wooden chains and cages that bewildered younger workers and earned him respect for his handwork. A skill and tradition he remembered from childhood, the carvings were more puzzles than figures, for they forced viewers to figure out how he managed to get the links interlocked or the balls in the cages without the use of screws. He expanded his activities into retirement, and besides

George Blume displaying his carved chains,
Huntingburg, Indiana. *Photograph by Simon J.
Bronner.*

making the traditional chains and cages, he carved buildings, figures, and
implements reminding him of his rural childhood home. When I came
into town and asked about old-timers working in wood, several people
pointed him out immediately.

George was like many other woodcarvers I met along my journeys in
southern Indiana, northern Utah, and central Pennsylvania. Typically elderly and male, raised in rural areas, transplanted to urban or industrial
settings, they drew attention for their work, especially from other old men.
Repeatedly I found that their workshops were social centers for gatherings
of men, and they gave away carvings to mark social ties among them. Except in some urban "clubs," I did not run across communities of carvers,
as much as I encountered carvers at the centers of men's gatherings. Many
of them were other blue-collar men who worked in manual trades and
appreciated the handwork; they discussed tools and tricks used as much as
the end product. The carver in these traditional communities held a spe-

cial role—social energy congealed around him as he displayed their memories in material form. It was customary for him to make things for his home and to give carvings to friends and family. He helped create social bonds and always sparked inquiry into his craft, and tradition, when he gave away his handwork. That inquiry often explored the role of such work in a youth-oriented technological society, from which the carvers and his allies felt alienated.

Carvers were customarily men. That is not to say that women could not carve, but strong associations were evident between masculinity and working in the hardness of wood. And if women indulged in craft, the expectations were that women in these communities worked in soft fabric and food. Carving suggested the outdoor realm of men and a connection to the source of the *hard*ened forests and *hardy* farms. Often carvers expressed to me that the cutting and piercing tools used and the firmness of the wood appealed to them as men. They judged men's character by looking at their hands and seeing if their thick, calloused appearance marked manual toil; handwork in wood to them meant hard work, and that made men. Unlike the communal gatherings of their crafting wives, carving was an individual, even competitive, endeavor that could be extended to, and shared with, others. For the old men, and children, who seemed to be the prime beneficiaries of their skills, the carvers produced items that were novel in their presence among commercial products and traditional in their associations.

The production of woodcarvings was symbolic in its very essence, because it was not meant for utility and therefore invited inquiry on its representation. It drew attention to itself, particularly as simulations of real-life items made out of natural wood. The carvers often "played" with the appearance, producing miniature versions of pliers and animals or overly fat chain links and left them unpainted so as to emphasize their handcrafted quality rather than metal models. By drawing attention to something out of the ordinary, the carver's alteration of scale and material visually set up various paradoxes meant to be resolved. The carving was new, yet old, real, yet unreal, artificial, yet natural.

I knew that the carvers had a sense of this "visual riddle/puzzle" because there was a performance that many of them engaged in when showing their carvings to others, initiated by "Bet you don't know how I did this!" The clash of categories challenged the cognition of the object's location and source; as anthropologist Marcel Danesi suggests, "riddles also warn us of the power of metaphor to deceive" (Danesi 2002, 41). Ethnographers have found that puzzles are "small-scale experiences" of the larger questions that life poses to us (Perkins 2000, 27; Danesi 2002, 36). Danesi observes that "in a fundamental sense, puzzles provide a means of 'comic relief,' so to speak, from the angst caused by the unanswerable larger questions (Danesi 2002, 36). The visual puzzles and riddles, sometimes deliv-

Ron Baker holds chain given to him by
woodcarver Earnest Bennett after being told,
"Bet you don't know how I did this!"
Indianapolis, Indiana. *Photograph by Simon J. Bronner.*

ered as comic pranks, direct the viewer to the answers—a different
perception of old age and manliness—or at least provide commentary in
the relative security of secret play.

Casting the carving in the realm of puzzle draws the viewer to take the
object in his or her hand and appreciate the magical transformation
wrought by the carver. It is a challenge to figure out the "trick" of the
trickster, to make the improbable probable. The answer to the puzzle of
how the object as a metaphorical concept was held together was that they,
as old men, still held power, still had vitality. The seemingly opposite forces
combined in an artistic object that was fragile, and perhaps impractical, yet
drew more attention because of its preciousness. In their workshops in
roughened basements and garages, the men maintained their productivity
and surrounded themselves with manly reminders of tools, sawdust, and
industriousness. In the ritual displays of their objects with others, they
played with and performed their meaning.

Often such art when presented in collections stood for community, regional and ethnic, and there is a sense in which there certainly can be that
reference in the invocation of tradition. But in the process of craftwork
that I witnessed, I saw the significance of carving as the expression of old
men and their maintenance of manliness as their bodies declined. Al-

though the scholarship I consulted associated carving with a man's activity, such a process did not receive the interpretation that, say, quilting did as a woman's expression of feminine symbolism. The carvers never claimed that all men would carve in their male experience, but they understood that talking about carving drew them to other men because of the hand-work involved. In the creation of chains, cages, pliers, and fans based on the concept of a visual riddle, they grasped the symbolic potential for their expressions for youthful viewers, for family members, and, as I later discovered, for other men.

I presented a case in *Chain Carvers: Old Men Crafting Meaning* (Bronner, 1985) for carving forms such as chains, cages, pliers, and fans as statements of the psychological states of elderly men (see also Bronner 1996). It was no coincidence, I maintained, that most chain carvers were old, anxious about being frail and idle, and alienated from modern technological life. Their perception of being removed from the youthfulness and commercialism of mainstream society in part motivated them to take up a traditional, relaxing practice that reassured them as they contemplated the end of life. Channeling this disturbing thought into creativity, they often created playful items, which in the levity, and relative safety, of fictive play suggested symbols of their repressed thoughts. Many carvers told me of their fears of approaching death after we got past talking about the mechanics of the object's construction. Alois Schuch, a Jasper, Indiana, wood-carver, rhetorically explained, "I would die just sitting here if I didn't carve, and then what would be left of me?" He carved old-time furniture, agricultural implements, playthings, and, yes, chains. I also think of Leonard Langebrake, a cane carver from Huntingburg, Indiana. I sat on Leonard's porch asking him about his life of craft. He put one of his hand-carved canes in my hand. "Take that. I'll be dead soon and then you'll know what that cane means and where it's from." Two weeks later he died. But he left the world knowing his objects would endure. Canes were special to him, he told me, because while he felt hunched over because of advancing age, the canes stood firm and erect. Actually, he did not use one for walking, but would sit on his porch and hold it much as a nobleman would hold a scepter to convey authority.

By making chains and other folk forms, and by showing their knowledge to younger generations, old carvers feel that they will be remembered after death as practitioners of a custom that represents traditional, often rural, values. Frequently, the carvers feel that such values need reinforcement, especially in the industrial milieu of their elderly years. Carvers often learned from an elderly neighbor or family member, and they in turn try to bridge the generations. As children they were trained to assume skills they would need later as men. They learned the proper masculine use of tools, became familiar with work and production outside the woman's domain (to their way of thinking, the home), and learned about the outdoors and the challenge of woods. Late in their lives, carving reminded them of their young experience, and they let others know its value.

By having the special knowledge of woodwork, carvers imagine that they increase their status, for creating technical and perceptual puzzles displays a carver's exceptional skill, patience, and creativity. It was a way, as they often said, to be "productive"; they sensed that many people expected them to disappear in retirement, so they seized the opportunity to make carving their personalized "work" on their terms. Although capable of manual utilitarian skills such as carpentry, metalwork, flooring, and plumbing, many carvers would show their creations to display their imaginative abilities to go beyond necessity with their handwork. Their utilitarian skills were for the purpose of maintenance, necessary service for others, while the woodcarving drew aesthetic responses. Indeed, they realized the expectation of their utilitarian trade as pragmatic, routine, and replaceable, but in woodcarving there is an element of mystery, even magic, in the individualized artifice displayed. As woodcarver Floyd Bennington of Huntingburg, Indiana, remarked, "If it's something that's out of the ordinary, it attracts lots of attention. Oh yes, I feel better when somebody comes along with 'I don't see how you did it.'" In the playful drama that takes place between the creator and the viewer, the viewer not only looks at the object but touches and handles it. An air of play attached to showing the chain conceals some of the deeper messages that chains and cages hold, even as it gives abstract clues to them and allows the viewer to come away with some lessons from the object.

Out of the associations of the carvings with the non-commercial and the past outside of the modernistic moment, symbols emerge. Because craft is not part of the machinery that runs daily life, the craftsman is free to be abstract. He is himself an abstraction of work, or what work once was, and because the things he makes are free of utility, they can take on many dimensions of meaning. Open to interpretation, the things he makes decorate and challenge, surprise and puzzle. Carvers may give chains as love and friendship tokens and refer to the symbol of linking, a common image of love and marriage. The chains and cages can also dramatize feelings of imprisonment, restriction, and containment. Wooden chains, cages, pliers, hooks, and locks may be unconscious, but not coincidental, symbols for the carvers. Such forms are often projections of carvers' mental conflicts or uncertainties not easily conveyed in conversation. The common addition to the chain of a caged ball gives a ball, a chain, and a cage—all symbols of imprisonment. In this regard, Vernon Shaffer from Malad, Idaho, showed me a carving he called "The Convict," with a whittled chain attached to a ball, and the distraught, bent-over figure of the prisoner made from a burnt matchstick. The behavioral restrictions an elderly carver feels as a result of his anxieties or fears may be symbolized in the restrictive chain and in the structured procedure of chain carving. At the

Carved chain with slip joint and rattlesnake by Earnest Bennett, Indianapolis, Indiana. Bennett reported learning to carve from a neighbor he described as "an old man with a joker's personality." Like most traditional carvers, he dropped the craft upon reaching manhood, but resumed it as an older adult, at which time he added creative features to the chains, such as rattlesnakes, belt buckles, and slip joints. *Photograph by Simon J. Bronner.*

same time, the "release" of chain carving compensates for the restrictions. Indeed, when I asked Wandley Burch of Bloomington, Indiana, how he chose the times he would carve, he replied, "When I feel chained, I make chains; when I feel caged, I make cages."

The chain's connectivity represents continuity, the opposite of disruption produced by conflict. The solution to the puzzle of how the carver manages to link the chains or get the ball in the cage is that he applies a process of "cutting in" with his knife. Carving "in" the ball, pivot, and hinge, rather than "cutting out," is a statement, too, about alienation. The audience is deluded by the chain and caged ball, because the viewer's expectation is that the object is cut out. But the carver has cut the object in, much as he wants to cut himself in to society. He shows himself and the audience that cutting him out, because of his age and outmoded skill, is not the answer. He has skills that the uninitiated cannot grasp. Carvers often talked metaphorically about *releasing* or *freeing* connected links from

"The Convict" carved by Vernon Shaffer, Malad, Idaho. *Photograph by Simon J. Bronner.*

a solid *block* of wood. They recognized, however, that forces, stresses, and tensions exist that can drive the links *apart*. Another indication of chains as a projection of anxieties is a typical pose assumed by carvers when I photographed them with their chains. Many carvers spontaneously put their chains around their necks and bodies, symbolic of confinement.

Still, I needed to explain why these carvers were so drawn to these forms and activities. Examining not just the forms of chains and cages, but also the process of creating them, I argued for the similarities of carving with injection, especially as a response to emotional withdrawal. The men reported feeling withdrawn, sometimes depressed, and often insecure. Carving, like injection, is a repeated activity that gives quick results, which in turn encourages further repetition. Chain carving, especially, is a sustained, open-ended activity, because the chain extends as far as the carver wants to take it. Also recalling the thrust of an injection are activities that require piercing, cutting, and penetrating. Carving, with its symbolic cutting and piercing, reduces the withdrawal distress of the men I met. The carver's knife injects changes into the wood, having been preceded by changes in concepts in the carver's mind. The image of change in the wood before him, and the change that he imagined around him, kept carvers like George Blume going. He stopped his carving years later when it began tormenting him, reminding him of his frailty rather than his control. Still it was not a habit easily abandoned. He did, as he said, get "homesick" for the carving. He did not always know what drove him so, but in carving he found a manly activity worth repeating, for it brought him into the web of his mind and body, nature and culture, past and present.

Woodcarver Wandley Burch showing technique
of "cutting in" on caged ball, Bloomington,
Indiana. *Photograph by Simon J. Bronner.*

Elderly men, unlike women who are characterized by more continuities
in craft activities through their lives, often revive practices remembered
from childhood. I have referred to the typically male pattern as a "regres-
sion-progression behavioral complex"—a mouthful of a label but useful in
describing what is going on (Bronner 1985, 139; see also Mullen 1992,
2–3; Jabbour 1981). When a carver resumes chain carving in old age after
a long hiatus, he reactivates conduct that in earlier and supposedly simpler
stages of his development helped him adjust from boyhood to manhood.
Faced with adjustments to old age, retirement, death, or an alien industrial
or urban environment, the carver nostalgically revives a creative behavior
which helped him adjust as a child to adulthood. The repetition and pre-
dictability of making the traditional form eases fears of the unpredictable
or threatening situation. That is the "regression" part. The "progression"
part comes in because the carver feels renewed and alive with the sense of
discovery. The carver's mind is uplifted by taking on a new challenge, setting a goal, and experiencing the thrill of innovative, creative activity.

I review this fieldwork and interpretation here because it establishes the connection of the forms and processes of woodcarving with the anxieties of old men and their creative ways of resolving them. I recognized in *Chain Carvers* the response of carving to crisis, and I gave special notice to alienation from society and family, lack of productivity, frailty, illness, loneliness, fear of death—their friends' and loved ones' and their own. I believe I was headed in the right direction in revealing the motives of the carvers as elderly men, but I had further to go (and seniority to gain) in the interpretation of their need to express their stature of manliness as they became painfully aware that their bodily appearance no longer conveyed youthful vigor. I revised my interpretation as I considered the meaning of prevalent traditional forms beyond the chain, fan, pliers, and cage that carvers shared not with younger generations or public audiences, but only with other old men in private settings.

The privatized forms I found share the theme of the hidden or surprising penile erection. It was George Blume who first drew my attention to them. Besides carving chains that many old men remembered from their childhoods on the farm, George carved horses and wagons, rural churches, and various toys. One that caught my attention was a chamber pot that had a removable lid. George told me he took delight in the fact that whenever he handed it to someone, they always looked inside, as if he was "giving them shit." Then he told me about one piece he never showed to strangers, a chamber pot cut in half that he had inscribed with the words "For My Half-Assed Friends." I duly photographed what I could and recorded his explanations of what he made.

I became more curious about these private risqué carvings and his personal association with them. He often included representations of himself in his carvings, and I queried him, for example, on the replacement of the traditional ball with a human figure in a cage. "Is that you?" I asked, and he replied, "That's what an old man feels like." He paused, as if unsure of whether he should confide in me, and then he blurted, "A lot of these old fellers won't admit it, but the worse thing about old age, well, that's your dick not getting hard no more." Then he pulled a small object out of his pocket. As he often said about his puzzles, "Bet you never seen this!" And he was right.

What I saw was a small figure of a man inside a barrel. As he did with so many other objects, he put the carving in my hand and let me figure it out. Seeing my fumbling with it, he said "Go ahead, push his head down." As I did, a carved wooden penis sprang up suddenly as the barrel lifted toward the head. I instinctively twitched and said, "Oh my goodness," and George had a good laugh. "Now that's a woody," he gleefully chimed, arousing my curiosity about the connection of his little object to his feelings about sex and death. Upon closer inspection of the object, I saw that he had rigged the penis to spring up with the help of a rubber band, which

Half of a chamber-pot, pliers, and chamber pot carved by George Blume, Huntingburg, Indiana. *Photograph by Simon J. Bronner.*

pulled it up when the head was pushed in. "He's still living, I figure," George said as he slapped my shoulder. Although one would not conclude that the figure was of an old man, George saw him as such, and other elderly men with whom he shared it understood the expectation of impotence, which was denied with a reminder of his manly vitality.

Although not often talked about, the prospect of impotence with advancing age is a common anxiety, especially among old men. I thought it conceivable that the caged balls and chains-on-shafts could also symbolize sexual restriction or impotence much as the barrel did. In America and Great Britain, wooden chains are frequently attached to spoons, and spooning is a slang term for courting or sexual intercourse, based on the metaphorical "fit" of overlapping spoons. Wandley Burch was fascinated, he told me, by his ability in carving to "make a piece of wood longer than its original size." Retired, at home with his wife, or all alone, the carver looked to creativity to reaffirm his manliness, because he realized that others looked at him, as well as his carving, as disempowered and therefore frail and limp. Using sexual metaphors in the safety of humor, the carver reminds others of the surprise they are likely to find when they check for his vitality. The structural incongruity causing the humor is the surprise of the discomforting erection after the expectation is established of the unattractive or confined figure in the old man's hand.

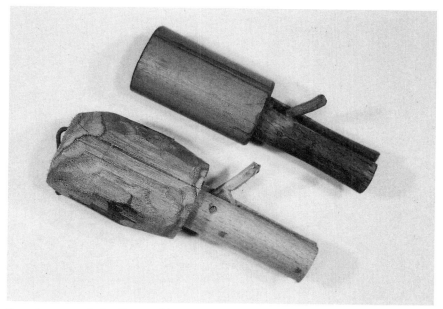

Barrel men made by George Blume, Huntingburg, Indiana. *Photograph by Simon J. Bronner.*

The structural incongruity appeared especially strong in a related form I encountered in relationships I developed with other carvers after meeting George. They hand me a carved coffin. Sometimes, a man's carved head would be exposed lying in the small coffin. The carver invites me to slide the lid open. Upon doing this, an oversized wooden penis springs up, again with the help of a rubber band or sometimes a metal spring connecting the penis to the body. The incongruity is the representation of death and its association with withdrawal and decay, and yet the viewer discovers an active, if hidden, member. The size of both the coffins and barrels would usually be small, and carvers liked to be able to pull them out of their pockets, as if to emphasize the privately shared joke as well as the source from the groin area.

The male carvers were aware that the risqué forms they made could be perceived as toys and therefore more appropriate to childhood than old age. Some handled this image by defining part of their repertoire as toys for childhood use, while elaborating the forms of chains, cages, fans, and pliers to the point where they were seen as artistically adult. Indeed, one challenge to interpreting the material I found was that the psychological and ethnographic literature categorized carving under childhood rather than considering such behavior across the life course. Erik Erikson's (1963) application of Freudian psychology to human development associ-

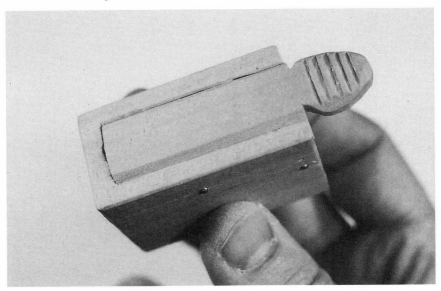

Box as it might be handed to a fellow man, carved by Bill Medlin, New Cumberland, Pennsylvania. *Photograph by Simon J. Bronner.*

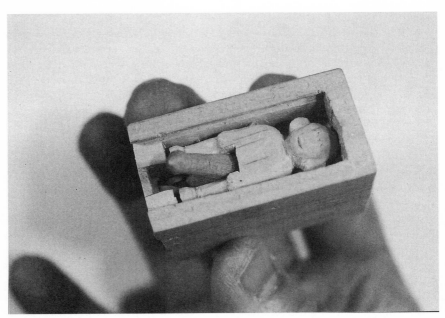

Opened box revealing man with wooden penis that pops up, carved by Bill Medlin, New Cumberland, Pennsylvania. *Photograph by Simon J. Bronner.*

ated toys with the "play sphere" of childhood. He suggested that dramatization with toys permit one to imagine that he or she is master of a life predicament, and in so doing the child develops identity. Brian Sutton-Smith also associated toys with childhood in his important book *Toys as Culture* (1986). He wisely offers the context of toys, however, within the *family* dynamic and allows that play can be enacted by adults even as they may disavow playfulness because it may appear "childish." Unlike Erikson, who espoused that children play with what in reality has been done to them, Sutton-Smith suggested that play is a vehicle for antithetical purposes. He writes, "It is play's very nature to assert a difference, an antithesis, an opposition" (Sutton-Smith 1986, 252–53). Aside from these very different views of the signification of toys as symbolic objects is the agreement that the objects are important to the formation and maintenance of identity and, by extension, the processing of culture.

Carvers arguably conceptualized one set of miniature carvings that could be construed as a "toy" as adult because of its display of a penis or a sexual act. There is a thematic connection with other carvings, because as with the chains, cages, fans, and pliers, a visual riddle was present of figuring out how the carver managed to create the form. There are differences, however, with the chains and cages. The risqué material was privately rather than publicly presented. An air of secrecy surrounded the presentation, raising the anticipation of an uninitiated viewer. Typically, the carver would keep the small carving in his pocket, and after feeling comfortable with me, he would show it to me inside his workshop. The action involved was different, too. The effect of the risqué material relied on the action of the erection or sex. With the chains, fans, and cages, the forms took center stage. The risqué material is separated from the chains, fans, and cages as something shared in secret among intimate peers. It would not be appropriate to show women, the carvers say, because they would be offended, imagining that men naturally understand, and appreciate, the humor or the hidden message. Although they intimate that showing the risqué forms to women may represent them as brutish, another consideration is that it also would risk leaving them vulnerable to ridicule for the connection of the erection to themselves or the infantilization represented in the showing of the "toy."

The ritual performance of pulling the object out of the pocket and showing it to another man also comes with some risks. While intended to be humorous, that is, serious issues couched in the safety of play, the surprise of the erection may be taken as a homoerotic act. In at least one tame version of the coffin man I have collected, the entire body rises rather than an erect penis. The maker told me that he knew about rigging a penis to arise out of the coffin, but thought that some people, as he said, "would take it the wrong way."

The reason it probably is not perceived as threatening in the contexts I

Coffin man in which the whole body rises, carved by Alois Schuch, Jasper, Indiana. *Photograph by Simon J. Bronner.*

witnessed is that the incongruity is not an arousal because the viewer is pulling down the barrel or pulling back a lid exposing the penis, but a contrasting vitality to the figure in the box or barrel. It is rare to have female versions of the barrel man to emphasize the heterosexuality of the figure, but these pairs are found when the figures are made out of beer cans and bottle caps (sometimes playing on the wordplay of female figures made out of "Busch" and male figures out of "Bud" beer cans). Typically, the embellishment of a man made out of a "basic" beer can associated with men's social gatherings adds to the manliness of the image. In some cases, other symbols of a hardened life, such as smoking a cigarette or sporting a stubble, are added to the figures.

The air of secrecy surrounding the object may be one answer to the risks of revealing vulnerabilities in the male display. The secrecy of the performed ritual of pulling the barrel man or coffin from the carver's concealing pocket sets up what sociologist Georg Simmel calls a "second world" in which external realities are separated for examination. In this world, a life frame and its problems are playfully enlarged, male bonds are privileged, and unsympathetic others are excluded (Simmel 1950, 320). Unlike the childish stage in which "every conception is expressed at once, and every undertaking is accessible to the eyes of all," the secret under-

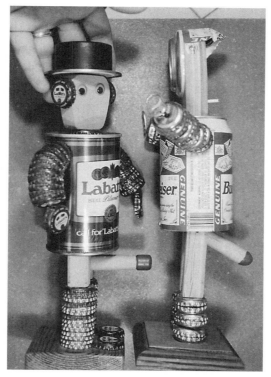

Two variations of barrel men made from beer cans. *Photograph by Simon J. Bronner.*

scores adult relationships (320). In an analysis that can apply to the performances of the barrel and coffin men, Simmel argues that the second world protects those who act in secret by making their actions invisible and disconnected from the external reality (see also Loeb 1929). At the same time, it serves to focus on a specific problem drawn from a life frame. Protection is needed, because the reference to secrecy suggests that a problem or threat exists. Sharing the secret among old men establishes some important contrasts between an external reality perceived as being modern and therefore not given to precedent. The modern is associated with being youthful, future-oriented, feminized, and unsympathetic. In the second world established within the ritual performance, the frame for the event is traditional, elderly, experience-oriented, manly, and empathetic. Particularly in American society noted for its future-orientation, its celebration of upward progress, optimism, and the "fresh start," coupled with denigration in lore of "old-fashioned," "old-hat," "has been," "behind the times," and "backward thinking," the cultural expressions of tradition may be denigrated (Dundes 1980, 69–85; Bronner 2002). A contrastive pair may be set up, in fact, between sure and optimistic hardness or growth (e.g., in folk speech, "firming up plans," "bigger and better," "tall oaks from little acorns grow") and uncertain and pessimistic softness or decline (e.g., also in folk speech, "soft argument," "soft as shit," "slippery slope," and "going downhill"). Realizing that the basis for the social capital of old age is in the past even while youthful modern American society venerates the future, the elderly narrator, prankster, carver, or jokester creates in the second world a setting in which experience and tradition are paramount. The presenter of the object is confiding, and therefore vulnerable, but at the same time powerful since he knows in advance the pranking outcome.

The secret, it should be noted, is not told, but displayed in an air of play and drama. The pranking "erection" of the carved corpse invites a comparison with commonly reported "resurrection" or what Ilana Harlow (2003) calls "the revival of the seemingly dead," as practical jokes at traditional Irish and American wakes. In such accounts, the deceased is consistently described as a man, the prankster a boy or man, and the audience may include women, who seem particularly horrified at the incident. Harlow summarizes one exemplary account:

> A man died sitting on the ground leaning against a wall with his knees pulled up to his chest. Of course, once rigor mortis set in they couldn't fit him in a coffin, so they built a coffin in which he could be placed sitting up—a coffin that was higher than usual, more of a cube shape than a rectangle. Someone managed to rig up a string to him and at the wake, when one of the women was saying the Rosary, he pulled it and that made the corpse turn over and face the woman. Everyone was upset, especially the woman. (Harlow 2003, 94)

The "shock" to the woman, at least in narrative, suggests not just the thought that the dead is really alive, but the man's bodily movement is threatening. In my gendered interpretation of the narrative, which differs from Harlow's, the symbolic castration of cutting off a finger causes the sitting up. In one session she recorded, an Irish hosteler tells the story of the corpse of an old married man whose finger was sliced to get his ring, "the guy woke up immediately . . . he woke up and he rose up more or less out of the coffin and the guys nearly shit themselves—like really. He jumps out of the grave anyway and they run away." The contrast is set up of the erect corpse and the infantilized grave robbers covered in feces. In apparent search of revenge for the castration, the revived corpse raps on his wife's door, and "she dropped dead" (87).

In available American versions of "the seemingly dead revive," the sitting up occurs by accident rather by intention, suggesting the perception that the erection was spontaneous, even natural. The other notable feature in American legends and jests collected through the twentieth century is that the man is described as a "hunchback," adding to the contrast between the decrepit state of being curved down and the vital manly position of being erect (Harlow 2003, 107–108; Baker 1982, 50; Montell 1975, 202–204, Dorson 1967, 330). Often tellers emphasize, in fact, that the corpse does more than sit up, it "shoots up" (Baker 1982, 50). The erection is in defiance of constraints put on the corpse such as "straps" or "strings" (the strings often form a chokehold around the corpse's neck). In the versions collected by Ronald L. Baker in Indiana, where many of the carvers I found resided, one type is in a religious setting similar to many Irish narratives in which "people flee" on seeing as well as hearing the sacred reminder that "this body will rise again" (Baker 1982, 50). Another type describes the erection as initiated by a feminine cat ("pussy") that jumps on the hunchbacked corpse, causing the strap holding him down to break (Montell 1975, 202–204).

Harlow quotes an Irish teller of the "seemingly dead revive" story explaining that the practical joke "creates a situation" (Harlow 2003, 84). Harlow elaborates that the playful situation is a social frame in which "fabrication occurs." Citing sociologist Erving Goffman, she explains that the fabrication is an intentional effort to manage activity so that "others will be induced to have a false belief about what it is that is going on," leading to a "falsification of some part of the world" (Harlow 2003, 109; Goffman 1986, 83). Jokers, pranksters, and carvers manipulate features of the situation or frame and create fabrications, appearances, designed to elicit reactions (Harlow 2003, 109; Bauman 1988, 39). Appropriate to the discussion of the carvers' "second world" in the presentation of coffin and barrel men, the social frame of the "seemingly dead revive" is especially notable for its encouragement of a schism and emphasis of the disjuncture of external appearance and internal reality (Harlow 2003, 108). In the frame, the communicated text may ridicule what is held sacred, and as Harlow ethnographically observes, it "mocks the oppression of death" (108). The falsification of the part of the world that is significant to the elderly carver is that of death and impotence.

While I made ethnographic observations of carving from the 1970s to the 1990s, the exhibition *Folk Erotica: Celebrating Centuries of Erotic Americana* by Milton Simpson (1994) featured historic examples of the risqué types. The hidden erection type is found in a coffin man hailing from Indiana, dated between 1875 and 1880. Simpson's comment is, "Novelty items such as this one, in which a facade may be removed to reveal a naughty view, were popular during this period. Closed, it is simply a miniature coffin, but once opened, the alleged corpse springs to life" (Simpson 1994, 39). While many of the forms I observed were abstractions of men, some of the historic forms represent specific renowned figures. A ten-inch barrel man is dated 1880 and bears the likeness of Abraham Lincoln. "Upon removing a small front section," Simpson writes, "the sixteenth president is revealed to be sporting a sizable erection" (42). On the historic occasion of Germany's defeat after World War II, one Nova Scotia carver created a coffin man that revealed Hitler sporting a darkened penis in contrast to his whitened body (Art Gallery 1976, 55). These political uses of the barrel man tend to humanize the lofty figures by showing their natural urges underneath their heroic exteriors. The historic examples also show the longstanding circulation for the carvings as part of folk tradition.

The folk examples are undoubtedly sources for commercial novelties produced for humor or political comment. The "Merry Monk" manufactured in Hong Kong and distributed in the United States around the 1990s features a plastic penis which rises behind the pietistic monk's robes when the head is pushed down. The packaging advertises the "fun raising action." The fun raised is as a result of mocking the presumably isolated, devoted religious figure who is revealed to be distracted. An item with political connotations for the American market is the "Women's Lib Doll." It is a female figure that sports a penis when the head is pushed down, and therefore is shown to be really manly and aggressive. While the folk forms I collected tended, like the chains, to emphasize the complexion of the natural wood, some commercial forms in plastic featured black stereotypes as barrel men with hidden erections. One was sold as a fishing lure while another from the 1950s was encased in a box emblazoned with the words "Not Homo!" Playing up the hypermasculine stereotype of African American men, the novelties may also be a reference to the potential for the objects to be perceived as homoerotic in their display among men.

Other commercial examples are produced to appeal to American tourists in the Caribbean, Philippines, and South America. The Kinsey Institute for Research in Sex, Gender, and Reproduction at Indiana University also has in its collections examples of tourist arts with the hidden erection from the Fiji Islands and Thailand (see Johnson, Stirratt, and Bancroft 2002, 144–52).

Although such items were not made by American carvers, they may often be placed in men's "areas" such as workshops, hunting lodges, or bars and shown as pranks to the uninitiated. Many of these manufactured tourist arts depict primitives (I have items in my collection from South America hawked as "Indian dolls," darkened natives from the Caribbean, and indigenous figures from the Philippines) as sexual objects, as primal men apart from women. As a tourist object consumed primarily by Western men from modern industrialized countries, they offer a reference to men not controlled by modern women. Celebrating the unrestrained sexual image of anti-modern tradition in stereotyped ethnic depictions, they usually have little relation to indigenous crafts. But what they do suggest is the Westerners' perceived contrast of the primitive to feminized or emasculated modern culture. Nelson Graburn has called this non-Western material "ethno-kitsch," and appropriate for our discussion, Gillo Dorfles has

Barrel men from northern Thailand. *Photograph by Tom Bertolacini. Courtesy of the Kinsey Institute for Research in Sex, Gender, and Reproduction.*

referred to it as "porno-kitsch" because it conforms to consumers', often Americans', popular notions of the lusty characteristics of the primitive group as sensual, erotic, and uninhibited (Graburn 1976; Dorfles 1969). None of the carvers I interviewed was aware of these tourist arts, or ethno-kitsch; for them, the barrel and coffin men had a local reference to an old-time tradition. Still, the kitsch is relevant to this discussion because of American male responses to them, particularly when it became headline news in America.

The incident that touched off this media attention occurred in 1990 when then vice-president Dan Quayle purchased a risqué South American Indian souvenir. It became highly publicized in newspapers, the *Doonesbury* comic strip, and radio talk shows. The vice-president bought a "macho doll," as it was described in the press, on a visit to Chile ("Quayle Taking a Macho Doll" 1990). According to press reports, the four-inch woodcarving was an "anatomically correct wooden Indian statuette that displays its virility when its head is pulled," and fit the pattern of the barrel men I found in America. Quayle blundered not only by his public display of the risqué item but also because he defied the custom of secretly sharing the object among men. In front of reporters, he showed it to his wife and said, "I could take this home, Marilyn, this is something teenage boys might find of interest." "You're so sick," Marilyn replied in disgust. Despite her protests and insistence that he purchase a copper flowerpot instead, he acquired the item. Newspapers and talk shows across America had a field day ridiculing Dan Quayle after the incident, further sullying an already tarnished image for the vice-president. The revelation on talk shows that the "doll" had a connection to a folk art tradition well known in the vice-president's home state of Indiana did not do much to help Quayle's case. Calling the carving "lewd" and "risque, if not obscene," the *Washington Post,* in fact, referred to the incident as a "nightmare" for Quayle's publicity corps (Devroy 1990b). In response, and not without humor, the vice-president's press secretary did damage control with a humorous explanation for the purchase: Quayle was on a secret buying mission for the National Endowment for the Arts (Devroy 1990a). (The comment was a jab at criticisms of the endowment for supporting offensive art.)

Quayle's view that it was adolescent in its appeal rather than among old men was probably due to the stereotypical Western image of the primitive as having childlike qualities and strong sexual urges. One might also speculate that he might have been responding to perceptions of him as childish and dumb (reinforced, many said, by his feminine blonde looks and inferiority to Marilyn), and, to quote the press, an "impotent leader" (see Thomas 1997). Even Marilyn Quayle commented on his need to use the phallus as a reassertion of his aggressive manliness when she was asked by the reporters about what he planned to do with it. She responded, "When he's having a press conference, he'll pull it out at the appropriate time" ("Quayle Taking a Macho Doll" 1990).

In light of the international spread of the form, what distinguishes the American examples? Field-collected examples consistently are hand carved and unpainted. They seem to be intentionally kept crude, so as to reinforce their local connection and spontaneous performance, and represent elderly men, sometimes rustics, rather than an exotic other of indigenous people. Barrel men collected by folklorist Gregory Hansen from a woodcarver from Harlan, Iowa, who gave his carving of a barrel man the title of "A Farmer's Tuxedo" (personal communication with author, July 8, 2002), and examples of "hillbilly" coffin men given to folklorist Charles Zug in North Carolina by Appalachian woodcarvers (personal communication with author, July 18, 2002; see also Zug 1994) support this view. And the folklorists reported, as I found, that the carvings were given to them in confidence after the carvers knew them for a while, as a token of their conversations "man to man." The carvings are typically small, no more than six inches, and consistently are made by men, often elderly men, and shown to other men.

The most common form in the United States is the barrel man, followed by the coffin man. I would hypothesize that this is because the coffin man may be too direct an admission of the fear of death, whereas the barrel man is more of a reference to the less disturbing process of aging. The humor of the barrel may also evoke images of the naked man in a barrel who was a comical folk type depicted in stereographs, postcards, and

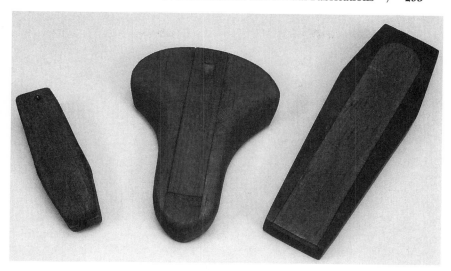

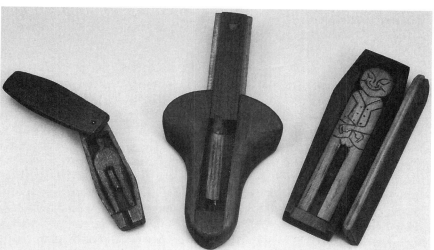

Carved coffin men in collections of the Kinsey Institute. *Photograph by Tom Bertolacini. Courtesy of the Kinsey Institute for Research in Sex, Gender, and Reproduction.*

films of the early twentieth century. The man wore a barrel because he was destitute (wealth as a sign of manly status) and to an extent embarrassingly effeminized by a dress-like barrel, but in the risqué carving of the barrel man, an implicit narrative is that the man is actually well endowed physically if not materially. The contrast is of the apparently inactive man in the barrel, who is belittled as a result, but who, when the viewer looks beneath the barrel, is actually quite active, vital, and enlarged.

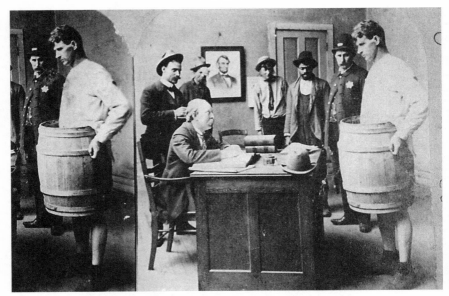

Stereoview entitled "Dey wuz stole, yer honor" by C. L. Wasson, 1901.

The emasculated external image of the man in the barrel is particularly evident in a widely circulating print from the beginning of the nineteenth century showing a man in a barrel in the unmanly act of crying with the caption "Take Me Home to My Mamma!" A disapproving erect policeman holding a firm club hovers above the crouching man. It thus relates the image of the man in the barrel with a childish, feminized stature and is a visual reminder of the contrast between the manly erectness of the authoritarian policeman and the cowering limpness of the man in the barrel. In a stereograph from the period, an impoverished man in the barrel faces an official clerk with another policeman and rough-looking attendants looking down at his barrel. Suggesting the barrel as a symbol of class, the main contrast in the scene is between the haves represented by the official and the have-nots in the characterization of the barrel man.

The barrel man as a portly aging figure appears in advertisements for Talon slide fasteners appearing in the *Saturday Evening Post* during the 1940s. To the blushing surprise of two thin clerks, a rotund, aging man in a barrel marches in. The text reminds men of the embarrassing consequences of having unreliable slide fasteners, namely the exposure to the groin because of a jammed open zipper on the trousers.

Bringing the image up to date, the shape of the barrel man also has a relation to the visual representation of the aging office worker in what Alan Dundes and Carl Pagter call "folk cartoons" or photocopier-transmitted

Postcard entitled "Take Me Home to My
Mamma!" c. 1900.

folklore. In the popular illustration below the caption "You'll Always Get
Your Reward," one finds a hand-drawn picture of an unattractive, bulbous
man with a screw piercing his flabby midsection. Dundes and Pagter interpret the image to be one of the man being passively or femininely
"screwed," probably by "someone in a position of authority." They call
the image of the aging worker "a rather benighted creature and not very
masculine" (Dundes and Pagter 1978, 146). The figure's aging is connected to his rotund belly, overhanging and therefore hiding his penis and
groin area. He is hardly the active or athletic figure, since he appears tied
to a sedentary lifestyle, and as a result his stomach rises higher than his
penis.

In contrast, the barrel man carving gives the shaft instead of getting it,
reminding the viewer to not count the figure, or the carver, out just yet. In
versions of the coffin man, this view is reinforced by the inscription "A
Good Man" on the coffin. Referring to the common description of the
deceased having completed a domesticated family life ("goodman" is an

Advertisement for Talon slide fasteners.

antiquated term for husband) or demonstrating decent moral character, the inscription of "A Good Man," like a photocopy caption, reveals the hidden reality as being satisfied or thinking sexually, and therefore his erect manliness is triumphally iterated. In the photocopy lore, however, the good (hardworking), if unathletic and limp, man is feminized and belittled.

The coffin man has a basis in oral tradition, especially what Gershon Legman calls the identification of impotence with death and old age with impotence. The erection of the dead man in the coffin symbolizes strength and vitality, which is often compromised in jokes by a vindictive woman who turns his penis up his anus, suggesting the embarrassment of being defiled as well as homosexual attack as punishment for infidelity in manly defiance of the woman. Turning this anality into a revenge motif, one illustration accompanying the photocopied lore of "To My Critics" often found on bulletin boards of furniture factories such as the one where George Blume worked, showed the deceased man face down. The text reads "When I am in a sober mood, I worry, work, and think. When I am in a drunken mood, I gamble, fight, and drink. But when all my moods are over, And the world has come to pass, I hope they bury me upside down, So the world can kiss my ass" (Dundes and Pagter 1991, 210).

Related to George Blume's creation of chamber pots, there is also a suggestion of anality in connection to the infantile presence of feces. It was

Coffin man carving inscribed with "A Good Man," collected 2003. *Photograph by Simon J. Bronner.*

common, for example, for the old men to mock themselves in their group as "old farts" or "old shits." Such images in old age offer exposure of the soft buttocks as a preview of death and a sharp contrast with the hard penile vitality of life. In photocopied lore, the appropriate image is of the child on a potty or decrepit aging worker on the toilet above the caption "No job is finished until the paperwork is done" (Dundes and Pagter 1978, 160–62).

The critical comment on bureaucratic or industrial culture with reference to feces is also found in a commonly made carving, often called a "Bullshit Grinder." It is a square block attached to a crank, and the viewer naturally is inclined to turn it. When he inevitably asks, "What is it?" the answer of the trickster carver is "a bullshit grinder," or if he wants to be more polite, "a do-nothing machine." Like handing over the barrel man, it is also a pranking gesture because it mocks the viewer while commenting on youthful technological society. It shows that turning the technological crank is an empty gesture and reminds the viewer of the false allure of external appearance. The viewer is put in the position of being inactive or impotent in contrast to the productive carver.

The symbolic connection between technology as a male embodiment is common in modern lore. In such humor, the failure of the main body part, the penis, is a sign of the machinery falling apart. There is often an assumption of the independent existence of the penis from the rest of the body, although it is clear that the functioning of the part affects the disposition of the whole. Humor, particularly on impotence, circulates in toasts and recitations that found their way into photocopied lore, such as the following verse from oral tradition on retirement:

> My nookie days are over,
> My pilot light is out.
> What used to be my sex appeal,
> Is now my water spout.
> Time was of its own accord,
> From my trousers it would spring.
> But now I have a full time job,
> To find the blasted thing.
> It used to be embarrassing,
> The way it would behave.
> For every single morning,
> It would stand and watch me shave.
> As old age approaches,
> It sure gives me the blues,
> To see it hang its withered head
> And watch me tie my shoes. (Dundes and Pagter 1991, 203–205)

The oral recitation of "When a Man Gets Old," still commonly collected among American men, playfully addresses impotence with reference to coldness, color, and erection:

Woodcarver Wandley Burch showing "bullshit grinder" he made, Bloomington, Indiana. *Photograph by Simon J. Bronner.*

When a man gets old his balls grow cold
And the end of his pecker turns blue,
When he begins to diddle it bends in the middle
Did it ever occur to you? (Randolph 1992, 666)

It is not coincidental that many of the same metaphors of coldness, blueness, and crumpling are also frequently uttered references to death.

The contrast in death symbolism between the submissive, infantilized anus and the aggressive, independent penis is exemplified in the joke of the wife filling her husband's death certificate. The woman requests that the cause of death be given as gonorrhea. "But he didn't die of gonorrhea," the doctor expostulates; "it was *dia*rrhea." "I know," says the widow, "but I'd rather have people remember him as the playboy he wasn't than the shitass he was" (Legman 1968, 655). In another traditional story, a manly Texan (or some other hardy figure) dies, and the undertakers cannot fit him into their largest coffin. His wife (or the governor) tells them to give him an enema, after which they can bury the remains in a cigar box

(Legman 1968, 655). Freudian interpretation would also hold that the woman's reduction of the man and her revenge, or the symbolic fear of it, is especially effective because it represents infantilization of the man with reference to the immersion in feces (see Freud 1955; Mechling 1984; Mechling 2001, 199–205). Legman, for example, reports a story of two men urinating by the side of a country road when a farm girl passes by. "One of the men waggles his prick at her and says provocatively, 'Say, you're from the country. What ought I do with a cucumber like this?' 'Stick it up your friend's ass,' says the girl coolly; 'I hear they do well in shit.'" (Legman 1968, 656).

In a joke collected in Arkansas by Vance Randolph and discussed in relation to the Freudian "castration complex" in infancy by Legman, the male fear of castration as punishment for excessive sexuality (and attachment to the woman) in the development of manhood is evident (Gay 1989, 460–61; Taylor 2002, 21–32).

> Tom Burdick's body was laying in a pine box, but his pecker stuck up like a fence-post. Hard as a rock, too, and it stood so tall they couldn't put the lid on the coffin. The folks never seen a corpse act like that before and they figured Tom's pecker would crumple soon as the evening sun went down. But the goddam thing just stood there, and seemed like it was getting harder all the time. So finally Sis Hopper went and told the widow. Old Lady Burdick come in the parlor where they had Tom laid out, and she seen how things was. "What do you want we should do about?" says one of the granny-women.
>
> The widow-woman just stared at old Burdick's pecker. "For all I care," says she, "you can cut the thing off and stick it up his ass." The folks was all surprised to hear such talk about her own husband. "Surely, you don't mean that!" says Sis Hopper, which everybody knowed she had laid up with Tom Burdick herself, whenever they got a chance. The widow Burdick looked at Sis mighty hard. "Why not?" she says. "Even when he was alive, Tom wasn't none too particular where he put it." (Randolph 1976, 93–94; see also Legman 1968, 655–57)

The distinction of the erection in the coffin with youth and old age is apparent in contemporary belief legends collected from adolescents. The carved coffin as a symbol of the diseased, dangerous penis of the virile youthful body rather than the vital penis of the decayed elderly body appears in contemporary legends dubbed "AIDS Harry." The story is usually about a woman who meets a man in a bar on a vacation and they make love. On the day she has to leave, the man sees her off at the airport and gives her a present which she is not to open until she gets home. Often it is a carved coffin with a note inside stating "Welcome to the World of AIDS." In contrast to the humor of old age told by men, suggesting the preciousness of potency presented in the coffin man, this contemporary legend offers a cautionary tale primarily expressed by women for the dan-

Carved pop-up phallus, American. *Photograph by Tom Bertolacini. Courtesy of the Kinsey Institute for Research in Sex, Gender, and Reproduction.*

ger of entering too quickly into intimacy with, and trust of, young men (Fine 1987; Brunvand 1999, 134).

In the material forms of the barrel and coffin men I found among elderly men, the primary reference was the insecurity of old age. In the figures the erect penis as an inversion of impotence is the repressed feature, and the release of the erection appears aggressive. More than identifying the vitality of the figure, whether in a deathly coffin or a destitute barrel, the erection sets up a particularly male answer to the visual riddle resolving exterior appearance of decline and internal strength. One can especially view this riddling in objects of the coffin type that invite the viewer to ask "What is it?" because it is not clearly a coffin. It may be a plain box or a container with two ovals. When the viewer opens it, a stick pops up, and the embarrassed viewer realizes that what he was holding was a representation of the man's genitals.

In the representations of the coffin, the structural incongruity of the corpse brandishing an erection or the destitute man showing a physical endowment rising depends on the cultural expectation that in a youth-oriented society, sexual and therefore social roles for the elderly are marginalized (Kinsey, Pomeroy, and Martin 1948, 235–38). While their body strength may be in decline, they point out their virility, and hence manliness, in their penile erection. The humor, though, may be appreciated more by men for whom the figures act out an antithetical role in play, to use Sutton-Smith's terminology. The figures can be interpreted for their representation of the use of handwork as one form of play through the life course to resolve anxieties of aging and maintain the identities of men as their bodies decline.

Related, for example, to the barrel and coffin men are other carved depictions of sexual activity that I categorize as hidden intercourse rather than hidden erections. This type involves sex between two figures and operates more like a whirligig with hinges that are worked mechanically. There is still the element of surprise because in a common subtype the embracing couple pop out of an ordinary box, while in the other they engage in sex on a platform. The image is of virility where one would not expect it. Sometimes the platform comes with a partition, so that on one side is a woman facing forward hiding the man who is penetrating her from behind. The position underscores the incongruity of the external appearance and internal strength and emphasizes the superordinate position of the man, or the submissive position of the woman.

While sex in these adult carvings are explicit, they share with a folk toy sometimes called "The Pecking Chickens" a mechanism that supports a surprising movement of chicken heads bobbing for pieces of corn on a paddle (see Dundes 1989, 83–91). The carver attaches a weight to the paddle and by moving it around in one hand, he can make the chicks "peck." The bobbing heads have some force to them and create a knocking sound on the wood. This action triggered in some gatherings of old men in a dusty Pennsylvania workshop I witnessed joking comments made on several occasions about holding active "peckers" or "cocks" (i.e., folk speech for penises) in your hand.

With the paddle held out from the body in one hand in an almost masturbatory stance, the holder of the paddle symbolically brings the inanimate wooden peckers to life by activating their heads and showing kernels on the paddle as evidence. The conspicuous working part is the head, suggesting a Freudian substitution for the penis (Carroll 1993; Dundes 1993), as in the bawdy song "Bang Away, Lulu" sometimes reported with the verse,

> Lulu gave a party.
> Lulu gave a tea.
> Then she left the table
> To watch her chicken peck. (Cray 1992, 182)

In a different socially constructed frame, say in giving the paddle to a child, the object becomes a "toy" admired for its amazing creation of barnyard movement; in the second world of old men, it often became another fabrication in hardy wood of the carver's erotic vitality.

Supporting this interpretation of the importance of expressing erectness as a sign of virile manliness into old age is my observation of the use of hand-carved canes associated with old men. Many canes incorporate

Alois Schuch's workbench with "pecking chickens," Jasper, Indiana. *Photograph by Simon J. Bronner.*

chain and ball-in-cage designs as well as images of nature and fierce animals. Like the chains, the walking sticks were made from sturdy wood and particularly appealed to men. The cane can be connected historically to various symbolic references—to defense, age, travel, authority, healing, and individuality—but in use among the carvers I met, it primarily imitated and extended the man's body. Arguably, this took phallic form that emphasized vitality embellished often with fanciful decorations. Unlike other pieces a carver provides, the cane has connotations less of public use than of private association. Its form is traditional, but its elaboration is personal. Held by a single hand, it is a threatening extension of the body; given by one man to another, it must be offered with caution.

Interviews with carvers reveal cane making to be most often a matter of self-discovery—like carving the wooden chain, an experience of hand-wrought creativity within tradition. Being able to turn a simple stick into an eye-catching work of art is a sign of transformative mastery. Unlike other linear art forms, the cane forces artistic elaboration into an unusually narrow range. Young boys in city and country today, as in the past, seek to make canes to resemble models they have seen. The carved cane, probably made with a pocketknife from a found tree branch or a discarded piece of lumber, offers the satisfaction of extending oneself through craftsmanship. As with other boyhood props, from bull-roarers to stilts, a cane allows a boy

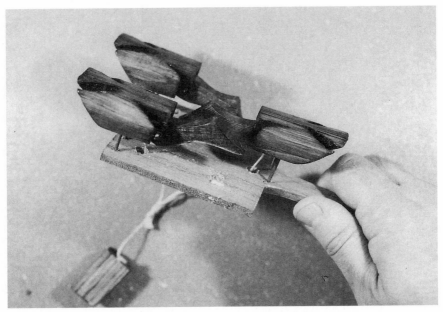

Variation of pecking chickens with rectangular board, collected 2003. *Photograph by Simon J. Bronner.*

to announce a growing presence, to explore and intrude into the world. He uses the carved stick to walk in the woods, swipe at foes along the way, fence with buddies, declare authority, and imagine the power of manhood. In adulthood, the cane is less apparent and useful, for a man realizes his strength and strikes at his foes in other ways. In old age, the cane allows rediscovery of a man's creative potential or at least it artistically provides support.

In encounters with others, the carver uses a decorated cane to invite conversation. An elaborate cane simultaneously announces the frailty and strength of an elderly maker. Embellished as an instrument of support, the carving encapsulates the wisdom of age and conveys vitality through its erectness and artistry. Although the old cane carver might rely on his creation to help him walk, and so direct attention to his body's feebleness, the flights of fancy displayed in the decoration can reveal a lively, imaginative gait. Going beyond the bounds of the utilitarian cane with a design all his own, the elderly carver tells himself and others that he is not to be lumped with a stereotypical group of oldsters but is an individual brandishing the power to create. For some, carving stories and symbols on the wooden canvas of the cane might be one way to review an individual life. Others may prefer the plainness of a useful cane, polished to perfection and given to a

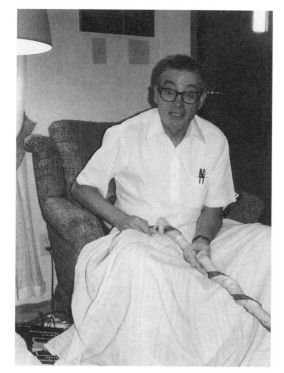

Philip Owen carving a cane, New Providence, Pennsylvania. *Photograph by Simon J. Bronner.*

grandchild, perhaps to ease the transition from one generation to another—to be passed from the man to the boy and to the man again. In boyhood, the stick is thrown away; in old age, the distinguished support is preserved and memorialized. In both, the cane, like the barrel and coffin men, is often a tool of passage.

Passersby used to stop Wandley Burch during walks and ask him about his cane with hanging chains. These moments gave him the opportunity to explain his carving and carpentry background. Although he would have hesitated to decorate his own body or clothes to announce himself in public, his stick seemed to him and others an acceptable, conservative way to herald his accomplishment. Well aware that his years were numbered, he gave me a cane and commented that it would stand up straight long after he was lying in the ground. Supporting the human form in life, before the final memorial of the grave marker, the erect cane carries the mark of individual and social human experience with physical rather than spiritual force.

I am not suggesting that every time a man holds a cane he is thinking

Philip Owen with examples of his carved canes, Lancaster, Pennsylvania. *Photograph by Simon J. Bronner.*

he has a penis in hand. In fact, if he did, it would probably be troubling. The point is that the symbolic significance of the erectness of the cane may carry associations with the embodiment of a man in the firmity of the penis. The creation and decoration of the cane as a walking stick makes it acceptable to the holder and the public viewer in a way that a more direct representation of the penis would not. Thus one often encounters sacred and patriotic symbols carved into sticks, giving them spiritual or religious meaning. Other common elaborations such as human heads and bodies on top of the cane, as well as chains, cages, snakes, alligators, dogs, and reptiles on its body add to the symbolic associations with the stick as a natural masculine extension (see Meyer 1992). In one special form of the cane, the carver will locate a root that is curled rather than straight, but it is often elaborated as a phallic snake or chosen for its enlarging illusion of giving the erection extra width. Unlike some other carvings previously mentioned, canes are connected to owners and are therefore frequently personalized with decoration. Canes tend to have male heads more than

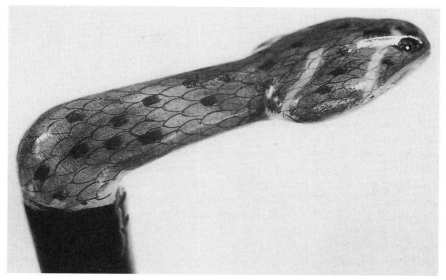

Cane with handle in snake form. *Photograph by Simon J. Bronner.*

female forms on top of the long shafts. Erotic canes also are found in folk art collections, but not usually with the male genitals on top. Emphasizing the erection of the cane, the erotic canes show women penetrated by the cane and were meant to be displayed privately (Simpson 1994, 114; Meyer 1992, 68, 80). In many canes that have woman figures on or near the top, a phallic snake or other reptile climbs up toward her (Meyer 1992, 79). A cane displayed in Milton Simpson's *Folk Erotica* shows a woman on her head with her vagina exposed, suggesting that she is penetrated by the holder's fingers (Simpson 1994, 40–41). One exceptional cane with a penis at the top included in the exhibition is, significantly, attributed to a woman (Simpson 1994, 41).

I know of at least one type of cane fashioned by men that actually is a penis, but appropriate to this discussion of old age is the fact that it is used in the secret world or social frame of a manly prank symbolically connecting sex and death. At male-dominated butcher shops such as the one described by Yolanda K. Snyder in Pennsylvania, men often expressed uneasiness about killing and dismembering bulls (Snyder 1987, 9). One humorous "fabrication" that served to create a playful situation out of a potentially disturbing procedure was to cut out the bull's penis to make a cane: "They would hang it over a pipe with weights for several weeks until it was 3 or 4 feet long, and then use the canes to drive the herd. They were more durable than sticks" (Snyder 1987, 9). In a ritual foisted on the uninitiated, the butcher-prankster would privately show the cane and exclaim, "I bet you don't know what this is!" The initiate would be asked to handle, smell, and bite the cane to figure out its origin (9). These responses would result in howls of laughter from the experienced butchers. In the socially constructed frame of this play, and its homoerotic undertones, the butchers worked through the conflicts of their killing and castrating the bulls, with whom they identify as extensions of themselves.

The connection between the butcher and the bull symbolized by the penis is also displayed verbally in jokes about the size of genitals removed from the bull. "Wouldn't ya like to have one like that!" she reported hearing on the floor. Snyder also observed men carving faces in the testicles of the bulls. In this cultural scene, the external appearance is one of a wooden stick even though the reality is that it is made of a penis. Distance is created between the natural bull and the butcher because the transformation is an exaggeration of the consumer products resulting from the butchering process. Used to "drive" the herd, it pronounces the butchers' dominance over the animals while also offering admiration for them. In the process of castrating the bulls, the butchers need to face their own sexual vulnerability and human mortality.

Castration and impotence are also evident in the symbolic references fabricated by elderly carvers as part of facing larger questions. Working in wood is certainly not the only means of playfully expressing the anxieties of old age for men, but it is a powerful one because of the traditional association of manhood with wood. The carver also realizes that woodcarving, especially rough and unpainted, connotes tradition and age associated with a faded pre-modern period; that makes the presentation of vitality all the more convincing. I realized this when a retired metalworker shared with woodcarver Bill Medlin a metal bookmark he made in the shape of an old man with a giant penis forming a clip on the marked page. It thus was in keeping with the idea of the secret erection, since the reader only saw the man's head rising from the page until the book is opened up. The men enjoyed it but preferred the springing effect of the wooden erection since it seemed more unexpected coming from an "old-fashioned" carving. In sharing risqué carvings with others, usually with an air of secrecy, the carver or prankster is revealing himself, perhaps displacing thoughts of life's end, and questioning the connection of sexual potency represented in the erect penis with the vigorous, self-confident man.

Some examples from oral tradition go further in connecting the loss of erectile function with death. In a recitation that I occasionally heard from adolescents and old men, the sexual man is defiant to the end:

> Johnny died an' went to hell.
> He said, "Now Mr. Devil, while I'm at rest,
> Place my dick upon my chest.
> Place a naked woman up over my head.

If my dick don't rise, you know I'm dead!" (See Roberts 1965, 155)

Further, one can hear in contemporary jokes about Viagra the assumption that elderly men may be able to have erections but still cannot be sexual:

> A son came to a nursing home and asked how his ailing father was doing. "Oh just fine, we give him a Viagra tablet every night and he's great in the morning." "Surely, he's not using it for sex," he replied in disbelief. "Oh no, but it prevents him from rolling out of the bed." (Collected 2004)

> An elderly man went to the pharmacist and asked for Viagra pills. "How many?" the pharmacist asked. "Oh just a few, but cut them each into quarters." "Oh, they won't do much good that way," the pharmacist said. The old man told him then, "Well, I can't use them for sex, but with that much, it'll stick out far enough so I don't pee on my shoes!" (Collected 2004)

These contemporary narratives of old age, often told by youth, deal with changing possibilities for elderly men having sex and appear to mock such potency in old age as incongruous or even threatening. Significantly, the narratives about this drug meant to treat erectile dysfunction essentially become humor about the special anxiety of old age for men, linking such dysfunction with physical decline and approaching death (see Friedman 2001, 286–307; Loe 2004, 63–94). Part of that anxiety is caused by awareness of a general pattern that women, and often their partners, will live longer than men. A common theme of replacing the expectation of using the drug for ejaculating semen with eliminating urine underscores the inability of the old man to give, and have, life. In such narratives, and in the perceptions of youth of coffin and barrel men made by elderly men, it is easy to dismiss them as products of "dirty old men" who can only fantasize rather than enact sex. Setting them in a profane category further marginalizes them in contrast to the centrality and sacredness of "clean" or "neat" looking youth. Yet for the carvers, their second worlds created by the ritual presentation of the erectile objects gives old age centeredness; their symbolically presented vitality is an erotic *denial* of death.

Based on my conversations with elderly carvers, the humor they express in carving and narrative represents sex as a sign of continued hardiness. The hardness of the erection, they realize, is perceived as a sign of youthful vitality at a time when they try to displace thoughts of death. It is a distinctly manly symbol, one that announces that if their worth, their manliness, is measured by the springing firmness of their penis, they can through a transformation in wood use that perception to refer to the skills, the power, they possess yet. In humor, aged storytellers and pranksters (such as the woodcarvers) confront the equivalence of the end of sex with the end of life and seek confirmation of their significance in modern life. When George Blume told me about other men fearing their "dicks not getting hard," he was talking of his own trepidations about his fading strength. In his wisdom, he understood the tendency to perceive the penis, or "little man" in folk speech, as the embodiment of the larger, or enlarged, man. In his narratives and carvings, he sought other embodiments, other ways to show me he fit, as an old but productive and creative man, into a manly tradition. He had to believe that his experience should not leave him a wilted thing of the past, but an erect figure and a vital presence.

REFERENCES

Art Gallery of Nova Scotia. 1976. *Folk Art of Nova Scotia.* Halifax: Art Gallery of Nova Scotia.

Baker, Ronald L. 1982. *Hoosier Folk Legends.* Bloomington: Indiana University Press.

Bauman, Richard. 1988. *Story, Performance and Event: Contextual Studies of Oral Narratives.* Cambridge: Cambridge University Press.

Bronner, Simon J. 1985. *Chain Carvers: Old Men Crafting Meaning.* Lexington: University Press of Kentucky.

———. 1996. *The Carver's Art: Crafting Meaning from Wood.* Lexington: University Press of Kentucky.

———. 2002. "Questioning the Future: Polling Americans at the Turn of the New Millennium." In *Prospects: An Annual of American Cultural Studies,* vol. 27, ed. Jack Salzman, 665–85. New York: Cambridge University Press.

Brunvand, Jan Harold. 1999. *Too Good to Be True: The Colossal Book of Urban Legends.* New York: W. W. Norton.

Carroll, Michael. 1993. "Alan Dundes: An Introduction." In *The Psychoanalytic Study of Society: Essays in Honor of Alan Dundes,* ed. L. Bryce Boyer, Ruth M. Boyer, and Stephen M. Sonnenberg, 1–22. Hillsdale, N.J.: Analytic Press.

Cray, Ed. 1992. *The Erotic Muse: American Bawdy Songs.* 2nd ed. Urbana: University of Illinois Press.

Danesi, Marcel. 2002. *The Puzzle Instinct: The Meaning of Puzzles in Human Life.* Bloomington: Indiana University Press.

Devroy, Ann. 1990a. "Dan Quayle Pussyfooting in Paraguay." *Washington Post,* March 16.

———. 1990b. "Quayle Buys a (Blush) Souvenir: Purchase of Off-Color Doll in Chile Amazes Marilyn, Onlookers." *Washington Post,* March 12.

Dorfles, Gillo, ed. 1969. *Kitsch: The World of Bad Taste.* New York: Bell.

Dorson, Richard M. 1967. *American Negro Folktales.* Greenwich, Conn.: Fawcett.

Dundes, Alan. 1980. *Interpreting Folklore.* Bloomington: Indiana University Press.

———. 1989. *Folklore Matters.* Knoxville: University of Tennessee Press.

———. 1993. "Gallus as Phallus: A Psychoanalytic Cross-Cultural Consideration of the Cockfight as Fowl Play." In *The Psychoanalytic Study of Society,* vol. 18, ed. L. Bryce Boyer, Ruth M. Boyer, and Stephen M. Sonnenberg, 23–66. Hillsdale, N.J.: Analytic Press.

Dundes, Alan, and Carl Pagter. 1978. *Work Hard and You Shall Be Rewarded: Urban Folklore from the Paperwork Empire.* 1975. Reprint, Bloomington: Indiana University Press.

———. 1991. *Never Try to Teach a Pig to Sing: Still More Urban Folklore from the Paperwork Empire.* Detroit: Wayne State University Press.

Erikson, Erik H. 1963. *Childhood and Society.* 2nd ed. New York: W. W. Norton.

Fine, Gary Alan. 1987. "Welcome to the World of AIDS: Fantasies of Female Revenge." *Western Folklore* 46: 192–97.

Freud, Sigmund. 1955 [1918]. "From the History of an Infantile Neurosis." In *The Standard Edition of the Complete Psychological Works of Sigmund Freud,* vol. 17, trans. James Strachey, 72–75. London: Hogarth Press.

Friedman, David M. 2001. *A Mind of Its Own: A Cultural History of the Penis.* New York: Penguin.

Gay, Peter, ed. 1989. *The Freud Reader.* New York: W. W. Norton.

Graburn, Nelson H. H., ed. 1976. *Ethnic and Tourist Arts: Cultural Expressions from the Fourth World.* Berkeley: University of California Press.

Goffman, Erving. 1986. *Frame Analysis: An Essay on the Organization of Experience.* 1974. Reprint, Boston: Northeastern University Press.

Harlow, Ilana. 2003. "Creating Situations: Practical Jokes and the Revival of the Dead in Irish Tradition." In *Of Corpse: Death and Humor in Folklore in Popular Culture,* ed. Peter Narváez, 83–112. Logan: Utah State University Press.

Jabbour, Alan. 1981. "Some Thoughts from a Folk Cultural Perspective." In *Perspectives on Aging,* ed. Priscilla W. Johnston, 139–49. Cambridge, Mass.: Ballinger.

Johnson, Catherine, Betsy Stirratt, and John Bancroft, eds. 2002. *Sex and Humor: Selections from the Kinsey Institute.* Bloomington: Indiana University Press.

Kinsey, Alfred C., Wardell B. Pomeroy, and Clyde E. Martin. 1948. *Sexual Behavior in the Human Male.* Philadelphia: W. B. Saunders.

Legman, G. 1968. *Rationale of the Dirty Joke: An Analysis of Sexual Humor.* New York: Grove Press.

Loe, Meika. 2004. *The Rise of Viagra: How the Little Blue Pill Changed Sex in America.* New York: New York University Press.

Loeb, Edwin M. 1929. *Tribal Initiations and Secret Societies.* University of California Publications in American Archaeology and Ethnology, vol. 25, no. 3: 249–88. Berkeley, Calif.: University of California Press.

Mechling, Jay. 1984. "High KYBO Floater: Food and Feces in the Speech Play at a Boy Scout Camp." *Journal of Psychoanalytic Anthropology* 7: 256–68.

———. 2001. *On My Honor: Boy Scouts and the Making of American Youth.* Chicago: University of Chicago Press.

Meyer, George H. 1992. *American Folk Art Canes: Personal Sculpture.* Bloomfield Hills, Mich.: Sandringham Press.

Montell, Lynwood. 1975. *Ghosts along the Cumberlands: Deathlore in the Kentucky Foothills.* Knoxville: University of Tennessee Press.

Mullen, Patrick. 1992. *Listening to Old Voices: Folklore, Life Stories, and the Elderly.* Urbana: University of Illinois Press.

Perkins, David. 2000. *Archimedes' Bathtub: The Art and Logic of Breakthrough Thinking.* New York: W. W. Norton.

"Quayle Taking a Macho Doll Back from Chile." 1990. *San Francisco Chronicle,* March 12.

Randolph, Vance. 1976. *Pissing in the Snow and Other Ozark Folktales.* Urbana: University of Illinois Press.

———. 1992. *Blow the Candle Out: "Unprintable" Ozark Folksongs and Folklore.* Vol. 2: *Folk Rhymes and Other Lore.* Ed. G. Legman. Fayetteville: University of Arkansas Press.

Roberts, Roderick, Jr. 1965. "Negro Folklore in a Southwestern Industrial School." M.A. thesis, Indiana University.

Simmel, Georg. 1950. *The Sociology of Georg Simmel.* Ed. and trans. Kurt H. Wolff. Glencoe, Ill.: Free Press.

Simpson, Milton. 1994. *Folk Erotica: Celebrating Centuries of Erotic Americana.* New York: HarperCollins.

Snyder, Yolanda K. 1987. "Butcher's Bull: A Study in Occupational Folklore." *Mid-America Folklore* 15: 1–13.

Sutton-Smith, Brian. 1986. *Toys as Culture*. New York: Gardner.

Taylor, Gary. 2002. *Castration: An Abbreviated History*. New York: Routledge.

Thomas, Jeannie B. 1997. "Dumb Blondes, Dan Quayle, and Hillary Clinton: Gender, Sexuality, and Stupidity in Jokes." *Journal of American Folklore* 110: 277–313.

Zug, Charles G. 1994. "Buddy Fisher, Woodworker." *Voices: Newsletter of the North Carolina Folk Art Society* 3: 10–11.

12

"Letting Out Jack": Sex and Aggression in Manly Recitations

RONALD L. BAKER AND SIMON J. BRONNER

Lady Lil

Lil was the best our camp perduced;
And of all the gents what Lillian goosed,
None had no such goosin', nor never will,
Since the Lord raked in poor Lady Lil.
We had a bet in our town
Thar warn't no geezer that could brown
Lil to a finish, any style—
And no bloke ever made the trial
'Cept Short Pete, the halfbreed galoot,
Who wandered in from Scruggins' Chute.
His takin' it surprised us all,
For Pete he warn't so big nor tall,
But when he yanked his tool out thar,
And laid it out across the bar,
We 'lowed our Lil had met her fate,
But thar warn't no backin' out that late,
And so we 'ranged to have the mill
Behind the whore-house on the hill,
Where all the boys could get a seat
And watch that half-breed brown his meat.
Lil's start was like the gentle breeze
That swayed the noddin' cypress trees,
But when het up, she screwed for keeps
And laid her victims out in heaps.
She tried her twists and double biffs,
And all such m'neuvres known to quiffs,
But Pete war thar with every tack,
And kept a-lettin' out more jack.
It made us cocksmen fairly sick
To see that half-breed shove his prick.
She gave short Pete a lively mill,
And wore the grass half off the hill;
'Til finally; she missed her shot,
And Short Pete had her on the pot,
But she died game, just let me tell,
And had her boots on when she fell,
So what the hell, Bill, what the hell!
Gentleman About Town, *Immortalia*

The above text is the first appearance in print of a poem under the title of "Lady Lil," but many subsequent collections of even more explicit variants in oral tradition, many of whose performers claimed learning the material from friends well before the publication, raise questions about its textual symbolism, historical context, and social-psychological meaning. The sophisticated-sounding title of "Lady Lil" disguises raunchy content meant primarily for male ears, but that incongruity is also part of the "inside" joke among men of knowing what this poem is about. Because of its erotic content, "Lady Lil" is probably the most popular poem you are likely *not* to see in print. Even folklorists devoted to documenting oral tradition shied away from reporting it because of its erotic content or a lack of access to the masculine settings where it was commonly performed. Renowned folklore collector Vance Randolph, for example, recorded many versions beginning in the 1930s, but the material was not published until 1992. Absent from Stith Thompson's motif-index of folk literature along with most other widely circulating narratives deemed "obscene," it was significantly recognized in oral tradition and dispassionately assigned motif X735.9.2.2, "Lie: Celebrated whore who claims to be able to take on any man meets her match," in folklorist Frank Hoffmann's *Analytical Survey of Anglo-American Traditional Erotica* (1973). Attesting to its popularity, the renowned bibliographer and collector of international erotica Gershon Legman called it "the best-known erotic rhymed recitation in America" and pointed out its variation as a four-line toast or epitaph as well as an epic narrative in American oral tradition (1964, 417–18). He found antecedents for it in bawdy folksongs of a much older and more "polite" kind and used this lineage to show that the modern version is "the standard sadistic concept of coitus" that displays male aggression, but he did not analyze further its variant texts, functions, or performance contexts collected from oral tradition (1964, 418; see also Legman 1976, 98–102; Baker 1987).

Collected from whom? Consistently in the reports that provide contextual information, the tradition-bearers are teenage boys and young men, and the performance settings are mostly in all-male settings. One limitation of collecting the material is that it has often been recalled by older adults, but when queried, they usually point out that it was primarily learned and performed in adolescence.

And as what? It is typically reported being recited by males to other males in bars, pool halls, summer camps, hunting camps, military bases and ships, jails, bachelor parties and other "stag" events, and fraternity and club houses. It is recognized as fantasy, and its tall-tale descriptions of the fallout from the fornicating couple are taken in performance as humorous. It might be accompanied by bawdy songs and "dirty" jokes in narrative sessions that express at once male sexual conquest as essential to a man's social empowerment and the insecurities that accompany coming-of-age.

"Lady Lil" deserves a closer reading, and analysis, than it has received, not only as an example of a persistent, popular folk poem—probably *the* most popular manly recitation—but as an expression of American sexual bravado and manliness performed mostly by young men for their fellows at a transitional time in their lives. In addition to examining the content of the recitation as it has been reported in orally collected variants, we consider the important details of who tells it and the time of life told for clues to the poem's signification of developmental issues at the folk roots of the often-difficult transition to manhood. In fact, we find it noteworthy in the frequently noted absence of a common rite of passage in America for turning boys to men that recitations are ritualized performances geared to settings associated with coming-of-age (Raphael 1988).

"Lady Lil" first appeared in print in 1927 in *Immortalia,* a privately published anthology of erotic verse by "A Gentleman About Town" (Gentleman 1969 [1927], 8–9; Mackay 1952 [1927], 8). The extensive *Immortalia* text reproduced at the start of this essay is thirty-seven lines long and is set in a "camp," often attributed to mining by later commentators. As a result of a wager that no one could "brown Lil to a finish, any style," only a character by the name of "Short Pete, the halfbreed galoot, Who wandered in from Scruggins' Chute" steps forward to take on the formidable Lil. Although appearing not big enough for the job, "when he yanked his tool out thar, And laid it out across the bar, We 'lowed our Lil had met her fate." Once the contest in intercourse begins before an audience, the damage that ensues is epic, especially from Lil's gymnastic "m'neuvres." But the eye-popping culmination of the contest, and Pete's ultimate triumph, occurs when "Pete war thar with every tack, And kept a-letting out more jack" (Mackay 1952 [1927], 8).

In the *Immortalia* collection, "Lady Lil," as well as seven other poems, is ascribed to the American journalist Eugene Field (1850–95), who apparently had a reputation for writing erotic poems and issuing them privately for friends. But Legman, having searched "the very complete" collection of Field's manuscripts without finding a trace of "Lady Lil," doubts the claim (Randolph 1992, 669–70). While it is possible that Field wrote "Lady Lil," it is more likely that the text in *Immortalia* is adapted from oral tradition, since most of the texts in the collection are well-known folk songs and recitations. In fact, the author of the introduction to *Immortalia,* who calls himself or herself "A Friend" of the anthology's compiler, writes: "Literature with a capital 'L' has all the stabilizing factors of the printed word and of learned tradition to perpetuate it—folk-lore lives only in the voices of the people themselves—the source from which the material in this book has been drawn, from cover to cover" (1969, 1). Regardless of the author-

Illustration by John Held Jr., published in *More Pious Friends and Drunken Companions*, "collected" by Frank Shay, 1928. *Reproduced with permission from the estate of Mrs. John Held Jr.*

ship of "Lady Lil," its appearance in *Immortalia* shows that the folk poem was known as early as 1927.

Just a year after *Immortalia* was privately published, in fact, John Held Jr. published his illustration entitled "Nell was the Best the Camp Produced," a variation of the first line of the "Lil" poem in *Immortalia*—"Lil was the best our camp perduced"—in *More Pious Friends and Drunken Companions* (Shay 1928, 141). The volume consisted of songs and verses collected from oral tradition by Frank Shay in bars and saloons. Although he did not include a text to accompany the engraving, probably because of the recitation's erotic content, the inclusion of the illustration is a strong indication that he thought readers would recognize the reference to a widely circulating set of bar-room verses following that first line. The illustration of a western scene depicts the buxom Nell "turning the heads" of four old miners, apparently gazing lustfully at her sexually suggestive raising of her dress. Considering the toning down of many of the songs in Shay's collection for the commercially published volume, it is understandable that Held chose not to portray the fornication contest between the "half-breed" and Nell/Lil.

The earliest documented recording of Lil from oral tradition in the field is by Ozarks collector Vance Randolph. In 1934, he jotted down as quickly as he could the following uncensored verses as they were recited by "Mr. S. N." in Pineville, Missouri, under the title of "Lady Lil."

> Little Lil taught school when she first came West,
> But she soon give it up to fuck and rest,
> There was a standin' bet around our town
> That no living man could hold Lil down.
>
> Across the street come a half-breed brute
> From over the top of Mount Janute,
> He slowly strode across the street
> And says no whore has got *me* beat.
>
> He layed his jong out on the bar,
> By God, it stretched from thar to thar!
> We knowed that Lil had met her fate,
> But to back out then was too damn late.
>
> So we decided to hold the mill
> Behind the shit-house on the hill,
> Where every man could get a seat
> And watch the half-breed sink his meat.
>
> Lil started like a little breeze
> That blows the tops of cypress trees,
> Then she jumped and flounced which was plenty slick
> Till the half-breed lost control of his dick.
>
> She pumped and pumped and double-pumped
> With tricks unknown to a common cunt,
> But he called her hand on every trick
> And just kept pouring on the prick.
>
> At last poor Lil she missed a shot
> And the half-breed pinned her to the spot;
> The sod was tore for miles around
> Where Lil's old ass had plowed the ground.
>
> But she died brave, I want to tell,
> She had her boots on when she fell,
> So we cut off Lil's drawers all full of gore,
> And nailed 'em on the shit-house door. (Randolph 1992, 667–68)[1]

The feature of an endless supply of penile power described as "pouring on the prick" and "letting out jack" is prominent in most "Lil" recitations, serving structurally to compensate for Pete's diminutive, and often unattractive, body and to match Lil's impressive athletic moves. When the informally named "Pete" uncovers his penis, there is the suggestion that his name is connected with "peter," used to designate the penis. He is remarkable, or heroic, because he defies the male insecurity about losing an erection; indeed, his erection appears to keep growing.

The multiple meanings of Pete's "jack" as penis, tool/weapon, and vigorous or wild youthful male (or "little man," as a diminutive form of the adult "John") are also apparent in texts with a masturbation ending of "jacking off." Not satisfied with merely winning, Pete with his "jack" attacks Lil with a ferocity that suggests sexual hatred or a revenge motive. Developmentally emerging in adolescence, such recitations told by males appear fantastically sadistic to unequivocally signify separation from the maternal/feminine.[2] In many narratives, Pete and his jack finish off Lil by humiliating her and even draw more power from her demise. In some versions in which Pete threatens or replaces older men, there is even a hint of patricide to mark the independence of the youth.

The earliest public printing of the poem, according to Legman, was an expurgated text that appeared three years later in George Milburn's *The Hobo's Hornbook* (1930) adapted from recitations of tramps and hobos he personally met. Like the text in *Immortalia*, "Our Lil" is described as "the best the camp produced," and Milburn presumes that the action takes place in a "western mining camp" (Milburn 1930, 140). Lil's adversary is "Greaser Pete . . . from Sugar Creek," and he, too, is described as "sawed-off," or diminutive. The key verse for "letting out jack" has been replaced with asterisks, drawing attention to it as dramatically explicit, and probably adding to its importance. Indeed, Legman comments that the verse ending with "And kept a-lettin' out more jack" is "a principal focus of variants collected in the field" (Randolph 1992, 670). While Milburn clearly recognized the recitation's circulation in oral tradition, folklore collector Vance Randolph documented background information in 1940 from a teller indicating its circulation as early as the 1890s. Recalling learning it in childhood, the informant related the verse, "She started like a gentle breeze, That bends and sways the cypress trees . . . The way Lil bucked was plenty slick, But he just kept letting out his prick" (668).

Randolph recorded four other texts, the longest of which at thirty-two lines is the one from Mr. S. N. reproduced earlier. The main variant he introduced was the narrative theme of Lil being a "schoolmarm" in Mr. S. N.'s poem. In another version Randolph recorded, the text begins, "Lil was a schoolmarm from the West, That's where she found the fuckin' best, The word it come from miles around, That no two men could hold Lil down" (Randolph 1992, 668). Significantly for male reciters, the construction of "School*marm*," emphasizing the maternal authority of the teacher, combines two powerful symbols of female authority for the school-age boy.

Presumably, Lil goes west because of its association with wildness. In a version of "Lady Lil" collected by Reynolds Morse from the same period, Lil gives up teaching to indulge her voracious sexual appetite, and this detail precedes the "camp" reference:

Our Lil was a school teacher till she came out west,
But she warn't a teacher long 'cause she liked fuckin' best.
O Lil was the best our camp produced,
And of all the gents what Lillian goosed,
None had no such goosin', nor ever will,
Since the Lord raked in our Lady Lil.
We had a bet in our gambling town
Thar warn't no geezer that could brown
Lil to a finish any style
And no bloke ever made the trial
'Cept Shorthorn Pete, the halfbreed galoot
Who had wandered in from Scruggins' Chute. (Morse 1945, 79)

The symbolism of age comes into play in the text, since his name of Short-horn, usually representing someone young or newly arrived, is contrasted with "geezer," associated with old age. A clue, in fact, to the identity of the reciter is the finding by linguists Harold Wentworth and Stuart Berg Flex-ner that "short-horn" was often used by American college students during the first half of the twentieth century (1967, 472).

Despite the popular image of the schoolmarm as sexually repressed, Lil is sexually unrestrained. She at first appears irrepressible, but she succumbs in Randolph's texts to "Piss-Pot Pete" from "Bare-Ass Creek," yet another diminutive figure. In an added coda that is found in two versions, Pete arrogantly displays his prowess in victory by masturbating: "The ground was tore up for miles around, Where Lil's old ass had plowed the ground, And Lil passed out with a sigh and a cough, While Piss-Pot Pete started jacking off" (Randolph 1992, 668). The detail of her ass as "old" appears to fit into the schoolmarm image and provides a structural contrast besides tall and short, of Pete's youth and the schoolmarm's maturity. Two of the informants recalled learning the recitation in childhood, and one was a college student at the time Randolph recorded him. The college student adapted the "camp" opening for college life by relating "she's the best this *town* ever produced" and adds the comment after "I'll swear it reached from thar to *thar!*" of "And stink—God damn! It stunk" (669; emphasis in original). Legman speculates that this reference to a strong odor and goos-ing may be thinly veiled allusions in an all-male group to the awareness, or threat, of homosexual intercourse (669).

Six versions of "Lady Lil," apparently collected from young men, have been found by Simon Bronner in the unpublished papers of the folksong collector Sam Eskin and date from 1936 to 1958. Although Eskin does not give precise informant data, he notes that three versions were collected during World War II, one of these in 1944 from "horny Marine Corps personnel." Another version, according to Eskin, circulated "in central Pennsylvania [in] 1957–58 in college circles." In this text, Lil again is a schoolmarm until she went West, where "she found that she liked fucking best." "Short-Horn Pete" meets Lil "lick for lick, And kept on reeling out more prick." The text also features more descriptive detail than other versions on Pete's aggressiveness and the damage he inflicts:

> And only once she missed a shot,
> And Pete, he nailed her on the spot,
> And stuck his prick into her twat.
> He drove his cock clear through her ass
> Until it wiped upon the slimy grass.
> The ground was torn for miles around.
> Where Lil's fair ass had hit the ground.
> And in her belly were great ruts
> Where Pete's big dong had ripped her guts.

Besides these versions from Eskin's collections, a further indication of the recitation's circulation among young adults are nineteen other versions of "Lady Lil," told by white American college students from 1964 to 1983, located in the Indiana State University Folklore Archives.

While the general setting is vague in eight of these twenty-five versions, twelve versions are set in the West, two versions are set in Louisville, and one version each is set in Terre Haute (Indiana), up north, and in the Lehigh Valley (presumably in Pennsylvania). In thirteen versions the female is named Lil—including Old Lil, Diamond Lil, Big-Ass Lil, and Whorehouse Lil. In six versions she is called either Nell, Old Nell, or Powder Mountain Nell. The only other names appearing in a version each are Old Kate and Lou. In nine versions, mostly early ones, Lil is a schoolteacher. In three versions, though, she is a whore, and in the other versions her occupation is not given. Generally, Lil is described as sexually dominant, unfeeling, insatiable—and combative. Typical lines in nearly half of the versions are: "When Ol' Nell fucked she fucked for keeps / And left her victims all piled in heaps." Another popular line in about half of the versions is a variation on "There weren't ten men who could fuck Lil down." And most give details on the remarkable length of Pete's penis, particularly when he is "pouring," "letting," "stretching," "reeling," or "hauling" it out.

The version with a reference to the Lehigh Valley suggests a relation to a bawdy folk song usually reported with the title "The Lehigh Valley":

> I've been up in the Lehigh Valley,
> Me and my old pal, Lou,
> A pimpin' for a whorehouse
> And a God damned good one too.
> It was there that I first fucked Nellie;
> She was the village belle.
> I was only a lowdown panderer
> but I loved that girl like hell. (Cray 1992, 199)

Milburn, in fact, reports that hobos "merged" ribald recitations from "Down in the Lehigh Valley" with "Our Lil." But the Lehigh Valley song is about hunting down the man who steals Nell away rather than a fornication contest between Nell and a young or diminutive man. Still, awareness of the song may explain the temptation to place the action "down in the Lehigh Valley," where, as D. K. Wilgus begins a recitation from his memory of his teenage years,

> Lil was the best our camp produced,
> And of all the gents that Lillian goosed,
> None had such goosing, and never will,
> Since the lord took to his bosom our lady, Lil. (Cray 1992, 200)

The name of Lil hardly connotes lady-like features, however. It suggests "Lilith," popularly known as the demon of the night. She is mentioned in the Bible as a kind of wild demon consorting with vicious animals: "Wild-cats shall meet hyenas, Goat-demons shall greet each other; There too the lilith shall repose, And find herself a resting place" (Isaiah 35:14). In many religious texts, Lilith is the symbol of sexual lust and is especially dangerous to children. In Talmudic legend, she is the wife that Adam is fabled to have had before Eve, and who refused to submit to him. The recitation of "Lady Lil" captures many of these qualities about her, since she is characterized as demonic, dominant, independent, and erotic.

Another erotic, if more light-hearted, character that appears in recitations to take on Pete is "Lulu." The bawdy character of Lulu appears frequently in children's and adolescent songs, so it is not unprecedented to see her appear in Piss-Pot Pete recitations (see Cray 1992, 173–82; Opie and Opie 1985, 472–73). Lulu meets her demise, for example, in "Lulu Had a Steamboat," frequently collected with the lines "Behind the refrigerator, There was a piece of glass, Lulu sat right on it, And bust her silly, Ask me no more questions, And I'll tell you no more lies, And that is the story of how Lulu died, died, died, died, died" (Bronner 1988, 61). Also using the cutoff line to indicate a taboo word, but with much more erotic imagery, is the song "Bang Bang Lulu" frequently reported being sung by adolescent boys in all-male settings about a whore named Lulu: "Bang bang Lulu, Lulu's gone away, Who we gonna bang bang, Since Lulu's gone away? Lulu's got a rooster, Lulu's got a duck. She put them in the bathtub, To see if they would . . ." (Cray 1992, 181).

Uses of Lou and Nell, and bar-room settings of the Pacific Northwest, are probably inspired by oral recitations of Robert W. Service's early-twentieth-century "bar-room ballads" set in Alaska and the Yukon, including "The Shooting of Dan McGrew" and "The Ballad of Touch-the-Button Nell." As folklorist Robert D. Bethke found in upstate New York bars, men frequently committed Service's poems to memory and then adapted them for bar-room recitations (Bethke 1976). Exotic locales, colorful characters with memorable names, simple ballad meter, as well as powerful themes of love and revenge, heroic adventure, and primal instincts in Service's poems made them popular sensations when they were published in the first decade of the twentieth century. Several scholars have noted that their easily remembered rhyming structure and the recounting of male bravado on the wild frontier invite manly public recitation and their entrance into oral tradition (Bethke 1976; Hirsch 1976; Leeds 1999).

In the cultural practice of using the bar-room setting as a stage for manly humor, Service's narrative poems also invited parody and ribaldry. The last lines of the fifty-nine-line poem "The Shooting of Dan McGrew" (1907), for example, are:

> These are the simple facts of the case,
> And I guess I ought to know.
> They say that the stranger was crazed with "hooch,"
> And I'm not denying it's so.
> I'm not so wise as the lawyer guys,
> But strictly between us two—
> The woman that kissed him and—pinched his poke—
> Was the lady that's known as Lou. (Service 1993, 7–8)[3]

Sam Eskin collected one parody of "Dan McGrew" recited to him in 1948. Like recitations about Piss-Pot Pete, it also features an unlikely stud, short in height but not in penis length.

> Then out of the night that was black as a bitch
> And into the din and smoke
> Stepped a shaky old prick just in from the creek
> With a rusty load in his poke.
>
> As he shouldered his way through the flea-bitten crowd
> He clutched at the crotch of his pants
> He looked like a chap with a dose of the clap
> And the girls wouldn't take a chance.
>
> In his ragged clothes he stood ready to hose
> Any bitch that came his way
> He dangled his dong, a horny prong
> And he howled that he wanted to play.
>
> His face was as red as a baboon's ass
> And his balls were so hot that they burned
> Then he lugged out his cock to display to the flock
> And everyone's asshole squirmed. (See Morse 1945, 78; *Shitty Songs* 2004)

As in some variants of "Lady Lil," once the unlikely stud "lugged out his cock," men as well as women feel threatened by sexual attack. Indeed, the parody changes the last lines of the original "Dan McGrew" to:

The lights went out, and I ducked to the floor
As the stranger sprang in the dark.
His aim was true, and the sparks they flew
As his donnicker found its mark.
With might and main, and a scream of pain
A man's voice filled the room.
With sighs and moans and farts and groans,
Three forms lay stacked in the gloom.
Then the lights went on, and the stranger rose
With a satisfied look on his pan,
For there on the floor with his ass all gore
Lay poor old corn-holed Dan! (See Morse 1945, 78)

Commenting on the text of "The Grooving of Dan McGrew" in his anthology of "folk poems and ballads," A. R. Morse observed that it is a "companion" to "The Ballad of Lady Lil." He stated, "Both have a real kinship with the other works of the Klondike poets and relate to a definite period in our social history when we looked to Alaska as the last frontier" (Morse 1945, 120).

It may be possible that the male figure of "Piss-Pot Pete" in many of the Lil and Nell folk poems derives from a mispronunciation of, or parody of, "Pious Pete" from Service's poem "The Ballad of Pious Pete" (Service 1940, 98–102). Yet the name "Pious Pete" appears only in the title, and it is a narrative about two antagonistic male neighbors, not a combat between a man and a sensual woman. Still, some of the colorful language of Pete touting a phallic gun in an angry struggle is reminiscent of the fornication contest in folk poems:

> As I rested my gaze in a misty amaze on the scurvy-degenerate wreck,
> I thought of the Things with the dragon-fly wings, then laid I my gun on his neck.
> He gave out a cry that was faint as a sigh, like a perishing malamute,
> And he says unto me, "I'm converted," says he; "for Christ's sake, Peter, don't shoot!"

The male hero in the twenty-five oral versions of the "Lady Lil" recitations is always named Pete, except for two versions in which he is nameless. In a dozen versions he is Pisspot Pete, but he also appears, generally in single versions or at the most in two versions, as Shitpot Pete, Half-Assed Pete, Yukon Pete, Short-Horn Pete, Sloppy Pete, Shaggle Pete, Sig Ep Pete, and simply Pete. Reinforcing the image of the figure's social marginality and profanity, Pete comes from such undeveloped or unrefined places as Tar-Ass Creek, Shag-Ass Creek, Bare-Ass Creek, Bare-Ass Street, and "From Shithead Mountain, 'Cross Piss-Fed Creek." In fourteen versions Pete is some kind of half-breed. In eight of these versions he is simply identified as a half-breed, but he also appears as a half-breed galoot, a half-breed

Injun, a one-eyed half-breed, a one-balled half-breed, a sawed-off half-breed, and a half-breed Greek (or Creek).

The "half-breed" identifies him as the offspring of white and Indian intercourse, implying in its colloquial usage inferior quality and liminal social status. It also can connote the fact that he is dangerous, even monstrous or uncontrollable, because he is "unnatural" (see Malchow 1996). He also is called a half-assed Greek, a bare-assed Greek, a bald-headed bastard, a blue-balled bastard, a little bastard, and a worthless miner. Sometimes he is physically repulsive, with "Snot on his head and shit on his feet," "Spit on his head and shit on his feet," and "Shit oozing between his toes." While such descriptions of his disgusting appearance may make him more uncaring, perhaps more primitive, and certainly more profane, in some versions there is also the insinuation that this might be the result of "goosing" or anal attacks. The racial epithet and the description of his social marginalization in the derogatory names for places he resides may also structurally explain in the narrative the motives for his ferocity. Implied in his attack is his pent-up anger, presumably from being ostracized, that he releases upon Lil. His unrefined appearance and home in profane, feces-filled surroundings further reinforce his image of immaturity compared to the "old" miners/geezers or even to the sophisticated *Lady* Lil/ Nell.

Nearly all versions describe his enormous penis, which he displays to the astonishment of goggling men. Some version of the lines "He stretched his dick along the bar, / And I'll tell you it reached from thar to thar" is found in nearly half of the variants. Other descriptions of his organ include: "99 pounds of dangling meat," "18 feet of swinging meat," and "As long as your arm and as big as your wrist, And a knot on the end as big as your fist." While Lil exhausts her opponents and is extraordinary because she performs "shunts and bunts, And stunts unknown to common cunts," Pete's organ ultimately acts as a superior weapon nailing, pinning, and mounting her, followed by sinking, shoving, and sticking "his meat" in her. The sadistic coitus theme, as Legman calls it, may be linked to his avenging Lil's rejection of the watching men. Even though there is an indication that the men have a low regard for Pete, he takes up their cause of dominating Lil as conflated symbols of maternal authority and unbridled female sexual power.

In the oral versions, the fornication contest is held in unbecoming places such as "behind the shithouse on the hill," "behind the shack, behind the hill," "between the whorehouse and the mill," in a "hall behind the schoolhouse on the hill," and (in one version) "upon the hill, behind the shithouse, behind the mill." The unseemly secrecy of being behind the shithouse, and the salacious betting that occurs on the fornication contest has the markings of a dogfight or cockfight in which gambling takes on masturbatory qualities (Dundes 1994 and his afterword in this volume).

This Freudian idea that gambling and masturbation are similarly compulsively driven repetitive acts that rise to a climax takes on added significance in the narrative action of "Lady Lil," since the reciter states that the bettors failed at intercourse with Lil but delighted in voyeuristically watching the fornication. It may be that the ending in several versions of "Lil" in which Pete masturbates after vanquishing his foe, presumably resulting in further frustration for the bettors who put their money on the imposing Lil, implies a connection between Pete's concluding action and the gambling at the beginning of the recitation.

In all twenty-three complete versions of "Lady Lil," Pete wins the fornication contest, and in a dozen versions he masturbates after defeating Lil, thus showing his inexhaustible potency. Whereas males feel vulnerable because they ultimately lose their erections and therefore have to prove their virility again, Pete appears to be hyper-masculine because he never goes soft. In one of the two fragments, Pete's animalistic manliness is exaggerated in his mounting Lil "like a Belgian stud," a phrase found in six other oral versions. As one male informant said, "That's a powerful line. Anyone who ever saw a Belgian stud in action can feel how Pete tackled Lil" (Mitchell 1969). He elaborated:

> As a country boy who remembers when horses were in and studs were travelled (i.e., brought from farm to farm for breeding purposes), let me point up the picture of the Belgian stud. A Belgian is a heavy horse, about a ton, and when the old stud was unloaded and he smelled the mare, he'd go wild. As a kid I watched in awe and appreciation when a ton of horse with nearly two foot of tallywhacker would charge the old mare. He'd rare up, his handler would grab his penis (the stud's) and make sure he drove it in the proper place. My brother and I used to muse about what would happen if he missed. (Mitchell 1969)

Versions of "Lady Lil" collected from African American males reported by Roger Abrahams, Bruce Jackson, Roderick Roberts, and Onwuchekwa Jemie show continuities in theme with the white versions, with a notable exception in the ending. In *Deep Down in the Jungle* (1970) Abrahams reports a single version, "Schoolteacher Lulu and Crabeye Pete," from the streets of Philadelphia. Typically Schoolteacher Lulu is insatiable, for "ninety-nine men couldn't fuck her down"; characteristically Crabeye Pete, though physically repulsive, has a huge organ, for he is described as having "Crab to his head and dick to his feet." The pimps and conventionists at Carnegie Hall bet that Crabeye Pete can get the best of Lulu, but in the contest that follows, Lulu with her "bulldog twist," is too much for Pete and kills him (Abrahams 1970, 164–65). Abrahams identifies the teller as a young man and connects the text to other "male entertainment" performed "on the street corners with the gang on long summer evenings, in the poolhall after everyone has run out of money, and occasionally at parties" (111). Although collected from black tradition-bearers, Abrahams observes that the text is representative of "common lore in the Anglo-American tradition" (164).

In *Get Your Ass in the Water and Swim Like Me* (1974), Jackson gives three versions collected in Texas and New York from black American males, mostly in prisons, in 1965 and 1970. Although he does not identify the ages of the informants, he quotes one who reported learning it from "a *boy* way back in '36 I believe it was" (Jackson 1974, 150; emphasis added). While Jackson agreed with Abrahams that such recitations are often told in male settings "at parties, lounging around bars and streetcorners, on a troopship crossing the boring ocean," he claimed that "they seem to be told in county jails more than anywhere else." His reasoning is that a great portion of the prison population is lower-class black, and the recitations, filling time, relate the risky, illegal street roles and activities that landed the jailhouse tellers in prison. With the tellers constrained in jail, he surmises, the toasts are fantasies relying on sexual symbolism that expresses tellers' freedom, dominance, and power.

Two full versions entitled " 'Flicted Arm Pete" collected by Jackson from the same informant seven months apart are set in Louisville and deal with a fornication contest between a "fast-fucking whore" named Lil and a "long-dicked creep" called 'Flicted Arm Pete, a super-stud with a damaged arm.[4] When Lil sees Pete's enormous organ, she realizes that "at last she'd met her mate." After hours and hours of going at one another, "Lil keeled over and died," leaving Pete masturbating. Pete brags that he has "fucked everything from the Gulf of Colorado to the rocky shores of Maine, / mules, cows, horses, and every goddamned thing." That evening after the fornication contest with Lil, one animal does Pete in, however, for "Pete topped him a mountain goat, / but Pete's backbone cracked and that was all she wrote." The third version in Jackson's collection is a fragment about Pisspot Pete, and the suggestion is that Pete loses the sexual contest with an unidentified woman, as this version concludes: "For days and nights the fuck went on / now Pisspot is dead and gone" (Jackson 1974, 150–52).

As Legman has observed of the different conclusions in black and white versions, "Almost none of the recitations printed by Abrahams and Jackson are found among whites, and conversely only two or three of the bawdy rhymed recitations common among whites appear in their books, in particular a highly reworked text of 'Our Lil' and one or two set pieces. Black and white repertories in this line therefore cannot be considered identical and do not derive from the same inspiration except perhaps as to their British origin and the defiant underlying emotion" (Legman 1976, 63–64). While not identical, black and white versions frequently share variations of the verse of "They fucked and fucked for hours and hours / Tearing up trees and shrubs and flowers / The earth was torn for miles around / Where Lil's poor ass had hit the ground." Another common connection is the age of the tellers in a transition to manhood and the description of the characters as the diminutive or "'flicted" man meeting his match against the potent woman. The main difference is the outcome of the fornication contest; while Pete dominates the woman in both black and white versions, in black versions Pete typically dies.

Giving more attention than Abrahams and Jackson to the age of the performers, Roderick Roberts recorded five versions from five different teenaged black men between the ages of seventeen and nineteen residing in an all-male industrial school, but apparently he heard it many more times, because he writes, "This was the most popular item among this group of informants," further underscoring the significance of the recitation in a typical folkloric repertoire of young men (Roberts 1965, 171). All his texts were set in the "West," probably a reflection of the teens relating to their location in Arizona. In all five texts, the female character is Lulu, but she is identified neither as a schoolteacher or a whore, but a woman who "went out West, Where she thought fuckin' was the best." In one version, the female character is introduced as "Mama," and the opening line is reminiscent of what Roberts hears referred to as "sounding," or rhymed insults delivered in playful contests (Abrahams reports them as "dozens"). Compare, for example, the first text collected as "sounding" and the second as a "toast," both from the same seventeen-year-old informant:

Well, I was walkin' through the jungle, ya know,
In the deepest grass;
Fuck aroun' an' stepped in your mama's ass.
Mama jumped up an' started ta swing;
I put my other foot dead in that thing;
She throwed a little ol' right,
But it was jus' too slow.
I hit her up 'side the head;
It was a TKO. (Roberts 1965, 186)

I remember when your mama went out West,
Where she thought fuckin' was the best.
She went from town to town;
No big-dick fucker could fuck her down.
Across the river and across the creek
Lived this half-breed Indian named Piss-Pot Pete,
Forty-two inches a breedin' meat.
He fucked little Lulu for hours an' hours,
Tearin' down trees an' rootin' up flowers.
Lulu killed Pete, the dirty bitch;
The next night she died with the overnight itch.
An' on Lulu's grave could plainly be seen:
"Here lies the bones of a great fuckin' machine." (173–74)

The difference between the two genres is that in the sounding the man beats the female character and arguably sodomizes or degrades her, since he penetrates her from the rear. Sounding is also associated with a younger stage of development in preadolescence, although informants "remembered" them in performances for Roberts. Both texts given above, however, convey the male-female encounter as combative. The toast is also consistent with sounding that portrays the other person's mother as insatiable and powerful. In the following sounding text from another informant, for example, the opening formulaic line "I remember" found in "Mama of the West" repeats:

> I remember when I fucked your mama.
> I fucked your mama on a bale of hay;
> When I got through, my nuts were gray.
> I got your mama behind a tree.
> The tree split, an' she shit,
> An' I didn't get nothin' but a little bit. (Roberts 1965, 185–86)

The male character in the versions Roberts collected is always "Piss-Pot Pete." Narrators describe him as "a half-breed Negro" in one version and "a half-breed Indian" in the other four. Emphasizing his hyper-masculine attributes, Pete's "breeding meat" is measured at its shortest at "thirty-two inches" (two versions) and at its longest at "forty-eight inches" (one version). Other versions give it as thirty-nine and forty-two inches. They all agree that Lulu kills Pete after fornicating remarkably "for hours and hours." All the narrators unequivocally call her "a dirty bitch" for getting the best of Pete, but he would have his revenge. All the tradition-bearers say that she ends up dying herself with the "overnight itch." The final lines of all their performances follow the pattern of "And on her grave could plainly be seen, 'There lies the bones of a great fuckin' machine'" (Roberts 1965, 171–74).

The destruction of Pete by a machine in African American versions suggests a relation to black recitations about John Henry, who is remembered for sexual feats in oral tradition and like Pete dies at the end (Abrahams 1970, 75). In many recorded polite versions, the "contest" which Henry loses is with a steam drill machine, while the African American figure swings his phallic hammer. Similar to the boast of "no whore has got *me* beat" in many versions of "Lady Lil," John Henry refuses to let any "steam drill beat me down" (Williams 1983, v). Roger Abrahams also points out that Henry channels his aggressions toward the machine attempting to emasculate him. In addition to recording versions of Piss-Pot Pete, Abrahams also recorded "John Henry" as a coming-of-age oral recitation emphasizing the sexuality of the black hero performed by African-American men in a Philadelphia ghetto:

When John Henry was a baby,
You could hold him in the palm of your hand.
But when he got nineteen years old,
He could stand that pussy like a man.

John Henry told his father,
A man ain't nothing but a man.
But before he'd let a piece of pussy go by,
He'd die with his dick in his hand,
Yeh, he'd die with his dick in his hand.

Now John Henry took his girl friend
He layed her 'pon the rock.
When he got through he looked at her,
"Umm, such good cock,
Umm, such good cock."

Now when John Henry died
They say he died from shock.
But if you want to know the truth
He died from too much cock.
Yes, the boy died from too much cock.

Now they took John Henry's body,
And they layed it in the sand.
People come from far and near
To see that good fucking man,
Yeh, to see that good fucking man. (Abrahams 1970, 75)

In Onwuchekwa Jemie's collections from young African American reciters of Piss-Pot Pete in New York City, the recitations similarly end with a
pronouncement of the hero being given respect upon death for his sexual
prowess. In the first version he published, the last lines are "With his ass
still pumping and his dick still hard, They drug his black ass to the nearest
graveyard, Pete's last words on his dying day, Was, 'Good pussy brought
me, now it has taken me away'" (Jemie 2003, 247). Pete in the second
version was, like John Henry, "a man big and strong, Had a dick on his
body eighteen inches long." As in the texts Roberts collected from African
American informants, the whore "killed poor Pete, the dirty bitch, But she
shall die of the seven-year itch." The ending is a variation of Jemie's other
text, "When they carried old Pete to the graveyard, His ass was still wiggling
and his dick was still hard, Last words old Pete was heard to say, 'Lord,
pussy brought me here, and it sure took me away'" (248).

Following Abrahams's argument that the black adolescent male in the
urban ghetto has special cultural pressures on him to demonstrate his manhood in a matrifocal society as well as suffering infantilization from mass
society, a developmental reading of the distinctive ending in texts from
lower-class African Americans suggests that the maturing male hero lashes

out with sexual bravado at the forces—matrifocal and mass-cultural—that emasculate him. From the matrifocal society, he feels disappointment, and from mass culture, he feels prejudice and lack of opportunity. In ringing tones of fatalism, the recitation concludes with his death while maintaining the resistant vitality of "his ass still wiggling, and his dick still hard." Perhaps this last paradoxical image symbolizes the artificial oppression of his social potency, while reminding his male tellers of the inner strength, and manliness, expressed naturally through sexuality. Part of his separation from the maternal/feminine is not to show any romantic sentiment or any sentimentality for death. He assumes the emotionally, and socially, detached "hardman" or the violent "badman" figure. Jerry H. Bryant adds that violent "badman" recitations serve to explain his "sorry state" in performance, because the badman led this street "Life" which he cannot escape. He writes, "The genre requires a 'framed' opening in which the narrator addresses an audience, perhaps in jail, more often in a barroom where his listeners have not yet been chastened by failure" (Bryant 2003, 96). A tone of resignation is apparent in many toasts, he finds, but there is also an affirmation of the *bad*man values by which he lives, plays, and suffers (98). Implied in the bitterness of Jemie's and Jackson's texts, in fact, is blame for the man's downfall or imprisonment on the strong woman figure and her association with a dominant culture.

African American toasts most intensively collected during the 1960s and 1970s are often referred to as the "roots" of rap and hip-hop that emerged as a commercial form during the 1980s, suggesting not only similarities in recitation style, but thematic continuities of sexual bravado, misogyny, egotistic self-assertion, and ferocious attack in contests to the death (Keyes 2002, 24–28). "Before there was rap, there were street rhymes," one contemporary account recalls (Metzger 2003). The writer reflects on the similarity of badman heroes, one of whom he remembers as Piss-Pot Pete: "They swagger endlessly. They fight and swear and use their sex appeal like a deadly weapon. They live on in folk rhymes, told again and again. The names shift and the exploits mutate each time the story is told. But as long as someone remembers these loud, vulgar, hilarious word-of-mouth poems, the heroes will live on" (Metzger 2003). Rappers found public outlets became available for the erotic content that had been privately shared on the street. To be sure, in hyper-masculine rap and hip-hop more original, obscenity-ridden rhymes with more gunplay and anti-police content can be heard. There are faster, more demonstrative rhythms overall, and what one prominent critic calls "dull-witted rage" (Metzger 2003). Indeed, that critic blames rap and hip-hop for swallowing up "a vital element of folk culture" of the street rhymes, and the declining number of reported Piss-Pot Pete texts at the end of the twentieth century may confirm this opinion. Or it may be possible that some of the functions of toasts in expressing male adolescent anxieties, as well as aggression, in the black ghetto are being more publicly, and commercially, incorporated into rap (Bennett 1999; Keyes 2002, 22–38).

As with women breaking through into the male-dominated rap, there is in its folk roots a female tradition, albeit a minor one, referring to Piss Pot Pete. The only version of Lady Lil or Lulu of the West in the Indiana State University Folklore Archives told by a female informant was collected on December 9, 1971, from a nineteen-year-old white student residing in Indiana. Her short version goes:

> There once was a girl named Sally Brown,
> Who claimed no man could get her down,
> When over the hill came Pissball Pete,
> Forty-five pounds of swinging meat.
> He got her down in the grass,
> Stick his dick up in her ass.
> She cut a fart and blew it apart,
> And over the hill went Pissball Pete,
> Forty-four pounds of shredded wheat.

Other versions with "hanging meat" instead of "shredded wheat" and "Jenny Brown" rather than "Sally Brown" circulate in oral tradition, judging from material submitted to humor sites on the Internet. The name "Sally Brown" is a stock folk character appearing in old bawdy folksongs about a promiscuous mulatto (Shay 1928, 146–47). It also has a connection to a sexual figure in limericks, a form alluded to in the opening line of "There once was a. . . ." Indeed, in limericks recorded from oral tradition by Legman, Sally farts while fornicating:

> There was a young man named O'Malley
> Who was fucking his gal in the alley,
>   When right at the start
>   She let a small fart,
> Said O'Malley to Sally, "Now r'ally!" (Legman 1969, 346)

Inversing Pete's sexual prowess in the contest of potency in Lil poems, Sally appears in feminine limericks as a lustful "matron" disappointed by her impotent, younger partner.

> There was a young matron named Sally
> Who went with her groom up an alley.
>   She was quite out of luck,
>   The young boy didn't fuck,
>   And she muttered, "How Green Was My Valet." (Legman 1977, 324)

And a "young lady named Brown" could perform remarkable bodily feats such as teaching her "vagina to clown," so it could "nibble" or castrate a "plum" and "chew JuicyFruit gum" (Legman 1977, 55).

The Sally Brown who destroys Pissball Pete has a decidedly feminine take on the narrative since the source of Pete's power in his penis is shattered, as well as soiled, by the woman's anus. Flatulence in such narratives turns the tables on the would-be attacker by humiliating him, indeed infantilizing him with feces. The name of Sally *Brown* is further evidence of her fecal/anal attack, an inversion of male narratives in which Pete "browns" or sodomizes Lil, thereby showing brutish domination (see Partridge 1970, 1032; Dundes 2002, 45–46).

With its association with violent contamination and feminine/homosexual revenge, the ultimate insult to the male of being farted upon during fornication shows up in African American soundings such as the following collected by Roderick Roberts from teenage males:

> I took your mama to a party
> Ta meet my friends an' all.
> The fart from her body
> Blowed a hole in the wall.
> I took her in the alley
> Ta fuck her in the ass;
> The fart from her booty
> Blew the green off the grass.
> I took her down ta the well,
> Jus' ta get some tail'
> The fart from her booty
> Blowed the bottom outa hell. (Roberts 1965, 186–87)

Moreover, a related connection exists between the imagery of feces "behind the shit-house by the mill" and Pete belittling Lil by throwing her "poor ass" "down into the mud." An example is this text collected by Sam Eskin in Colorado during the 1950s, with a note saying that it was also heard in Logan, Utah, during World War II.

> **Our Nell (Lil)**
> Down in Looeyville on the hill
> There lived a gal, her name was Lil
> The fact was known for miles around
> That no two men could hold her down.
>
> Then down from the hills came a bare-assed Greek
> That son of a bitch was Piss-pot Pete.
> Now Piss-pot and Lil, they chose a spot upon the hill
> Behind a shit house by the mill.
>
> When Piss-pot Pete hauled out his cock
> Lil knew that she'd met her fate
> But to back out now was too late.
>
> For people came miles to gain a seat
> And see that half-breed take his meat

He threw her down into the mud
And mounted her ass like a Belgian stud.

They fucked and fucked for hours and hours
Tearing up trees and shrubs and flowers
The earth was torn for miles around
Where Lil's poor ass had hit the ground.

Lil passed out with a sigh and a cough
While Piss-pot Pete stood jacking off. (Eskin [1936–1958])

If audience responses are any indication of the significant actions in the verses, then three moments are typical in performances recorded by Simon Bronner as part of his study of college student folklore (Bronner 1995, 139–40). In recitations observed in fraternity houses, the loudest reaction from the audience was first to the introduction of the name "Piss-pot Pete" and his action of "hauling out his cock," "letting out jack," or "pouring on the prick." The second is the staccato rhythm created, often accompanied by aggressive bodily thrusts of "they fucked—and fucked—for hours—and hours," and the third is the final line, delivered like a punch-line emphasizing the rhymed couplet of Lil's submissive "sigh and cough" and Pete's "jacking off." The emphatic performance thus stresses the sexual dominance of the male member despite the diminutive bodily appearance; in bodily gestures, the penis becomes a weapon of destruction. It also becomes significant developmentally because the performer is dramatizing with bodily motions and hand gestures his power, which is not evident from his appearance. The important features to convey to the audience in his onanistic movements are the performer's attributes, not the woman's responses.

Gershon Legman similarly notes the "highly dramatic fashion" in which recitations of "Lady Lil" in an earlier period were performed. He observes that reciters use "an insistent rhythm," and surmises that it is "a rather ancient style of delivery" (Legman 1964, 418). "Some reciters," he writes, "inject various bits of local business, such as pausing to spit imaginary tobacco juice at a spittoon, and in this text even an explanatory aside (*'But wan't fer long'*). When the 'lean galoot,' who is usually referred to as a 'half-breed' or 'greaser' (Mexican), takes out his penis before the saloon idlers in some texts, and *'the damn thing stretched from thar—to thar,'* the teller's hands always measure off a wondering two-foot gauge or more" (Legman 1976, 98–99). In his performance notes, Legman intimates that the American frontier mystique of a crude, wild setting is re-created through gesture. Related to the adolescent concerns for coming-of-age, the frontier setting enacted through bodily movement and speech has associations with demonstrations of manliness in the cowboy figure (perhaps related to legendary Oklahoma cowboy "Pistol Pete") and the symbolism of breaking away from home to have a fresh start.

In the open, tall-tale West, or the untamed wilderness of the Yukon, as the following recitation underscores, sexuality is free and easy, unbridled by anxiety, and potential for growth is limitless. From the confining, grim "Drag-Ass Creek," Pete crosses over into Lil's "Free-Fuck Saloon." Conquering her, even if violently, allows him to regenerate.

> Ol' Lil was a book worm 'till she went west,
> And there she learned that fuckin' was best.
> And then one day out of Drag-Ass Creek
> Came a half-shot bastard named Piss Pot Pete.
> Pete strolled into Lil's Free-Fuck Saloon.
> He slapped his meat across the bar.
> I swear to God it stretched from thar to thar [gesture]
> It stunk, my God it stunk! [gesture]
> There ain't no soap this side of hell
> That could wash away that cunt-soaked smell.
> They fucked and fucked and fucked for hours,
> Tore up roots, trees and flowers.
> The ground was plowed for miles around
> Where Ol' Lil's ass drug the ground.
> He fucked her sittin', he fucked her lyin'.
> Had he some wings, he'd a fucked her flyin'.
> Ol' Lil gave Pete a Yukon squeeze
> That dropped that half breed to his knees.
> Pete replied with a Yukon grunt
> That popped out her eyes and split her cunt.
> Ol' Lil died with a sigh and a cough
> That left that half breed just a jackin'-off [gesture].

The reciter of the above text elaborated to Ronald Baker on the context of his rendition of "Lady Lil" as a college student residing in a fraternity house at Indiana University, Bloomington (referred to in his narrative as "IU"). The performance of this recitation that emphasizes the points at which the extraordinary penis and imposing smell come into play shows the role of Pete as standing apart, coming into his own in an arrogant display of manliness:

> I was introduced to this saga in the fall of 1966 while living in the Alpha Tau Omega fraternity house at IU. The tradition was for this saga to be recited in the style of an elaborate oration with considerable dramatic facial expressions, gestures, and animations. The person who could perform it the best was hailed to perform at all social functions. Can you believe it, that I was the one dubbed to act out the saga? Upon the call to perform, I'd stand on a chair and let it rip. The call started as rumble calling for, "Ol' Lil." The rumble would build up to a crescendo, and the crowd was then ready for the presentation. Also, in the ATO tradition, certain parts had a required gesture. As an example, when Piss-Pot Pete stretches his meat across the bar it's necessary to demonstrate the length by extending

both hands at least three feet apart. When it comes time to refer to the stench of Pete's unit, the performer must crinkle up the nose and close the eyes and do whatever is needed to accentuate the offensive odor of the appendage. Finally, when Ol' Lil dies with a sigh and a cough, and leaves Piss Pot Pete just a jackin'-off, the performer demonstrates the act of male masturbation as if there were a pole present, at least 12 inches in diameter. (Collected December 19, 2003)

Fornication contests in folk literature are not uncommon, though early analogues of "Lady Lil" are hard to come by since erotic folk poetry has been neglected or suppressed. Legman, however, regards folksongs like "Fair Janet" (Child 64), in which a woman dances down endless partners (Motif H1501, "Endurance test: long dancing"), as polite parallels to poems involving fornication contests and the sadistic concept of sex—the dancing symbolizing sexual intercourse (Legman 1964, 418–19). Tales of sexually dominant women are older than "Fair Janet," however. The connection in some texts of Pete mounting a goat, another demonic symbol, suggests again a psychogenic relation to the she-demon Lilith, who consorts with mountain goats sporting devilish hooves. In Talmudic legend, Lilith refuses to acknowledge Adam as her master and leaves Paradise for the Red Sea, a place of ill repute, where she became extremely promiscuous with innumerable demons and bore more than a hundred offspring a day. Becoming attracted to Adam again, the insatiable Lilith returned to Adam and sleeps with him against his will. Later in medieval Jewish folklore Lilith becomes the succubus, the cause of nocturnal emissions, and roams the world seducing men, awake as well as sleeping, and killing her many victims (Patai 1964, 296–97).

A much closer analogue appears in *Immortalia* (Mackay 1969, 43–45) along with the first printed version of "Lady Lil." This anonymous poem, called "Hookshop Kate," runs 112 lines, or three times as long as "Lady Lil." "Hookshop Kate" deals with a prostitute whose "one pet brag . . . was that she'd never met her mate." Kate goes first to Fairbanks, Alaska, during the gold rush, but there "all the miners who tested her power / were frigged to a whisper inside an hour." Consequently, Kate heads for the Hawaiian Islands, where again no man can satisfy her. The Hawaiians crown Kate "queen of the Frigging Zone," and she reigns for two years, though she still longs to be satisfied. Finding her in tears, the Hawaiians decide to find her a proper match by placing an advertisement in a magazine. A bookseller sees the ad and recommends a man who he claims "could outfrig great Hookshop Kate":

'Twas a sheep-herder from a distant Isle,
   Who had never been tempted by woman's wile;
But had spent his life with his wandering flock,
   Developing by hand his phenomenal cock.

'Twas a daily thing for him, they said,
　　To frig sixty sheep ere he went to bed.

The bookseller convinces the sheepherder "that frigging sheep / was an action base, profane and cheap," and persuades him to take on Hookshop Kate. Amidst great celebration, including a parade led by the sheepherder, the contest between Kate and the sheepherder is arranged "in a chamber with curtains drawn." The next morning when the bookseller checks on the outcome of the match, he finds:

> With a happy smile, propped up in bed,
> 　　The famous Hookshop Kate was dead.
> While under the bed the sheep-herder guy
> 　　Jacked off at the post without batting an eye.[5]

An even longer analogue of "Lady Lil" is "Eskimo Nell," which, in the longest of three manuscript versions in the Indiana State University Folklore Archives, runs 96 lines. A version running 228 lines, cited as "Anonymous/20th century," is included in a British collection of erotic verse and includes the figure of "Mexico Pete" (Bold 1978, 208–14). In the narrative poem, Pete avenges the death of Deadeye Dick at the hands of the mighty whore named Eskimo Nell. In rhetoric reminiscent of "Lil," Pete rams "his tough-nosed colt with a savage jolt . . . right up her cunt" (213). According to Legman, "Eskimo Nell" is a British imitation of "Lady Lil," and it may well be, since apparently it is not as common in the American oral tradition as "Lady Lil" and is called "the famous 'Eskimo Nell'" in a collection of British rugby songs (Green 1967, 12). Several collections note the perception that many verses exist, beyond the power of an oral reciter's memory, suggesting a broadside origin (Anderson 1983; Baker 1987). Into the twenty-first century, "Eskimo Nell" appears to be a modern broadside, or one of those long poems that circulate in typescript and since the 1990s on the Internet as well as through oral performances (see Green 1967, 57–66). Prefacing the following final five verses (there are sixty-two in all) on an Internet homepage, the collector states, "There are many small variations on this classic rhyme, and this one seems to me to be the best" (Nicholson 2004):

> "They'll tell this tale on the Arctic trail
> Where the nights are sixty below,
> Where it's so damn cold the jonnies are sold
> Wrapped up in a ball of snow.

> "In the Valley of Death with baited breath,
> That's where they'll sing it too,
> Where the skeletons rattle in sexual battle
> And the rotting corpses screw.

"Back to the land where men are Men,
I'll say 'Terra Bellicum,'
And there I'll spend my worthy end,
For the North is calling: 'Come!' "

Then Dead-Eye Dick and Mexican Pete
Slunk away from the Rio Grande,
Dead-Eye Dick with his useless prick,
And Pete with no gun in his hand.

When a man grows old and his balls grow cold,
And the tip of his prick turns blue,
And the hole in the middle refuses to piddle,
I'd say he was fucked, wouldn't you?

The last verse appears to be tagged on to Nell from another oral source and can be frequently collected by itself from American men. Legman identifies it with the medieval "Madrigals" tradition of humorous prognostications (Randolph 1992, 666–67).

The central motif in "Eskimo Nell" differs from that in "Lady Lil" and "Hookshop Kate," too. In Hoffmann's index its motif is X735.9.3.1, "Eskimo Nell. Lecherous man squeezed dry by renowned whore." Thus, in "Eskimo Nell" the female wins the fornication contest, and the central figures appear to be old, rather than young. Another striking difference in "Eskimo Nell" is an apparent doubling of the hero, representing the threat of sex and death in two pals, Deadeye Dick and Mexican Pete, instead of appearing as one central figure. For example, verses early in the poem are:

When Deadeye Dick and Mexican Pete
Go forth in search of fun
It's Deadeye Dick who slings the prick
And Mexican Pete the gun.
When Deadeye Dick and Mexican Pete
Are feeling depressed and sad
It's mostly cunt that bears the brunt
Though the shooting ain't so bad.

Deadeye and Pete leave their home by Dead Man's Creek, where they find things rather slow, and head for the banks of the Rio Grande, where in a saloon "forty whores tore down their drawers / At Deadeye Dick's command." Deadeye intends to take on all forty of them, but before he is well into the second, Eskimo Nell enters the saloon, insults the forty whores as well as Deadeye's manhood, and takes on Deadeye. Though Deadeye performs admirably in the fornication contest, Nell defeats him:

Nell lay for awhile with a subtle smile
And the grip of her cunt grew keener

Then with a sigh she sucked him dry
With the ease of a vacuum cleaner.

Even when Mexican Pete attempts to avenge his pal Deadeye's affront by sticking his Colt in Nell's vagina and firing three times, Nell simply "smiled in ecstasy" and tells Mexican Pete, "I should have guessed that that was the best / You two poor punks could do."

Although Nell wins this fornication contest and does not get killed in sexual combat as Lady Lil generally does, the sadistic concept of intercourse is apparent with Pete's firing his pistol in Nell's vagina. Moreover, with the doubling of the hero in "It's Deadeye Dick who slings the prick / And Mexican Pete the gun," the symbol of the penis as weapon in versions of "Lady Lil" is explicit, becoming even literal, in "Eskimo Nell." Legman interprets the narration of the penis as a weapon as a compensation for anxieties that the penis in an admission of impotence will not perform. In the case of adolescent narratives, this concern becomes enlarged because of the resistance to confess inexperience. Therefore, Legman hypothesizes, "The penis is almost invariably understood in folklore to be primarily a weapon, and not an instrument of pleasure" (1982, 1:268). Speaking of the "sweet death," Legman writes:

> Unless he dies in the act of intercourse . . . no man is ever assumed in jokes to be sexually satisfied. The man's ability to satisfy and oversatisfy the woman is, however, taken for granted. One would imagine that this is intended to give her pleasure, but jokes make clear that there is no such intention. She is forcibly oversatisfied to prove the man's virile status, and, if possible, to kill her in the process. Oversatisfaction is therefore strictly sadistic, in an extension of the idea of the penis as a weapon that harms and may destroy the woman. (1:272–73)

Boasts about large penises, according to Legman, "are intended as reassurance against the castratory notion that one's own penis is too small" (1982, 1:270). Further, this boast can also be a compensation for inexperience by avoiding the association of the small penis with infancy. In "Eskimo Nell," and other folk poems set in the far "north" or "Yukon," the castratory diminution of the penis is achieved from the cold or the association with old age. After Pete fails to ejaculate, Nell ridicules Pete with the line "You cunt-struck shrimp of a Yankee pimp! You call that a tool?" It is probably a sign of ethnic prejudice that Mexican Pete falls first, followed by the supposedly superior white western hero Deadeye Dick, a name familiar in popular dime novels of the early twentieth century. He literally is castrated by the "grip" of her vagina and the "squeeze" of her thighs. The result is that "his cock fell out," "stripped right down to a thread."

That the man sees himself as undersized, or an underdog in sexual relations, is suggested in the hero of "Lady Lil." The "little man" is the penis as well as the figure of Pete. We have an example of the little man's revenge in male versions of the poem. Pete not only is diminutive, but he is also a bald, dirty half-breed with "snot on his head and shit on his feet." He is clearly unpromising until he reveals his extraordinary weapon. Pete as an unlikely hero is akin to dirty Boots in "The Princess on the Glass Mountain," who rips off his rags and becomes a knight in shining armor. He is like mild-mannered Clark Kent in the comic books, who takes off his glasses and business suit and becomes powerful Superman. In "Lady Lil," Pete drops his pants and becomes the hard, mean ("bad") Penisman, thus succeeding where all others have failed. Apparently, men who recite and listen to "Lady Lil" use humor to refer to insecurity in sexual dominance, and its association with manliness, but vicariously through Pete's accomplishment are able to retain some self-esteem. When considered in the context of adolescent settings, Pete's exploits as an underdeveloped body with great sexual power relates to adolescent male yearnings, and frustrations, since he may feel that females are not available to him or will reject him as undesirable. The female, he surmises, enjoys the position of power because she is consistently desirable, particularly to older males.

Besides the liminal status afforded Pete in being identified as a "half-breed," another explanation of the reference to "half" as in "half-pint" is that Pete is not fully developed. Pete, in fact, is depicted as being much more of an animal than a human, indicating that he still needs to evolve, which helps the contrast of his wildness, and raw sexual energy, compared to the civilized, mature, educated "Lady Lil." Compared to the old geezers who fail with Lil, he has extraordinary youthful vigor, even if he is unattractive. He not only has "shit oozing between his toes," but "his balls hung down like a Jersey bull."

In some folk narratives the hero is not merely a man but a "human fucking machine," as in the following recitation in the Indiana State University Folklore Archives, which was collected from a male student in an Indiana State University dormitory in May 1967:

> I'm a mean motherfucker from the savage land,
> Going through the jungle with a cock in my hand,
> Came across 100 women against the wall.
> For 400 dollars I'd fuck them all.
> Well, fucked 98 till my balls turned blue,
> I backed off and jacked off and shot the other two.
> On his grave it was written, it was written in green,
> He wasn't a man but a fuckin' machine.

The unnatural, enduring machine, like the hyper-masculine Pete, never loses an erection, as nature would suggest. As the "savage," the "mean motherfucker" acts on instincts considered unsuitable in public society. Yet he also represents typical male desires and symbolizes the idea that his sexuality is the sign of his vitality. The conflict between the unethical, but understandable, actions of the savage expressed by the male reciter is rationalized in his attribute of being "not a man but a fuckin' machine" and in his death, even if he appears to be admired for his formidable sexual feat in life. In some related recitations such as "Little Johnny Fuckemfaster," the women occupy a specified authority role of the schoolteacher:

> Little Johnny Fuckemfaster
> Was a fuckin' fool;
> He fucked all the teachers
> In grammar school.
> He lined ninety-nine teachers
> Up against a wall.
> He swore to God
> He'd fuck 'em all.
> He fucked ninety-two
> An' his balls turned blue;
> Swore ta God
> He'd fuck the other few.
> Little Johnny died an' went ta hell.
> He say, "Now, Mr. Devil, while I'm at rest,
> Place my dick upon my chest.
> Place a naked woman up over my head.
> If my dick don't rise, you know I'm dead!" (Roberts 1965, 155; see also
>   Bronner 1988, 134; Baker 1986, 191–95)

In some modern folksongs commonly reported being performed in fraternity settings, such as "Big Fucking Wheel," the fucking machine is no longer a metaphor but literally has replaced the man in sadistic intercourse. In verses circulated in handwritten and photocopied copies to fraternity members as *Shitty Songs of Sigma Chi,* the woman, like Lil, is insatiable:

> There once was a man from across the sea
> And this is the tale he told to me
> About a maid with twat so wide
> She never could be satisfied
>
> So they fashioned for her a big fucking wheel
> With balls of brass and a big prick of steel
> The balls of brass were filled with cream
> And the whole fucking issue was run by steam
>
> Around and around went the big fucking wheel
> And in and out went the big prick of steel
> Until at last the maid she cried
> Enough enough I'm satisfied

But that was not the end of it
There was no way of stopping it
And the maid was split from twat to tit
And the whole fucking issue went up in shit. (*Shitty Songs* 2004)

Ronald Baker collected a short variant of "The Great Wheel" from a male student at the University of Illinois in November 1964:

'Round and 'round went the big fucking wheel.
In and out went the big prick of steel.
Tore that poor maiden from twat to tit,
And covered the walls with shit.

The moral of the narrative is that the woman suffers for her onanistic self-centeredness of replacing a man with a machine. She is symbolically punished for her insatiability and independence with contamination by feces. The singer or reciter, usually a young fraternity brother, is reminding the audience that he cannot be replaced, with perhaps the implication that women need to be domesticated or tamed.

The domestication theme is evident in at least one variant type of the Lady Lil recitation in which she "gives up" rather than dies. In this version transcribed from oral tradition by a young Navy man based in San Francisco, the following verses are added to the typical contest for sexual dominance between the vulgar Piss-Pot Pete and the whore Lil.

Now Lil is no longer a well known whore
And Pete is the father of four or more
They no longer do it behind the mill
For now they do it on the window sill

Pete better teach his kids [to tell] right from wrong
Or they will go about a [singing] this song. ("Lil the Whore" 2004)

One could read in the verses that the young reciters are relating to their audience that this age is appropriately a time of sexual exploration and male conquest, but either that pregnancy is a risk or that with maturity comes responsibility. The imagery of domestication after previous descriptions in the recitation of the male need to mount and subdue the whore Lil carries the ring of "breaking" a wild, bucking horse to assert male patriarchy. Indeed, one of Vance Randolph's versions intentionally uses the phrase "The way Lil *bucked* was plenty slick, But he just kept letting out his prick" (Randolph 1992, 668; emphasis added).

In the fornication contest tradition, the male figure, if he is victorious over the sexually dominant female, often is either animalistic, socially liminal, or mechanistic, something different from an ordinary man. In *Eros Denied,* Wayland Young reflects further on this pattern: "It seems to me that an amazing amount of what men in our society think about women is folklore tinged with projection mechanism. Often in the Christian erotic tradition, they appear to be simply foreign men; creatures superficially like us but underneath it all tremendously addicted to fucking, far more than we could ever be" (Young 1966, 295). Significantly, in the earliest versions of "Lady Lil," the female antagonist is a schoolmarm, a symbol of female dominance as well as a model of moral authority. Since the female school-teacher is a dominant figure in the classroom, schoolboys also envision her as a dominant figure in the bedroom. Still, in schoolboy fantasy, especially as reflected in American joke lore, the schoolmarm is the subject of sexual desire and conquest, almost always by the bad boy, who represents the Outsider, someone different (see Legman 1982, 1:65–76). In some narratives, in fact, the schoolmarm is linked with the prostitute, explaining perhaps the linkage in "Lil" characterizations as whore or teacher. An example is "Why Schoolmarms Make Good Prostitutes," collected from an eighteen-year-old teller:

> This guy ran a whorehouse, and on the first floor he had the housekeepers, on the second floor he had the models, and on the third floor he had the schoolteachers. And it seemed like the third floor was getting all the business. And he couldn't figure out why the schoolteachers were gettin' all the business. So he went to the first floor, and he listened to the housekeepers, and they said, "Come in. Hang up your clothes! Don't mess up the bed!" So then he went up to the second floor, and he listened to the models, and they said, "Don't mess my lipstick up! Don't mess my hair!" So then he went up to the third floor where the schoolteachers were. And he listened in, and they said, "If you don't do it right the first time, you'll have to do it again." (Baker 1986, 195)

In the punch line, the schoolteacher embodies the authoritarian feminine figure or mother after other maternal images of housekeeping and grooming. But in the final line, the men are invited to satisfy themselves sexually, as if they were being instructed as adolescent "schoolboys."

Most generally learned in adolescence, "Lady Lil" serves important psychological and expressive functions in the transition to manhood. Its recitation by young males reduces male fears and anxieties about sex since a woman considered sexually dominant is defeated in a fornication contest by an unpromising male hero. Versions with the schoolmarm as antagonist may also serve to reduce male hostilities toward the oppressive moral authority of adults since an authority figure, the schoolmarm, is presented as not so moral—thus relieving young males from the pressure of a too ideal model. As other related examples of folklore such as jokes, songs, and limericks show, this function may be found in other enactments of male fantasies, shared with other young men so as to avoid the vulnerability of male anxieties (Theweleit 1987, 63–108).

Other clues to the significance of "Lady Lil" in the sexual anxieties of adolescent males are in the contrast of Lil as a grown "lady" or experienced "whore" and Pete as still connected to the pisspot and shitpot. He is the galoot or awkward, inexperienced rustic compared to the self-confident Lil, who presumably comes from the cosmopolitan East. He reveals a childish insecurity in descriptions of him as sloppy, little, punk, sawed-off, and short-horned. In some texts he is the "son of the bitch," while Lil is the "dirty bitch." He is childishly mired in muck and seems not able to clean himself, as indicated by lines of "Snot on his head and shit on his feet," "Spit on his head and shit on his feet," and "Shit oozing between his toes." Linking the extension of the arm with the extension of his penis, he has a " 'flicted arm." He is disabled, or not quite whole, since he is half-breed, one-balled, and half-assed. The symbolic connection is between Pete as representative of the "peter" or penis and a stage of toilet training in the shitpot.

The places he comes from such as Bare-Ass Creek, Shithead Mountain, and Piss-Fed Creek are also representative of the toilet training stage, not only in which he is immature but also in which he is dependent on the mother. Significantly in many of the descriptions he has his rear end exposed as a "bare-ass," for which he must compensate by aggressive sexual attack. Underscoring his ferocious pent-up energy and aggressive dominance, he may indeed be sexually threatening to men and women alike. He responds angrily to the ridicule that the whore hurls at him for being a "punk," slang used not only for someone young and small but also passively homosexual. Indeed, in several versions he is a half-breed Greek, half-assed Greek, or a bare-assed Greek suggesting the ethnic stereotype of homosexual tendencies that must be suppressed. There are mixed messages about his puberty and sexual potency. His head is bald or lacking pubescent hair, and he is a blue-balled bastard, suggesting his inability to ejaculate. Yet typical of adolescence, he has uncontrollable erections and "breeding meat." He exaggerates its length as an indication of its contrast to what was there before in an earlier childhood stage. In the poem, he is separating from the mother/feminine or authority figure by making her submit to his manhood, even though she still holds power over him. He shows her his ability to dominate as a man, sexually.

In the versions collected from African American youth, Pete puts up a good fight but is ultimately vanquished. Yet he is triumphant, precisely because he is unclean. His youthfulness and recklessness subversively win the day in the end. The significance of versions entitled "Mama Went Out West" is perhaps akin to a Freudian slip whereby the ambivalence of separating from the mother becomes verbalized. The function of dozens or sounding as separating from while declaring loyalty to (and dependence on) the mother may apply, although analysts have not previously made the connection between the toasts and contests-in-insults. To be sure, Roger

Abrahams in his study of African American street performers proposed that the two may be related developmentally with verbal dexterity formed in the dozens in prepubescence blooming into the pubescent toasts (Abrahams 1970, 48). He insightfully found that "black males find themselves in a totally male environment in which the necessity to prove one's masculinity (and to reject the feminine principle) recurs constantly" (54).

Particularly in situations in the all-male black contexts in which Lulu or Mama of the West were collected, the need to show sexual bravado while respecting the maternal hold in a matrifocal society is apparent. Earlier in performances of dozens, the lower-class black youth entered into contests-in-insults so that he can separate by insulting, or symbolically fornicating with, someone's else's mother, while respecting the maternal hold by defending his mother from attack. Simon Bronner maintains in his comparison with white contests-in-insults that the black dozens focus on the mother more and are particularly aggressive because of the strength of the matrifocal social structure (or the absence of the strong father figure) in ghetto culture (Bronner 1978a, 1978b). In the dozens, the mother is still at home, while in the mature toast, the mother is leaving home, as the boy has left. He is, as many versions say, "way across the street." He is aware that he can procreate and uproot ("rooted up trees and tore down flowers"), and he seeks to be on an equal sexual footing. While admired for her power, Lulu or Lil in the end is dreaded as diseased and dehumanized as a "machine."

Since the 1990s, texts typical of white versions of the recitation are abundant on the Internet, though they are frequently called "The Legend of Pisspot Pete" and are found in relatively fixed form. Yet in their new electronic mode of circulation, they may affirm yet anew privatized adolescent needs to come of age in a society such as America's that seems to lack socially agreed-upon public rituals for turning a boy into a man (Raphael 1988). In recitations and narratives, there is evidence that sexual humor is used by the man to signal, or fantasize, separation from the feminine as a symbol of authority over the boy, but not without ambivalence for the deed. Ironically, the sexual bravado of the manly tradition of reciting "Lady Lil" also shows the insecurity of the man's independence and is therefore performed with the support of his fellows.

NOTES

1. Vance Randolph collected this recitation from Mr. S. N., Pineville, Missouri, July 20, 1934. His notes state that it was "recited," and it was the most complete text of the Lady Lil poems he collected. In his notes to the text, Legman cites a commentary by A. R. Morse, suggesting that the bouts may have a basis in reality:

"In Nevada one time I witnessed a fucking bout, but not as spectacular a one as described in 'Lady Lil.' We left the mine, and walked some seven or eight miles to the nearest saloon, a lonely desert saloon with a gas pump out in front, kept by an old woman and her daughter. There an argument ensued about whether an old miner could still get an erection, and bets were made. The old lady and miner in question repaired to a pile of rags by the pot-belly stove, and for about 45 minutes the old fellow did his best, with the old girl's help. But nothing happened [meaning, the man could not 'perform,' or ejaculate], and he lost the bet. Thus among our people are found all the roots of their poetry given here" (Randolph 1992, 670; see also Morse 1945, 120–21).

2. It can be pointed out in relation to the metaphor of the name Jack that many British-American "Jack tales" such as Jack and the Beanstalk have a coming-of-age component of the sexually awakened boy who enters contests with formidable larger foes such as giants and devils (Lindahl 2001; McCarthy 1994). Similar to Bruno Bettelheim's observation that Jack moves beyond the sexual potency of youth, thereby signaling the end of infancy, by becoming phallically satisfied in contests to the death, Pete begins as the underdog, the unlikely contestant, until he shows his hidden weapon that defies expectations (Bettelheim 1976, 183–93).

3. It appears to be the basis for the suggestive "Hula Lou," occasionally mentioned in relation to Lil texts and recorded by "hot mama" Sophie Tucker in 1924, and the figure of Dan McGrew replaced by Dan McCan:

You can talk all you want about women
Said a sailor known as Dan McCan
And if you really want to know about women
You've got to talk to a sailor man.

Now I don't know how many women the sailor met
And I hope there isn't any that he'll regret
For if he'd only met me I'd a given him some trimmin'
I'm one gal he'd never forget.

Who am I? I'm Hula Lou.
I'm the gal that can't be true.
I do my nestin' in the evenin' breeze
'Neath the trees
You oughta see me shake my BVDs.
I never knew
A man who wouldn't hula dance or woo
And sail across the briny blue to who
The lady known as Hula Lou

Lou is here associated with the extreme of heat and the erotic suggestiveness of the exoticized Pacific islands, just as Lou and Nell also were set in recitations in the extreme cold of the Yukon with its suggestion of wildness. Indicating Hula Lou's basis in oral tradition is the fact that its lyrics were claimed by at least three lyricists, two in 1916 under the title of "My Hula Hula Lou" (Buster Santos) and "Hula Lou" (Edward Grossmith), and the above song in 1924 (Jack Yellen). The important point to remember is the association of the bar-room with oral recitations. An advertising campaign in 2004 by Coors Light beer, for example, featured an ordinary guy by the name of "Dave" reciting bar-room verse in praise of the product, although men hearing it will undoubtedly think of the form rather than the content of the commercial recitation.

4. Jackson's 1966 recording of "'Flicted Arm Pete" recited by eighteen-year-

old "Peter" in Texas is available on the audio CD *Get Your Ass in the Water and Swim Like Me: Narrative Poetry from Black Oral Tradition* (Rounder Records CD 2014, 1998; originally released in 1976 as an LP).

5. Essentially this same version of "Hookshop Kate," though slightly reworked and shortened, appeared in the December 1982 issue of *Playboy* (p. 205), where it is called an "American folk verse, circa 1900."

REFERENCES

Abrahams, Roger D. 1970. *Deep Down in the Jungle: Negro Folklore from the Streets of Philadelphia.* Chicago: Aldine.
Anderson, June. 1983. Letter to Ronald L. Baker, Terre Haute, Indiana, November 11, 1983.
Baker, Ronald L. 1986. *Jokelore: Humorous Folktales from Indiana.* Bloomington: Indiana University Press.
————. 1987. "Lady Lil and Pisspot Pete." *Journal of American Folklore* 100: 191–99.
"The Ballad of Hookshop Kate." 1982. *Playboy,* December, 205.
Bennett, Eric. 1999. "Rap." In *Africana: The Encyclopedia of the African and African American Experience,* ed. Kwame Anthony Appiah and Henry Louis Gates Jr., 1589–91. New York: Basic Civitas Books.
Bethke, Robert D. 1976. "Verse Recitation as Barroom Theater." *Southern Folklore Quarterly* 40: 141–68.
Bettelheim, Bruno. 1976. *The Uses of Enchantment: The Meaning and Importance of Fairy Tales.* New York: Alfred A. Knopf.
Bold, Alan, ed. 1978. *Making Love: The Picador Book of Erotic Verse.* London: Picador Pan.
Bronner, Simon. 1978a. "A Re-examination of Dozens among White American Adolescents." *Western Folklore* 37: 118–28.
————. 1978b. "Who Says? A Further Investigation of Ritual Insults among White American Adolescents." *Midwestern Journal of Language and Folklore* 4: 53–69.
————. 1988. *American Children's Folklore.* Little Rock, Ark.: August House.
————. 1995. *Piled Higher and Deeper: The Folklore of Student Life.* Little Rock, Ark.: August House.
Bryant, Jerry H. 2003. *"Born in a Mighty Bad Land": The Violent Man in African American Folklore and Fiction.* Bloomington: Indiana University Press.
Cray, Ed. 1992. *The Erotic Muse: American Bawdy Songs.* 2nd ed. Urbana: University of Illinois Press.
Dundes, Alan. 1994. "Gallus as Phallus: A Psychoanalytic Cross-Cultural Consideration of the Cockfight as Fowl Play." In *The Cockfight: A Casebook,* ed. Alan Dundes, 241–84. Madison: University of Wisconsin Press.
————. 2002. "Much Ado about 'Sweet Bugger All': Getting to the Bottom of a Puzzle in British Folk Speech." *Folklore* 113: 35–49.
Eskin, Sam. [1936–1958]. File of erotica marked with delta sign. Sam Eskin Collection, AFC 1999/004, American Folklife Center, Library of Congress.
Gentleman About Town, A. 1969 [1927]. *Immortalia: An Anthology of American Ballads, Sailors' Songs, Cowboy Songs, College Songs, Parodies, Limericks, and Other Humorous Verses and Doggerel.* Venice, Calif.: Parthena Press.
Green, Michael. 1967. *Why Was He So Beautiful, and Other Rugby Songs.* London: Sphere Books.

Hirsch, Edward. 1976. "A Structural Analysis of Robert Service's Yukon Ballads." *Southern Folklore Quarterly* 40: 125–40.

Hoffmann, Frank. 1973. *An Analytical Survey of Traditional Anglo-American Erotica.* Bowling Green: Bowling Green University Popular Press.

Jackson, Bruce. 1974. *Get Your Ass in the Water and Swim Like Me: Narrative Poetry from Black Oral Tradition.* Cambridge, Mass.: Harvard University Press.

Jemie, Onwuchekwa. 2003. *Yo' Mama! New Raps, Toasts, Dozens, Jokes and Children's Rhymes from Urban Black America.* Philadelphia: Temple University Press.

Keyes, Cheryl L. 2002. *Rap Music and Street Consciousness.* Urbana: University of Illinois Press.

Leeds, Robert X., ed. 1999. *Doctor Leeds' Selection of Popular Epic Recitations for Minstrel and Stage Use.* Las Vegas: Epic.

Legman, G. 1964. *The Horn Book: Studies in Erotic Folklore and Bibliography.* New Hyde Park, N.Y.: University Books.

———, ed. 1969. *The Limerick: 1700 Examples, with Notes, Variants, and Index.* New York: Bell.

———. 1976. "Bawdy Recitations and Monologues." *Southern Folklore Quarterly* 40: 59–123.

———, ed. 1977. *The New Limerick: 2750 Unpublished Examples, American and British.* New York: Bell.

———. 1982. *No Laughing Matter: An Analysis of Sexual Humor.* 2 vols. Bloomington: Indiana University Press.

"Lil the Whore." 2004. Typescript found among 1944–1946 letters. http://www.immortalia.com/html/recitations/long-recitations/lil-the-whore.htm. Accessed September 28, 2004.

Lindahl, Carl. 2001. *Perspectives on the Jack Tales and Other North American Märchen.* Bloomington: Folklore Institute, Indiana University.

Mackay, Arthur, ed. *Immortalia: An Anthology of American Ballads, Sailors' Songs, Cowboy Songs, College Songs, Parodies, Limericks, and Other Humorous Verses and Doggerel.* 1969. New York: Karman Press.

Malchow, H. L. 1996. "The Half-Breed as Gothic Unnatural." In *The Victorians and Race,* ed. Shearer West, 101–11. Aldershot, UK: Scolar Press.

McCarthy, William Bernard. 1994. *Jack in Two Worlds: Contemporary North American Tales and Their Tellers.* Chapel Hill: University of North Carolina Press.

Metzger, Th. 2003. "Funky Tongue: Street Rhymes and the Roots of Rap." *City* (Rochester, N.Y.), October 8. http://www.rochester-citynews.com/gbase/Gyrosite/Content?oid=oid%3A2152. Accessed September 28, 2004.

Milburn, George. 1930. *The Hobo's Hornbook.* New York: Ives Washburn.

Mitchell, Roger. 1969. Letter to Ronald L. Baker, Terre Haute, Indiana, December 1969.

Morse, A. Reynolds. 1945. *Folk Poems and Ballads: An Anthology.* Mexico City: Cruciform Press.

Nicholson. 2004. *Poems and Prose.* "Eskimo Nell." http://homepages.tcp.co.uk/~nicholson/index.html. Accessed February 16, 2004.

Opie, Iona, and Peter Opie. 1985. *The Singing Game.* New York: Oxford University Press.

Partridge, Eric. 1970. *A Dictionary of Slang and Unconventional English.* New York: Macmillan.

Patai, Raphael. 1964. "Lilith." *Journal of American Folklore* 77: 295–314.

Randolph, Vance. 1992. *Blow the Candle Out: "Unprintable" Ozark Folksongs and Folklore.* Vol. 2: *Folk Rhymes and Other Lore,* ed. G. Legman. Fayetteville: University of Arkansas Press.

Raphael, Ray. 1988. *The Men from the Boys: Rites of Passage in Male America*. Lincoln: University of Nebraska Press.

Roberts, Roderick J., Jr. 1965. "Negro Folklore in a Southwestern Industrial School." M.A. thesis, Indiana University.

Service, Robert W. 1940. *The Complete Poems of Robert Service*. New York: Dodd, Mead.

———. 1993. *The Shooting of Dan McGrew and Other Poems*. New York: Dover.

Shay, Frank. 1928. *More Pious Friends and Drunken Companions: Songs and Ballads of Conviviality*. New York: Macaulay.

Shitty Songs of Sigma Chi. 2004. Transcribed from handwritten text by John Mehlberg. http://www.immortalia.com/html/books-OCRed/1960s-shitty-songs-of-sigma-chi/index.htm. Accessed September 28, 2004.

Theweleit, Klaus. 1987 [1977]. *Male Fantasies*. Vol. 1: *Women, Floods, Bodies, History*. Trans. Stephen Conway. Minneapolis: University of Minnesota Press.

Wentworth, Harold, and Stuart Berg Flexner, eds. 1967. *Dictionary of American Slang Based on Historical Principles*. New York: Thomas Y. Crowell.

Williams, Brett. 1983. *John Henry: A Bio-Bibliography*. Westport, Conn.: Greenwood Press.

Young, Wayland. 1966. *Eros Denied: Sex in Western Society*. New York: Grove Press.

AFTERWORD

Many Manly Traditions—A Folkloristic Maelstrom

ALAN DUNDES

Simon Bronner deserves a lot of credit for assembling this outstanding selection of essays all treating aspects of the cultural construction of masculinity in various American ethnic and other subcultures. Each essay contains important raw data as well as valuable insights. As a totality, the volume demonstrates the wide range of definitional issues in the formation of masculine identity in a praiseworthy variety of different contexts. This volume will surely serve as a unique and indispensable source book for anyone with a serious interest in exploring the relationship between folklore and identity formation with a special emphasis on manliness.

That said, it might be observed that despite the range of topics by diverse scholars, the volume could be profitably expanded beyond American cultures. Surely the issue of what constitutes masculinity is cross-cultural, and one could develop considerations of folkloristic factors in masculine identity formation across a wider span of time and space. Many of the classic pioneering works with an international scope are worthy of consideration. For example, Jacques-Antoine Dulaure (1755–1835) published in 1805 *The Gods of Generation: A History of Phallic Cults among Ancients & Moderns.* He drew on classical mythology as sources for his study. This material has led to a host of modern studies of phallic influence in classical antiquity, such as Eva C. Keuls's *The Reign of the Phallus: Sexual Politics in Ancient Athens* (1985) and Giancarlo Carabelli's *In the Image of Priapus* (1996). The literature on male sexual symbolism in cultures is way too immense to survey here, but the reader should at least be aware of the existence of Roger Goodland's old but still useful 750-page *A Bibliography of Sex Rites and Customs* (1931).[1] There are many classic works that one could consult, including Thorkil Vanggaard's *Phallos: A Symbol and Its History in the Male World,* first translated from the Danish in 1972, and Klaus Theweleit's two-volume *Male Fantasies,* translated from the German (1987, 1989).

If I were teaching a course in folklore and masculinity, I would adopt *Manly Traditions* as a required text, in addition to my colleague Stanley Brandes's brilliant analysis of Andalusian folklore, *Metaphors of Masculinity* (1980), along with James M. Taggart's invaluable *Enchanted Maidens* (1990), which compares male and female Spanish versions of the same Aarne-Thompson tale types. I might also assign Daisy Dwyer's less folkloristically sophisticated *Images and Self-Images* (1978) for purposes of comparison. I would probably also have as required reading Peter F. Murphy's *Studs, Tools, and the Family Jewels: Metaphors Men Live By* (2001), which covers many important items of relevant folk speech.

For cross-cultural consideration of ritualized speech play among adolescent boys in their demonstration of manliness, one could also compare American contests-in-insults, particularly the African American "dozens" with Turkish verbal dueling, discussed in "The Strategy of Turkish Boys' Verbal Dueling Rhymes" (Dundes, Leach, and Özkök 1970; see also Abrahams 1962; Bronner 1978, 1987). Unlike in the African American dozens, one finds in the Turkish tradition a major theme of homosexuality. A distinctive feature to account for the difference is the symbolic castration of circumcision, conducted without anesthesia, for Turkish boys when they are between *four and eight years old*. I suggest that the circumcision may lead to confusion concerning sexual identity such that boys may later tend to assume feminine traits (see Cansever 1965). Like most—if not all—puberty initiation rites, the duel allows the young boy to repudiate the female world with its passive sexual role and to affirm the male world with its active sexual role. The fact that the repudiation of the female role seems to involve the partial enactment of that role by males is in accord with the theory that initiation rites are those in which males, envious of female organs, seek to usurp female sexual powers and activities. The verbal duel, in keeping with Turkish predisposition in childhood for "dependent-aggressive" conflict, offers the opportunity of penetrating one's fellow male but also the danger of being penetrated in turn by that same fellow male. The homosexual relationship involves dependence coupled with mistrust: dependence upon friends who will not attach, but mistrust in the fear that they might attack. Just as the "higher powers" upon whom the young boy depended suddenly launched an emasculating attack (circumcision), so one's peers upon whom one depends may suddenly threaten one's masculinity. In the verbal duel, a boy must try to aggressively hand out at least as much as—and hopefully a bit more than—he is forced to take. To the extent that Turkish worldview contains an oppositional contrast between fatalistic, passive dependence and individualistic, active aggression and American worldview emphasizes more individualism, the presence of both kinds of behavior in the Turkish verbal dueling situation and the emphasis on phallic aggression in American examples come more clearly into relief.

I might also immodestly assign my own essay "Gallus as Phallus: A Psychoanalytic Cross-Cultural Consideration of the Cockfight as Fowl Play" which was reprinted in *The Cockfight: A Casebook* (1994). Since the cockfight is a form of folklore with cross-cultural distribution from Asia (China and Indonesia) to the New World (especially Latin America and the Caribbean), the analysis of the homoerotic and onanistic masculinity component might prove to be cross-culturally valid. In the United States, cockfighting is legal only in Louisiana and New Mexico but nonetheless is reported being practiced across the country as an "underground industry with a devoted following" despite the protests of animal welfare groups (Pacelle 2004; Bilger 1999). In most states, cockfighting is punishable only as a misdemeanor (in thirty states as of 2004), and in places such as Tennessee and Kentucky, one investigative journalist found, many venues have "the tacit or active consent of local law enforcement" (Simbeck 2000; see also Parker 1986). A thrilling sport and manly tradition to its admirers, cockfighting is "inhumane and barbaric" to protesting organizations such as the Humane Society of the United States and the Fund for Animals. Frequently critics cast cockfighting as "dark and shadowy," or addictive, like the practices of drinking and gambling that usually accompany it. The point of my analysis is that cross-culturally the practice defines and asserts masculinity, as well as drawing criticism, because it is metaphorically a masturbatory display of cocks as phalluses in public.

Cockfighting fits into the theme of all-male preserves in which one male demonstrates his virility, his masculinity, *at the expense of a male opponent.* One proves one's manliness by feminizing one's opponent. Typically, the victory entails (no pun intended!) penetration. In American football, the winning group of males get into their opponents' "end zones" more times than their opponents get into their end zones (see Dundes 1980a). In the bullfight, the battle of man against bull is to determine whether the matador penetrates the bull or whether the bull's horns penetrate the matador. The penetrator comes away triumphant and with his masculinity intact; the one *penetrated* loses his masculinity. In the case of the bullfight, the expertise and skill of the matador can be rewarded with different degrees of symbolic castration of the bull. The bull, if penetrated cleanly and dexterously, may have his hooves, ears, or tail cut off to be "presented" to the successful matador.

The cockfight is, I maintain, a thinly disguised symbolic homoerotic masturbatory phallic duel, with the winner emasculating the loser through castration or feminization. If one accepts the premise that the genus Gallus can symbolically be a phallus, it follows that the cockfight is an all-male event, and in many cultures women are intentionally excluded. The separation from women in cockfights is also signaled by the fact that the roosters are not permitted access to hens during the period immediately preceding a cockfight. This form of quarantine is surely analogous to the modern-day football coach's forbidding his players to spend the night before a game

Postcard of cockfight in Mercedes, Texas, 1907. *Photograph courtesy Simon J. Bronner.*

with their wives or girlfriends, or to a bullfighter's sexual abstinence the night before a bullfight. Here is an account of the training of roosters in the Texas-Mexico border area:

> The most important experience of the young stage commences when his trainer moves him from his solitary cage and places him in a hennery. There he bosses his harem of hens, living and learning the meaning of his cockhood. Later, when the trainer takes him away from the pullets, the cockerel turns into a bird of Mars. Now he has a lust to fight, his lust arising from his strong sex drive. (Braddy 1961, 103)

The question is: To what extent, if any, is it legitimate to interpret the cockfight (and the gambling that accompanies it) as a symbolic form of male masturbation? Here we may turn to cross-cultural data to find an answer. Time and time again, we read reports of how much time a cock handler devoted to grooming and stroking his bird. The present argument illuminates the fact that cockfights are illegal in many countries. No doubt being outside the law makes cockfights more exciting for those men participating. In other words, it is illegal to play with cocks in public; hence, one must do it sub rosa, in secret, in "dark and shadowy" venues, as critics often point out. That authorities ban cockfighting but then allow it to take place in secret locations seems to confirm its symbolic value. Masturbation is typically proscribed by parents, but masturbation occurs nonetheless. For

Stereoview entitled "Betting on the Cockfight," Luzon, Philippines, 1900. By B. W. Kilburn. *Photograph courtesy Simon J. Bronner.*

Postcard entitled "Cockfight on board U.S. Man O' War" by Enrique Muller, 1906. *Photograph courtesy Simon J. Bronner.*

those skeptics who may not be able to see the possible symbolic meaning of a handler's massaging the neck of his cock, I call attention to the fact that in American slang "to choke the chicken" is a standard euphemism for male masturbation and that a "chicken-choker" is a male masturbator.

Betting, often considered a male activity, accompanies cockfights in almost all parts of the world where cockfighting occurs. Usually the betting is one-to-one, that is, one person will call out a bet and another person will accept it (Parker 1986, 24). In this way, the betting scenario mirrors the one-on-one action of the fighting cocks. A cocker turned academic describes betting in his thesis on cockfighting in Utah as follows: "Betting at cockfights is an overt expression of machismo. The larger the bet the bigger the man. . . . In a cockfight the betting opponents are in a face-to-face confrontation, a man-against-man contest so to speak" (Walker 1986, 49).

Ever since Sigmund Freud's brilliant paper "Dostoevsky and Parricide" (1928) the psychoanalytic community has been aware of the possibility that gambling is a symbolic substitute for masturbation. "The passion for play is an equivalent of the old compulsion to masturbate; 'playing' is the actual word used in the nursery to describe the activity of the hands upon the genitals," Freud wrote (1961, 193). Psychologist Robert Lindner discussed the gambling-masturbation equation with clarity: "Now gambling and masturbation present a wide variety of parallels—Both are repetitive acts, both are compulsively driven, and the nervous and mental states accompanying the crucial stages in the performance of each are almost impossible to differentiate" (Lindner 1953, 212). A characteristic of gambling that is perhaps most reminiscent of masturbatory activity is the "inability of the gambler to stop," even when winning (Fuller 1977, 28). Here I cannot help but be reminded of the Filipino manual on cockfighting that warns against "holding-handling" the cock in public, as "handling is habit-forming and once acquired, it is hard to get rid of" (Lansang 1966, 97–98).

The cockfight might be construed as a metaphorical performance of a phallic brag session: "My cock is stronger than yours" or "My cock can outlast yours." This view is confirmed by the further observations of cockfighting in Utah: "As a man's own penis or cock is the staff of his manhood so by extension is his fighting cock an extension of himself. The man whose cock lasts the longest and thus wins the fight is judged the better man. A man's own sexual prowess is largely judged by how long he can maintain an erection. The obverse helps prove this statement. A man who is plagued with premature ejaculation is someone to be pitied and given professional counseling. Thus by association a man who has a battle cock with staying power [and] pride and [which] fights to the end is macho indeed" (Walker 1986, 59–60).

If my analysis of the cockfight as a symbolic, public masturbatory, phallic duel is sound, one should be able to understand why participants might be reluctant or unable to articulate consciously this symbolic structure. In

effect, the cockfight is like most folklore fantasy: its content is largely unconscious. If the participants consciously realized what they were doing,
they would in all probability not be willing to participate. It is precisely the
symbolic facade that makes it possible for people to participate in an activity without consciously understanding the significance of that participation.

My most important contribution to the study of masculinity in folklore,
in my opinion, is the title essay in *From Game to War* (1997) in which I try
to show that in the continuum running from competitive games to actual
warfare, males demonstrate their masculinity at the expense of male opponents whom they feminize.[2]

The question to be addressed in relation to the demonstration of masculinity is, Why should males want or need to feminize their opponents on
a playing field or in a war combat zone? The adolescent male need or
inclination to feminize an opponent through actual or symbolic penetration in war or game is thus a result, not a cause. And determining ultimate
causes of human behavior as opposed to merely describing human behavior, American or universal, is always a daunting and demanding intellectual
challenge.

I believe that there may be a number of possible contributing factors
which lead to the pattern in male competitive sports and warfare I have
sought to describe. The first and perhaps foremost has to do with the nature of child rearing in the vast majority of human societies. I am speaking
of the fact that it is primarily women who bear the responsibility for infant
and small child care. Part of the reason for this is, of course, biological. It
is women who carry and bear babies, and until relatively recently, it was
women's breasts which provided the basic initial nourishment for the new-
born. The existence of a strongly female-centered world for most infants,
both male and female, has important consequences, *differential* consequences for infants. Little girls from the start have a role model to observe
and emulate; little boys do not. In sexually segregated societies, little boys
are raised in a world of women for the first impressionable years of their
lives even to the point in Western societies of using women's bathrooms in
public facilities. What this critical infantile conditioning means—to
males—is that at some point, usually in early adolescence, they must break
away from the world of women to join the world of men. This is usually
accomplished through some form of all-male puberty rite (Ong 1989,
130).

So whereas young girls do *not* have to shift away from any undue influence of the opposite sex, young boys do. Boys therefore become obsessed
with (1) asserting their masculinity and (2) denying or repudiating any
hint of effeminacy. A mama's boy, that is, a "sissy," is portrayed in American culture as being "tied to his mother's apron strings," which may be a
symbolic continuation or replication of the initial umbilical cord which

connects mother and infant (Ong 1989, 70). Boys are thus urged by peers and perhaps their fathers to "cut the cord," that is, to break away from the all-powerful maternal environment which threatens to keep them from attaining their manly identity.

Another contributing factor, I believe, is the enforced sexual segregation imposed in so many societies. Certainly in circum-Mediterranean cultures, we find a high premium placed upon female chastity accompanied by strict rules of sexual separation. In cross-cultural comparison, it is worth considering whether the emphasis placed on co-education, and sexual integration, in twentieth-century America alters patterns of demonstrating manliness. In relation to one another, human males are thought to reach their sexual peak much earlier than females. It is significant that at the age when male sexuality peaks, they may be denied access to women other than prostitutes. The only sexual objects immediately available are *other males*. The point here is that all-male competitive sport teams (and the military) are thus organizations where sexual energies can be expended only via males either within the group or in the case of sports on members of the opposing team. I am convinced that male competitive games and verbal duels, like juvenile gangs of males, are part of adolescence. The existence of professional sports teams where slightly older men participate is merely an extension of an activity which is fundamentally one of adolescence.

So to sum up my reasoning thus far: young boys raised in a "suffocating" maternal-female environment are encouraged by society to move into all-male (gang or team) groups where they feel obliged to prove their masculinity to the satisfaction of their male peers. If male A tries to do so by forcing male B into a female role or position, and if male B does not want to be in this role, male B may try to force male A to assume the female role instead.

There is yet one additional possible contributing factor, and that is the biological nature of the male phallic erection. Male anatomy and physiology is such that an erection is a temporary, not permanent, state. Accordingly, males feel the need for proving, repeatedly, that they are able to achieve this indisputable demonstration of masculinity. Thus winning one match or one game may not be enough. One has to prove one's ability to feminize or emasculate one's opponent again and again. Whether male aggression is innate or acquired (my own feeling is that aggression is learned by individuals as they experience the pleasure principle running smack into the reality principle, and hence babies soon experience frustrations of various sorts and thus anger), the fact is that in many Western societies aggression is forbidden or at least frowned upon. Superego through parents and the church does its best to inhibit aggressive behavior. As a result, the only socially sanctioned outlet available for males is through games, contests, sports, and warfare.

As folklore, manly traditions often offer a form of escape for the people who tell tales, sing songs, play games, and so on. In this sense, folklore offers a socially sanctioned outlet for the expression of taboo and anxiety-provoking behavior. One can do or say in folkloristic form things otherwise interdicted in everyday life. Many different types of interpretation are possible, and in theory I certainly subscribe to the desirability of multiple interpretations. In practice, my own interpretations tend to fall along structural and psychoanalytical lines. I favor analysis of metaphors as folk roots of behavior. I assume that metaphors are meaningful, not accidental, and that there are consistent patterns of metaphor in every culture. These patterns may be cognitive or symbolic. Thus Americans may be three-determined in reporting the number of shots they allegedly heard fired in an assassination attempt or in designing multiple choice examinations, but these same Americans may not be consciously aware of the importance of the number three in American culture (Dundes 1980b).

I believe that by analyzing folklore we discover general patterns of culture, and I would maintain further that a knowledge of such patterns can provide the means of raising levels of consciousness. So my analysis of metaphors of male dominance is intended to show how folkloristic patterning acts as a critical cultural force in shaping opinion and prejudice. Accordingly, my analysis of the possible symbolic content and function of American football and other male combat rituals is not simply a delineation of metaphorical patterning, but rather an implicit commentary on a facet of American society that typically discourages men from expressing physical affection toward one another. Folklore furnishes a socially sanctioned outlet for cultural pressure points and individual anxieties. Further, as reflections of "worldview," it reveals how individuals perceive their world and their place in it. By analyzing the folklore of a group such as men, then, we may well succeed in the laudable goal of making the unconscious conscious.

And this brings me to my final comment. What is the value, if any, of studying masculinity as manifested in folklore? To what extent, if any, can it illuminate or help solve actual problems in the real world outside the sanctity of the ivory tower?

Let me present one illustrative example. In May of 2004, graphic photographs and videotapes revealed that Iraqi prisoners detained in the Abu Ghraib prison outside Baghdad were seriously abused by American military and civilian personnel. Upon viewing the images, President Bush called them "disgusting" and definitely "un-American." The images were also shown to the public on American television, and even though pundits and high government officials claimed that Americans did not indulge in such barbaric behavior, the "ocular proof," to quote Shakespeare's Othello, proved otherwise. There were distressing scenes of piles of naked Iraqi prisoners in a jumbled mass on the floor while American military personnel looked on, smiling and sometimes shown making a mocking thumbs-up gesture. One video seemed to show a GI preparing to sodomize a male detainee. Another photo zeroed in on the face and torso of a detainee smeared with what appeared to be feces (McGeary 2004, 46). The American public was embarrassed and perplexed by this shocking incident. How could it possibly be explained? The typical rationalization offered was that these techniques were intended to soften up terrorist prisoners so that they might be induced to provide critical intelligence to the interrogators. Photographs were taken so as to intimidate other prisoners who would see what was in store for them and thereby persuade them to cooperate with the American authorities.

In an essay co-authored with my sociologist daughter, Lauren Dundes, entitled "The Elephant Walk and Other Amazing Hazing: Male Fraternity Initiation through Infantilization and Feminization," we demonstrated that all-male college fraternities and male sports teams carry out precisely the same acts. Stripping the Iraqi prisoners of their clothing reduced them to the level of naked helpless infants. Smearing them with feces further reduced them to an un-toilet-trained phase of infancy. The implied threat of sodomy along with forcing the prisoners to don women's undergarments surely constituted a form of feminization. The piling up of naked Iraqi prisoners is remarkably similar to a fraternity ritual known as "Dog Pile" (Dundes and Dundes 2002, 115). This behavior might not have been in compliance with the Geneva Convention with respect to the rules governing the humane treatment of prisoners of war, but it was certainly not un-American, not at all.

But the theory can explain more than just American behavior. Shortly after the revelation of the Abu Ghraib scandal, a small group of Iraqi terrorists showed a videotape of their own in which an American civilian, Nick Berg, was shown sitting and bound in front of five masked black-garbed men. He mentioned the names of his parents, and then suddenly without warning, one of the men "took a long knife from his shirt, grabbed a screaming Berg by the hair and cut off his head" (Rawe 2004: 43). Why was Berg beheaded? He could have been shot, or strangled or even beaten to death. The question is: Why was he decapitated? In male competitive games as well as in many of the jokes contained in the essays in this volume, we find an emphasis on castration and the fear thereof. Moreover, in war, winning males often seek trophies. A flag in the game "Capture the Flag" is one thing, but in warfare, soldiers will often confiscate weapons (swords or guns—basic male symbols) and occasionally actual body parts. Capturing the head of a male opponent is symbolically possessing the masculinity of the opponent, much as the bullfighter can claim one of the extremities of a conquered bull if he has fought very skillfully and by this means pleased the crowd in attendance, so that they demand he be rewarded with the bull's tail or hooves. There is also the practice of "headhunting" in some parts of the world, a practice which surely has some symbolic significance. The sexual meaning of "head" is obvious enough in American folk speech. A man who deflowers a virgin is said to have taken her maiden *head*. In the folktale of the forbidden chamber (Aarne-Thompson tale type 311), the heroine opens the forbidden door, thereby causing an egg or key to become bloody, and inside the room, she finds the decapitated bodies of her sisters (who had evidently opened the [vaginal] door of the forbidden chamber earlier and thereby lost their maidenheads?). Etymologically speaking, there is also the possibility that the words "head" and "hood" are cognates (Thass-Thienemann 1973, 2:50) so that "manhood" was equivalent to "manhead." If so, then if a man lost his head, he would accordingly lose his manhood or genitals.

We know that "Disenchantment by decapitation" (motif D711) is common enough in folklore. And heroes in fairy tales are often required to decapitate giant or dragon foes to conquer them. But perhaps the most persuasive evidence for the symbolic meaning of decapitation comes from an application of the principle of "symbolic equivalence." One of folklore collector Vance Randolph's (1976) prize informants had two versions of the same Aarne-Thompson tale type 570, the Rabbit Herd. In the version he told to mixed audiences (men and women), the king threatened to cut off the hero's head if he lost control of the rabbit or rabbits, but in the version for "men only," the king threatens instead to cut the boy's pecker off. These two motifs (allomotifs) are symbolically equivalent. So clearly in this case decapitation is a symbolic substitute for castration. One may reasonably assume that the same symbolic equation holds for Arabic folklore.

In any case, the terrorists did behead Berg, a seemingly inexplicable act of brutality. The terrorists wanted to castrate a token American as a celebration of a kind of minor victory. This theoretical speculation in no way condones or excuses either the treatment of the Iraqi prisoners or the beheading of Nick Berg, but I hope it shows how the academic study of masculinity through folklore can help to explain what would otherwise appear to be totally bizarre and irrational behavior.

NOTES

1. For an entrée to some of the abundant contemporary anthropological literature devoted to the subject, see Matthew C. Gutmann, "Trafficking in Men: The Anthropology of Masculinity" in the *Annual Review of Anthropology* (1997).

2. My most recent illustration of this thesis consists of an analysis of a modern Greek version of a traditional game known in the Euro-American world as "How Many Horns Has the Buck?" (Dundes 2002a). I have also continued my investigations of male verbal dueling in proposing an Old Norse origin of the English term

"bugger" (2002b) and in an analysis of an obscene anti-Islam joke about Muhammad (2004).

REFERENCES

Abrahams, Roger D. 1962. "Playing the Dozens." *Journal of American Folklore* 75: 209–20.

Bilger, Burkhard. 1999. "Enter the Chicken—On the Bayou Cockfighting Remains Undefeated." *Harper's Magazine* (March). Available at http://articles.find articles.com/p/articles/mi_m1111/is_1786_298/ai_54 018061. Accessed September 30, 2004.

Braddy, Haldeen. 1961. "Feathered Duelists." In *Singers and Storytellers*, ed. Mody C. Boatright, Wilson M. Hudson, and Allen Maxwell, 98–106. Dallas: Southern Methodist University Press.

Brandes, Stanley. 1980. *Metaphors of Masculinity: Sex and Status in Andalusian Folklore.* Philadelphia: University of Pennsylvania Press.

Bronner, Simon J. 1978. "A Re-examination of Dozens among White American Adolescents." *Western Folklore* 37: 118–28.

———. 1987. "'Who Says?': A Further Investigation of Ritual Insults among White American Adolescents." *Midwestern Journal of Language and Folklore* 4: 53–69.

Cansever, Gocke. 1965. "Psychological Effects of Circumcision." *British Journal of Medical Psychology* 38: 321–31.

Carabelli, Giancarlo. 1996. *In the Image of Priapus*. London: Duckworth.

Dulaure, Jacques-Antoine. 1933 [1805]. *The Gods of Generation: A History of Phallic Cults among Ancients & Moderns*. Trans. A. F. N. New York: Panurge Press.

Dundes, Alan. 1980a. "Into the Endzone for a Touchdown: A Psychoanalytic Consideration of American Football." In *Interpreting Folklore*, by Alan Dundes, 199–210. Bloomington: Indiana University Press.

———. 1980b. "The Number Three in American Culture." In *Interpreting Folklore*, by Alan Dundes, 134–59. Bloomington: Indiana University Press.

———. 1994. "Gallus as Phallus: A Psychoanalytic Cross-Cultural Consideration of the Cockfight as Fowl Play." In *The Cockfight: A Casebook*, ed. Alan Dundes, 241–82. Madison: University of Wisconsin Press.

———. *From Game to War and Other Psychoanalytical Essays on Folklore*. Lexington: University Press of Kentucky.

———. 2002a. "The Greek Game of *Makria Yaidoura* [Long Donkey]: An Adolescent Articulation of a Mediterranean Model of Masculinity." In *Bloody Mary in the Mirror: Essays in Psychoanalytic Folkloristics*, by Alan Dundes, 122–36. Jackson: University Press of Mississippi.

———. 2002b. "Much Ado about 'Sweet Bugger All': Getting to the Bottom of a Puzzle in British Folk Speech." *Folklore* 113: 35–49.

———. 2004. "'What If Mahomet Won't Go for the Mountin': An Analysis of an Arabic-Islamic Joke." *Midwestern Folklore* 30: 5–14.

Dundes, Alan, and Lauren Dundes. 2002. "The Elephant Walk and Other Amazing Hazing: Male Fraternity Initiation through Infantilization and Feminization." In *Bloody Mary in the Mirror: Essays in Psychoanalytic Folkloristics*, by Alan Dundes, 95–121. Jackson: University Press of Mississippi.

Dundes, Alan, Jerry W. Leach, and Bora Özkök. 1970. "The Strategy of Turkish Boys' Verbal Dueling Rhymes." *Journal of American Folklore* 83: 325–49.

Dwyer, Daisy Hilse. 1978. *Images and Self Images: Male and Female in Morocco*. New York: Columbia University Press.

Freud, Sigmund. 1961 [1928]. "Dostoevsky and Parricide." *Standard Edition* 21: 173–94. London: Hogarth Press.

Fuller, Peter. 1977. Introduction to *The Psychology of Gambling*, ed. Jon Halliday and Peter Fuller, 1–114. New York: Penguin.

Goodland, Roger, 1931. *A Bibliography of Sex Rites and Customs*. London: George Routledge & Sons.

Gutmann, Mathew C. 1997. "Trafficking in Men: The Anthropology of Masculinity." *Annual Review of Anthropology* 26: 385–409.

Keuls, Eva C. 1985. *The Reign of the Phallus: Sexual Politics in Ancient Athens*. New York: Harper & Row.

Lansang, A. J. 1966. *Cockfighting in the Philippines (Our Genuine National Sport)*. Atlag, Malolos, Bulacan, Philippines: Enrian Press.

Lindner, Robert. 1953. "The Psychodynamics of Gambling." In *Explorations in Psychoanalysis*, ed. Robert Lindner, 197–217. New York: Julian Press.

McGeary, Johanna. 2004. "Pointing Fingers." *Time* 163, no. 21 (May 24): 44–47, 50.

Murphy, Peter F. 2001. *Studs, Tools, and the Family Jewels: Metaphors Men Live By*. Madison: University of Wisconsin Press.

Ong, Walter J. 1989. *Fighting for Life: Contest, Sexuality, and Consciousness*. Amherst: University of Massachusetts Press.

Pacelle, Wayne. 2004. "Down for the Count: Cockfighting Is Wobbling on Its Last Two Legs." Humane Society of the United States. http://www.hsus.org/ace/21073. Accessed September 30, 2004.

Parker, Gary L. 1986. "An Outlet for Male Aggression: The Secret Fraternity of the Southern Cockfighter." *Tennessee Anthropologist* 11: 21–28.

Randolph, Vance. 1976. *Pissing in the Snow and Other Ozark Folktales*. Urbana: University of Illinois Press.

Rawe, Julie. 2004. "The Sad Tale of Nick Berg." *Time* 163, no. 21 (May 24): 42–43.

Simbeck, Rob. 2000. "Feathers and Blood: The Shadowy Allure and Complicated Politics of Cockfighting." *Nashville Scene* (June 12). http://www.weeklywire.com/ww/06–12–00/nash_cover.html. Accessed September 30, 2004.

Taggart, James M. 1990. *Enchanted Maidens: Gender Relations in Spanish Folktales of Courtship and Marriage*. Princeton, N.J.: Princeton University Press.

Thass-Thienemann, Theodore. 1973. *The Interpretation of Language*. Vol. 2: *Understanding the Unconscious Meaning of Language*. New York: Jason Aronson.

Theweleit, Klaus. 1987 [1977]. *Male Fantasies*. Vol. 1: *Women, Floods, Bodies, History*. Trans. Stephen Conway. Minneapolis: University of Minnesota Press.

———. 1989 [1978]. *Male Fantasies*. Vol. 2: *Male Bodies: Psychoanalyzing the White Terror*. Trans. Stephen Conway. Minneapolis: University of Minnesota Press.

Vanggaard, Thorkil. 1972. *Phallos: A Symbol and Its History in the Male World*. New York: International Universities Press.

Walker, Jesse Lloyd. 1986. "Feathers and Steel: A Folkloric Study of Cockfighting in Northern Utah." M.A. thesis, Utah State University.

CONTRIBUTORS

ANTHONY P. AVERY is a doctoral candidate in American Studies at the University of New Mexico and has taught courses in "History of Sexuality" and "Hip Hop and Rave." He has published in the *Journal of Men's Studies* and is the editor for the online men's studies annotated bibliography for the American Men's Studies Association. He received the Gerald Davis Memorial Research Award from the American Studies Department at the University of New Mexico.

RONALD L. BAKER is Chair of the English Department and Professor of English at Indiana State University. He is author of *Jokelore: Humorous Folktales from Indiana; Hoosier Folk Legends; Folklore in the Writings of Rowland Robinson; Indiana Place Names; From Needmore to Prosperity: Hoosier Place Names in Folklore and History; Homeless, Friendless, and Penniless: The WPA Interviews with Former Slaves Living in Indiana;* and *French Folklife in Old Vincennes.* He has also served as editor of *Midwestern Folklore, Indiana Names,* and the *Folklore Historian.* He was awarded the Lifetime Achievement Award from the History and Folklore Section of the American Folklore Society and the President's Medal in recognition of exemplary performance as a faculty member at Indiana State University.

SIMON J. BRONNER is Distinguished University Professor of American Studies and Folklore at Pennsylvania State University, Harrisburg. He is author of over a dozen books, including *Following Tradition: Folklore in the Discourse of American Culture; Grasping Things: Folk Material Culture and Mass Society in America; The Carver's Art: Crafting Meaning from Wood; Folk Nation: Folklore in the Creation of American Tradition; American Children's Folklore; Piled Higher and Deeper: The Folklore of Student Life; Old-Time Music Makers of New York State;* and *American Folklore Studies: An Intellectual History.* He has received the Wayland Hand Prize in Folklore and History and the Peter and Iona Opie Prize for best book on children's folklore.

NORMA E. CANTÚ is Professor of English at the University of Texas, San Antonio. She is author of *Canícula: Snapshots of a Girlhood en la Frontera,* a winner of the Premio Aztlán for literature, and co-editor of *Chicana Traditions: Continuity and Change* and *Telling to Live: Latina Feminist Testimonios.* She has published numerous articles and book chapters in both English and Spanish. She has served as chair of the National Association of Chicana and Chicano Studies.

ALAN DUNDES was Professor of Anthropology and Folklore at the University of California, Berkeley. He published more than thirty books, including *Interpreting Folklore; Folklore Matters; Analytic Essays in Folklore; From Game to War and Other Psychoanalytic Essays on Folklore; Bloody Mary in the Mirror: Essays in Psychoanalytic Folkloristics; Cracking Jokes; Two Tales of Crow and Sparrow: A Freudian Folkloristic Essay on Caste and Untouchability;* and *Parsing through Customs: Essays by a Freudian Folklorist.* A former president of the American Folklore Society and member of the American Academy of Arts and Sciences, he received the Pitre Prize's Sigillo d'Oro (Seal of Gold), the premier international award for lifetime achievement in folklore, in 1993. He died in 2005.

GARY ALAN FINE is John Evans Professor of Sociology at Northwestern University. He is author of *With the Boys: Little League Baseball and Preadolescent Culture; Talking Sociology; Shared Fantasy: Role-Playing Games as Social Worlds; Morel Tales: The Culture of Mushrooming; Manufacturing Tales: Sex and Money in Contemporary Legends; Kitchens: The Culture of Restaurant Work; Everyday Genius: Self-Taught Art and the Culture of Authenticity;* and *Gifted Tongues: High School Debate and Adolescent Culture;* and co-author of *Whispers on the Color Line: Rumor and Race in America and Rumor.* He has served as president of the Society for the Study of Social Problems and the Association for the Study of Play.

GREG KELLEY is Assistant Professor of Folklore and Women's Studies in the English department at Indiana State University. He has published articles in *North Carolina Folklore, Western Folklore, Pennsylvania Folklife, Contemporary Legend, Swift Studies, Hamlet Studies,* and *Folklore and Literature: An Encyclopedia.* He is editor of the journal *Midwestern Folklore.*

HIDEYO KONAGAYA is Associate Professor of American Studies at Siebold University in Nagasaki, Japan. She has written in both Japanese and English. Her English articles include "The Christmas Cake: A Japanese Tradition of American Prosperity" in the *Journal of Popular Culture,* "Taiko as Performance: Creating Japanese American Traditions" in the *Japanese Journal of American Studies,* and "Breaking the Barriers through Origami: A Perspective on the Japanese American Experience," in the *Journal of the*

Popular Culture Association of Japan. She received the Richard Reuss Prize from the American Folklore Society for an outstanding essay in the history of folklore studies.

W. K. MCNEIL was Folklorist at the Ozark Folk Center, Mountain View, Arkansas. He published sixteen books, including *American Proverb Literature* (with Frank de Caro); *The Charm Is Broken; Ghost Stories from the American South; On a Slow Train through Arkansaw; The Life and Adventures of an Arkansaw Doctor; Ozark Mountain Humor; Southern Folk Ballads; Southern Mountain Folk Songs;* and *Appalachian Images in Folk and Popular Culture.* He was elected a fellow of the America Folklore Society in 1996. He died in 2005.

JAY MECHLING is Professor of American Studies at the University of California, Davis. He is author of *On My Honor: Boy Scouts and the Making of American Youth* and co-editor of *American Wildlife in Symbol and Story* and the *Encyclopedia of American Studies.* He is past president of the California Folklore Society, former editor of the journal *Western Folklore,* and chair of the California Council for the Humanities.

TOM MOULD is Assistant Professor of Anthropology and coordinator of the Program for Ethnographic Research and Community Studies at Elon University. He is author of two books on Choctaw narrative: *Choctaw Prophecy: A Legacy of the Future* and *Choctaw Tales.* He has also produced video documentaries for public television. He has served as president of the Hoosier Folklore Society.

W. F. H. (BILL) NICOLAISEN is Honorary Professor of English in the School of Language and Literature at the University of Aberdeen, Scotland. He is also Distinguished Professor Emeritus of English and Folklore at Binghamton University (New York). He is author of *Scottish Place-Names: Their Study and Significance,* which won the Chicago Folklore Prize, and *The Picts and Their Place Names.* Past president of the American Folklore Society and the American Name Society, he received the American Folklore Society's Lifetime Scholarly Achievement Award.

MICKEY WEEMS is a folklorist, journalist, and scholar of religions and sexuality studies. He teaches world religions at Columbus State Community College, writes for various gay newspapers, and is completing his doctoral degree in Somatic Studies at Ohio State University. He is cofounder of Qualia, an annual conference for the study of gay folklife.

INDEX